Samuel Beckett in the Literary Marketplace

Irish Studies
James MacKillop, *Series Editor*

OTHER TITLES IN IRISH STUDIES:

Catholic Emancipations: Irish Fiction from Thomas Moore to James Joyce
Emer Nolan

The Irish Beckett
John P. Harrington

An Irish Literature Reader: Poetry, Prose, Drama, Second Edition
Maureen O'Rourke Murphy and James MacKillop

Irish Orientalism: A Literary and Intellectual History
Joseph Lennon

Irish Women Writers Speak Out: Voices from the Field
Caitriona Moloney and Helen Thompson

Modern Irish Drama: W. B. Yeats to Marina Carr, Second Edition
Sanford Sternlicht

Party Pieces: Oral Storytelling and Social Performance in Joyce and Beckett
Alan Warren Friedman

A Reader's Guide to Samuel Beckett
Hugh Kenner

Trapped in Thought: A Study of the Beckettian Mentality
Eric P. Levy

Writing Irish: Selected Interviews with Irish Writers from The Irish Literary Supplement
James P. Myers, Jr., ed.

SAMUEL BECKETT *in the* Literary Marketplace

Stephen John Dilks

With a Foreword by S. E. Gontarski

SYRACUSE UNIVERSITY PRESS

Syracuse, New York 13244-5290

First Edition 2011
11 12 13 14 15 16 6 5 4 3 2 1

∞ The paper used in this publication meets the minimum requirements of the American National Standard for Information Sciences—Permanence of Paper for Printed Library Materials, ANSI Z39.48-1992.

For a listing of books published and distributed by Syracuse University Press, visit our Web site at SyracuseUniversityPress.syr.edu.

ISBN: 978-0-8156-3254-2

Library of Congress Cataloging-in-Publication Data

Dilks, Stephen.
Samuel Beckett in the literary marketplace / Stephen John Dilks ; with a foreword by S. E. Gontarski. — 1st ed.
p. cm. — (Irish studies)
Includes bibliographical references and index.
ISBN 978-0-8156-3254-2 (cloth : alk. paper)
1. Beckett, Samuel, 1906–1989—Criticism and interpretation. 2. Publishers and publishing—Ireland—History—20th century. 3. Authorship—Marketing—History—20th century. 4. Authors and publishers—Ireland. I. Title.
PR6003.E282Z62484 2011
848'.91409—dc22 2010052233

Manufactured in the United States of America

My Mum and Dad, Joan Mary Dilks and Maurice William Dilks, DFM, were unequivocal in supporting the career I chose, and I remain loyal to their memory, doing my utmost to express the best of each of them in everything I do, including the composition of this book. They live through me.

Donna, Griffin, and Sara-Jessica give me unconditional love, daily joy, and constant stimulation: I dedicate this book to them.

Stephen John Dilks is associate professor of English and Irish literature at the University of Missouri–Kansas City. In addition to publishing articles on Beckett, Joyce, and college-level teaching, he teaches discourse analysis, Irish history and literary culture, and courses on popular and world literature. He is coauthor of *Cultural Conversations: The Presence of the Past* (2001), cofounded the Faculty Center for Excellence in Teaching at UMKC, and is director of Universal Design for Learning for an NSF grant serving students with disabilities, including veterans.

Contents

Illustrations

Following page 166

Foreword

Custodian of His Own Image

S. E. GONTARSKI

Amid the intense theorizing of "Three Dialogues with Georges Duthuit" sits Beckett's acknowledgment of a materialist theory of art, "The realization that art has always been bourgeois, thugh [*sic*] it may dull our pain before the achievements of the social progressive, is finally of scant interest" (Beckett 1984b, 144). Despite Beckett's casual dismissal, the statement seemed important enough for him to revise and reprint it in two subsequent publications, one in French and one in English, tributes to the struggling painter Bram van Velde.[1] In fact, Beckett leads with this simultaneous admission and dismissal, with only the subordinate clause, the quasi-Freudian acknowledgment of art's potential palliative effect "to dull our pain," expunged. Although the relation of art to bourgeois culture may have seemed "of scant interest" to Beckett as he focused on other features of the artwork, particularly the paradoxical relation between the artist and his occasion, even that quasi-psychological argument seemed to double back on itself, as a denial of occasion itself, as Beckett admits, constitutes something of an occasion. Evading the material and bourgeois, Beckett recognized, may be futile, his evasion itself simply a return to the terrestrial world.

The issue that Beckett skirts in his commentary, the politics of art, its uneasy, often occluded association with commodity and commerce, is, of course, most evident in theater, where property is rented from its owners, presumably an author (or designate), packaged, and resold to the public, but

1. First in *Bram van Velde*. Texts by Jacques Putman, Georges Duthuit, and Samuel Beckett. Collection: Le Musée de Poche. (Paris: Editions Georges Fall, 1958) and then in English by Grove Press in 1960 as an Evergreen Gallery Book, book 5 (E-174).

it remains a defining feature of all art. Like painting, writing is thus inextricably tied to the quid pro quo world of commerce. Most literary publication and theatrical performance, especially in late capitalist societies, require investors, those bourgeois replacements for patrons, who exhibit something less than altruism in their economic support for the arts. They expect something tangible in return for their outlay. As uninterested as he appeared to be in the quid pro quo world he so castigated in *Murphy,* Samuel Beckett himself, like the unfortunate Murphy, was tied ("ti-ed") to it, and the arc of his literary reputation was inextricably linked to the world of commerce. Murphy avoided that world as best he could; Beckett, on the other hand and for a time, flogged his wares almost door to door. That this link between art and commerce has been underexamined by cultural critics is surprising given the trend in contemporary culture to rate creative achievement in terms of cash value, sales, and attendance figures: platinum CDs, the weekly box office take, Christie's sale prices, and best-seller lists. Barney Rosset, Beckett's first and only American publisher, took on Beckett, son of a successful Dublin entrepreneur, as an author in June of 1953 for his aesthetic and political qualities, but Rosset, son of a wealthy, successful Chicago banker, was always a commercial publisher who expected to, who needed to earn a return on his investment, even from avant-garde authors. His publishing enterprise was funded by a personal fortune, but it would soon run dry, as it did in the 1970s, without substantial capital return.

Samuel Beckett's alliance with Grove Press was literary and aesthetic, certainly, but the association was also commercial, a relationship Beckett acknowledged and accepted. The dearth of analysis of that relationship suggests something of a critical blind spot, a refusal to confront the material circumstances of art. In *Institutions of Modernism: Literary Elites and Public Culture,* for instance, Lawrence Rainey traces the assimilation of art and commodity, or art by commodity, to the social provocations of the Futurists in 1912–14 as the artist had "to come to terms with the new institutions of mass culture and assess their bearings on the place of art in the cultural marketplace." Such reassessment precipitated "a permanent collapse of all distinctions between art and commodity, [and effected] the perceptible and irreversible leveling of both within the single and amorphous category of commodity" (1998, 38–39). Beckett's recognition "that art has always been bourgeois" reaches further, to suggest that to be an artist was not only to fail on the highest of aesthetic planes, but to be something of a huckster as well.

A neophyte publisher, Rosset saw the economy of publishing, and so of literature, clearly and early on. He built his enterprise, which would feature Beckett and other writers of the European avant-garde, as something of a second phase of modernist publishing with emphases on a little literary review, *The Evergreen Review,* later just *Evergreen* in its glossier, more commercial format (with issue no. 32 [April-May 1964]), and on limited editions, author-signed artifacts designed as cultural and commercial investments. Grove's marketing strategy for *Waiting for Godot* in 1954 was decidedly populist, Rosset offering the paperback *Godot* for $1.00, a strategy to broaden sales, particularly among the young and particularly at performances.[2] Beckett was enthusiastic about such market expansion that accompanied low-cost books. But Rosset also targeted another market, this one more upscale. In 1956 Grove published *Malone Dies* in an Evergreen paperback format (E-39), but also as a hardbound limited edition of five hundred copies (selling for $3.75). In March 1957 Rosset began printing signed editions of Beckett's work, first with *Murphy,* publishing it in hard and soft covers, but also offering a specially bound, limited edition of one hundred copies signed by the author, and even *Endgame* appeared in four editions that same year: an Evergreen Book (E-96), a hardbound edition, a specially bound limited edition of one hundred copies, and a special edition of twenty-six copies signed by the author. By 1958, the economic stakes increased as *The Unnamable* was published in five editions, that is, as both a cultural and an overtly commercial artifact: an Evergreen book (E-117, $1.45), a clothbound edition like *Malone Dies,* a specially bound limited edition of one hundred numbered copies, a specially bound and signed edition of twenty-six copies lettered A through Z, and a specially bound and signed edition, hors commerce, numbered 1–4. The publishing pattern of *The Unnamable* was repeated the following year for *Watt:* a trade paperback (E-152, $1.75), a clothbound book ($3.50), a specially bound limited edition of one hundred numbered copies, a specially bound and signed edition of twenty-six copies lettered A through Z, and four copies hors commerce, numbered 1–4. Rosset thus set about encouraging investment in the avant-garde in general and in Beckett's work in particular. For that he needed

2. Substantial expense was saved by eliminating the production photos of the hardcover edition and reducing the size of the 1951 publicity photograph of Beckett, the latter originally published internally (eliminated) and on the back cover (reduced in size).

Beckett's participation, and so Beckett went into what Rosset's assistant, Judith Schmidt, called the "autograph business." For Rosset's books-as-investment strategy Beckett signed and promoted books: numbered and limited editions for the collector's market and personalized autographs of general editions for special clients. And Rosset prevailed upon Beckett to write, even if not directly, the occasional book blurb, in this case for Beckett's friend Robert Pinget, whose novel *The Inquisitory* is called in a blurb attributed to Beckett, "One of the most important novels of the last ten years." Admittedly, the prose sounds little like Beckett, but his name is linked to it on the cover of the hardback edition. He thus became part of the Grove Press marketing strategy. What Rosset seems to have understood, instinctively perhaps, was that an antibourgeois art needed substantial and broad bourgeois support, and that Beckett's name already had considerable commercial cachet by the 1950s. That cachet would only increase with the award of the International Publisher's Prize in 1961 (which he shared with Jorge Luis Borges) that Grove Press engineered for its author, and the Nobel Prize itself in 1969.

In his study *Samuel Beckett in the Literary Maketplace,* Stephen John Dilks details what he takes to be Samuel Beckett's complicity not only in the business, the marketing of his books but in the shaping and marketing of his own image as an ascetic, anticommercial author. That is, Dilks poses the paradox that Beckett commercially exploited his image as an anticommercial artist. As he notes in his introduction, using Beckett's association with the *Index on Censorship* as a prime example:

> Against those who treasure the idea that Beckett was a saint (as John Calder suggested with no apparent irony in an article, "A Saint Born on Good Friday," in *The Independent* on April 13, 1990), unique in his indifference to "the favour of the multitude" (Joyce 1989, 71), we assert that Beckett's life as a writer is most productively seen in terms of the materialist approach inaugurated by Virginia Woolf in *A Room of One's Own* (1929) and brought into the modern academy by D. F. McKenzie in *Bibliography and the Sociology of Texts* (published in 1985). In the context of Huyssen's analysis of the collapse of the division between art and commerce, and seen in terms of the sociology of texts, Beckett's participation in the campaign Index on Censorship is far from being "emblematic of the theatre of the absurd" (Kyncl 1989, 39). Instead, understood in the context of Beckett's professional life as a writer, it becomes symptomatic of a

relationship with the literary marketplace that goes back to the beginning of his career in the late 1920s.

The degree of Beckett's complicity in the marketing of his own image, particularly for the Index on Censorship campaign with its compelling image of the author gagged, is still open to some debate, although Dilks argues convincingly for such complicity. What is abundantly clear, however, is Beckett's understanding of the business of authorship and of book selling. The marketing of Beckett's image, now perhaps run rampant, is very much of a piece with the larger question of the marketing of the avant-garde and, in Beckett's case, the almost inexplicable number and levels of celebratory activities that marked the centenary of his birth in 2006, the publicity for almost all of which was dominated by his iconic face.

Judith Schmidt, who joined Grove as Rosset's personal assistant in April 1956 and went on to become head of Grove's subsidiary rights division, was Beckett's principal liaison with Grove during the growth years of both Grove Press and the Beckett business, and she fully understood the economic requirements of publishing and what was required of Grove authors. On September 15, 1962, Beckett wrote Schmidt that he would sign books, as requested, for the cast of Alan Schneider's Cherry Lane production of *Happy Days,* John Becher and Ruth White, and pass them on to Grove editor Richard Seaver, who would relay them to the actors. The copies, however, went missing; on December 6, 1962, Schmidt wrote Beckett:

> John C. Becher called this week to say that he never received the signed copy of HAPPY DAYS. Unfortunately, I had mailed the book to him about three months ago, so it was too late to check with the Post Office. Would you mind inscribing another copy and mailing it whenever it is convenient? Mr. Becher sounded so disappointed when he heard that the book had been mailed, and was presumably lost. (SUL)

On December 12 Beckett replied to Schmidt and agreed to sign another copy for Belcher.

In January of 1964 Schmidt wrote to Beckett:

> Please sign as many copies of POEMS as you can spare. I think we sent you about 20, but if you have given some away, or would like to keep some, it doesn't matter. Ten or fifteen will do for us. Barney would like to give them to a few people—mainly people at Grove, I think. He would also like you

> to sign about 10 copies of HOW IT IS. I'll send them on to you. Hope it's OK. (SUL)

Beckett was away in London rehearsing *Endgame* with Jack MacGowran and Patrick Magee, which he deemed "very exciting. They are both marvelous." He got back to the publishing business in Paris and replied to a series of Schmidt's letters on February 7, referencing her letter of January 27 by expressing his regrets about failing to sign the book of poems and promising to sign and send them after the weekend. He also promised ten signed copies of his latest novel, *How It Is.* On March 7 he confirmed he had completed the work, acknowledged receipt of his royalty check, and noted that he had sent a handwritten note to Mrs. Cole and that he had recently sent the ten signed copies of *How It Is.*

By 1967 the signings had become a business, big business, and Schmidt wrote to Beckett on August 23:

> It looks as though the autographing business is picking up. I have a letter from a man and enclosures of the last page of *Godot* and the same for *Happy Days,* plus a typed copy of a poem by you, for which he wants three signatures. I frankly hesitate to send these on to you, and I fear that we may be getting many of these in the future. I can tell people that you do not give out autographs—shall I do that? Please let me know your decision.
>
> I'm afraid that you may soon be swamped with these requests. (SUL)

And swamped he was. Such was the business of authorship, particularly with Beckett's American publishing house, all of which exploded after the Nobel Prize was awarded. This prefatory look at Beckett going about the business of authorship, the business of being Beckett, is the subject that Stephen Dilks explores extensively, as fully and in as much detail as currently possible given restrictions on the uses of primary material imposed by protectionist overseers of the legacy. Moreover, Dilks theorizes Samuel Beckett as one "Samuel Beckett," something of a cultural icon, an almost theatrical construct, which perspective allows a different Beckett to emerge and opens an avenue to approach Beckett's social production, his literary output, in ways hitherto unthinkable. The material, the nuts and bolts, the bourgeois Beckett is thus hardly "of scant interest," as Dilks demonstrates on nearly every page. Looking at Beckett functioning in material culture clears a space to ask question hitherto obscured by myth and performance. It is in that space that Dilks works to show a richer, fuller, more human, and so less sanctified Beckett.

Acknowledgments

Samuel Beckett has been part of my life since 1979. Efforts to understand his work shaped me as I learned to use literature as a tool for understanding culture through the analysis of discourse conventions and as I figured out how to teach. My primary debt is, then, to Samuel Beckett.

I owe considerable gratitude to Lance St. John Butler, my advisor at Stirling University in 1979–83. Dr. Butler introduced me to the deep philosophical analysis of Beckett's texts, guiding me through a Sisyphean struggle that allowed me to imagine what had been unimaginable, not just in academe but also in life. Derek Attridge, George Kearns, and Tom Van Laan, my patient and open-minded teachers at Rutgers University, deserve my sincere thanks for letting me explore what Beckett took from Samuel Johnson: without their input I would not have begun to see how Johnson's vision of positive annihilation became, for Beckett, an instrument of self-fashioning.

▪ ▪ ▪

Since I began this project in 2003 I have had help from many quarters. The English Department and Arts and Sciences Dean's Office at UMKC have been generous in providing leave time and other support, secretarial and collegial. Joan Dean and Tom Stroik have been especially supportive. Librarians at the Harry Ransom Humanities Research Center in Austin, Texas; the Beckett International Foundation at Reading University; the Bird Library at Syracuse University; and the Lilly Library at the University of Indiana facilitated the process of research. Richard Workman at the HRHRC and Brian Ryder at the Beckett archive in Reading deserve special mention. Edward Beckett graciously allowed me to purchase a copy of the McGreevy Correspondence from Trinity College and has allowed me to quote extensively from Beckett's published work. Nicci Cloke at Faber and Dara Hyde at Grove/Atlantic worked tirelessly during a protracted permissions process. From the early days of the project Rohan Jayasekera at Index on Censorship has been very helpful, and Philip Spender answered numerous questions as I established the key point that Beckett took an active role in constructing the advertising poster for the organization. Finally I acknowledge my deepest gratitude to my editor, D. J. Whyte, and to Glenn Wright, James MacKillop, Lisa Kuerbis, and Annelise Finegan at Syracuse University Press for their commitment to this book.

. . .

Quotations from *The Unnamable* by Samuel Beckett, translation copyright © 1958 by the Estate of Samuel Beckett, used by permission of Grove/Atlantic, Inc. and Faber and Faber Ltd.

Quotations from *How It Is* by Samuel Beckett, copyright © 1964 by Grove Press, Inc., used by permission of Grove/Atlantic, Inc. and Faber and Faber Ltd.

Permission to quote material from *Damned to Fame: The Life of Samuel Beckett* by James Knowlson, copyright © 1996 by James Knowlson, has been granted by Bloomsbury Publishing Limited, Grove/Atlantic, Inc., and James Knowlson. Permission to quote material from *Samuel Beckett: A Biography* by Deirdre Bair, copyright © 1978, 1990 by Deirdre Bair, has been granted by Simon and Schuster and EMLA (UK), Ltd. Permission to quote from a letter written by Jack Yeats to T. M. Ragg dated November 22, 1937, has been granted by A. P. Watt Ltd on behalf of Grainne Yeats. Permission to quote from a report issued by Oliver Warner and Ian Parsons of Chatto and Windus on July 2, 1936, held by the Chatto and Windus archives, has been granted by The Random House Group Ltd. Permission to quote from letters by Abraham "Con" Leventhal has been granted by Andrew Woolfson. Permission to quote from Barney Rosset's correspondence and from a summary royalty statement has been granted by Barney Rosset.

Permission to quote from materials from the Grove Press Archive 1953–1985, Syracuse University Library, has been granted by Grove/Atlantic, Inc. and Grove Press Records, Special Collections Research Center, Syracuse University Library.

Permission to quote from the Calder and Boyars archives has been granted by John Calder and The Lilly Library, Indiana University, Bloomington, Indiana.

Permission to quote from Samuel Beckett Archives at the Beckett International Foundation Library, Reading University, UK, has been granted by Special Collections/Beckett International Foundation, University of Reading.

Permission to quote from the Samuel Beckett and Carlton Lake Archives courtesy of the Harry Ransom Humanities Research Center, The University of Texas at Austin.

Abbreviations

Unless otherwise cited, all references to Beckett's writings are to the four-volume Grove Centenary Edition, abbreviated thus:

GCE I *Samuel Beckett: The Grove Centenary Edition*, volume 1: *Novels.* Edited by Paul Auster with an introduction by Colm Toibin. New York: Grove Press, 2006.

GCE II *Samuel Beckett: The Grove Centenary Edition*, volume 2: *Novels.* Edited by Paul Auster with an introduction by Salman Rushdie. New York: Grove Press, 2006.

GCE III *Samuel Beckett: The Grove Centenary Edition*, volume 3: *Dramatic Works.* Edited by Paul Auster with an introduction by Edward Albee. New York: Grove Press, 2006.

GCE IV *Samuel Beckett: The Grove Centenary Edition*, volume 4: *Poems, Short Fiction, Criticism.* Edited by Paul Auster with an introduction by J. M. Coetzee. New York: Grove Press, 2006.

Letters that appear in the first volume of Fehsenfeld and Overbeck, *The Letters of Samuel Beckett (1929–1940)* are cited with the abbreviation *Letters* and a page number.

Unpublished letters and other archival documents are cited with a date and/or title and an abbreviation of the library at which they are held, as follows:

HRHRC Samuel Beckett and Carlton Lake Archives. Courtesy of the Harry Ransom Humanities Research Center, University of Texas at Austin.

Lilly Calder and Boyars Archives. Courtesy of John Calder and the Lilly Library, Indiana University, Bloomington, Indiana.

RUL Samuel Beckett Archives at the Beckett International Foundation library, Reading University, UK.

SUL Grove Press Records, Special Collections Research Center, Syracuse University Library. Courtesy of Barney Rosset and Grove/Atlantic, Inc.

TCD Tom McGreevy correspondence in special collections at Trinity College College, Dublin.

WUL Henry Wenning correspondence at Washington University Library, St Louis.

Samuel Beckett in the Literary Marketplace

Introduction

Selling Beckett

> The isolated, estranged images of alienation and loss, the narrative discontinuities, have become the easy iconography of the commercials, all authors have become inescapably enmeshed in commercialism.
>
> —Williams, *The Politics of Modernism*

"Havel, Beckett: The Intolerable Shirt of Fame," an article by Karel Kyncl published a week after Beckett died on December 22, 1989, begins, "The most obvious personal feature of the late Samuel Beckett was his profound dislike for publicity that would intrude on his privacy" (Kyncl 1989, 39). Kyncl's perspective is that of an educated layperson who accepts the separation between art and commerce and who sees Beckett as a prime example of the anticommercial artiste. Kyncl, a Czech radio and television journalist, became an assistant editor at *Index on Censorship* in December 1982 after being released from a term of imprisonment occasioned by his support for the civil rights movement Charter 77. He lays no claim to being a Beckett scholar. And, unlike the majority of those who wrote obituaries in the days after Beckett's death, he lays no claim to a personal relationship with Beckett. He is not a member of "the Sam Club," a club comprising those "insiders" who had sufficient contact with Beckett to call him "Sam." Instead, he writes from the point of view of an editorial assistant whose position allowed him to witness "an absurd exchange between a new president, Vaclav Havel, and the late Samuel Beckett." The whole point of the article is to explain Beckett's unexpected "willingness to be shown with a gag" (fig. 1). Because he accepts one of the most powerful myths in Beckett studies (that Beckett had a "profound dislike for publicity" and was intensely private to the point of being "reclusive"), Kyncl's explanation depends on the proposition that Beckett and Havel shared a coping mechanism for dealing with a situation they did not want to be in; they shared a "sense of the absurd" and preferred a life of solitude to the public life to which they seemed condemned.

The problem for Kyncl is that he cannot reconcile his received understanding of Beckett with the "rather undignified picture" that dominates his article and that "[Beckett] agreed . . . might be used in the most banal field imaginable, in advertising." Kyncl's assumption is that, because the adjective "reclusive" was "the most often used word" in the obituaries published after Beckett's death, Beckett could only have participated in advertising because he was driven, against his will, by a deep sense of the absurd. In the tributes to which Kyncl refers, we learn many intimate details about Beckett's "private" life (and thus begin to suspect that Beckett was much less private than his long retinue of friends and acquaintances suggest). Most stridently, we are told that Beckett is "The Celebrity no one knew" (MacRuairi 1989, 7), a "shy" man (Wallach 1989, 3) who experienced "recognition" as a "burden" (Montague 1989, 13), "shunned the spotlight" (Smith 1989, 12), and "had a horror of interviewers" (Kenner 1989, D2).

The sheer number of articles published by close friends and those who had "encounters with the author" (as Kenner [1989, D2] puts it) is consistent with the fact, underlined in John Pilling's *Samuel Beckett Chronology* (2006), that Beckett was far from reclusive. Even during the famous "siege in the room" (to use Kenner's influential phrase for the period between 1946 and 1950 when Beckett wrote the texts that would establish his international reputation), he was in constant contact with Georges Duthuit, Tom McGreevy, Geer van Velde, Jacoba van Velde (aka Toni Clerkx), George Reavey and, of course, Suzanne Deschevaux-Dumesnil (whom I will refer to as "Dumesnil"). Further, a quick survey of Pilling's entries for the period between 1946 and 1950 shows that during this period of "siege" he went to numerous art exhibitions and plays, visited Dublin annually for long spells of four to eight weeks, went on a number of vacations with Dumesnil (including a nine-week trip to Menton in 1947, two weeks in Fontainebleau in 1948, and a two-month trip to Ussy in 1949), and spent much of the time when he was in his Paris apartment not only writing the prose and drama that would make him famous but also writing numerous letters. Many of these letters are personal, but they frequently address professional matters. As Pilling points out, Beckett was a prolific letter writer: "There are more than fifteen thousand Beckett letters either still in private hands or in the public domain. . . . This is roughly the equivalent of a letter a day for almost fifty years!" (xiv). But, as Kyncl's opening line suggests, these signs of professional and social engagement are at odds with the public persona of a man who, as the December 1989 obituaries tell us, "refused to don the mantle of the great man of letters" (*Times* [London] 1989, 44), lived a "secretive lifestyle" (Braun 1989, 1), and "hated all forms of self-promotion" (Knowlson 1989, 19). The obvious material evidence that Beckett enjoyed regular contact with numerous "intimates" who knew him well enough to publish obituary accounts of his "private" life was occluded by the repeated assertion that Beckett "is best remembered as a secular monk" (Nightingale 1989, 16) who "was a figure of great austerity and hermetic elusiveness" (Gussow 1996, 12) and whose life was "sheathed in mystery" (Billington 1989, 13). Al Alvarez, John Calder, Mel Gussow, Jocelyn Herbert, Hugh Kenner, James Knowlson, Peter Lennon, Jérôme Lindon, John Montague, Tommy Murtagh, Harold Pinter, Barney Rosset, Francis Stuart, and Billie Whitelaw are among those who published obituary accounts: each records an intimate personal friendship with Beckett. But biographical accounts to date have been overwhelming to the point of tedium in their repetition of a narrative placing Beckett on a pedestal, cut off from market forces, preferring prisonlike solitude to publicity and celebrity. As the obituaries were followed by fuller biographical studies, the idea that Beckett was a fish out of water in his role as an international celebrity solidified into the assertion that he was "damned to fame," a reluctantly famous man who "declined to surround himself with a coterie of admirers" (Gordon 1996, 1). In the process, the author was elevated above other artists, becoming an exception defined by his isolation and his absolute disengagement from the literary marketplace: Bruce Arnold suggests Cronin's Beckett "achieved the apotheosis of solitude" (2003, 93); Ronan McDonald raises him to the level of a saint, describing him as "a saintly artist untainted by grubby self-promotion or by the coarse business of self-explication" (2006, 1). In this process, any contrary evidence is either neglected or it is treated as an anomaly; the myth of Beckett's absolute isolation from the marketplace is so strong that any hint he engaged in advertising is dismissed and any evidence he expressed interest in money or success is pushed aside. Worse, those who point to this evidence are treated with disdain. As Beckett's correspondence becomes public, the myth of Beckett will change because his deliberate efforts to craft a marketable persona; his determined use of contacts in the publishing industry to further his career; and his ongoing interest in money, contracts, copyright control, and the business of literary marketing will become increasingly evident. His letters reveal an obsessive interest in the public reception of his work. But until those letters become public, and with the Beckett estate continuing to exert rather excessive control over what we are allowed to publish, we must begin the process of revision with the evidence we *are* permitted to use.

Having spent more than two years of my life struggling to gain approval to publish the material used in this book, and having devoted a sabbatical to revision in response to a blanket denial by the Beckett estate to publish any quotations from Beckett's correspondence, published or unpublished, I can testify to the ensconcement characteristic of the received understanding of Beckett's authorial persona. There is unequivocal and direct evidence demonstrating Beckett's engagement with all aspects of the literary marketplace from 1929 to 1989, but there is a fortress mentality by a powerful contingent of Beckett's personal acquaintances and professional colleagues in defense of his image as a man "damned to fame."

McDonald is on solid ground when he suggests that "[t]here is . . . a unique cult of veneration amongst Beckett's followers, imitators and devotees" (2006, 2). And he is correct to caution "the vigilant Beckett reader" about "the Beckett myth, the aura of artistic integrity, elemental truth and existential bravery that surrounds him" (2). McDonald begins to challenge the sanctimonious image constructed by Beckett and his acolytes. But his "non-specialist general reader" (3) does little to put "Beckett's life and work" in the context of his subject's sixty-year career as a hard-working professional writer: in other words, McDonald suggests the need for a reevaluation of Beckett's "myth" and "aura," but he leaves this work undone, giving only a brief summary of "Beckett's Life" and "Cultural and Intellectual Contexts" before turning his attention to the plays, prose works, and criticism. True to a pattern that has been constant in Beckett studies from the earliest postwar reviews, he preserves Beckett's authorial persona as a man with a "determined reclusivity" and "a horror of publicity" (1), who "guarded his privacy with intense vigilance" (3), and who was "persistent" in the "shunning of publicity" (19). McDonald thus holds back from the long-overdue analysis of the myth that has placed Beckett in a hermetically sealed box on a commercial-free pedestal. My experience with the Beckett estate during the production of this book suggests that they would prefer Beckett to remain on this pedestal; their decision to block the publication of evidence illustrating Beckett's career-long interest in advertising, publicity, commercial book production, and money is, in fact, entirely consistent with the strategy used to market Beckett's work after he signed with Jérôme Lindon in 1951.

Despite the resistance I have encountered during my research, I remain committed to my thesis because I sincerely believe Beckett would have appreciated my candid analysis of his life as a professional writer. He was, after all, willing to puncture his myth with photographic portraits and material references to his commercial context in his works. Unfortunately, his "sentinels," as Peter Lennon calls them (1990), are invested in a less complex image of the fortress they defend. In light of the analysis in this book, we begin to recognize that received accounts of Beckett's life as a writer not only overlook the facts of his professional life, but that they also disregard one of his most significant contributions to the critical analysis of contemporary culture. It is not just that, as Bruce Arnold notes, Beckett is "big business" and the hottest international literary property of the late Twentieth century" (2003, 90), but that his life and work are a powerful challenge to the idea that art and commerce are incompatible. In this sense Beckett provides a career-long example in support of Andreas Huyssen's thesis in *After The Great Divide: Modernism, Mass Culture, Postmodernism* that "modernism's insistence on the autonomy of the art work, its obsessive hostility to mass culture, its radical separation from the culture of everyday life, and its programmatic distance from political, economic, and social concerns was always challenged as soon as it arose" (1986, ix). From this perspective, the photograph of Beckett that forms the basis of Kyncl's article is entirely consonant with a career that illustrates Beckett's unrelenting challenges to the shibboleths of modernism and new criticism and that situates him with the "postmoderns" who interrogate the discourse of "subjectivity and authorship" (Huyssen 1986, 213). The advertisement for *Index on Censorship* is best seen as a continuation of Beckett's deep investment in strategies highlighting the "tension between tradition and innovation, conservation and renewal, mass culture and high art, in which the second terms are no longer automatically privileged over the first" (216); rather than "absurd," Beckett's agreement to allow the modified "gag" photograph to be used in an advertising campaign is a logical addendum to a career marked by a series of texts that challenge stable understandings of the relationship between art and commerce, blurring distinctions between literary genres and forms, and exploring the expressive opportunities offered by the latest developments in mass media and communications technology. Beckett's sentinels are, I would argue, too focused on defending the fortress they think preserves his sanctity to appreciate the ironic gag he pulled when he allowed Saatchi and Saatchi to superimpose a fake gag over his clenched gob; we do not need to stretch too far to appreciate Beckett's irreverent attitude toward such resolve. Over a period of three decades Beckett pushed the bounds of self-representation, using minimalist techniques to expose and exploit the limits of recording technology (as in *Krapp's Last Tape*), radio technology (as in *All That Fall*), television technology (as in *Eh Joe*) and theater technology (as in *Play*); it is no anomaly that a man capable of such mini-revolutions in a wide range of genres and media would play with representational strategies in an advertising poster, exposing and exploiting the process of self-fashioning and self-representation, ironicizing the authorial image constructed in his name as part of the process designed to establish and perpetuate his career as a professional writer (see figs. 2, 3, and 4).

By focusing on the self-conscious invention and marketing of Beckett's authorial persona in the context of his unrelenting examination of the processes of image-construction and self-representation in his work, and in the context of his authorial persona and his legacy as a writer, we gain insights into the business of literature during a period when, as Raymond Williams puts it, "the anti-bourgeois stance" of modernism "achieved comfortable integration into the new international capitalism" (1996, 35). In short, a critical inquiry into Beckett's life as a professional writer tests Williams's argument that modernist aesthetics, together with "complicit academic endorsements," created a "selective tradition" that turned "marginal or rejected artists" into the "classics of organized teaching and of traveling exhibitions" (31–34). Such an inquiry must take into account Beckett's ongoing interest in "self-writing" (Abbott 1996), focusing on his concerted efforts to fashion a viable authorial persona, to establish a niche in the publishing industry, to protect and preserve his status and legacy, to do so without seeming to do so, and then, crucially, to expose his participation in "the most banal field imaginable, advertising" (Kyncl 1989, 39).

There is no question Beckett became one of the classics of the second half of the twentieth century and that he did so with the approval and support of a number of friends, publishers, and scholars who perpetuated the idea he was averse to publicity and fame. This book provides a preliminary documentation of the process through which he achieved international celebrity status without sacrificing his reputation as writer uninterested in success, fame, and the marketplace. While it begins by accepting, with Bruce Arnold, that Cronin and Knowlson's biographies "provide a splendidly rich account of a key literary figure of this century" (2003, 94), it is specifically intended to supplement this account by focusing on his professional career, foregrounding what Beckett's professional life teaches us about authorship and the business of literature. My thesis is supported by letters that are in research archives in Atlanta, Austin, Bloomington, Dublin, Reading, and St. Louis. Many of these letters have been quoted by Beckett's previous biographers and many more will become publicly available as Cambridge University Press goes ahead with the publication of Beckett's correspondence in four volumes. My argument is no less valid for the "protracted" and "complex" process of negotiations the editors of *The Letters of Samuel Beckett* narrate in their "General Introduction" (Fehsenfeld and Overbeck 2009, xv–xvi). Clearly the Beckett estate remains nervous about which aspects of Beckett they wish to enter the public domain: their decision to block my use of direct evidence from Beckett's correspondence after seeing my manuscript suggests the executors of Beckett's estate continue to defend the received understanding of Beckett's authorial persona. Indeed, that they chose to censor my use of correspondence, published or unpublished, is a sign to me that they see my thesis as a legitimate threat to the image of Beckett as a man "damned to fame": Beckett's "Catholic Truth Society" (1984b, 86) has been reincarnated by the Beckett estate as the "Beckett Truth Society." But the evidence will eventually become public; for example, a letter published in *The Letters of Samuel Beckett* from February 23, 1937, unequivocally indicates Beckett's desperate urge to succeed in the literary marketplace. I am not permitted to quote from the letter, but I refer my patient reader to the second paragraph on page 454 of the first volume for evidence of Beckett's callous willingness to exploit a family friend when he was trying to find a publisher for *Murphy* (2009, 454).

In "The Day of the Rabblement," Joyce asserts that "Until he has freed himself from the mean influences about him—sodden enthusiasm and clever insinuation and every flattering influence of vanity and low ambition—no man is an artist at all" (Joyce 1989, 71–72). If we accept this argument at face value, accepting the possibility of an irreconcilable opposition "between high art and mass culture" (Huyssen 1986, ix), we might see Beckett's participation in a marketing campaign as confirmation of his shared legacy with Havel as the master of the absurd. From this point of view, Beckett's part in the campaign would be "absurd," laughably unreasonable, because Beckett was the least likely person on earth to seek the public spotlight and was even less likely to seek public attention through a T-shirt. Because Beckett's image lies in the realm of artistic, noncommercial purity and integrity, any implication he stepped outside this realm is perceived as an unwanted intrusion, subjecting him to "intolerable" suffering. The title of Kyncl's article points to the idea, repeated in the main biographies of Beckett and taken as a defining principle of the "sole authorized biography," *Damned to Fame,* that fame was, for Beckett, not just unwanted but "catastroph[ic]" (Knowlson 1996, 505). Kyncl links Beckett and Havel through their shared intolerance for public attention, turning them into martyrs suffering the intolerability of fame; he thus suggests that they suffer from what Huyssen calls "the anxiety of contamination by . . . an increasingly consuming and engulfing mass culture" (1986, ix). The strong implication is that they have been chosen by forces beyond themselves to perform a major public function against their private will. Again, Kyncl is entirely consistent with the authorized version of Beckett's persona that had been in circulation since the 1950s, courtesy of Beckett's business colleagues, and that would be turned into "the" narrative of his life in *Damned to Fame.* For example, Knowlson would interpret Beckett's "appalled reaction[s]" to the Nobel award in 1969 as evidence that "[h]e saw only too clearly how much his long-term future would be disrupted by the celebrity, in addition to his present peace being shattered" (Knowlson 1996, 505). In order to stay consistent with a thesis demonizing fame so as to elevate the artist above the hoi polloi, Knowlson downplays Beckett's careful professionalism. As we see in chapter 8, by doing so he overlooks how the "publicity-shy author" (506) used the on-site help of Suzanne Beckett (née Dumesnil) and Jérôme Lindon, and frequent and detailed business-focused letters to John Calder, Barney Rosset, and a host of other acquaintances who were invested in his work (including Ruby Cohn, Jack MacGowran, Henry Wenning, and Samuel Zacks), to take control over the press coverage of his Nobel award and to manage his life and work from sites in Northern Africa and Southern Europe until late January 1970, three months after the award was announced. Beckett's approach, supported by a loyal professional network, enabled him to accept the Nobel Prize without being overwhelmed by the media circus that came with it; for three months he stayed out of the public spotlight and ran his professional life remotely, through his surrogates.

In keeping with an authorial image fashioned in the postwar years, during a period when Beckett was dependent on the professional services of Toni Clerkx and George Reavey, and when Dumesnil provided crucial support, Knowlson underplays the extent to which Beckett's professional minders effectively reduced the "disruption" and "stress" accompanying the Nobel. This tendency to downplay the role of Beckett's professional assistants has the entirely intended effect of reinforcing the idea that Beckett was isolated, bolstering the impression that he was ensconced in a noncommercial world and that any incursions he made into the marketplace were anomalous, "absurd."

Against those who treasure the idea that Beckett was a saint (as John Calder suggested with no apparent irony in an article, "A Saint Born on Good Friday," in *The Independent* on April 13, 1990), unique in his indifference to "the favour of the multitude" (Joyce 1989, 71), we assert that Beckett's life as a writer is most productively seen in terms of the materialist approach inaugurated by Virginia Woolf in *A Room of One's Own* (1929) and brought into the modern academy in 1985 when D. F. McKenzie first published *Bibliography and the Sociology of Texts*. In the context of Huyssen's analysis of the collapse of the division between art and commerce, and seen in terms of the sociology of texts, Beckett's participation in the campaign for *Index on Censorship* is far from being "emblematic of the theatre of the absurd" (Kyncl 1989, 39). Instead, understood in the context of Beckett's professional life as a writer, it becomes symptomatic of a relationship with the literary marketplace that goes back to the beginning of his career in the late 1920s. Although it does not sit comfortably with the idea that he was an unknown celebrity, damned to fame while remaining indifferent to success and money, the professional and commercial life this image invokes is entirely consistent with the method through which this idea was put into circulation. Like me, most Beckett critics accept that Beckett demands deep analysis of interactions between words and images as they construct and constrain the representation and misrepresentation of beings in time. I would argue that his work invites us to apply this kind of analysis to the persona referred to with the label "Samuel Beckett," suggesting we challenge the use of "*The*" in the title of Knowlson's biography by putting his art-focused account alongside a more pragmatic account of Beckett's life as a professional writer.

A quick summary should suggest the relevance of this alternative account. While Beckett conducted his business affairs in ways that distanced him from any hint of "vanity or low ambition" (Joyce 1989, 72), we can still begin our analysis of his professional persona with Beckett himself, with the fact he launched his career by reflecting on "the prospect of self-extension in the world of Mr. Joyce's *Work in Progress*" (*GCE IV*, 495). In 1929–38 Beckett did a lot of creative writing. But he also stomped the streets and knocked on doors in search of people who would support his authorial ambitions; he sat down to eat and drink with a long list of potential allies in the publishing industry. And, as Fehsenfeld and Overbeck's collection of letters *selected* from the period 1929–40 demonstrates, he wrote more than six hundred letters that fit the criterion of "having bearing on my work" (2009, xvi). His correspondents were, typically, well placed in the publishing industry, and the letters often address specific moves he was making to establish a professional career. Every trip through London brought him into contact with agents and publishers. After his move to Paris in 1937, he dedicated his life to building the foundations of a viable career, experimenting during the war, then working hard in 1946–50 to define a new approach to prose and drama, creating a body of work that would sustain him well into the 1950s. In the prewar phase, Beckett benefited from the support of Richard Aldington, Nancy Cunard, Mary Manning Howe, James Joyce, Charles Prentice, George Reavey, Edward Titus, and Jack Yeats. In the postwar phase he was boosted by Dumesnil's loyal support, together with the professional services of Clerkx, Reavey, and Pierre Bordas. Then, in November 1950, he entered the world of long-term publishing contracts, signing with Jérôme Lindon at Les Editions de Minuit. And in June 1953 his career became supercharged when he signed with Barney Rosset at Grove Press. After 1950 he posed for an increasing number of publicity shots that would become central to the Samuel Beckett "brand," creating the resilient image of a private man thrust reluctantly into public life; it is interesting to note that many of these iconic photographs were taken in his "private" rooms and all were taken with his full consent (figs. 3 and 5).

Beckett had been signing collectors' editions of his texts since the release of *Whoroscope* in August 1930 and *Echo's Bones* in 1935; but after he contracted with Lindon and Rosset, and later when he contracted with John Calder, this particular marketing technique became both routine and lucrative. After Lindon signed Beckett, every text he published was available in at least one limited edition, signed by the author, with a special binding and, often, on special paper. In the wake of the success of *Godot,* the increasingly famous author substantiated and expanded his public reputation through careful attention to his contractual obligations; he also kept in close contact with those who organized the marketing and other campaigns waged in his name, participating (though always behind the scenes) in a series of events that established and furthered his international prestige. Although the author did not join the lecture circuit touring bookstores and universities to propel sales, he actively supported and encouraged those, like John Calder and Jack MacGowran, who *did* make presentations designed to expand the market for his books. Beckett actively supported these "Evenings with Beckett" while camouflaging his involvement. Numerous letters to Calder and Rosset demonstrate that he suggested readings and the order of presentation and wrote guidelines for actors who would present author-approved extracts from his work. He thus supported events where his presence was indicated without being realized. By the end of the 1960s he was directly involved in fund-raising for the Samuel Beckett Theatre at Oxford, and it is arguable that the wide net cast in search of donors for this theater, together with the numerous promotional events held in Beckett's honor, fueled the process that culminated in the award of the 1969 Nobel Prize for Literature (fig. 6). In the years after the Nobel Prize he actively supported the development of a Samuel Beckett Festival, a Samuel Beckett archive, the Beckett International Foundation, and an authorized biography that represented him as a man "damned to fame": it is not insignificant that both the first major festival and the archive were presided over by the man who would become his "sole authorized" biographer, James Knowlson.

Much of the promotional work on Beckett's behalf was done for, not by, Beckett. But there is significant evidence of active self-promotion. As he became known, Beckett enhanced interest in, and access to, his work by releasing personal commentaries at key moments. When he was trying to launch his postwar career in France he published "Three Dialogues" (1949), providing a number of phrases that have become standard interpretive frameworks for his texts; when the first New York run of *Waiting for Godot* was on the horizon in 1956, he provided Israel Shenker with phrases that continue to shape readings of his work, especially in relation to Beckett's aesthetic as it differs from Joyce's; and when the 1958 Cherry Lane production of *Endgame* promised to demonstrate his longevity in the literary marketplace, he "reluctantly" allowed the play's director, Alan Schneider, to publish his letters. From these texts we get some of the most important ideas in Beckett studies: he preferred failure; he felt obliged to write even though he had no desire to do so; he focused on impotence and ignorance; his work speaks for itself; critical analysis is undertaken at the reader's own risk. One way of understanding the structure of Beckett's life as a professional writer is, in fact, in terms of the pattern he adopted of publishing ostensibly peripheral texts that would have an enormous influence on subsequent interpretations of his work. And the pattern has the features of a deliberate strategy: each of these commentary texts was deliberately presented so Beckett could deny any hint of complicity in literary marketing and personal publicity: the Duthuit conversation is presented as a fictionalized drama and is, anyway, about painting, not literature; the words in the Shenker report are not verbatim and can be dismissed as the fanciful product of a reporter's memory; the Schneider letters were, we are told in the headnote, published against his will.

Beckett's participation in what Kyncl calls the "banal field of advertising" is, then, entirely consistent with a career during which the author created and managed his public image without apparent effort and with minimal evidence of his participation, preserving the image of isolation even as he wrote hundreds of letters that reveal deep engagement with every aspect of the literary marketplace and even as he facilitated the publication of material designed both to boost and to influence the reception of his work; as I have suggested, this image management and disguised self-promotion is also in keeping with the analysis of image-making and self-representation in his literary texts. It is to be expected that an author who engaged in such intense analyses was supremely conscious about the construction and deployment of his authorial persona. As we'll see, his success in controlling and protecting his private life and public image was possible not only through his ability to frame interpretations of his work through indirect (and deniable) means, but also because he worked diligently to create a manageable professional life and to enlist the support of a long list of professional actors, agents, directors, painters, photographers, producers, publishers, and scholars who would work, *in his name,* to protect and preserve his authorial persona. Again, my experience with Rosica Colin Limited, agent for Edward Beckett, who became Beckett's executor when Jérôme Lindon died in April 2001, is a good illustration of how the Beckett estate continues to protect this image. In the absence of any explanation on their part, I must conclude that their refusal to grant permission to quote Beckett's letters after they had insisted on seeing the full manuscript of this book is due to a disagreement with my thesis: even though they do not have control over access to the letters, they are determined to control what is done with the content of the letters. This conclusion is supported by the fact that the material I asked to use from Beckett's correspondence is readily available to anyone who travels to Reading University, the Harry Ransom Humanities Research Center in Austin, and the other archives, and much of the relevant correspondence is already available in the three main biographies (Bair, Cronin, and Knowlson) or will become available through the four-volume *Letters of Samuel Beckett.* Further, the Beckett estate willingly sold me a complete copy of Beckett's letters to Tom McGreevy held by Trinity College Dublin. Access is not the problem; the problem is how I interpret the evidence and what I choose to emphasize. Because my book focuses on Beckett's construction of an authorial persona, challenging the "authorized" representation of Beckett as a man "damned to fame," and because it threatens to take Beckett off the pedestal of artistic noncommercialism, the Beckett estate made the rather extraordinary decision to deny permission to use Beckett's correspondence *published or unpublished.* This decision has led to some awkwardness in how I present my evidence; but I would argue that the decision reinforces my thesis, supporting the assertion that there is an ongoing effort by Beckett's representatives to control representations of his authorial persona and literary legacy.

In many cases the professionals responsible for protecting and perpetuating Beckett's legacy are deeply invested in the idea that Beckett "loathed all forms of self-exposure or self-promotion" (Haynes and Knowlson 2003, 1). To borrow a metaphor from Stan Gontarski's "Greying the Canon: Beckett in Performance" (Gontarski and Uhlmann 2006, 141–57), the received Beckett legacy emphasizes the idea that "he recoiled from the role of omniscient author, projecting for himself instead an image of authorial impoverishment, indigence, and impotence" (142–43). In this projection his career is defined in terms of a "diminished author-ity" (143), his interactions with publishing, advertising, and other aspects of literary commerce foisted upon him from the outside, his tolerance for money-making and the other "trappings of fame" more to do with his generosity to friends than any desire on his part to make a successful living as a professional writer. However, when we dig into the details of his professional life it becomes evident that his Nobel-winning career was not so "white."

As this broad summary suggests, a greying of Beckett's image happens when we highlight specific evidence of his ongoing engagement with literary marketing and the profession of writing. Exactly because Beckett was so careful in controlling his public persona, and exactly because his professional network of sentinels remains invested in the protection and preservation of his purity as an artiste, it is very difficult to build a comprehensive understanding of Beckett's relationship with the literary marketplace. The Beckett estate and other "authorized" and approved guardians and representatives remain deeply invested in what can only be called a quixotic mission to control the legacy of a man who worked exceedingly hard to nurture contacts in the publishing industry; who spent many years crafting and "exploiting" (to use a word attributed to him in Shenker's 1956 report) a literary approach that would distinguish him from Joyce and other modernists; who engaged in prolific correspondence with literary agents and publishers throughout his career; who willingly posed for publicity photographs in public and private spaces; who participated enthusiastically and diligently in the creation of collectors' editions of his texts and the sale of high-priced manuscripts; who exerted careful control over representations of his life as a writer by issuing strategic interpretive frameworks that continue to shape readings of his work; who managed his representation in newsprint by imposing strict rules on interviewers from magazines and newspapers; who provided extensive advice and support to actors, publishers, and scholars as they orchestrated countless festivals, evenings, galas, fund-raisers, and soirees dedicated to the promotion of his plays and novels; who created and managed his own archival library in a way that is unprecedented except, perhaps, by American presidents; and who spent the last precious months of his life setting the stage and defining the terms for his "authorized biography." There is, I think, sufficient evidence to suggest Beckett was deeply invested in the construction, dissemination, and protection of a commercially viable and sustainable public persona.

But let's return to the supposedly anomalous advertising poster commissioned in 1983 (fig. 1). As we will see in my concluding analysis of *Catastrophe,* which Beckett had written a few months before his agreement with *Index on Censorship,* the image used in the journal's marketing campaign forms an emblematic connection between Beckett's ostensible reaction to the Nobel Prize, his personal experience of celebrity, and his understanding of the relationship between an artist's private life and his public persona. Whether or not we decide to accept Kyncl's argument that the image is an example of Beckett's sense of the absurd, we should not overlook the direct evidence confirming Beckett's agreement to allow the journal to create this image, which superimposes a gag on a photograph of his face with the express purpose of advertising a commercial product. In addition to Karel Kyncl's article, which explains that Beckett "agreed . . . to be shown with a gag," we have confirmation from Kyncl's immediate boss at the Index, Philip Spender (godson of W. H. Auden and brother of Stephen Spender). Spender was an associate editor at the journal in 1983 and became its director and production editor in 1988. In e-mail correspondence with me on June 14, 2004, Spender explained, "Beckett agreed a photo could be used," writing that Beckett "sent a supportive postcard to George Theiner, editor of Index." Unfortunately I have not been able to track down this postcard, but we can fully trust Spender's recollection, accepting without question his December 18, 2007, confirmation that "Samuel Beckett gave permission to Index . . . to use that photo and to superimpose the gag."

The image of Beckett that accompanies Kyncl's article is a modified version of a photograph purchased by *Index on Censorship* from John Minihan in 1984 for one thousand pounds. The original photograph was taken by Minihan in the privacy of Beckett's room in 1980 at the Hyde Park hotel, when the author was "in London to direct *Endgame* at the Riverside Studios with the San Quentin Drama Workshop" (see Minihan 1996 for shots from that session: frontispiece, 52, 53, 56–57, 58). Like numerous photographs taken after Beckett signed with Les Editions de Minuit in 1950, the original photograph is a professionally commissioned portrait deliberately composed to situate Beckett as a private man in a private space; in other words, it publicly documents a moment in his private life in order to reinforce his public image as a man averse to intrusions into his private life. And, while it is an excellent photograph, the pose is, again like many photographic portraits of Beckett taken during the last four decades of his career, worthy of a Hollywood star. Minihan presents Beckett as "Samuel Beckett," the mythic author. And he does so by conforming to the established Beckettian persona, presenting him as though he is an intensely private man. Blurring lines between Beckett the man and Beckett the author, the original photograph thus participates in a process of image-construction that is part-and-parcel of the process that made Beckett "un célèbre inconnu," Madeleine Chapsal's term for Beckett in a February 1957 article for *L'Express* (26). But it also exposes this process *as a process:* it is not a photograph of Beckett; it is a photograph of Beckett the man *posing* as Beckett the author.

As a deliberately situated and posed representation of Beckett, the Minihan photograph suggests a different reading of the line from Pope's *Dunciad* that became the title of Beckett's authorized biography. Knowlson interprets Beckett's citation of "damned to fame" as evidence that Beckett "took steps to avoid what he considered the worst of fame's trappings" (1996, 567), emphasizing his tendency to retreat from the limelight into a carefully guarded private sphere. But I think the strategic process to which Knowlson points also underscores Beckett's deep investment in the myriad ways in which his private life became an extension of his public "fame." And vice versa. A student of Joyce when Joyce was the most famous author in Europe and a successful author who would eventually equate himself with his erstwhile mentor, Beckett was acutely aware that no successful author can hope to escape such trappings. Control, yes. Avoid, no. As Knowlson suggests, Beckett would spend a great deal of energy exerting control over his professional reputation, taking steps designed to protect his ability to compose new work and to enjoy gardening, swimming, traveling, drinking in pubs, fine dining and all the other pleasures of a life considerably improved by the substantial proceeds from his literary endeavors. By invoking the line, Beckett invokes the full implications of a complex epic-comedy written to expose the nature of fame (as a verb-driven process) in London's literary marketplace. He thus signals his awareness that published authors struggle "in vain, in vain" to resist "the pow'r" that compels "all" to "draw near on bended knees" in "Homage to a King" (Pope 1984, *The Dunciad* 4, ll. 514–656). Whether he understood the "King" as fame itself or the channel that allows the author to control his fame by "mak[ing] a long Posterity thy own" (l. 334), Beckett was too humble and too pragmatic to imagine that he, alone among authors, was immune to "Ambition" (l. 623), to the active pursuit of new readers and new sources of revenue. In fact, when we examine his career from the point of view of his development as a professional writer, it is clear Beckett took an active part in the shaping of his reputation and "posterity," doing everything he could to direct how his fame functioned, collaborating in the creation of an archive and a biography, controlling his personal and professional lives as best he could.

When it first appeared, the Saatchi poster resonated with Beckett's most recent play, *Catastrophe* (1982), which had been published a few months earlier in *Index on Censorship* and which remains his most explicit analysis of image manipulation. The poster is, in fact, anticipated by the play's reference to a "gag," and it clearly evokes the image of the protagonist's face that forms the play's "catastrophe." At the same time, the play demonstrates Beckett's intense concern with his persona as an intensely private man reluctantly forced into public view by a futilitarian urge to express himself. With its title the play also refers directly to an established shibboleth of Beckett studies, referencing the received idea that he experienced the Nobel award as a "catastrophe." The "greying" effect on Beckett's reputation as a pure artiste happens when we recognize that the Saatchi campaign and the play it reinforces are consistent with the career of a man who, in 1938, contemplated the most effective ways to find an audience for his work without damaging his professional prospects (Beckett to Reavey, February 20, 1938, *Letters,* 604); who made specific recommendations to Grove Press about the layout and cover art for the first English edition of *Waiting for Godot* (Beckett to

Rosset, December 14, 1953, SUL); who told Tom McGreevy on April 9, 1956, that his only interest in the New York opening of *Godot* was the money it would give him (TCD, 198); whose face advertised the fall 1958 Grove Press catalog (fig. 7); and who featured in a 1966 Evergreen Press advertising campaign alongside "Barbarella" (February 28, 1966, Lilly) (see fig. 2). This greying may not always be as dark as his sometimes desperate efforts in the 1930s to get his work in circulation, but no matter how subtle, it is in keeping with the oeuvre of an author who, in 1934, addressed "the relations between purveyor and consumer" (*GCE IV,* 104) and who, in one of the last plays he wrote, explored "how it looks from the house" and from "the front row of the stalls" (*GCE III,* 487).

Beckett's agreement to participate in the campaign for *Index* invites us to develop an approach to Beckett and his work that celebrates both his self-fashioning and his deliberate exposure of the devices that went into this self-fashioning. As we develop this new way of thinking about Beckett, we will inevitably encounter those who cling to the idea that Beckett was exceptional in his indifference to the literary marketplace, that his life and work are best understood in terms of monkish asceticism. But we must remind ourselves that, like anyone else who makes a living with the pen, he was "a professional working, from first drafts onwards, in a professional world" (Willison, Gould, and Cherniak 1996, xiii). We must also remind ourselves that Beckett had known this pragmatic fact about his livelihood since he worked with Joyce and Jolas in 1929. And we must acknowledge that he was careful *to let us know that he knew:* he was smart enough to know that "to live completely outside market relations was no more possible than breathing without air" (Rainey 1998, 170). I would argue that the *Index* advertisement provides evidence of his willingness to call attention to the fashioning and marketing of his authorial image. Further, I would argue that he had already provided explicit evidence in the form of posed photographs documenting moments in his professional life where his "private" and "professional" lives merged: Roger Pic's 1977 photograph of him signing a collectors' edition of *Imagination Dead Imagine* in his Paris apartment exemplifies this self-revelation (fig. 3); Jerry Bauer's 1973 portrait of him sitting on garbage in an alley during a break from his work with the Royal Court production of *Not I* underscores his willingness to reveal his participation in the fashioning of the authorial persona known as "Samuel Beckett" (see fig. 4).

Index commissioned Saatchi and Saatchi to develop an advertising campaign when its frequency increased from six to ten times a year. Even though it used a black-and-white photograph of Beckett (a choice consistent with the "no-glamour" publicity photographs published after Beckett signed with Lindon), the Saatchi campaign was in keeping with the magazine's relatively expensive, "glossy" cover: Saatchi was, after all, the leading ad agency of the day, its most famous recent client Margaret Thatcher during her June 1983 reelection bid. Saatchi's modified photograph represents Beckett in the way proposed by the "female assistant" in *Catastrophe* (1982) to ensure the "Protagonist" does not "utter" (*GCE III,* 487). It is significant, of course, that the "Director" immediately rejects the idea to use a gag:

> **A** [timidly] What about a little . . . a little . . . gag?
>
> **D** For God's sake! This craze for explicitation! [*sic*] Every i dotted to death! Little gag! For God's sake! (*GCE III,* 486)

In the play there is no need for an actual gag because the Protagonist has no lines to speak: a gag would be gratuitous and, more important, it would lessen the impact of the show-stealing moment when "P raises head, fixes the audience" (*GCE III,* 489). While this moment functions as the play's "catastrophe," it is, from the point of view of the Director, an anti-catastrophe because it is an act of defiance against *his* catastrophe, the image of a "bowed head." The play becomes an expression of the tension between different ways of representing the "Protagonist"; it thus analyzes how a subject's public image is constructed and received. The threat of speech from the Protagonist, a threat made possible because of the decision not to use a gag, is sufficient to silence the prerecorded applause of the audience. Because there is no gag, the action of the play scripted and staged by the on-stage author-director collapses: in an instant of time the script is flipped and the staging directed by the man ostensibly in control is overturned. The director's game of image manipulation is thus challenged by "P"'s silent but show-stopping resistance. Had the director used more "explicitation" by employing a gag, the catastrophe would have been more likely to remain under his control; without the gag, control is permitted to shift to the supposed victim, creating an image of defiance rather than resignation.

In the poster, which was mainly used in the London Underground on trains and in stations, the gag provides the "hook," catching the eye and drawing the casual passerby to a tagline: "If Samuel Beckett had been born in Czechoslovakia we'd still be waiting for Godot." Intrigued by this rather odd statement, potential customers would be likely to read the more detailed selling proposition: "Samuel Beckett's *Waiting for Godot* is banned in Czechoslovakia. In fact, any writing that differs from the opinions of the Czech government is banned in Czechoslovakia. Luckily, Beckett does not live in Czechoslovakia. But what of those writers who do? Fortunately, some of their work can be read in *Index on Censorship*." Beckett, who provided a graphic description of a complex Bovril advertisement in *More Pricks Than Kicks* (*GCE IV,* 108) and who had entertained the idea of becoming an adman when he was struggling to earn a living in the 1930s, knew how marketing works and would have understood why Saatchi wanted to superimpose the gag. By 1984, he had sat through hundreds of photo shoots and portrait paintings, and he had been featured on countless posters advertising his work. He knew from all the posed photographs and caricatures of his face that graphic art requires the dotting of i's, depending on visual impact of the sort he had written about when he imagined the narrator of *The Unnamable* functioning as "a kind of landmark, not to say an advertisement" (*GCE II,* 322). We do not know whether or not Beckett approved the text for the poster, but we *do* have Philip Spender's word that he approved the use of the Minihan photograph and gave permission, through Tom Stoppard, for the gag to be superimposed.

Given his well-documented and assertive, but indirect, control over his work, which was largely accomplished through personal letters and postcards, private meetings and telephone calls, and given that he spent so much time contemplating tensions between written discourse and visual representation, we can assume Beckett would enjoy the complex nexus of references gathered in an image portraying Ihab Hasan's postmodern icon of silence begagged in the name of free speech (Hasan 1967). In addition to publishing *Catastrophe* in the same journal his modified image was used to advertise, Beckett had recently contributed to Sean O'Mordha's *Silence to Silence,* an RTE documentary completed in 1984 featuring Jack MacGowran, Patrick Magee, and Billie Whitelaw. These three actors had, with Beckett's full support, established themselves as his public representatives, proselytizing his work in seminar rooms and on stages across Britain, Ireland, and the United States. In other words, they were author-approved guardians who facilitated Beckett's ability to remain aloof, protecting his image as an author who preferred to remain silent about his work. Their professional viability boosted by the association with Beckett, these and other actors were willing to speak for him in a documentary that is, essentially, a promotional advertisement with its main subject, Samuel Beckett, absent. This absence illustrates Beckett's ability to keep his mouth clenched in public without actually remaining silent. Clenched or gagged, he spoke eloquently and effectively through actors (and others) who were willing, as Whitelaw put it, to function as "the mouthpiece of the greatest playwright of the twentieth century" (1995, 133).

The success of this carefully crafted strategy perhaps explains why Kyncl glides over the complex nexus of biographical threads gathered in the "gag" image. However, if we connect the image with Beckett's professional career we can see that it invokes the author's life (through the Minihan photograph) and work (through the connection to *Catastrophe*) at the same time it reveals the process of media management and the array of professional "mouthpieces" that made him "larger than life," turning him into his own "Godot." Beckett becomes a symbolic, but absent, character with a public image manipulated according to the requirements of a marketing strategy that worked by juxtaposing selected details from his private life with "classic" moments from his work. The photographic portrait of Beckett's clenched mouth underscores the link between the author and the silent "Protagonist"; it thus calls attention to the tension between Beckett's ostensible integrity as a commercially averse "artiste" and his willingness to engage with his publishers in the development of marketing materials. This link between Beckett and his subject was already embedded in *Catastrophe* through the reference to a disease Beckett suffered, "Fibrous degeneration" of the hands (*GCE III,* 486), also known as Dupuytren's syndrome, and it implies that Beckett and the Protagonist share the fate of being on a pedestal subjected to manipulation for the sake of public applause ("He'll have them on their feet," *GCE III,* 489). In this scenario, any private needs or dignity have been sacrificed to accommodate the needs of the paying audience. By invoking this connection between author and character, the poster thus crosses lines between Beckett's private and public lives, connecting the purist Aquinian aesthetics articulated by Joyce in "The Day of the Rabblement" and by his youthful hero, Stephen Dedalus, in *A Portrait of the Artist as a Young Man* (Joyce 1916) with the consumer-based needs of the theater and the fee-paying audience. The greying of the relationship between private and public selves has a profound effect on Beckett's canon. This effect has been fully explored in relation to his aesthetics in H. Porter Abbott's *Beckett Writing Beckett: The Author in the Autograph.* Abbott illustrates how Beckett creates "narrative self-writing" by engaging in a "thorough transmutation of autobiographical sources" (1996, 1–2). The book persuasively undermines the long-established tendency to describe "Beckett's world" as though it is hermetically sealed, the product of a head cut off from the material world (see fig. 8). It thus connects Beckett with Joyce's pragmatic immersion in the marketplace: just as critics have taken note, since the summer/fall 1993 issue of the *James Joyce Quarterly* and the 1996 publication of *Marketing Modernisms* (Dettmar and Watt 1996), of Joyce's efforts to sell *Ulysses,* complicating how we understand the career of a man who has, too often, been read as though his work is shaped by his position in "The Day of the Rabblement" and Stephen Dedalus's exposition of Aquinian aesthetics in *Portrait,* critics can now begin to notice and analyze the "greying" of Beckett's relationship with literary commerce.

The advertising poster for *Index* makes public use of a photograph taken in a private hotel room and, through the gag, it crucially invokes the "quelle catastrophe" story that dominates received understandings of Beckett's "private" reaction to the award that cemented his public role as a twentieth-century icon. Further, by using the gag the Director in *Catastrophe* had rejected, the poster gives the author the appearance of being a public victim of enforced silencing, turning a public "utterance" into an expression of subjectivity. The poster thus plays with Beckett's reputation as a silent author, calling attention to the fact that his exploration of silence was a choice taken in the context of his relative freedom to speak and write exactly as he pleased with little fear of external interference and with no obligation to speak when he chose not to. The censorship message of the poster might have had some direct relevance to Beckett's life as a writer early in his career, when *More Pricks Than Kicks* was banned by the newly installed theologians in the Saorstat. At a stretch it also applies to the period in 1954 through 1958 when he suffered the pedantry of Britain's Lord Chamberlain's decision to declare a few words in *Waiting for Godot* and *Endgame* "blasphemous." But the truth of the matter is that Beckett was unusually free of external controls over his work. His editors made the occasional suggestion, but they always deferred on even the most minor point of punctuation: in the case of *The Lost Ones* this editorial deference to Beckett's authorial autonomy allowed a serious mathematical miscalculation to persist through a number of editions. We can conclude, then, that if the poster speaks of the absurd, it does so through the absurd idea that Beckett himself was gagged in any way. In other words, in a reversal analogous to the shift from catastrophe to anti-catastrophe at the end of the play Beckett dedicated to Havel, the poster highlights the fact that, while Havel was enduring a prison sentence as punishment for his writing, Beckett was almost entirely free of any form of censorship. In this sense it is also analogous to the photographs, such as those by Roger Pic documenting Beckett's signing of collector's texts and the Bauer photograph of Beckett with garbage, because it self-consciously reveals the process of image manipulation that transmuted the private life of a man writing in a room into the professional life of a famous man in the public spotlight.

Beckett's decision to participate in an explicitly political marketing campaign designed to attract international attention to the cause of those imprisoned for their support of Charter 77 required little more than his agreement with the request to use and modify a photograph taken three years earlier. In Philip Spender's account, Beckett mainly wanted assurance that *Index* was a legitimate publication. But because he had a firmly established reputation for silence on political matters *and* was framed as though he were "notoriously elusive throughout his life" (Minihan 1996, flyleaf), and because his prior involvement in publicity and advertising had been effectively downplayed, the poster remains important to our understanding of Beckett's public image. Despite his minimal effort—which may explain why Tom Stoppard has no recollection of his role as intermediary in negotiations between Beckett and *Index*—the campaign had commercial and political impact. The gagged face is visually dramatic exactly because it is Beckett's face. His authorial image was so firmly established in terms of his reluctance to participate in any form of publicity, political, commercial or otherwise, that his appearance in an advertisement draws attention. In this sense it connects with the Grove Press campaign in 1964 using a photograph of Beckett with the caption, "Samuel Beckett will be appearing at your local news-stand" (fig. 2). As with the Grove campaign—which worked because Beckett himself was unlikely to appear at a local newsstand in New York and because his work was associated with specialty bookstores rather than local sellers of magazines and newspapers—the advertisement gains potency exactly because his participation is unexpected and surprising.

True to a pattern that developed in the 1930s when George Reavey acted as his agent—a pattern that became increasingly sophisticated after 1945, when Suzanne Dumesnil functioned as an intermediary between Beckett and potential publishers; when Lindon, Rosset, and Calder became the main conduits between Beckett and his public; and when Magee, MacGowran, Whitelaw and other actors became his "mouthpieces"—his participation in the campaign was indirect, leaving little trace of his complicity aside from the very fact of the poster itself. Fortunately, Philip Spender distinctly remembers that Beckett authorized the use of the photograph and the gag. By participating, however minimally, in the Saatchi campaign, Beckett acknowledged his engagement with an image-driven medium he had recently parodied in *Catastrophe*. He managed to do so without uttering a public word, expressing his views on politics *and* participating in advertising without appearing to do so. As we will see throughout this study, this participation that gives the impression of resisting participation is one of the hallmarks of Beckett's authorial persona: it led Ronald Hayman to conclude his article "The Most Courageous Writer Going" by writing, "I can think of no one who deserves a Nobel Prize more—and no one who will care less about having won it" (1969). Beckett's brilliance is evident from his ability to manage his affairs so he could accept the prize while giving the impression he preferred not to; in this sense he inherited James Joyce's strategic use of the antimarketing marketing campaign, a use of "stealth advertising" (as it is called in the industry) specifically designed to appeal to those who resist mainstream marketing techniques. Contemporary examples of this strategy include Honda's series based on the slogan "The Car That Sells Itself" and Nextel's television campaign with a star using a Nextel phone to tell his agent, "I don't do advertising." In this context the gagged image underscores the process of antimarketing marketing that turned Beckett's face into an iconographic representation of the Beckettian aesthetics of silence. His clenched mouth was reproduced with such frequency and such consistency after the success of *Godot* in 1956 that it eventually "spoke for itself," advertising his work with the efficiency of a "brand." As we'll see in chapter 1, this brand reached its expressive crescendo with the photograph by John Haynes used on the cover of the first edition of *Damned to Fame* (1996), but it was created over a twenty-year period and can be seen through a series of publicity photographs beginning with the side profile used in the playbill for the first production of *En Attendant Godot*. Representing Beckett as "a man in a void" (November 1956 review of "Malone Dies," SUL), this image established the idea that Beckett was in a world of his own, isolated from the "rabblement," his head floating free of the sordid, grubby world of money and publicity, self-promotion and fame (fig. 8).

In Kyncl's view, the next stage of development by *Index* truly pushed Beckett's involvement in "the most banal field imaginable, advertising," into the realm of the absurd, producing the "intolerable shirt of fame" and "a little story . . . which seems to resemble absurd moments in the plays of both Beckett and Havel" (1989). Tempted as we are to connect this quintessentially postmodern episode with Beckett himself, the evidence suggests

Beckett played no role in the T-shirt episode (though the fact *Index* was free to use the image in a subsequent campaign confirms its ownership and, thus, Beckett's approval; given his reaction to the American Repertory Theater production of *Endgame* in 1984, we can be certain Beckett or, more likely, his representatives in London, would have challenged *Index* if his copyright interests had been violated). Still, it is an episode worth exploring because it points to the postmodern character of the fame Beckett achieved during the course of his long professional career.

Philip Spender recalls that in November 1989 David Holden at Index commissioned a T-shirt using the image and copy from the poster. He proposed giving the T-shirts to famous people, creating advertisements from photographs of them wearing the shirt. At the top of the list was Vaclev Havel, a friend of Beckett's who had risen to international fame after his January 1989 release from a Czechoslovakian prison. The first issue of the shirt sold quickly, but the collapse of the Soviet Union and Havel's ascension to the presidency made it obsolete. In response, Holden redesigned the shirt to include an advertisement on the back with an image of Havel on a postage stamp, and a caption saying "We helped give Vaclev Havel a licking he'll never forget" (private letter from Philip Spender, June 14, 2004). This second version of the shirt was advertised in 1990–1991 in a series called "Eminent Persons in Index T-shirts" (see back cover of *Index* 19, no. 6, June–July 1990). The campaign was launched in April 1990 with the tag line, "Far be it from us to use one man's good fortune for personal gain. . . . We'll use three" (back cover of *Index* 19, no. 4, April 1990). Composed from the 1985 poster with the gagged Beckett, the new Havel postage stamp, and a photograph of Stephen Spender wearing the T-shirt, the advertisement in volume 19, number 4 of *Index* (April 1990) inaugurated a series to include photographs of Lothaire Bluteau (June–July 1990) and Michael Heath (September 1990). The plan had been to use a fourth advertisement featuring Havel, but Havel refused once he heard about Beckett's death. In February 1991, however, the inside front cover of the magazine finally included a photograph of Havel wearing the shirt (*Index* 20, no. 2, February 1991).

Beckett's face works in the advertisement, both on the poster and on the T-shirt, because he had already achieved iconographic status as *the* man of silence in the years after *Godot* brought international fame. His face was instantly recognizable because it had appeared with some regularity since 1953 on book covers, in newspaper articles, and in theater promotion. While it is clear the advertisement gave Beckett no direct commercial benefits, and while *Index* was never a money-spinner, even when Saatchi used Beckett's face to boost sales, the poster underscores the marketability of his face. And, crucially, it does so by representing him as someone orally silenced *and* pictorially eloquent. As such, the advertisement takes advantage of a paradox central to literary commerce and to every text Beckett wrote after World War II: the writer "speaks" as an absence through a silent medium, representing speech and presence with written marks that allow his absence and that are as silent as dried ink. To use advertising-speak, the unlikelihood of Beckett speaking publicly is the main selling proposition.

In Kyncl's received understanding of Beckett's public image, the most obvious implications of the Saatchi image are displaced by the suggestion that Beckett's decision to participate in an advertising campaign was "incredible." Unable to see past the authorial image created during Beckett's early years of fame in the 1950s, an image reified in the hundreds of obituaries published across Europe and America in the week after Christmas 1989, Kyncl adds another biographical tale to what would become the authorized representation of Beckett as someone with "a phobia about appearing in public situations," who "could not bear intrusions into his private life," and who quoted "Damned to fame" from *The Dunciad* "as he took steps to avoid what he considered to be the worst of fame's trappings" (Knowlson 1996, 567). As I have begun to suggest, in the process, Kyncl reiterates the basic principles of the 1950s marketing campaign that made Beckett internationally famous as "un célèbre inconnu" (Chapsal, 1957). This representation was firmly established in the English marketplace by March 1958, when an anonymous writer for the *Daily Mail* wrote: "Seldom photographed, never interviewed, Beckett . . . has a deep revulsion against personal publicity" (fig. 5).

Anticommercialism was, of course, par for the course for Beckett's predecessors and peers. As Huyssen argues convincingly, it was a central credo of the modernist manifesto writers that "modernism and mass culture" are opposed (1986, ix). The editors of *Transition,* Eugene Jolas and Elliott Paul, loyal to Beckett from June 1929 to 1938, repeatedly attacked "the encroachment of commercialism upon the field of art" (April 1927, 135), "the businessmen of literature" (March 1928, 142), and "the salesmen in the marketplace hawking their messages" (March 1932, 248). As Lawrence Rainey has suggested in *Institutions of Modernism,* these editors were clinging to an "adversarial model of culture" with "the belief that only cultural activity inimical or in opposition to dominant social values can be genuine or true culture" (1998, 8). In keeping with this belief, and as part of the "revolution of the word" proclaimed repeatedly in the journal, in June 1927 to June 1929, the editors chose not to capitalize the first letter of the journal's title; when Jolas turned the magazine into a quarterly in fall 1930, he changed the name, now using the conventional capital letter. Jolas and his co-editors failed to see how their own work engaged in a process of commodification whereby the works of art they published were "integrated into a[n] . . . economic circuit of patronage, collecting, speculation, and investment" (3). True to Raymond Williams's thesis in *The Politics of Modernism,* as modernist marketing managers worked to define a market share for a product that was, ostensibly anyway, pitched in opposition to commerce, anti-advertising became a necessary strategy. As "all authors" became "inescapably enmeshed in commercialism" (1996, 35), certain artists claimed to transcend the dross of commerce, defining their exceptionalism in terms of aesthetic purity. In modernism the opposition between art and commerce became a central defining principle; journals like *transition* made it their main selling proposition, pitching themselves to a niche in the marketplace that was holding out, "by the skin of its teeth," against "the loss of aesthetic autonomy" (Rainey 1998, 3). The fact that John Keats, who Beckett quotes freely in texts from *More Pricks Than Kicks* to *Happy Days,* saw the impossibility of avoiding commerce is a sure sign that any possibility of absolute artistic integrity had faded long before Beckett set pen to paper: in a letter to P. B. Shelley, Keats acknowledged that, despite living a "monastic life, . . . an artist must serve Mammon" (August 16, 1820, Keats 2002). Beckett clearly knew this sobering fact from the beginning of his career. Between 1929 and 1937 he was directly involved in Joyce's campaign to find an audience for "Work in Progress." Beckett's first publication, "Dante . . . Bruno . Vico . . Joyce," was part of this campaign, and his developing understanding of what it meant to be a professional writer was forged in proximity to a host of literary agents, patrons, and publicists (Nancy Cunard, Peggy Guggenheim, Eugene Jolas, Tom McGreevy, Charles Prentice, Samuel Putnam, George Reavey). Even as Joyce explored advertising in *Ulysses* (1922) and remained chief orchestrator of books designed to promote his own work—most notably Gilbert's *James Joyce's Ulysses* (1930) and Shakespeare and Company's *Our Exagmination Round His Factification for Incamination of Work in Progress* (1929)—and even as Virginia Woolf revealed the inextricability of money and creativity in *A Room of One's Own* (1928), the ideal artist remained on a pedestal, indifferent to celebrity, oblivious to material success, and uninterested in public opinion. Beckett inherited both sides of this equation and would construct his public image in terms of a preference for failure (Beckett 1958) and "artistic integrity" (Gruen 1969). While he was careful to cleanse himself of "contamination" from the promotional business he did for Joyce by purging any direct connection to the Joyce circle, freeing himself from "the association with Joyce," he knew he could only sustain a viable and livable professional career by developing a network of his own that he could control with his own protocols: this is what he did in 1950–72. He became a sort of amateur professional, offhanded about certain things but extremely strict about others, shifting between repeated confessions of his confusion and stupidity about copyright issues and other aspects of the literary marketplace and long passages establishing his intentions and expectations. For example, in a May 6, 1958 (RUL), letter to Rosica Colin of Faber and Faber, he was extremely precise in clarifying rights pertaining to future texts he would write for the theater or radio, using legal discourse to define his own jurisdiction and to distinguish between the contractual situation as regards John Calder and Faber. In the letter Beckett balances legalese with a casual attitude that allows for solutions and compromise as necessary. As he progressed from being a struggling writer determined to succeed to being a successful writer struggling to sustain this success, he gently but firmly established control over his publications, his contracts, his professional acquaintances, and his public image. But his ostensible aversion to publicity and self-promotion did not manifest itself in the ways it did for Thomas Pynchon and J. D. Salinger, who retreated so completely they retained their anonymity; unlike Pynchon and Salinger, Beckett avoided the "worst trappings" of fame while putting himself in a position to analyze how fame functions.

Before we conclude this introduction to our study of Beckett's life as a professional writer, we must note that the analysis of self-representation and persona manipulation we see in *Catastrophe* was preceded by a number of such analyses going back to the beginnings of Beckett's career. The amateurish professionalism of someone who writes for a living is, in fact, crucial to the framing narrative that sets up Beckett's major trilogy of novels. The opening of *Molloy* describes an author who, it seems, has achieved Virginia Woolf's ideal of a room and an income. But he is by no means independent or isolated. His "room" was his "mother's" and he admits he "was helped." He also admits he is part of an economic system of exchange: "So many pages, so much money." He works in a commercial system, serving "Mammon," but he sees himself as an amateur: he doesn't "know how to work any more," he doesn't understand the "signs" marked on the returned pages, and he doesn't "work for money" (*GCE II,* 3). While he depends on a professional network of third persons ("they" and "he" [3-4]) to provide transport, money, editorial assistance, creative advice, and literary criticism, he occupies a space in which it "doesn't matter apparently" whether he "know[s] how to work" or whether he can "spell" or remember "the words" (3). He is, then, a quintessential amateur surrounded by an enabling set of professionals: his ostensible isolation is enabled by his contacts in the commercial world. Molloy's progress, which somehow extends the imagined journey that connects Belacqua to Murphy to Watt to Moran, and which anticipates the imagined journeys pursued by all Beckett's subsequent prose characters, is the progress of a writer stuck in a "Denn." In a five-hundred-word paragraph that functions as a preamble, Beckett establishes the fact that Molloy's isolation from the world is enabled by his fortnightly contact with a go-between who connects him with the world of markets and money. In the context of the received myth, we can certainly understand how Enoch Brater would conclude that the trilogy sets out "to explore the boundaries of a totally hermetic sphere" (1986, 51). But we must insist that the grey-toned world of the marketplace is a constant backdrop not only in Beckett's "private" life, which engaged him in perpetual correspondence with his network of professional aides and led to numerous sessions with photographers, academics, and other professional colleagues in his Paris apartment and in his cottage at Ussy (as well as in hotel rooms like the one in Hyde Park that formed the setting for the Minihan photograph used in the Saatchi ad), but also in his entire oeuvre up to and including *Stirrings Still* (1988). Again and again, he punctures the "hermetic sphere," greying the idealized whiteness of his texts by reminding us of their material contexts.

Literary analysis is not the primary focus of this book, but we will delve into Beckett's texts to illustrate that his participation in advertising and promotional photography, his business-oriented correspondence, and his work developing collectors texts and archival repositories, are complemented by explorations in his published work. The "greying" effect that occurs when we cast aside received understandings of Beckett's legacy and take seriously the efforts he made to establish a successful professional livelihood is complemented by the literary references he made to the marketplace and the material contexts that make writing possible. In an economy of writing where the work ethic is diminishing but where "the obligation to express" remains, the mechanisms of the marketplace are never very far away.

A summary perusal of his texts to *How It Is* (1964) reveals his ongoing concern with economic and material situations that contextualize and enable characters that seem, otherwise, to be isolated and disabled. He is not as direct as Virginia Woolf in her pioneering work on the material contexts that make writing possible in "A Room of One's Own." But he is equally persistent, reminding us again and again that the apparently independent "I" is dependent on networks of people who provide various kinds of sustenance and support: Belacqua, Murphy, Watt, Molloy, Malone, Mahood, and the rest struggle to define themselves as autonomous beings, but they are as dependent on "outside" help as *Murphy*'s narrator is on "the gentle compositor" (*GCE I,* 141). The entire plot of Beckett's first published novel is, in fact, driven by the pressure on Murphy to get a job in the money-centered world of "quid pro quo" (*GCE I,* 1). Murphy prefers the solipsistic bliss of his rocking chair but is compelled "to cultivate the sense of time as money which he had heard highly prized in business circles" (45). Although, as we might expect of a "Beckettian" character, his flat on Brewery Road is next to Pentonville Prison, it is also next to "the Caledonian Market" (43). As he searches, or avoids searching, for a job, he traipses the same streets Beckett traipsed as he sought a publisher. He waits in the environs of commercial establishments in direct proximity to the publishing houses Beckett frequented in 1935–38: "The Perseverance and Temperance Yards, the Vis Vitae Bread Co., the Marx Cork Bath Mat Manufactory . . . waiting for the market clock to chime" (*GCE I,* 47). Like a modernist writer infused with the antimarket rhetoric of *Transition* and the other avant-garde magazines of the age, Murphy considers "all working for a living" to be "a procuring and a pimping for the money-bags, one's lecherous tyrants the money-bags, so that they might breed" (48). He has adopted "aloof able-bodied postures on the fringes of the better-attended slave markets" (48–49), exhibiting the modernist disdain for the job market. But even as he stands on the fashionable margins, observing the market from an elitist position and representing himself to himself as "a closed system . . . self-sufficient and impermeable" (68), his author underlines his dependence on the "big blooming buzzing" (5) and the world of markets, money, and "commerce" (7). Like Beckett himself, whose income from translations and other publications was generously supplemented by family money and, after 1938, by the earnings of his girlfriend, Suzanne Dumesnil, Murphy benefits from monthly contributions by his uncle, Mr. Quigley (89), and is partly supported by Celia's "savings" (42). Even though "Murphy's mind" proposes a theoretical ideal of "willlessness" (70), his life is defined by positive acts of will: for example, he uses his skills of deception and his facility with language to wheedle extra tea out of a waitress (51–53) and finds a "use for a pot poet" by tricking Ticklepenny into paying his bill (58–59). Even if we challenge the long-standing tendency in Beckett studies to equate Beckett's life with the lives explored in his fictional works, a tendency exemplified by Grove Press's use of a line from the end of *The Unnamable* as the title for a collection of his work (*I Can't Go On, I'll Go On,* 1976 and 1992), we have to admit that Murphy the character and *Murphy* the book are situated from beginning to end in commercial contexts. Murphy, and later Beckett characters, may think of themselves as hermetically sealed beings, but the books in which they are presented reveal that their solipsism is as false as the idea that an internationally famous writer had no interest in success, money, and the literary marketplace.

A quick survey of a few moments in Beckett's post-*Murphy* prose reveals that money and the workings of the marketplace remain a regular subject. For example, *Watt* is punctuated by the main character's purchase of tickets to get him to and from the house that forms the main setting of the novel. Enabled by a system of postindustrial travel, Watt is introduced in a context that emphasizes his economic position: soon after he arrives on the scene, he is defined in terms of how much money he owes Mr. Nixon (*GCE I,* 180); further, he enters Mr. Knott's house as a paid servant in "Mr Knott's establishment" (201). Beckett's interest in the economic basis of Watt's relationship with Mr. Knott is underlined by the fact that the narrator spends page after page calculating the economy of supply and demand, what he calls "the arrangement" (239–40), as it pertains to the disposal of leftover food, the dog that eats this food, and the family that keeps the dog (239–62). Even though Watt is entranced by the idea "that nothing could be added to Mr Knott's establishment, and from it nothing taken away, but that as it was now, so it had been in the beginning" (276), the narrator systematically documents the comings and goings of the various tradesmen who keep Knott's house functioning (222, 289). Again, the idea of an isolated, self-enclosed, hermetically sealed world is punctured by Beckett's attention to the commercial relationships that make this world possible. Whether it is Molloy standing in a shop doorway on a workday morning or inventing codes to get money from his mother; Moran sending his son to buy a bicycle or figuring out the chain of responsibility while he approaches "nutritional zero" (149); Malone contemplating "The market" and "the inadequacies of the exchanges between the rural and urban areas" as he compiles an inventory of his "chattels personal" (196); the "I" in *The Unnamable* contemplating his position as "a kind of landmark, not to say an advertisement" (328); or the "I" of *How It Is* "working" under the watchful eye of "a woman" who "stoops to her work again the needle stops in midstitch she straightens up and looks at me again" (10), market forces and the labor market are part of the ongoing pattern of Beckett's literary output.

But because the main thrust of Beckett's oeuvre is understood to be toward a form of puritanical asceticism typically defined as "minimalism" and anti-intellectual, the commercial marks Beckett imprinted on his texts have been downplayed. Instead, the emphasis has been placed on his "aestheticism" and "exotic and willful singularity" (Abbott 1996, 60–62), the "fictionality of fiction" and his tendency to write "about the process of writing" (Cohn 2001, 168), "the multiplication of interior voices" (Albright 2003, 4), and "the consciousness of surveillance" (Uhlmann 1999, 48). These elements, and more aspects associated with modernist and postmodernist, poststructuralist and deconstructive literary technique, are certainly evident in what Cohn calls "the Beckett canon." But the tendency to revere him as "a poet who has never made the slightest concession, never sought acclaim, never explained himself, who has never bowed to the demands of fashion or publicity" (Esslin 1982, 109), has made him seem more like a product of seventeenth-century feudal literary relations than someone with a deep and complex understanding of the ubiquitousness of market relations in the twentieth century and the role of the professional writer in the years after World War II. Despite the evidence from his texts, from his correspondence, from his indirect statements about his work, from his participation in advertising, and from work he did to augment the market value of collectors' texts and to create archival repositories designed to protect his long-term legacy, Beckett is represented as though he is as ignorant about publishing, marketing, and the world beyond the pure domain of artistic creation as his characters are about any order of discourse beyond their immediate experience (see Uhlmann's discussion of *Molloy* [1999, 40–57]).

Operating according to an ingrained work ethic that would emerge in his critical prose as "an obligation to express" (*GCE IV*, 556), Beckett represented himself as though he never worked hard enough, as though he never knew what he was doing when he did work, and as though he never knew what his work meant once it was done. Even during his most productive periods, Beckett repeatedly complained of his lethargy and failure. The "obligation to express" is part and parcel with the rhetoric of humility that leads "B," in "Three Dialogues," to assert a "fidelity to failure" and to conclude "I am mistaken" (*GCE IV,* 563). And it connects him with those who seek freedom through work in a world of vanity and the vanity of vanities. In this context we can draw a line connecting Beckett to a literary tradition that includes Bunyan, Johnson, and Carlyle. It is in terms of such a tradition that I read James Knowlson's choice of the title for *Damned to Fame: The Life of Samuel Beckett.* As I have suggested, the line from *The Dunciad* situates Beckett *in the marketplace,* in the parade of fools parodied by Pope; as such, it invites us to contemplate the difference between authorial self-representation designed to boost public interest and the actual life lived by a man who made a professional living from his writing. When Beckett represented an aesthetic persona in "Three Dialogues with Georges Duthuit," in his *New York Times* interview with Israel Shenker in 1956, and in the letters to Alan Schneider published in the *Village Voice* in 1958, he did so in the context of efforts to cultivate an audience for the work he had been doing since 1946 and to boost box-office receipts for the first New York run of *Waiting for Godot.* Beckett's efforts to represent his authorial persona also took place in the context of advertising campaigns marketing his Grove texts to booksellers (fig. 9) and boosting the New York premiere of *Endgame* (fig. 10). To emphasize his commitment to "failure" (see, for example, *As No Other Dare Fail* [Calder 1986]) is to ignore Beckett's actual experience as a professional writer; of course, the authorial persona created and perpetuated as part of the marketing strategy that brought him international success is designed to distract us from this experience.

And so back to the "absurd" Saatchi advertisement (fig. 1). Beckett's gagged face effectively communicates a set of specific messages about art and the artist in relation to politics and the political and in relation to commerce and the commercial. His reputation as an artist isolated from, and silent about, commerce and politics, art and the artist, is vital to the ad, giving the image its vitality and meaning. When commuters saw the poster in the London Underground in 1984, many would have instantly recognized Beckett's face, and anyone with any familiarity with European literature and/or theater would have recognized the reference to Godot. Many would have reacted as Kyncl did, reading the poster in terms of the absurd; but we can imagine they would also have paused as they reconciled Beckett's reputation with the image in the poster, recognizing that Saatchi and Saatchi and Index on Censorship were exploiting Beckett's reputed aversion to advertising, politics, and self-explication. Many would have realized that the advertisement created interest in the journal by taking advantage of Beckett's reputed position as a pure, independent artist best known for the aesthetics of impotence and silence. They would have seen that Beckett the author was being conflated with "Beckettian" characters who struggle to speak in imaginary worlds tending toward silence. And they would have known that it was "just an ad," a commercial plea for attention no different than the hundreds of celebrity-exploiting pleas they witnessed as they moved around the big blooming buzzing confusion of the London Underground.

1

Portraits of Beckett as a Professional Writer

Beckett "looked as Beckett should look."

—Gussow, *Conversations*

The Authorized Portrait

James Knowlson's "sole authorized biography" of Samuel Beckett, *Damned to Fame: The Life of Samuel Beckett,* provides the most comprehensive version to date of the authorial representation of Samuel Beckett that has dominated Beckett studies since he became internationally famous in the 1950s. Knowlson began the biography in the summer of 1989, six months before Beckett died. With the approval and cooperation of Beckett, through "weekly interviews" during which the author relaxed his erstwhile inflexible rule about note-taking, Knowlson laid the groundwork for an "authorized . . . not sanitized" biography (1996, 19). Perhaps responding to John Calder's effusive celebration in "Samuel Beckett: A Saint Born on Good Friday," where Beckett's London-based publisher asserts Beckett was an "ascetic" who "lived his last years in simple self-deprival" (1990, 7), Knowlson concludes his preface by saying, "Beckett would not have wanted to be treated like a saint." Instead, he explains how he set out "to paint the fuller portrait that he would have expected from me" (1996, 22). By "present[ing] the private man more than the public figure" (22), Knowlson gives us a portrait of the author as an artist. But by treating him as a man "damned to fame," he downplays the public and professional side of Beckett's life. In doing so, he reinforces representations of Beckett as an exemplary model of a noncommercial artist, marginalizing biographical details that underscore Beckett's protracted struggle to become a viable professional writer, to maintain a sustainable public image, and to establish a postdeath legacy. He thus reinscribes the image of Beckett as a man who preferred "quietistic self-effacement" (217) and avoided "threats to his privacy" (354), deemphasizing the fact that many of his closest friends (including Knowlson himself) functioned as conduits through which he controlled his professional reputation and legacy. In addition, he downplays Beckett's involvement in contracts, his joy at receiving royalty checks, the lifestyle differences effected by his celebrity status, his willingness to participate in publicity campaigns, and his deep engagement in the construction and preservation of the authorial persona that brought him fame. Knowlson's biography is itself evidence of the depth of Beckett's engagement with his public image *and* of his long-standing technique of disguising this engagement by delegating the job of image dissemination to a trusted guardian.

Working according to an idea of artistic integrity that separates the artist from the marketplace, and apparently fearing the implications if he were to acknowledge the occasions when Beckett expressed sheer joy at the receipt of royalty checks and revealed his keen interest in his business affairs, Knowlson chooses to overlook incidents in Beckett's life that reveal his engagement with activities designed to further the public prestige of his authorial persona. While he acknowledges the commercial side of Beckett's literary fame, suggesting, for example, that "Beckett went so far as to inquire what the precise contractual position [regarding the stage production of *Waiting for Godot*] was in the United States" (380), Knowlson typically does so in order to illustrate "his resentment of the constant intrusions" (414) occasioned by this fame. The overarching thesis of the book is that "in [Beckett's] own terms . . . all this success was an infallible recipe for disaster" (484). As a consequence, the portrait created in this highly influential biography is of a man who only "went so far as to inquire" about "contractual" issues when he had no choice. But this representation distorts the actual record: Beckett kept in close contact with his publishers and penned many letters in 1953–69 detailing, clarifying, specifying, and controlling his contractual position in relation to the publication and performance of his work. He also posed for numerous publicity photographs, helping create the image that became central to the Beckett "brand" and that was used on the front cover of the first edition of Knowlson's biography (fig. 8).

Crucial to Knowlson's biographical representation of what he calls "*the* life of Samuel Beckett" is the assertion that "money made almost no difference to Beckett's state of mind" (381). This particular assertion is made in the context of Knowlson's acknowledgment that the "Broadway production [of *Godot*] ran for over a hundred performances and brought in five hundred dollars a week as Beckett's personal share of the box office" (381). Knowlson does not point out that on April 9, 1956, Beckett told McGreevy he was only interested in the New York production because it would be financially lucrative (TCD, 198). Such direct statements of interest in money do not fit with a biography designed to show that Beckett was not "interested in the least kind of acquisition or display" (Knowlson 1996, 424) and who "in his own terms" experienced "success" as a "disaster." It is understandable, then, why Knowlson would overlook a letter Beckett wrote to Susan Manning on April 16, 1953, in which he explained how he had already made a considerable profit from *Godot* and was excited by the prospect of further profits in the future (HRHRC). Other letters, such as one he wrote on October 16, 1958, salivating over his royalty statements and a large check (SUL), also fall by the wayside in Knowlson's account. Even if the Beckett estate banned Knowlson from using quotations from these letters, we would expect some acknowledgment of Beckett's expressions of interest in the profits from his work; clearly Knowlson chose to protect his thesis rather than puncture Beckett's authorial persona.

Because the idea of fame was, ostensibly, anathema to Beckett, his three main biographers (Bair, Cronin, and Knowlson) choose to pass over a June 1, 1967, letter to Francis Warner in which Beckett explains the depth of his commitment to the project to build a Samuel Beckett Theatre at Oxford (RUL). The idea that Beckett only accepted tributes "as a gesture of forgiveness" and as a "belated justification" for a decision that hurt his parents—which is how Knowlson explains why he accepted an honorary doctoral degree from Trinity College in 1959 (1996, 416)—comes under serious scrutiny when we note that he had had no prior contact with Warner or with Oxford University: he accepted the honor because, despite his carefully cultivated reputation as a man averse to fame, he genuinely enjoyed public tributes. As we shall see in chapter 7, his involvement with Warner's plan to build a Beckett theater at St. Peter's College, Oxford, extended to advice on the architectural plans (in a minimum of seventy-one letters to Warner [Ezard 1970]); regular correspondence with the main donor, Samuel Zacks; and participation in fund-raising through dinners and sales of a collector's version of *Imagination Dead Imagine* (figs. 3 and 6). Knowlson and Cronin completely ignore this protracted episode in Beckett's life. A decade later, Knowlson's colleague at Reading University, John Pilling, released *A Samuel Beckett Chronology* with only passing reference to the theater, again giving the impression it was of little interest to Beckett; for June 20, 1969, he notes that Beckett wrote to Henry Wenning saying he planned to give the manuscript of *En Attendant Godot* to the theater (2006, 181); and for March 8, 1970, he notes that there was a "Gala Performance in Oxford in aid of the proposed (never completed) Samuel Beckett Theatre" (183). This is Pilling's complete record for the author's involvement in a complex project he fully supported by collaborating with the main organizer, the architect, the main sponsors, and the fund-raising campaign. A plan that occupied Beckett in meetings and other planning activities for over three years also receives very short shrift in the *Grove Companion to Samuel Beckett* (Ackerley and Gontarski 2004); again it is only mentioned in passing as part of the stage history of *Breath* (73). The fact Beckett gave Warner *Breath* for its English premiere and was prepared to help him raise money by donating his most treasured and jealously guarded manuscript illustrates how important the theater was to Beckett. However, the project was simply too ambitious from an architectural point of view and the substantial funds raised by the appeal—$170,000 Canadian from Zacks; $250,000 American from Richard Burton; plus well over $100,000 from other donors, including Prince Charles, Edward Heath, and Lawrence Harvey—were transferred to a charitable trust in 1976. This fund created the Samuel Beckett Theatre Trust Award in 2003 (a fund that gives substantial grants to innovative playwrights and drama collectives). The legacy of the fund-raising efforts goes on, but the episode has been turned into a footnote in Beckett studies.

As a result of his commitment to a thesis that requires Beckett to be passive except inasmuch as he had the urge to create art, Knowlson often passes over important incidents pointing to Beckett's engagement with the life of his work beyond its creation. This has the effect of exaggerating Beckett's "purity," making any success seem entirely accidental or, if we accept the theological implications of Knowlson's title, predetermined by an omniscient force over which he had no control. Again, Beckett is represented as though he is as passive as Molloy. The extreme representation of the author as "Saint Beckett" (as Matthew Hodgart titled his December 7, 1967, review of *Stories and Texts for Nothing*) is a development of the authorial persona Beckett cultivated after he moved to Paris in 1937. It was convenient for the author to project this image because it protected him from the chaotic lifestyle he had witnessed when he was on the edges of the Joyce circle in the 1930s. But as I have begun to suggest, these efforts to protect Beckett's anti-commercial persona go too far, creating a hagiographic myth that Beckett certainly helped create but that he was, himself, willing to puncture:

in his first interview with his first biographer, Deirdre Bair, he portrayed himself as a "charlatan" (1990, ix); in a 1977 photograph by Roger Pic he reveals his participation in the augmentation of market value through special signing sessions (fig. 3); and in *Catastrophe* he reveals his deep engagement with image making and manipulation. We have no interest in representing Beckett as either a saint or a charlatan. Still, Knowlson's portrait of a private man needs to be supplemented with an account that puts more emphasis on Beckett as a public figure, an account that explores the diverse ways in which "the supremely well-balanced pillar-hanging saint of literature . . . and saint in life" (Hodgart 1967, 3) engaged with his profession and his public as he built a career that would sustain him and his extended family and that would bring him the Nobel Prize for Literature.

The downplaying of Beckett's public and professional life in *Damned to Fame* (1996) is evident from the coverage of one of the key events in Beckett's ascension to international fame. Knowlson devotes a mere one hundred words to the moment when Beckett signed with Grove Press to publish an English translation of *En Attendant Godot.* Bizarrely, the biographer does not give the actual date of the agreement, which was drafted (with Sylvia Beach's assistance) on May 26, 1953, finalized on June 2, 1953, and turned into a binding "Memorandum of Agreement between Samuel Beckett, c/o Les Editions de Minuit . . . and Grove Press" on June 18, 1953. Instead, he focuses on Beckett's urge to preserve his "freedom and integrity" as an artist, again resorting to religious discourse: "A principle as sacred as that of artistic freedom and integrity, learned at the feet of the uncompromising James Joyce, was not easily to be sacrificed" (1996, 354). Further along in his narrative, Knowlson chooses to overlook Beckett's direct participation in the design of Grove's English translation of *Godot,* which included suggestions about the layout of speeches on the page and contact information for the copyright holder of the photograph used on the book's cover (as we see in a letter he wrote to Barney Rosset on December 14, 1953, SUL). We can, of course, read this direct advice as an effort on Beckett's part to express his freedom and maintain his integrity; but this reading only works if, unlike Knowlson, we accept that the packaging and marketing of a book are part and parcel of the life of writing. It is, of course, where the creative writer meets the audience, the photograph of the author and information about his life and work bringing his private life into the public sphere. The private struggle to create a viable work of art becomes a professional endeavor designed to produce a marketable product and to return profits to those contractually involved, from author to agent to publisher/producer to bookseller/theater (see figs. 2, 9 and 10). Beckett's correspondence with his publishers between 1953 and 1969 includes numerous examples of his engagement with finances and publicity, contracts and marketing strategies. When we look at Knowlson's account of "the early months of 1958," we see that he covers Beckett's work writing *Krapp's Last Tape* and translating *L'Innommable,* his withdrawal of *All That Fall* and *Act Without Words I and II* from the Dublin International Theatre Festival in protest over the exclusion of a play by Sean O'Casey, and his problems with England's Lord Chamberlain over some words in *Endgame* and *Krapp's Last Tape* (1996, 400–404). Again, his devotion to the idea that Beckett's ruling "principle" was a sacramental commitment to "artistic freedom and integrity" leads him to skip evidence of Beckett's direct participation in the definition and clarification of contractual details concerning the publication and performance of his work in the United Kingdom and the United States (March 25, 1958, SUL).

There is no question that the activities and events Knowlson recounts in his report on the early months of 1958 are significant to Beckett's life as an artist. However, they only tell one part of the story. During this period Beckett also wrote a series of extremely important business letters to Barney Rosset. On March 5, 6, 10, 25, and 30, 1958, he wrote letters clarifying his professional relationship with his English language publishers. Beckett's keen attention to his contractual obligations is suggested by the fact that the letters written on March 10 and March 25 respond to mail received from Grove Press that day. Beckett goes to great lengths to explain Grove's position as it is affected by region-specific contracts with Calder Publications, Faber and Faber, and the producer George Devine. He is obviously impatient, confessing in his fourth detailed letter on the subject that he feels incompetent about the business of literary rights and marketing (March 26, 1958, SUL). In the context of the authorized portrait of Beckett it is tempting to focus on this confession of stupidity and confusion about his professional affairs, overlooking the gratitude he expresses on the same page for the constant stream of royalty checks flowing in his direction. But Beckett was sufficiently invested in the effort to achieve clarity in his affairs that he adopted quasi-legal language whenever there was too much confusion (see letters to Rosset, March 5 and 6, 1958, SUL). To make sure the various contractual relationships are above board, he quotes a specific clause from his contract with Faber, underscoring Rosset's title to the Canadian rights to "From an Abandoned Text" (March 5 and 6, 1958, SUL). Returning to the issue on March 25, he explains the exact territorial extent of Rosset's rights to publish, noting that Curtis Brown and Rosica Colin have no jurisdiction in the United States, Canada, and other parts of the British Commonwealth (March 26, 1958, SUL). Letters written on May 5, 1959, and June 2, 1961, underscore his ongoing attention to his increasingly complex professional affairs. In the first, to Rosica Colin, he goes into great detail about who has Canadian rights, going on to insist on a distinction between radio and stage plays and nondramatic texts when it comes to rights to publish. He then explains who has German publication rights to *From an Abandoned Work, Krapp's Last Tape,* and *Embers.* All of this was written from memory when he was at Ussy, without the contracts (SUL). In other words, and despite his claims to incompetence, he was so involved in the business end of his career that he could recall the complex details of his commercial dealings when he was on the road. The June 2, 1961, letter to Judith Schmidt, business manager at Grove Press, provides detailed instructions about publication and performance rights for *Happy Days* in the United States, Canada, Latin America, Germany, France, and beyond. None of this evidence turns Beckett into a "charlatan"; but neither does it allow us to accept the adequacy of the portrait of Beckett as a man damned to fame. Instead it suggests he was keenly attuned to, and involved in, the long-term plan that transformed him from a struggling artist in 1937 into a Nobel laureate in 1969.

During a historical period in which most successful authors expressed their investment in their professional career by making public appearances on television, on the radio, on the lecture circuit, and at book signings, Beckett was a relatively withdrawn figure (though, as already noted, he was not as elusive as Thomas Pynchon or J. D. Salinger). We are not trying to put him on a level with Jack Kerouac, Jacqueline Susann, or other writers who played the media circuit for all they could get. However, just as we cannot ignore his behind-the-scenes orchestration of, and deep engagement with, his business affairs, neither can we ignore publicity, persona-building, and authorial promotion on his behalf, in his name, by those who reported to him regularly and who had his direct approval. When he acknowledged his debt to Grove Press in a letter to Rosica Colin on May 5, 1959, explaining that this debt was so great it made them his top priority when it came to the literary marketplace (SUL), Beckett was not only referring to the work they did on his behalf in terms of publication and performance. He was also acknowledging their work as marketing agents who developed a long-term strategy to sell his work and promote his name (fig. 11).

Starting in 1956 Grove Press had organized a series of "Evenings with Beckett" designed to promote Beckett's work. These evenings were developed with Beckett's direct input (see his letter to Rosset on August 30, 1956) and were adapted by Jack MacGowran, again with Beckett's direct input, for a one-man show initially performed as "End of Day" at the Tóstal in Dublin on October 5, 1962, and at the New Arts Theatre in London on October 16, 1962, eventually becoming "Beginning to End," a television show screened by the BBC on February 23, 1965. A revised version, *MacGowran Speaking Beckett,* recorded with Beckett's on-site participation, was released by Claddagh in 1966. The longevity of Beckett's interest in this project is apparent from the fact that in 1988 he signed 326 copies of a collector's text, *Beginning to End: A Selection of the Works of Samuel Beckett, Adapted by Samuel Beckett and Jack MacGowran,* with illustrations by Edward Gorey (1988). This sequence of events, which involved Beckett in various advisory functions, from behind-the-scenes guidance to active directorial control, drives home the importance of Rosset's role in advancing Beckett's cause. Further, it gives us a clue about Beckett's professional approach to his role as a public figure. By writing letters and holding private meetings, he could stay out of the limelight even as he guided how his work entered the marketplace. He could step forward to take a more active role whenever it suited him and could step back into relative seclusion whenever he chose.

In chapter 7 we'll examine Beckett's contribution to the various "Evenings with Beckett" organized to promote his work in London and New York. Suffice it to say here that he helped shape these events by selecting texts and actors and was not only interested in their outcome but was also active in publishing the most successful schedules of readings, providing specific input for a Calder collection in 1967 (*A Samuel Beckett Reader*) and the MacGowran/Gorey text mentioned above (fig. 12). Of course, Knowlson makes no mention of these carefully orchestrated, author-approved promotional events. A good example is his report about Beckett's bout of depression at the end of August 1956 (1996, 387). We would imagine that the last thing on the mind of a depressed man would be the details of his public life in New York. However, on August 30, 1956, he wrote a long letter to Barney Rosset making detailed proposals for readings and approving the introductory matter for a YM-YWCA program, going on to thank Rosset for a copy of Grove's new advertising brochure; to express his gratitude for being promoted so vigorously; to explain in great detail his analysis of the Columbia Recordings version of *Godot;* to comment on the possibility of an

African American production of the play; to give a blow-by-blow account of what is happening with the script of *Fin de partie* in France, the United States, and Germany; and to comment on Nicklaus Gessner's dissertation on his work (August 30, 1956, SUL). Presumably Gessner's thesis cheered him up. The letter begins with Beckett's confession of unhappiness, but it reveals that even in his darkest moments of malaise he was fully capable of engaging with the business of promoting his texts. Further, it demonstrates that Beckett was involved in developing an approach to the promotion of his work that would make a significant contribution to his celebrity status. A letter Beckett wrote to his friend Aidan Higgins is instructive on this point. He explains how indebted he is to Barney Rosset and invokes God in celebrating the increasing flow of royalty checks into his bank account (May 10, 1960, HRHRC). Seven years after signing with the Grove Press marketing machine, Beckett was well on his way to being regarded as the most important writer of the postwar period. It is time to recognize that he played a vital, though carefully controlled, part in this transformation and was happy with the hard-earned flow of money that came with his international success.

While he was helping with the Calder series of public readings, Beckett's life was dominated by an upcoming surgery on his mouth. In Knowlson's 250-word account of the five-month period between June 1965 and "the last day of October 1965" (475), he notes that Beckett distracted himself from the operation by taking a holiday in Italy. While there he translated *Eh Joe* into French and completed the translation of *Imagination morte imaginez* into English, returning to Paris for the surgery before he began to write a new work (475). Knowlson's summation of what happened in the summer of 1965 keeps the emphasis on Beckett's creative process, but the omission of any reference to the Calder series of readings dissociates Beckett's art from the professional context in which this creativity took place. Letters to Calder in June, July, August, September, and October 1965 illustrate Beckett's ongoing interest in these readings. Their promotional effect is clear. The newly translated *Imagination Dead Imagine* had its first public reading at the Arts Theatre series in September 1965. Two months later the text was printed for the first time in English in the *Sunday Times,* November 7, 1965. Calder successfully cultivated a wider audience for the previously unpublished text by inviting reviewers to the author-supported promotional event. That led to the *Times* publication; and this publication boosted interest in Calder's November 1965 release of *Imagination Dead Imagine* in a hors commerce collector's edition "on handmade paper, numbered and signed" by Beckett. Again we underline the fact that the readings were designed as a marketing tool with Beckett's regular input and full awareness. And, again, we note that Knowlson's biography makes no mention of these public readings. Perhaps a more serious omission from *Damned to Fame* is coverage of the Samuel Beckett Theatre at Oxford. Even though the Beckett archives at Reading University Library include a substantial file from 1967–70 with press cuttings describing the funds raised, with Beckett's full support, to build the Samuel Beckett Theatre at St. Peter's College, Oxford (MS 1792, RUL), Knowlson chooses not to document the process in his biography. Presumably Beckett's collaboration with Professor Francis Warner, which involved him in various fund-raising activities, strayed too far outside the storyline of a man who, ostensibly anyway, experienced success as "an infallible recipe for disaster" (Knowlson 1996, 484). Looked at through the art-focused lens of *Damned to Fame* it seems surprising Beckett should have written the enthusiastic acceptance letter to Warner on June 1, 1967. But read in the context of Calder's efforts to promote Beckett's work around the British Isles, Warner's project should be viewed as an instrumental part of the consolidation and promotion of Beckett's international fame in the years preceding the Nobel Prize award. Beckett's direct involvement in a fund-raising campaign generated at least five hundred thousand dollars and gathered contributions from a long list of dignitaries including Prince Charles, the Right Honorable Edward Heath, Buckminster Fuller, Henry Moore, Richard Burton, Edmund Blunden, and Graham Greene. The meeting with Warner on July 24, 1967, was the first of many meetings Beckett attended on the subject of the Oxford Theatre project; a photograph from one such occasion, May 19, 1969, shows Beckett at a table in the Closerie de Lilas with Francis Warner, a couple who donated $170,000 Canadian, and Sorel Etrog (fig. 6), who would illustrate a signed collector's edition of *Imagination Dead Imagine* to be sold as a way of raising money for the theater ("Experiments Under the Quad"). Between July 1967 and October 1969 numerous newspaper stories were published covering the project: the *Oxford Times,* the *Isis,* the *Irish Times,* the *London Times,* the *Guardian,* the *Daily Mail,* the *Daily Telegraph,* the *Financial Times,* the *Observer,* and the *Evening Standard* all kept up with developments, associating Beckett's name with a high society crowd of sponsors and donors including the future prime minister, the Prince of Wales, two famous actors (Burton and Harvey), the most famous British composer (Britten), four of the best known writers of the British postwar period (Greene, Osborne, Pinter, Wesker), and a host of prominent artists and celebrities including Peter Ustinov, Henry Moore,

Peter Hall, and, of course, Buckminster Fuller. Beckett's sponsorship by the British celebrity scene is only part of the story of his rise to international fame, but surely the project that galvanized this support is symptomatic of the author-approved efforts on Beckett's behalf that prepared the ground for the October 1969 Nobel award. To discount this project because it did not lead to the building of a theater is on a par with discounting the preparation that goes into the creation of the final image in *Catastrophe* simply because it does not produce the effect intended by the Director.

"Pour faire remarquer moi"

The cover of the original Bloomsbury press printing of *Damned to Fame* encapsulates the authorized portrait of Beckett as an ascetic and aesthetic icon who had an "appalled reaction" to the Nobel award (505). A "severed head" study by John Haynes with a brightly lit face against a dark background, the photograph distills the idea that Beckett was intensely private and reluctantly famous (fig. 8). Taken during rehearsals of *Not I* and *Krapp's Last Tape* at the Royal Court Theatre in January 1973, the original photograph isolates Beckett's head in a field of black, presenting him as a flesh-covered skull cut off from his body, from his background, from any context except that of his own head. In terms of the history of Beckett studies, it not only functions as a publicity shot of Beckett as a famous author, as a Nobel laureate who, to quote Mel Gussow, "looked as Samuel Beckett should look" (13), but it is also the product of a twenty year tradition of such photographs. In the case of the first edition of *Damned to Fame,* released on September 26, 1996, it functions as part of the packaging of a book that narrates "*the* life of Samuel Beckett," telling the story of an author who, ostensibly, had no history of self-promotion and no interest in fame; in this sense, the image seems to confirm the governing thesis of Knowlson's biography. In the second Bloomsbury edition, released in September 1997, the photograph is more obviously part of the packaging of the book: it is framed by the announcement that this is "The Authorized Biography" (presumably so potential buyers can distinguish it from Anthony Cronin's *Samuel Beckett: The Last Modernist,* released in December 1996). Across the bottom of the photograph a blurb from the *Sunday Times* describes it as "a literary biography of supreme distinction." By choosing this photograph, Bloomsbury tapped into the version of Beckett preferred by the Beckett establishment in Britain. It was taken three years after the Nobel had consolidated his international status; he was at the height of his powers in Britain.

As I have suggested, the media attention from Calder's "Evenings with Beckett" and Warner's "Oxford Samuel Beckett Theatre Appeal" culminated in "A Celebrity Gala" on March 8, 1970. Next on the agenda was a major exhibition of his work at Reading University in mid-May to the end of July 1971, with follow-up exhibitions in London at the Institute of Contemporary Arts and the National Book League in August to September 1971 and at the University of Essex in October through December 1971. On the heels of the exhibition, Beckett collaborated with Knowlson and the University of Reading to create an archive of manuscripts, correspondence, and other materials: again this made a big splash in the media. By the time Haynes went on the set of *Not I* for his photo shoot, Beckett's prestige was sufficient that the Royal Court had given him complete control over the premiere of *Not I.* It is not just that he directed the play with no interference from an in-house director or producer and that he had the authority to rid the theater of "all the lights . . . including the exits, the lavatories, and the aisles"; it is also that Billie Whitelaw, his chosen actor, surrendered herself so absolutely to his will that she suffered permanent mental and physical damage (1995, 118–31).

The 1973 Haynes photograph is, then, an emblem of Beckett's status as a celebrity who wielded immense authority over public productions of his work on the British stage; as such, it is an iconic representation of a reputation established in Britain during the two decades following the August 1955 English-language premiere of *Waiting for Godot* at the New Arts Theatre. As I have suggested, this reputation was consolidated through conversations and debates organized by producers and publishers who were in direct communication with Beckett about how the evenings should work. The emblematic power of the Haynes photograph is such that it works as a commercial brand, an image used, without comment, on the front cover of a glossy brochure produced in 1989 to solicit contributions to the Foxrock Foundation. In the brochure Beckett's head floats in the bottom center of an expansive black background with no reference to Beckett except through his "floating" head. Founded by Billie Whitelaw with the mission "to bring [Beckett's] work, especially his plays, to a wider British audience" (Foxrock Foundation 1990), the charity assumes that Beckett's head speaks for itself, without the need for words. Using the same photograph and the same black background as the Bloomsbury edition of *Damned to Fame* (1996), but without Beckett's name, the document testifies to the work of a "select group . . . chosen" by Beckett with "the generous support of James Knowlson" to preserve and disseminate "The spirit of Samuel Beckett." The Haynes photograph again functions as an iconographic distillation of the religious discourse adopted by a "privileged" group of insiders who claim "his blessing" (to quote the precise language used on the brochure). In this particular case, Whitelaw, as "patron," and Knowlson, as a source of "generous support," organized a "scheme" (as the brochure puts it) designed to perpetuate a particular version of Beckett's authorial legacy.

In her autobiography, *Billie Whitelaw... Who He?* (1995), Whitelaw gives a very clear sense of this version of Beckett: shaping her self-representation in terms borrowed directly from *Not I,* not only using a quotation from the play as a subtitle for her own memoirs but also using a facsimile of her annotated actor's script from the 1973 Beckett-directed production on the inside front and back covers of the hardback edition, she reveals a level of devotion that approaches religious worship. She applauds him for his "total integrity," his "natural quiet authority," his "artistic integrity" and "moral integrity," concluding with the familiar claim that "[h]e didn't give a damn about becoming more famous or getting more prizes, nor did he care for money" (134–35). The persistence of the legacy Whitelaw set out to preserve and protect through the Foxrock Foundation is apparent from *Images of Beckett* (2003) a collection of photographs by John Haynes with three essays by Knowlson. Released in 2003, the book uses a cover image from the same session as the Haynes photograph we have been discussing, reserving the "floating head" for the back cover and, again, for the first photograph inside the book. This time, however, the photograph is contextualized: in an essay beginning on the facing page, "A Portrait of Beckett," Knowlson uses the photograph to confirm Whitelaw's assertion that "Beckett had a horror . . . of publicity of any kind" (135), using it as evidence that Beckett "hated the trappings of fame," "loathed all forms of self-exposure or self-promotion," and "hated to be recognized" (1). Just as Whitelaw claims the authority of Beckett's "blessing" to "produce the plays in the author's own style" (Foxrock Foundation 1990), Knowlson underscores the authority of his essays by using the front flap to tell us, "The essays are the result of personal conversations with Beckett." The context for this startlingly graphic image of Beckett *as Beckett* is, then, tied directly to Knowlson's inside knowledge of Beckett's personal and artistic life. But just as Beckett the artist merges with Beckett the friend, so, too, Beckett the isolated author merges with Beckett the professional writer; the Haynes photograph testifies to Beckett's status as a famous author who looked exactly as he was supposed to look. It would be a mistake, however, to take this "look" at face value.

Presented in the context of *Damned to Fame,* the Foxrock Foundation brochure, and *Images of Beckett,* the Haynes photograph portrays Beckett as an isolated creative consciousness characterized by "[s]ilence and solitude" (Haynes and Knowlson 2003, 1). It thus reinforces the received understanding of Beckett as a pure, commerce-free artist who was "notoriously private" ("Playwright Pictured" 1987). In this sense it seems to confirm Patrick Bowles's 1958 assertion in the BBC's *Listener* magazine that the author lives in a "spiritual wilderness," exiled in "his own particular vision of the universe, original and uncompromising" (1011). In other words, the photograph reveals the resilience of the authorial image developed after Beckett emerged from "the siege in the room" (Kenner 1968, 20). It thus underscores the careful craftsmanship behind "the photographs which determine the public image of Samuel Beckett" (20–21), creating the impression that Beckett "looked as Beckett should look" (Gussow 1996, 13). To accept that Beckett looked as Beckett should look is, literally, to accept his authorial persona at face value, ignoring the artistry and business acumen that went into the creation of his image as a writer and ignoring the public-relations strategies that disseminated this image. It is tempting to do so. The Haynes photograph seems to lift Beckett out of any material context, giving his face the portability we would associate with Cindy Crawford; the image communicates such intense concentration that we can imagine it would remain unchanged in any context, whether on a book cover, a magazine, an advertising brochure, or a shampoo bottle. In Gussow's terms, "the intensity of his art was reflected in his gaze," his authorial persona a mirror image of his private self (13). But, as we have already begun to see with the Kyncl article and the *Index* poster and T-shirt, when we attend to the contexts that produced this image *and* reflect on the contexts in which it is used, we begin to see beyond its face value. Ultimately we recognize, through the Haynes photograph, Beckett's deep respect for the entire process of literary production and *his* understanding that "artistic integrity" takes place in time and space, in a material environment that demands compromise, forcing even the most ardent aesthete to engage with contexts beyond the silence and solitude of his workshop. Haynes, Knowlson, and Whitelaw functioned as mediators, or "conduits" (to use Whitelaw's word [1995, 120]), between the private man and this larger professional context, but their faith in his absolute artistic integrity should not distract us from an appreciation of this context.

In addition to being used as an anchor point by a network of individuals who worked on Beckett's behalf, with Beckett's "blessing," to preserve a legacy defined by "the unmistakable mark of the author's vision" (Foxrock Foundation 1990) and by his resistance to the "pressures that fame exerted upon him, especially the Nobel Prize for Literature" (Haynes and Knowlson 2003, 3), the photograph is part of a historical pattern of variously veiled publicity statements and posed photographs going back to 1948. In 1948, we detect the first glimmerings of the nascent public persona that would eventually bring international fame to Beckett. This persona is consistent with Beckett's early social and professional life, but it assumed a much more coherent shape after World War II. As he emerged from an intense three-year period of creativity, he began to establish himself in Paris literary society. He initially did so by going back to some of his old haunts. One of his first postwar publications was in the second issue of the newly revived (and now capitalized) *Transition,* an English-language journal with advisory editors including Georges Bataille, Max-Pol Fouchet, Stuart Gilbert, Eugene Jolas (who founded the magazine as *transition* in 1927), and John-Paul Sartre. Beckett's "Trois Poemes/Three Poems" appeared in French and, on the opposite page, in an English translation "by the author" (Duthuit 1948, 96). In the "Notes about Contributors," the editors contemplate why he "has adopted the French language as his working medium" (146), describing their efforts to get an answer on the subject and, albeit parodically, suggesting a market-oriented response:

> [W]e begged him to make a further effort, in his own interest and in that of literature as a whole. Drawing us then aside into the little frequented semi-circular Rue de Tilsitt, and having first looked round in every conceivable direction to make sure no doubt that we were not observed, he confessed at last in a strong or rather weak Dublin accent: "Pour faire remarquer moi" ["In order to get myself noticed"]. (147)

The parody in this scene comes from the implication that the barely known author is already protecting the image of himself as someone who has "quietly but uncompromisingly . . . avoided every form of personal publicity" (Reid 1971, 12). It is very likely we are supposed to laugh at the possibility Beckett would retreat into a back street to confess he wrote in French to get himself noticed. But even if the words and the situation are meant to be received ironically, there is still some truth in the idea that an Irish author trying to make a living in postwar Paris could bring attention to himself by writing in French and publishing through offbeat companies. The received representation by the time Beckett achieved fame was that "he has dodged the commitments of fame and the Literary Life as successfully as the dodged the Occupation"; and this idea is connected, in Kenner's representation, with the suggestion that he wrote in French because he "just felt like it" (Kenner 1968, 24). Kenner turns what was clearly a strategic move into a whim. In doing so, he passes over the fact that the postwar publishing industry in Paris was very difficult, especially for non-French authors: for a foreign writer struggling to make ends meet, the adoption of French was, in fact, a perfectly feasible way to get noticed. As we see when we examine the work done on Beckett's behalf by his life partner, Suzanne Dumesnil, Beckett's professional career benefited enormously from a network of French writers and intellectuals, a tight Left Bank community that knew him as a prewar associate of Joyce, that would notice his change of language, that would respect what he had done during the war, and that would be open to his association with Suzanne Dumesnil. It hardly needs to be said that an English-language play would never have attracted the attention of Roger Blin in 1950 and would never have received a grant from the French government in 1952. By writing *En Attendant Godot* in French, Beckett opened Parisian doors that would have remained closed to an Irish writer writing in English. In the light of Beckett's professional circumstances in 1946–50, the decision to write and publish in French was, then, highly pragmatic.

Whether or not it is part of an elaborate joke, the scenario described in the "Notes about Contributors" in 1948 suggests his next publication in *Transition,* "Three Dialogues: Tal Coat—Masson—Bram Van Velde," was also part of Beckett's very sensible strategy to get himself noticed. Typically reprinted as "Three Dialogues with Georges Duthuit" (see *Disjecta* and *GCE IV*), this piece has become a staple of Beckett criticism, providing numerous quotations used to interpret and analyze his work. In his highly influential book *Samuel Beckett: A Critical Study,* first published in 1961 and released in a second, revised edition in 1968, Hugh Kenner uses the text as evidence of Beckett's "one public appearance to discuss the theory of these operations" (28). He goes on to treat "Three Dialogues" as an aesthetic manifesto, footnoting his list of Beckett's works with a six-page essay explaining how it applies to Beckett's canon. Repeated in the introduction to the *Samuel Beckett Reader,* where John Calder argues that the dialogues "contain the key to all Beckett's work" (1967a, 15), and in numerous other texts, including one that uses a quotation from the text as its title, *As No Other Dare Fail,* critical statements made by Beckett in 1949 continue to shape Beckett studies: as recently as 2007 Sandra Wynands uses the text in *Iconic Spaces: The Dark Theology of Samuel Beckett's Drama* to set up her argument. She focuses on the short dramatized interview for an entire chapter.

The details of "Three Dialogues" have been adequately explored elsewhere; suffice it to say here that Beckett successfully framed the critical reception of his postwar work by suggesting that he had no interest in artistic expression or reception. As I have suggested, he did so obliquely, creating distance between the critical ideas expressed in the three conversations and his own literary output. By presenting his ideas as a three-part dialogue between "B" and "D," a technique that echoes Bishop Berkeley's *Three Dialogues Between Hylas and Philonous*, he associates himself with the discourse of philosophy; by focusing on pictorial art he associates himself with the discourse of art and art history. We could, in fact, argue that "Three Dialogues" has very little to do with Beckett's work as a writer because it is not literary criticism and does not address the genres with which he would become famous. In light of the long-standing dependence of Beckett scholars on the text, that would be churlish. Still, a question mark hovers over Kenner's suggestion that the text is an example of a "public appearance" in which he addressed "the theory" of his literary "operations" (1968). Again, suffice it to say that it is an oblique public appearance. I would argue, however, that this fits exactly with the authorial persona and strategy Beckett had begun to deploy in 1949: while seeming to be tangential, it provides a powerful theoretical context for his work, and it brings public attention without giving any impression that this is the desired effect. In short, "Three Dialogues" promotes the work he was actively shopping around Paris in 1949, but it does so in a way that is deliberately constructed to be deniable.

The argument that "Three Dialogues" functions as an oblique but effective promotional text becomes clearer when we see it as part of the history that produced his *New York Times* "non-interview interview" with Israel Shenker in 1956 and the *Village Voice* publication of his letters to the director of *Endgame* in 1958. Both publications appeared when he was establishing his reputation in New York, the gateway to the American literary marketplace. While the dramatized interview functioned as a primer for texts that would be published starting in 1951, these later publications coincided with important productions of career-defining plays. Even though both pieces are framed by Beckett's expressions of reluctance, both were instrumental in projecting his authorial persona into the public sphere, shaping his reception and image for the duration of his career and beyond. Further, both pieces demonstrate the effectiveness with which Beckett managed his public persona while giving the impression of passive unconcern: just as Billie Whitelaw would become "the vehicle for his art" (Lovenheim 1990), Shenker became the vehicle for his aesthetic philosophy. For his part, Alan Schneider provided the opportunity to publish private correspondence; although Beckett wrote in one of the letters that he was opposed to the publication of letters, he still gave his approval (Beckett 1958), bringing into public circulation a set of ideas that has had enormous long-term influence.

We can debate whether or not the Shenker article accurately reflects Beckett's views because any reference to it as an "interview" must be put in quotation marks (see Ackerley and Gontarski 2004, 287, and Pilling 2006, 130); but we cannot deny that he invited a *Time* magazine reporter into his home in spring 1956 and gave him sufficient information to write one of the most influential statements about his work, life, and thought. Shenker managed to place his article in the Arts section of *The New York Times* on May 6, 1956, at the end of the third week of the first New York run of *Waiting for Godot* at the Golden Theater. Inaugurating a subgenre special to Beckett, what we might call the "non-interview interview" because Beckett agreed to respond to questions but refused note taking or recording, the article explains that "Beckett is in no mood to offer explanations" and that "he has never been interviewed." "Moody Man of Letters" is bracketed by the admission that what is recorded is not what Beckett actually said, but what "he would say (he has said it all, in precisely these words)" if he were to "relax his rule on interviews." This strange situation, in which a man notorious for his inaccessibility spoke at length with a journalist but precluded direct quotation, is made even more bizarre by Shenker's insistence that Beckett is like one of his own fictional characters. Shenker is at pains to underscore the confusion between Beckett and his texts, confirming Beckett's image as someone oblivious to the material world because he is "lanced . . . in a situation that I can't extricate myself from." The effect, and Beckett must have known this would be the effect, was that audiences and critics latched onto the Shenker text as an authoritative description of his views about his work. At the same time, the effect is to project the public image of someone uninterested in developing a public image.

Most immediately, the "non-interview" with Shenker boosted ticket sales: the amount due to Beckett during the week ending May 12 was more than 20 percent higher than the amount due for the week ending May 5 (based on figures reported in letters from Rosset on May 18 and July 3, 1956). In addition, the article shaped long-term interpretations, not only of *Waiting for Godot* but also of the rest of Beckett's canon. Indeed, it competes with "Three Dialogues" as a source of the interpretive truisms that have come to define Beckett's place in literary history. "Moody Man of Letters" begins by setting the context for our approach to Beckett, describing him as "a gloomy despairing man" who is "no charlatan" but who has written a play that provokes "hardly more than enlightened puzzlement" (Shenker 1956, 1). After setting this context in 350 words, describing Beckett as "a fiery apostle" who "does not care what he looks like," implying that he is a bohemian, "uninterested in economics" with "clothes that look slept in," and "the vocation of degradation," he presents a seventeen-paragraph, almost 900-word text spoken by Beckett in "precisely this phrasing." Shenker notes that he "speaks exactly like his characters—with pained hesitation." After reinforcing this identification between author and text, the article concludes with a six-paragraph, 200-word summary, ending with a quotation from Beckett about those "who throw themselves out of a window after years of struggling" (1956, 3). Presumably Beckett is "moody" because, like his characters, "he has nothing."

The enormous influence of the Shenker article is evident from its construction of Beckett in terms of three main ideas that have become axiomatic: first, he is just like his characters; second, his method is directly opposed to Joyce's; and third, he is an artist uninterested in "achievement." One of the more influential, career-defining parts is Shenker's report that Beckett said "[Joyce is] tending toward omniscience and omnipotence as an artist. I'm working with impotence, ignorance. I don't think impotence has been exploited in the past" (1956, 3). In a book published shortly before Beckett was awarded the Nobel Prize for Literature, with a quotation from one of the Schneider letters as its title, Alec Reid uses these words to frame his entire project. His effort to go to "the heart of the matter" (1971, 11) in Beckett's theatrical work is defined using exact quotations from Beckett's non-interview with Shenker. Almost forty years later, Ronan McDonald also defers to Beckett's representation of himself in the Shenker non-interview and the Schneider letters. He concludes his introduction with a long quotation from a letter suggesting that those who wish to stress themselves by trying to decipher Beckett's texts should buy their own aspirin (2006, 5). And he uses a long quotation from the Shenker "interview" to justify his argument that the "key textual and thematic preoccupations" of Beckett's postwar work are "ignorance and impotence" (15). Fifty years after Beckett put these ideas in circulation, critics continue to focus on the words "impotence" and "ignorance," using them to define the core principle of "Beckettian" aesthetics as they differ from the "Joycean" aesthetic of "omniscience and omnipotence." Persuaded by the idea that Beckett lived his life "like his characters," they have, however, overlooked the word "exploited." Beckett's use of this word suggests an active effort on the part of the author to shape a viable creative strategy. For his part, McDonald omits the short clause containing the word "exploited" from his quotation. We can only assume he selectively deleted a problematic word because he wishes to emphasize what Beckett set out to explore rather than what he set out to "exploit." If we are to accept the statements in "Moody Man of Letters" as clues to "Beckett's mature style" (McDonald 2006, 15), we must also accept the text itself as evidence he was deliberate in identifying an area that had not been "exploited in the past" (Shenker 1956, 3), and we must see it as evidence he wished to promote his "little exploration" in the mainstream media (otherwise why would he invite into his home a correspondent for a magazine with a circulation of 2.4 million copies per week?).

For the record, Beckett facilitated two further "non-interviews" in the New York market, one in 1961 by Tom Driver for the *Columbia University Forum,* another in 1969 by John Gruen for *Vogue.* In the *Vogue* article Gruen, publicity manager in the early days of Grove, repeats the mantra that "Beckett did not want to be interviewed" and "shunned publicity" (1969, 210). We must ask ourselves how the Shenker, Driver, and Gruen articles came to exist. Again, Beckett must have known that these writers would "reconstruct his sentences from notes made immediately after our conversation." And he must have known that, even with the disclaimer that "what appears is shorter than what he actually said but very close to his own words" (Driver 1961, 21–22), the words published would become central to interpretations of his work, carrying the weight of his authority even though he made a deliberate move to destabilize the words by precluding the taking of verbatim notes. It was a case of an artist having his cake and eating it, too. In other words, Beckett was a superb manipulator of material who set out to "exploit" an area of artistic expression previously defined as "something by definition incompatible with art." Rather than being a passive experience to which he was "damned," this was a deliberate effort to which he applied himself diligently and persistently.

During the 1958 New York premiere of *Endgame,* which previewed at the Cherry Lane Theatre on Commerce Street on January 22 and opened on January 28, Beckett agreed to the publication of a series of letters he had sent the play's director, Alan Schneider. Published in the *Village Voice* on March 19, 1958, on pages 8 and 15, the letters span the period from December 27, 1955, to March 4, 1958. They include his reactions to the Miami production of *Godot,* his initial conception of *Fin de partie* and his response to Blin's Paris production, his thoughts about the translation process, and his views on the presentation of the play. In a strategy that parallels the use of nonverbatim interviews, the Schneider letters disseminate Beckett's approach to *Endgame* in particular and his work in general. Again, the views expressed in these letters have exerted a powerful shaping influence on Beckett's critical reception. Having expressed his refusal to offer any kind of critical commentary on his work, he goes on to explain the basic principles that shape his aesthetic. The "take it or leave it" approach expressed in this letter from December 29, 1957, would assume a central role as the Beckett industry flourished in the 1960s, providing the epigraph to Martin Esslin's *Samuel Beckett: A Collection of Critical Essays* (1965) and the title and epigraph for Alec Reid's *All I Can Manage, More Than I Could* (published in 1969). Of course, the strategy would not be true to Beckett's public image without a prominent disclaimer. The series of letters includes a January 9, 1958, letter expressing his reluctance about their publication before he gives the go-ahead. Beckett preserves the idea that "No writer of our time has more consistently refused to comment on, or explain, his own work," as Esslin would put it in the introduction to his collection (1965, 1), but he still manages to get his ideas in circulation at a key moment in his professional career. In the process of turning "private" correspondence into part of the public and professional record, a move that highlights the inextricability of one's private, personal, and public selves, he authorizes Schneider's production. And by asserting that the play is best performed in a small theater and that the critics are just imposing difficulties on a very simple text, he reinforces the ongoing advertising campaign for the play. In February 1958 the *New York Times* ran advertisements announcing *Endgame* as "the play that isn't for *most* playgoers," billing it as a play that avoids "crushing Broadway production costs" and the "appeal to huge masses of people to pay back the investors and make a profit," by being aimed at "the relatively small number of people interested in original, stimulating artistic theatre—the theatre of ideas" (*Endgame* advertisement, February 21, 1958, SUL). In a parallel publicity campaign, a Grove press advertisement for the book, which had been issued on February 1, 1958, proclaims it as "The play the critics didn't understand" (fig. 10). The ad quotes John McClain's "Beckett Fails in 'Endgame'"—"I'm afraid Mr. Beckett has lost me"—and Frank Aston's question "What did all this mean? I haven't the faintest idea" (*Endgame* advertisement, February 1, 1958, SUL). The preference for failure expressed in Beckett's once-private letters thus reinforces the advertising for the play. And the advertising campaign Beckett participated in through the publication of these letters is crucial to Beckett's career because the New York production of *Endgame* would demonstrate his ability to follow through on the success of *Waiting for Godot*, setting the tone for his rise to international fame. The campaign consolidated his long-term reputation in one of the world's most important markets for books and plays, underscoring his public image as an anti-intellectual intellectual.

A further example of the strategy used to disseminate specific models of understanding that would attract an audience for Beckett's work while providing ways of approaching this work is evident from an article by one of Beckett's closest professional acquaintances. Published in London in the midst of the censorship controversy between the Lord Chamberlain and director George Devine over plans to stage *Endgame* at the Royal Court Theatre, a June 19, 1958, article in *The Listener* by Patrick Bowles, "How Samuel Beckett Sees the Universe," describes Beckett as a man of "lonely obscurity" who "has finally led himself to his own particular vision of the universe, original and uncompromising" (1011). Without announcing his direct professional affiliation with Beckett, not to mention his financial stake in one of the books he reviews (Grove paid him $180 plus 2.5 percent in royalties for his work as co-translator of *Molloy*), Bowles articulates an understanding of Beckett that had already been asserted in New York in the Shenker "interview," in the Schneider letters, and in photographic portraits that had, by then, entered the British marketplace in publicity materials distributed by John Calder (fig. 5). After putting Beckett on the same level as Camus, Conrad, Joyce, and Kafka, Bowles gives Londoners a way to appreciate his "departure from the world of masterpieces and literary virtuosity" (1011). According to this view, "Beckett, once a professional litterateur, is here preparing himself to abandon literary writing," becoming an author who is so "close to his creations" that "they speak as it were from his image" (1011). Again we notice the collapsing of any distinction between Beckett and his characters. Expressed in terms of the "pervasive disintegration . . . of body and mind, of world and memory," this image is summarized in the assertion that "Beckett seems to have set the 'I am' of identity afloat" (1012).

As the Haynes photograph suggests (and as neo-Romantic conceptions of authorial genius require), the idea that Beckett is detached from "professional" and "literary" considerations becomes the main mark of Beckett's difference from his peers: he has "a destiny of his own to mark him out from others, in a separate space, with a separate mind" (1011). It is not just that he has set identity afloat in his texts; it is that his identity as an author has been set afloat from the world of literary professionalism. In a world consumed by commercialism and materialism, Beckett represents a noncommercial exception. Affirming Shenker's idea that Beckett is "precisely like his characters," Beckett's professional collaborator describes him in terms of "medieval austerity"; he thus amplifies Beckett's claim in the January 11, 1956, letter published on March 19, 1958, in the *Village Voice* that public fame was of no interest to him.

Marketing Failure

The publications we have been discussing, "Three Dialogues" (which appeared in *Transition* in 1949), "Moody Man of Letters" (Shenker 1956), the Schneider letters (1958), and the article by Beckett's co-translator (Bowles 1958), reinforced the advertising campaign that turned Beckett into a famous writer, creating the image summarized in the *Daily Mail* on March 8, 1958 (fig. 5),

> Seldom photographed, never interviewed, Beckett, an attractive cordial man with the beaky, intense glower of a sparrowhawk has a deep revulsion against personal publicity. . . . He has had to wait for fame with the fatalism with which his tramps waited for Godot. As the overdue acknowledgment now swells to world scale I suspect that Beckett is shrinking back from it at a corresponding rate—retiring to his last ditch."

The campaign that produced, established, and perpetuated this representation of Beckett began soon after he signed with Jérôme Lindon in November 1950. In an April 1951 advertisement in the Paris press, Lindon hailed the publication of *Molloy* as "Le Plus Grand Événement Littéraire de L'Après-Guerre," asserting that "Moins d'un mois après la parution de son premiere roman, la critique unanime salue l'apparition d'un grand écrivain français" ("Less than a month after the publication of his first novel, critics unanimously salute the appearance of a great French writer"). Lindon's publicity was effusive. By aligning Beckett with a long list of avant-garde French authors, including Celine, Proust, Quenau, and Sartre, he supplemented the work Beckett had already done in *Transition* by building Beckett's reputation in the indigenous marketplace in Paris. A fully fledged, more subtle, and expansive publicity campaign began when Barnet Lee Rosset signed Beckett with Grove Press in June 1953 (fig. 11). Rosset's effort to associate Beckett's name with a particular authorial image was part of a strategy that would turn an initial investment of $3,000 in 1951 into a company with gross sales of $1,062,000 in 1959 and a net worth of $17 million in 1970 (Gontarski 2000). The entrepreneur son of a Chicago banker, Rosset quickly gained notoriety as an "advance-guard" publisher, as *Newsweek* called him in a feature on March 30, 1953 ("Advance-Guard Advance"). In his determination to make "the project survive . . . on a commercial basis" (Clarksdale Press Register 1955), Rosset brought cutting-edge marketing skills into the postwar publishing industry. With Beckett as his lead author (he assured Beckett no other author would receive a better royalty agreement), he pioneered new techniques, including cross-Atlantic and international collaboration (by sponsoring, for example, a $1,000 contest for submissions by citizens of India) and scandal-driven publicity stunts. By publishing uncensored editions of *Lady Chatterley's Lover, Lolita,* and *Tropic of Cancer* (which he successfully defended in front of the Supreme Court in 1963–64), he created a high-profile trial and a boom in profits. Sales of Lawrence, Nabokov, and Miller had a domino effect, boosting sales of his other authors. By featuring beatniks on the cover of *Evergreen Review,* advertising the journal as an "Underground magazine," and using Roy Kuhlman's "beat-style," incredibly "hip" abstract expressionism for the covers of his books (including Beckett's), he targeted a very specific, generation-defined audience that specifically wanted to distinguish itself from its fuddy-duddy elders by asserting Euro-postmodernity against their prewar taste for passé modernism. By creating a special imprint of original paperback texts called "Evergreen Books," Rosset successfully exploited the market for cheap paperbacks opened by Doubleday in the postwar period. As a November 30, 1953, letter to Bowles suggests, Rosset had a keen eye for "the best possible way[s] to get Beckett known" and made a point of exploiting any opportunity that would "give interest in Beckett an additional boost" (SUL). As he put it in a December 7, 1953, letter to Bowles, throughout his campaign Rosset worked to "make a good impression in the American stores" (SUL). While he claimed, in a January 16, 1954, letter to Lindon, that he was not publishing Beckett out of a "profit motive," assuming "it can hardly be hoped that his books are going to be big sellers,"

Rosset remained true to the promise he made in his first letter to Beckett, dated June 18, 1953: "we will do what we can to make your work known in this country" (SUL) (fig. 11). As we have already seen from the critical texts he published and the "Evenings with Beckett" he organized, Rosset also remained true to representations that emphasized failure and impotence, isolation, and passivity.

Selling Beckett as a failure worked. This became clear in the first few months of 1956. Even though it grossed $22,000, giving Beckett a royalty check of $1,293 (enough to buy more than fifty state-of-the-art reel-to-reel tape recorders of the kind used in *Krapp's Last Tape*), the American premiere of *Godot* at the Coconut Grove on January 3–14, 1956, was shut down after two weeks. Based on the ongoing success of Donald Albery's production of the play in London, which began a successful nine-month run on August 3, 1955, Michael Myerberg, the American producer, was confident he could make the play work in New York; his advertising strategy emphasized its supposed failure. He took advantage of the Miami disaster, repeating a sentiment expressed by Beckett in a January 22, 1956, letter to Rosset, billing it as a "stupendous flop" in a *New York Times* interview with Arthur Gelb. Any self-respecting Greenwich Village beatnik would be itching to see a play regarded as a flop in the retirement communities of Florida. In the Gelb article, "Wanted: Intellects: Producer Myerberg Seeks 70,000 of Them to Support Plotless Play," published three days before the play opened on April 15, 1956, Myerberg emphasized failure: "On opening night in Miami, 60 per cent of the audience walked out in disgust after the first act" (Gelb 1956, 1). Gelb transmits Myerberg's message that "the success of "Waiting for Godot" . . . is dependent on an audience of 70,000 keen or curious minds to make it a paying proposition." And, despite billing the play in the drama section as "The International Tragicomedy Hit by Samuel Beckett" and as "Triumphant in every respect," Myerberg insists, "we aren't aiming . . . for popular appeal" (Gelb 1956, 3). The success of this strategy is evident from box office sales for the New York production, which began on April 19, 1956, at the eight-hundred-seat Golden Theater. On May 2, 1956, New York's *Variety* published a snippet noting that *Godot* took in "nearly $15,300" in the previous week after taking $10,000 during "its first four performances." On top of the $1,293 from the Miami production, *Godot* earned Beckett $6,422 at the box office in the first six months of 1956 (figs. 13, 14, and 15).

Beckett's expressed lack of interest in the success of the play was possible because both Myerberg and Rosset were determined to turn it into a money-spinner. Myerberg told Beckett he had "spent a good deal of money on publicity" with the hope he could keep the play "alive in the theatre for many years (Myerberg letter to Beckett, June 8, 1956). For his part, Rosset took advantage of the commotion surrounding Myerberg's production by publishing a one-dollar edition of *Godot*. This decision, which was brilliant because, as Myerberg pointed out, "four-fifths of our audience are young—under 24, and even girls and boys 17 and 18 are storming the box office for cheap seats," complementing the "careful handling" that ensured the play's "unique place in America" (Myerberg letter to Beckett, June 8, 1956, HRHRC). By December 1969, the Grove paperback, now selling at $1.75, had sold 536,195 copies, netting Beckett well over $75,000 at an average of $5,000 per annum. The data and information in the *Godot* editorial files of Grove Press at Syracuse provides ample evidence that, fiasco or not, the Miami production entrenched the main selling proposition for Beckett's work, branding his authorial persona by associating his once "nameless name" (Pope 1984, *The Dunciad* 3, l. 151) with a specific literary approach entirely in keeping with "Three Dialogues" and the other texts we discussed above. After the 1956 production of *Godot* in New York, the word "Beckettian" entered the literary vocabulary as a term directly connected with failure and unpopularity, defining a futilitarian form of literary expression not only exemplified by Beckett's texts but also entirely consistent with Beckett's own life. Because Beckett's narrators and characters wore scruffy clothes and lived in the midst of blind alleys, bicycles, and garbage cans, it became normal to represent Beckett himself as though he also wore frayed garments and as though his typical milieu was "a cul-de-sac which contained two ash-cans and a bicycle" (Kenner 1968, 11). As we have seen, obituary accounts of Beckett's life and work, written thirty-three years after Shenker's article and twenty-eight years after the first edition of Kenner's *Critical Study* appeared in 1961, memorialize Beckett in terms directly influenced by the material that established his reputation in 1949–58: according to one, he lived "a reclusive life in a Paris apartment overlooking a prison exercise yard" (U.S. News & World Report 1990); according to another, who happened to be a close friend and colleague, his "genuine" wish in later life was to have been "unknown . . . never heard of" (Montague 1989). We can take this at face value if we like; but to do so is to blinker ourselves to the overwhelming evidence suggesting there was a concerted effort in the 1950s and 1960s to fashion Beckett's image as an unknown celebrity who experienced fame and success but preferred anonymity and failure.

Portraits of Beckett as a Floating Head

In a pattern running parallel with the development of the public image we have been discussing, the period between 1951 and 1973 saw the creation of a series of formal portraits matching Beckett's face with his authorial persona and blurring the line between Beckett and his characters. As I have suggested, these portraits culminate in the 1973 Haynes photograph used on the front cover of the Bloomsbury edition of *Damned To Fame* (fig. 8). The specific characteristics associated with these portraits, characteristics defining Beckett's most distinctive "mark" or "brand" in the publishing industry, originate with acts and decisions by Beckett himself. Given the deferential nature of his participation in literary marketing, it is almost impossible to prove Beckett engaged in any direct form of self-promotion, but it is also hard to accept the argument that he "kept himself to himself" when it came to publicity and the promotion of his work and image. The fact is, "Samuel Beckett's face is as familiar as his characteristic images: a tree, a country road, tramps, dustbins, boots, tape recorder, bananas" (Minihan 1996, 20–23). The emphasis placed on Beckett's injunction to Minihan to leave his camera at home (22) must be put in the context of the fact Minihan took a regular series of photographs of Beckett in the period between 1980 and 1985. Further, Beckett made a habit of providing publicity photographs to his publishers; invited a long list of photographers to photograph him, often in the privacy of his home; and became one of the most recognizable writers of the twentieth century. Even though he gives prominence to the postcard in which Beckett told him to leave his camera, Minihan's "rare and intimate look into the life of this intensely private person" takes its place on a bulging shelf of texts brimming with photographs of the author. I cannot think of a twentieth-century author who was photographed more often than Samuel Beckett. Further, I cannot think of an author whose most distinctive photographs were taken in such intimate, private settings.

As I have begun to suggest, Beckett's long-term fame and success were made possible by a publicity campaign begun in April 1951 and entering high gear in June 1953: an April 10, 1951, letter to Jérôme Lindon makes evident Beckett contributed to this campaign from the beginning. Published in *Libération* as part of its December 27, 1989, tribute to Beckett, the letter acknowledges the advance of 25,000 old francs for the contract to publish *Molloy* and *Malone meurt* and promises he has just sat for the photograph requested by Lindon. The way Beckett describes the photograph suggests it was a one-off, done in a shop equipped to make identity photographs. Certainly it has the look of a passport photograph. A side profile showing Beckett's right ear, the photograph was forwarded to Rosset in 1953 and became Grove's main press release photograph until 1957, becoming the iconic image of Beckett as a writer "cramped in an island of self," as a caption on a photograph in *Time* put it on October 15, 1956 ("Molten Gloom"). This is the same photograph used in the March 8, 1958, *Daily Mail* article (fig. 5). Beckett's further participation in the process of publicity and self-promotion through photography is evident from a letter he sent Rosset on December 14, 1953: he proposes a shot by a company called "Foto Dönitz" to be used on the cover of the American edition of *Godot.* To streamline the process, Beckett went out of his way to find and send the contact address for the photographer. Beckett thus chose the cover photograph for the first American edition of *Waiting for Godot;* as already noted, this edition would earn him an average of $5,000 per year for the next fifteen years. His ongoing participation in the publicity campaign after he had achieved a level of success is evident from his immediate response to a February 27, 1957, letter from Judith Schmidt of Grove Press. Schmidt requested "another photograph" on the grounds that "The one we have has, I believe, been reprinted in half of the newspapers in the country. Now that MURPHY and PROUST are out, these same papers are again asking for your picture, and would like a new one" (SUL). Less than a week later Beckett confirmed he had arranged with Jérôme Lindon for a more recent photograph to be sent (March 4, 1957, SUL). It is hard to reconcile these facts with the repeated claim that Beckett "[h]ad not the slightest interest in celebrity" and "was shy of publicity" (Dukes 2002, 1).

The photograph he asked his French publisher to send his American publisher in March 1957 was the carefully crafted studio photograph attributed to Philippe Charpentier on the back cover of the *Evergreen Review* in fall 1957 and erroneously credited to Brassai on the back cover of the 1958 Grove edition of *Watt* (it also appears on page 45 of *The Essential Samuel Beckett: An Illustrated Biography,* 2003). This photograph dominated publicity for Beckett for more than a year. But more important, it established a tradition of publicity shots representing the author in black and white, his body cut off at the shoulders, his eyes staring directly at the camera. A direct descendant of the anonymous photograph Beckett sent to Lindon in 1951, but now with his head turned to face the camera full-on, this photograph is more obviously the forerunner to the series of "floating head" images culminating in the Haynes portrait. Used in Grove's spring 1958 campaign to sell *The Unnamable* and *Endgame,* and appearing, for example, in Kenneth Harrison's April 1958 review of *Watt* and *Malone Dies* in *Books and Bookmen* ("Mr. Beckett Finds Himself"), this photograph became the basis for a line-art drawing that initiated the strategy of representing Beckett's head as a free-floating image. But, important as it is, the Charpentier photograph was soon superseded by a higher quality shot.

Attributed to Brassai and used in a number of prominent places by Grove Press, including the front covers of the fall 1958 catalog, the hardback edition of *Three Novels by Samuel Beckett* (1958), and Michael Robinson's *The Long Sonata of the Dead* (1969), as well as advertising for the 1967 release of *Stories and Texts for Nothing,* this photograph is worthy of a photographer who had achieved international fame in the 1930s by capturing candid scenes of Paris street life (fig. 7). Beckett's respect for Brassai was such that his photographs were still at the forefront of his mind in December 1985 when he met John Minihan for a final photo shoot (Minihan 1996, 23). The advertising blitz for *Three Novels* used cropped versions of the Brassai photograph to assert the idea that Beckett was "a man who has fallen out of the world" (press release for *Stories and Texts for Nothing,* 1967, SUL), connecting him with the struggling urban people typically associated with Brassai by insisting on his detachment from the commercial world of jets and hotels, royalty checks and publicity hoardings, business contracts and professional correspondence. This world had, of course, become Beckett's familiar milieu by 1958: rapidly accumulating royalty income gave him the freedom to maintain and improve his custom-built house in the French countryside, to go on long vacations in southern Europe and northern Africa, and to support a number of struggling actors, publishers, writers, and other professionals. With a number of post-*Godot* productions under his belt and with his fame spreading across America, Europe, and beyond, Beckett had become an author worthy of a session with one of Europe's top photographers. His image as someone cut off from the world of literary professionalism had, of course, been reinforced by his assent to the publication of the Schneider letters, and it was, by 1958, so pervasive that Brassai accepted this image as a given, putting aside the main aspects of his own style (characterized by raw, unposed shots of urban streetscapes) in order to amplify an established mode of representation. Through Brassai's expert lens-craft Beckett was presented as "un célèbre inconnu"; his photograph posed the author in a way carefully calculated to encapsulate and perpetuate Beckett's established authorial persona.

The legacy created by Charpentier and continued by Brassai led to the creation of what I call the "inmate" photographs taken by Jerry Bauer in Beckett's "private" apartment in 1962. A version of one of the photographs from the session, with the background cut out, was used on the front and back covers of *Samuel Beckett Now* (Friedman 1970). Prepared by Bauer's mug shot, we are hardly surprised Friedman concludes his introductory essay by arguing that, for Beckett, "silence is the 'mother tongue'" (30): this to describe a writer who had, by 1962, completed four major post-*Godot* plays, who was working on commissions for the BBC, and who was in the process of translating a major post-*Unnamable* novel (*Comment c'est*). In the full-frame version of Bauer's publicity photograph, Beckett is carefully posed on a low ottoman in the bare corner of a room, the light diffused to minimize shadows, the angles designed to give the impression the subject is awkward in front of a camera (see Marie 1997, 22–23). As in so many photographic portraits, Beckett stares directly at the lens. He has a "short-back-and-sides" haircut, his top hair spiked, a tight-lipped expression on his face, his collared shirt buttoned to the top, his body slouched against the wall, the arms of his V-neck pullover twisted, his hands crossed at his groin with a half-burned cigarette in his right hand. It is a carefully posed shot intended to represent an indifferent author. The photograph is deliberately designed to communicate the blankness and awkwardness of the powerless; the author's body seems limp, his attitude resigned. But we notice the high quality of the wool trousers and pullover, the hand-sewn shoes, and we observe that the posed carelessness is offset by the cuff-linked shirt. Used on the cover of Grove Press's collection *I Can't Go On, I'll Go On: A Samuel Beckett Reader* (1976), the photograph directly connects Beckett's authorial persona with the ambiguous state of mind expressed in the last sentence of *The Unnamable:* the strong suggestion is that, like his narrators, Beckett is a reluctant subject hassled by a voice saying "you must go on" (*GCE II,* 407). As we see so often in commercial uses of Beckett's image, the photograph on the book jacket is cropped, the "cut-out-background" (c.o.b) technique emphasizing his isolation not only from other people but also from the world of things. It is an intentional photographic portrait of the artist described in the first sentence of Joyce's "Day of the Rabblement": "the artist, though he may employ the crowd, is very careful to isolate himself" (Joyce 1989, 69).

One of the most revealing representations of Beckett as a man who experienced success but preferred failure was taken in the same year he posed for Haynes against a black background wearing a black turtleneck. The session with Jerry Bauer produced the "photograph of author" used on the back cover of all Beckett books issued by John Calder and Grove Press between 1975 and 1985 (see, for example the 1975 Calder editions of *Molloy, Malone Dies* and *The Unnamable* and the 1983 edition of *Worstward Ho*). Beckett's expression is less severe than usual, his eyes and mouth hinting at a smile. A stylish tweed coat and wool muffler are balanced by the roughness of the brick wall behind him; again he is situated as though he shares the state of a character in one of his own books, this time Molloy at a near impasse in an alleyway in a city. But there is no question this "brick wall" photograph presents a portrait of the artist as a success: it is captioned on the back of every Calderbook with the phrase, "Nobel Prize for Literature 1969." At the same time, it is clearly intended to affirm the idea that "Beckett had suddenly been besieged on all sides by the rhetoric which has become an inevitable part of the [Nobel] award" (Friedman 1970, 30).

The "brick wall" image of Beckett as an author in a Molloy-like impasse takes on new meaning in light of two carefully staged photographs by Roger Pic. Reproduced on pages x and 133 of Gerry Dukes's *Samuel Beckett* (2002), Roger Pic's formal portraits, captioned "Beckett signing limited editions of his work in 1977" and "Beckett signing the deluxe, limited edition of *The Lost Ones* at his Paris apartment," demonstrate Beckett's willingness to display himself as a professional writer firmly situated in the professional world of literary commerce and authorial image making. Whereas the material we have analyzed so far suggests a deliberate effort to erase consideration of Beckett's private life, mystifying his position as an author by, paradoxically, collapsing lines between the author and the text, Pic's photographs expose the private space in which Beckett performs his function as a professional writer. The strategic publications and publicity photographs analyzed thus far have the effect of closing us off from "Beckett the man" because they represent him in terms of a carefully crafted "Beckettian" authorial persona. The Pic portraits deliberately puncture this persona by calling attention to his active and willing participation in a commercial enterprise.

In the first portrait Beckett is shown in right profile, the whole upper part of his body addressing an open book on a desk. The black pen in his right hand touches an indistinct page, a mini-cigar hangs from his mouth; our eyes focus on the hands of a writer, writing. On first glance, we might think the photograph shows Beckett hard at work on a creative project; but closer inspection, and the caption on the opposite page, makes it clear he is adding his signature to a printed text. We cannot tell much about the text he is signing except to observe it is oversized and printed, with about thirty lines of prose on the page: *The Lost Ones* is a likely candidate because it was published in a limited edition around the time of the photograph, but we cannot say for sure. In any event, Dukes's suggestion that the second Pic photograph in his photo-biography (133) shows Beckett signing an edition of *The Lost Ones* is a misidentification: the text is *Imagination Dead Imagine* (fig. 3). The photograph is distinct enough that, by comparing it with the copyright page of the "texte d'artiste" of *Imagination Dead Imagine* held by the Beckett International Foundation (copy number 1 of 50), we can be certain the photograph shows Beckett writing a dedication to Sorel Etrog (who was, incidentally, at the table at the Closerie de Lilas in the May 19, 1969, press photograph commemorating the Zacks gift to the Samuel Beckett Theatre in Oxford). The copy Beckett is signing is an hors commerce presentation copy set aside for the artist. Taken from a position thirty degrees right of front, the photograph shows the author leaning over a large printed text with white letters on a black page; he writes with a white pen in the bottom right-hand corner of the copyright page.

The valuable collectors' text he is signing was published with "ten original prints on Arches paper and a portrait of Samuel Beckett" in a limited edition of sixty, with "fifty copies numbered 1–50" and "ten copies hors commerce I–X" (Beckett 1979). This second photograph is significant because it provides historic documentation of the moment when Beckett dedicated a copy of a collector's edition to the artist who designed and illustrated it: close examination of the photograph lets us see he has written "For Sorel Etrog, With all good wishes, Samuel Beckett, Paris" and has just begun to write a new letter, presumably the date. As he works in the ostensible privacy of his study, augmenting the value—archival, monetary, and personal—of a museum-quality book, participating in a form of marketing driven by the desirability of hand-crafted, authorized special editions and, perhaps, by nostalgia for the days before mechanical reproduction, he deliberately reveals his close relationship with a specialized area of the literary marketplace, the rare-books market. Providing photographic evidence of his status as a creator of hors commerce and limited-edition texts, he proves that he did, indeed, personalize special versions of his books by dedicating them, in his own hand, to specific individuals. In other words, the photograph authenticates the signature Beckett is autographing, and it provides evidence he *did* sign copies of special editions of his books even though he was, ostensibly, opposed to such marketing strategies. These photographs by Roger Pic complicate Gerry Dukes's familiar comment in the introduction—Beckett "had not the slightest interest in celebrity, believing that it was the writing rather than the writer that should be the main focus of attention" (2002, 1)—by making him the main subject of portraits directly connecting him with the marketplace. This is especially true because the photograph connects Beckett with the fund-raising efforts for the Samuel Beckett Theatre at Oxford: Etrog's *Imagination Dead Imagine* was developed with the specific purpose of raising money for this project.

Rare because they show him in the physical act of writing, the photographs by Roger Pic call attention to a number of legacy-shifting aspects of Beckett's professional life as a writer: presenting him as a participant in the literary marketplace, as a professional writer actively engaged in a commercial enterprise, the photographs are graphic evidence of the need for a reassessment of his received reputation as a private man who was shy of publicity and uninterested in commerce. The photographs provide visual proof that Beckett invited professional photographers into his home. Further, they document autographic, author-scripted connections between his private and public lives. A quick glance through Cécile Marie's *Portraits d'auteurs* (1997) reveals that Pic was by no means the first to do his work in Beckett's private space: photographs by Lufti Ozkok in 1963 and 1966, by Gisèle Freund in 1964, by Jerry Bauer in 1973, and by Marc Trivier in 1983 demonstrate Beckett's openness to select photographers, to the professional practice of photography, to the practice of displaying his own participation in the business of public relations and authorial image making, and to the inscription of his private life on the iconography of his public persona. The collections by Gerry Dukes, John Haynes, and John Minihan underscore the craftsmanship that went into this image making. At the same time they demonstrate the ongoing effort to perpetuate Beckett's authorial image. And they provide adequate evidence that Beckett was content to underwrite and expose this image making. As always, he maintained firm control over his public persona, becoming irate when unapproved photographers captured his image, only allowing photo shoots he could plan in advance with professionals who would respect how he wanted to be portrayed.

Our reading of the Pic photographs as evidence of Beckett's willing participation in literary marketing is strengthened by a publicity photograph taken by Charles Altschul "in Paris on November 30, 1983" (SUL). This photograph was used in a 1984 brochure publicizing the New Overbrook Press edition of *The Lost Ones* with illustrations by Charles Klabunde, and it was sent out with the press packet publicizing Beckett's latest *livres d'artiste:* it appeared in a number of newspaper reports about the April 1984 publication. For example, in the *Los Angeles Herald Examiner* on April 11, 1984, the photograph appeared with the caption, "Beckett signs copies of books that will debut at $1,750." In the photograph the author is not, in fact, signing the book; rather he is holding the cleverly designed copyright page, emphasizing the fact that the lines of the text are shaped to match the circular abode of the narrative. His hands clenched, fingers overlapping (like the protagonist with "Fibrous degeneration" in *Catastrophe, GCE III,* 486), Beckett appears to be turning to page 1. The photograph again reveals Beckett's willingness to endorse, with his signature, and with photographic evidence of his active participation, a commercial enterprise; taken together, the photograph and the autograph become value-enhancing marks of authentication. In this case, Beckett's participation cannot be explained by friendship: while he gave Altschul and Klabunde a revised, "definitive" version of the narrative to typeset, he met neither man before they had completed their work on *The Lost Ones.* This contrasts, of course, with the creation of the limited edition of *Imagination Dead Imagine,* where he worked closely with both the publisher and the artist, Sorel Etrog, throughout the process.

Initially, these photographic portraits make us pause because it is rare to see photographs of Beckett writing, because he seems unusually oblivious to the camera's gaze, and because we do not expect to see evidence of Beckett engaged in literary marketing. The Pic photographs provide evidence counter to Beckett's reputation for shyness and an aversion to publicity because they suggest he was at ease with portrait photography and was comfortable with a genre of writing solely designed to increase the ownership value of legacy-enhancing, museum-quality texts. They situate him as a professional writer who was, in keeping with Rainey's thesis, actively engaged in the production of "consuming investments" that turn "the reader into a collector, an investor, or even a speculator" (1998, 53). As Rainey and others who study the sociology of texts have suggested, Beckett was simply participating in a practice standard among avant-garde writers in the twentieth century: he had, after all, been signing limited editions of his work since Nancy Cunard's Hours Press release of *Whoroscope* in 1930 (100 signed copies and 200 unsigned). While we take seriously James Knowlson's observation that Beckett "tolerated [having his photograph taken] for the sake of his friends or as a minimal concession to publicity for the sake of the theatre or the production" (Haynes and Knowlson 2003, 20), we must consider this observation in light of the indisputable evidence from numerous photographs revealing his willingness to invite professional photographers into his private abode. In the case of Roger Pic, he opened his study to a photographer who documented, and thus authenticated, the task of autographing a collector's text (fig. 3).

Beckett, always precise in his control of visual representations, obviously wanted Pic to photograph him as he put the finishing touches to a personal dedication destined, he surely must have known, to become immensely valuable. The commentary surrounding these photographs asks us to deny what is staring us in the face: rather than showing a man "averse to publicity" who is making a "minimal concession" to be polite, they reveal a self-confident author who is relaxed in front of a camera and who is comfortable revealing his active participation in the creation of rare, highly marketable artifacts. The cigar hanging from his lip suggests his comfort both as a photographic subject and as a writer of autographs.

Given Beckett's reputation as someone "damned to fame," and with unwavering respect for Beckett and those who helped create and maintain his public image, we can excuse Dukes for putting the entire book of photographs, which includes a "selection of formal portraits by some of the leading photographers of the time" (2002, 1–2), in the context of Dumesnil's reaction to the award of the 1969 Nobel Prize: "His wife regarded the award as a 'catastrophe' because it inevitably meant that attention was paid to his person rather than his work" (1). Even though it happened in a private telephone conversation between Dumesnil and Lindon, with only Samuel Beckett as witness, this "reaction" has become a firmly entrenched part of the Beckett myth. As I suggested in the introduction and as I argue later, this "private" moment quickly achieved mythic significance in representations of Beckett's public image. This is why Beckett used it as the source of his analysis of image manipulation, audience response, and the apparatus of the theater in *Catastrophe,* in a play connecting his public life as a famous author with the field of advertising. Even as it seems to reinforce the public image constructed as Beckett rose to international fame, the representation of Beckett as a floating head also serves to underscore the professional craftsmanship and authorial collaboration that went into the fashioning and advertising of this image.

2

"Fight"

Beckett's Social Agency, 1928–1934

> Beckett, like Malone, has sought unceasingly to divest himself of his identity by means of his art, but in the end he remains what he always was, an Irish gentleman of the professional classes, reared by a sporting father and an evangelical mother.
>
> —Mercier, *Beckett*

The Roots of Beckett's Ambition

During the 1973 photo session that produced the "brick wall" head shot used to promote Beckett's post-Nobel books published by John Calder, Jerry Bauer took a photograph of Beckett seated in an alley on a bag of rubbish (fig. 4). Clearly this "alley" portrait is designed to associate Beckett with characters and narrators in his work who struggle to "accommodate the chaos" (Dearlove 1982). The most immediate reference is to Beckett's "most 'popular' play," *Breath,* which had 1,314 performances on Broadway between February 1971 and August 1989 and was seen by eighty-five million people (Ackerley and Gontarski 2004, 73). The image also connects Beckett with Molloy's "blind alley . . . littered with miscellaneous rubbish" (*GCE II,* 55) and, less directly, the ash cans in *Endgame.* At first glance the photograph seems to provide support for the frequent tendency to treat Beckett as though he lived like the characters he created in his literary texts. But we then notice it is as carefully staged as any Beckett text. The empty cigarette and snack boxes and stuffed plastic bags are arranged precisely. He is clothed in well-made, hand-sewn leather shoes, new corduroys, a spiffy, buttoned tweed coat and an urbane muffler. His eyes are fixed on the ground below the camera, his right arm rests on a box positioned at exactly the right height for his arm to dangle without effort, and his index and middle fingers extend loosely to his right knee. His left hand rests palm-down on his left knee, the angle between his hands mirroring the angle of separation between his feet; the bag he is sitting on holds him at a height perfectly balancing the composition of the photograph, creating a triangle between his washed-out face, a black bag the same size as his torso, and his polished black shoes. Beckett's blank look, framed as it is by two distinctly black objects, seems to recede, the crowded scene overwhelming his ostensibly meek, but supremely self-confident, persona. The portrait is composed to communicate passivity, as though he accepts the lot of an author forever associated with trash cans, rubbish, and back alleys; but it also communicates the precise process of image construction that turned this association into a formula for long-term success in the literary marketplace.

Despite the effort to underscore Beckett's authorial association with alleyways and garbage, Beckett's well-made clothes and the professional composition of the image inspire us to ask how a man who was so well-regulated in his lifestyle and so careful in his clothing and behavior should become famous not only for representations of "low life" but also for being at home in rathskeller culture. The fact is, he was not. Or, rather, he was not at home in this culture after he settled in Paris in 1937–38; once he began to enjoy the lifestyle of an internationally famous author the life of basement bars and reckless debauchery was part of a past he had as little interest in reliving as he had in wearing frayed, castoff clothes. This can be seen through his relationship with Brendan Behan, a fellow Dubliner who rose to fame at the same time as Beckett, but who was from a very different social background and who expressed his success in ways that rubbed Beckett the wrong way. In Cronin's telling, when Behan showed up in Paris, proclaiming his fame and love of publicity with every shout on the way to Beckett's flat, Beckett and Suzanne responded by learning to "keep mum and still until the storm blew over" (Cronin 1996, 497). They turned the lights off, hunkered down, and waited for Behan to give up on his efforts to rouse them. From Beckett's point of view, Behan was too inclined to get caught up in the sordid life of backstreet bars and alleys. Even though he had his rathskeller moments, exploring the kinds of "crapulent den" (*GCE IV*, 103) preferred by Behan and using material gathered from these explorations in his early texts, Beckett was trained from youth to be master of his upper-middle-class domain: this is, perhaps, why he preferred drinking in the expensive bars of five-star hotels like the PLM, why he preferred to meet in Boulevard restaurants like the Closerie de Lilas, and why he chose the peace and quiet of his settled domestic life over the places to which he was likely to be dragged by Behan. At the end of a day spent posing against a brick wall, on a fire escape, and in an alley sitting on garbage, Beckett retired to the Hyde Park Hotel.

Behan, the product of a rough working- and nonworking-class area of North Dublin, was too crude in his habits, too seedy in his preferred locales, and too boisterous in his ways of expressing his particular brand of Irishness for Beckett, a product of the privileged South Dublin suburbs. Simply put, the working-class playwright was not Beckett's social type: he was too rambunctious, too loud, too much of an alley cat. Further, he was a threat to Beckett's highly guarded methods of engaging with "the public," calling too much attention to Beckett's carefully sequestered hideaway. Raised in a social class intolerant of public drunkenness, Beckett preferred to drink alone or in anonymous hotel lobby bars, in theater bars when they were closed except to those working in the theater, and in bars where the management and his inner circle protected him from unwanted interruptions by "admirers"; Behan's preference for much wilder, more open, more public drinking went against Beckett's social upbringing and threatened to disrupt his carefully managed life as a professional writer.

The comparison with Behan underlines what is apparent from Bauer's "alley" photograph: from beginning to end of his professional life, Beckett was guided by manners and forms of behavior in keeping with a socially privileged background, with an emphasis on propriety and moderation, self-effacement and self-control. His tight-lipped avoidance of Behan is entirely in keeping with his experience sitting with the upper-middle-class Irish from South Dublin, watching the Easter Rising from a suburban hill, keeping their heads low and their children out of the way until the smoke had cleared. Soon after the British brought in the "Black and Tans" in spring 1920, Beckett was sent to school in Enniskillen, well away from turbulent Dublin; Cronin suggests Beckett's household lived in a "political vacuum" during the period between 1916 and 1936. Beckett and his domestic partner had been dragged into Behan's drunken displays on a number of occasions, and Beckett had paid money to get him out of trouble with his landlord. But Behan and Beckett grew up in different worlds and had very different senses of what it meant to be famous writers. As Bair puts it, "They were a curious contrast: the lean, ascetic Beckett, product of lawn tennis and yacht clubs, public schools and good manners; Behan, the scruffy ex–Borstal boy from a tenement off the North Circular Road" (1990, 507).[1]

What we see throughout Beckett's professional life as a writer is an ongoing expression of his social class; his tight control of his public image and his legacy as a man averse to fame is consistent with his upper-middle-class upbringing. As he began to invent an authorial persona, Beckett downplayed his social status, describing himself with the same words he used to describe his first main character: "a dirty low-church Protestant" (*GCE IV,* 129). But his confidence and agency shone through, calling attention to the fact he was only partially "low-church" and only experienced the "dirty" through choice. He attended low-church services with his mother, but he had access to the privileges of the established church and the country-club life preferred by his father. He grew up in a very comfortable, well-appointed, custom-built house with the best Anglican education money could buy, playing golf, rugby, cricket, and other games associated with the high-church "ascendancy," tagging along with his father in one of Dublin's first automobiles (hardly the transport of a "dirty low-church P."), carousing with the wealthy clerk of the local racecourse, and racing expensive motorcycles and cars with the bravado of the social elite.

Clearly, the decision to pose in an alley with garbage had little to do with the actual life Beckett had lived or was living when the photograph was taken in 1973; it was entirely about the strategic reinforcement of a public image in which the author of texts about tramps and invalids, alleyways and backstreets, dustbins and trash associates himself with his characters so as to increase his credibility. In short, the photograph is a publicity shot designed to promote a specific authorial image, providing a deliberately crafted visual connection between Beckett the man and Beckett the author. The long-term planning behind the creation of this connection is evident when we backtrack four decades to the letter he wrote to Thomas McGreevy on October 18, 1932 (*Letters,* 133–36). The letter reveals Beckett began the process of self-fashioning when he was twenty-six, shaping his authorial persona by tapping aspects of his sociocultural context that would eventually allow him to define himself. Written to his main confidant during his formative years as a professional writer, the letter proves he had begun a serious effort to define a

1. Reprinted with the permission of Simon & Schuster, Inc. from *Samuel Beckett: A Biography* by Deirdre Bair. Copyright © 1978, 1990 by Deirdre Bair.

personal aesthetic not only by calling attention to a specific aspect of his life but also by framing this aspect as "dirty." The letter begins to articulate a "low church" aesthetic, directly anticipating the polar opposition to Joyce's method he would describe in his 1956 conversation with Shenker: as such, it suggests Beckett's early efforts to define a minimalist aesthetic were deliberately constructed in opposition to Joyce's Roman Catholic poetry (*Letters,* 134). Forty-one years later this aesthetic would take him into an alley to be photographed sitting on a pile of rubbish.

As is well known, Beckett's initial path to a literary career began in "the world of Mr. Joyce's *Work in Progress*" (*GCE IV,* 495). Soon after he went to Paris in 1928 to teach at the École Normale Supérieure, Beckett used his contacts and his urbane self-confidence to move himself close to the center of Joyce's "high-brow" circle, gaining access to the most cutting-edge publishers in Europe. Within months he was published in *transition,* had an essay in a book by Shakespeare and Company, and was developing personal and professional relationships with Richard Aldington, Nancy Cunard, Eugene Jolas, Charles Prentice, Samuel Putnam, and other literary pioneers. By the time he was twenty-six he had published a number of poems and stories in a variety of prominent avant-garde venues and had two independent publications, *Whoroscope* (1930) and *Proust* (1931). At this point in his career, it was in Beckett's interests to emphasize the more scholarly, high-brow side of his upbringing: "Dante . . . Bruno . Vico . . Joyce" and his early poems and stories are explicit demonstrations of his scholarly erudition. Intentionally or not, the title of the story he published alongside the essay on Joyce in *transition* in June 1929, "Assumption," suggests an arrogant intention to take over from Joyce.

His relationship with Joyce was never easy. "Home Olga," the acrostic he wrote on Joyce's name in 1932, seems to posit his fellow Dubliner as a sacred mentor, "Juvante Jah" (*GCE IV,* 8). But in the period between 1928 and 1932 Beckett engaged in a serious analysis of the job of the writer, beginning to weigh the short-term advantages derived from the association with Joyce against the long-term consequences of this association. He knew very early he would never establish himself as a writer in his own right so long as he followed the Joycean path. Hence his June 1932 postcard to Samuel Putnam in which he announced his plan to overcome Joyce's influence (*Letters,* 108); and hence the unmistakable irony in "Home Olga" when he seems to refer to himself as a "pickthank agnus," an ingratiated sheep (*GCE IV,* 8). He realized he was seriously enmeshed in Joyce's complex web and was willing to express this enmeshment in the effort to disentangle himself.

Sometime after the section that became pages 104–25 of *Finnegans Wake* was published in *transition* magazine in August 1927, Joyce added a paragraph with what might be a deliberate reference to Beckett's enmeshed confusion as he struggled to translate part of the novel into French: "You is feeling like you was lost in the bush, boy? You says: it is a puling sample jungle of woods. You most shouts out: Bethicket me for a stump of a beech if I have the poultriest notion what the farest he all means" (1939, 112). The word "Bethicket" contains all but the last "t" of Beckett's name; in *Wake* studies this is as close to a clincher as we get! But even if we remain skeptical about the idea that Joyce consciously refers to the young writer, we can use the word to describe how Beckett must have felt in 1928–32: bethicketted by "Work in Progress," caught in its thicket of meanings, struggling to escape from Joyce's "jungle" of words, his very name subsumed by Joyce's method.

In any event, as he set out to develop a coherent aesthetic method designed to sustain a viable professional career, Beckett engaged in a process of autobiographical image analysis. In the works he wrote before 1950 he explored the job of the writer through characters who situate themselves in relation to, and at an increasing distance from, landmarks in what Eoin O'Brien has called "The Beckett Country" (1986). As already noted, our main focus in this book is not literary analysis. But as "Home Olga" demonstrates, his literary texts from the period when he wrote this poem directly address his association with Joyce, his struggle to become a viable writer, and his barely veiled ambition to achieve social, professional, and aesthetic independence. The process, which is best understood as a novitiate effort to find a voice of his own by tapping the most viable aspects of his biography, is evident from *Dream of Fair to Middling Women*, the novel he drafted in February to June 1932, which would remain dormant until it was published posthumously in 1992. This effort is also evident in the collection of short stories salvaged from the novel. Between them, *Dream* and *More Pricks Than Kicks* (1934) are the most directly autobiographical texts he produced, illustrating both how his religious, economic, and educational upbringing shaped his understanding of the social function of the professional author and how he selectively explored specific aspects of this upbringing in his work. In the context of the October 18, 1932, letter to McGreevy in which he links his strict Protestant upbringing with his style as a writer, and given that he terminated his academic career in 1931 with the specific goal of becoming a writer, we can read these texts as the initial products of his decision to become a professional; they provide solid evidence of his autobiographic crossing of his own experiences *as a writer* with those of characters who are also writers.

Throughout both texts, plot is subservient to the baring of the formal mechanisms of storytelling. The analysis of authorial integrity is a constant: numerous narrative interruptions ensure the emphasis remains on the job of storytelling as the narrator and the narrated figure out how to act like writers and as Beckett figures out what kind of author he wants to be. For example, in *Dream* the narrator notes, "The fact of the matter is we do not quite know where we are in this story" (Beckett 1992, 9), "Why we want to drag in the Syra-Cusa at this juncture it passes our persimmon to say" (49), "Extraordinary how everything ends like a fairy-tale, or can be made to" (109), "The only unity in this story is, please God, an involuntary unity" (133), "At last the plot looks as if it might begin to thicken" (199). The plot never does thicken because the novel is an exercise, an experiment in which the main character, Belacqua, is a writer figuring out his relationship with "Mr Beckett" (141 and 186), and in which the narrator (apparently named "Mr Beckett") is described meeting his character "on the way back to the city after a disastrous day on the course." Later, he is in a position "to behold him as he was, face to face, even as he sometimes contrived to behold himself" (186). This self-reflective content will be displaced as Beckett defines a recognizably "Beckettian" authorial persona and as he deconstructs the concepts of "self" and "story" to create a style of writing Abbott calls "autographic" (x). But in these early texts, which Abbott does not address exactly because they are more autobiographical than autographical, his more self-conscious technique explicitly reveals the steps he was taking on his way to aesthetic and professional independence.

Although he toned down the self-conscious narrative intrusions in *More Pricks Than Kicks* as part of his effort to create a more marketable series of well-made stories he could send to a publisher (the metaphor he used in a May 13, 1933, letter to McGreevy suggests the stories would be self-enclosed microworlds of the sort perfected by Joyce in *Dubliners* [*Letters,* 157]), the stories retain their focus on tensions between inner perception and outer representation as these tensions play out in various mundane situations: shopping, making and eating lunch, picking up a lobster, riding back and forth on a bus, getting dressed, rehearsing a poem, seducing a girl, going for a walk. Again, plot is much less important than the self-conscious effort to figure out a viable approach to storytelling while taking into account the unstable relationship between the narrator and the narrated. Accepted in October 1933 by Chatto and Windus, who paid an advance of twenty-five pounds with a deduction of six pounds, five shillings against potential royalties (October 9, 1933, *Letters,* 166–67), the collection repeatedly returns to the job of writing: "Let us call it Winter, that dusk may fall now and a moon rise" (*GCE IV,* 86), "Who shall silence them, at last?" (94), "Notice the literary man" (147), "this old pen is gone to the dogs" (197), "he was at a loss to determine off-hand whether the scene was of the kind that is termed romantic or whether it should not with more justice be deemed classical. . . . Perhaps classico-romantic would be the fairest estimate" (226).

Throughout, his characters are exposed as posers who, like Belacqua in "Dante and the Lobster," wear "an expression of profundity" like a mask (85). If there is a claim to integrity, it is on the part of a narrative persona trying to create a story around a group of awkward, often loathable misfits: as I have indicated, the narrator repeatedly calls attention to the formal apparatus of the text, addressing the reader directly and making numerous self-conscious references to the craft of writing. The narrative voice builds credibility with the reader by exposing the literary devices he uses, turning self-representation and artifice into central subjects, bringing us into a shared conversation about relationships between form and content. Beckett was, crucially, concerned with the profession of writing as a matter of integrity; he would, in the 1969 *Vogue* "interview" with Gruen, identify "integrity" as the one thing he learned from Joyce. But his idea of integrity diverges from Joyce's as radically as "low church" Protestantism diverges from Roman Catholicism. Joyce had a Catholic notion of the priesthood and translated this notion during the course of *A Portrait of the Artist as a Young Man* into a hierarchically elevated author function, making artistic "integrity" a matter of absolute detachment: "The artist, like the God of creation, remains within or behind or beyond or above his handiwork, invisible, refined out of existence, indifferent, paring his fingernails." While Beckett had an ingrained sense of social hierarchy as a result of his elite social class, the artistic approach he crafted was based on an egalitarian model of understanding, putting the author on the same level as his characters and audience, exposing and deriding any authorial elevation. The notion of the author as a detached, priestlike artist is displaced by the idea that the only difference between the preacher and the congregation is the surplice thrown over her/his day clothes. And herein lies the difference between Beckett the person and Beckett the artist: in his professional and domestic life he retained the sense of class he learned from his parents and school teachers; in his creative life he worked to erase class distinctions by emphasizing the lowest common denominator.

The two distinct versions of Beckett—the one who lived an upper-middle-class life and the one who represented classlessness (which come together in the "alley" photograph and which are played out in the ongoing tension between Beckett's actual life as a successful author and his public persona as a man damned to fame)—are evident throughout *More Pricks Than Kicks,* where he explores the tension between inner consciousness and outer show, exposing an elite social class permeated with pretentiousness at the same time as he exposes a narrative apparatus increasingly inadequate to the inner consciousness he is more interested in exploring. If we were to frame this phase of Beckett's career in terms of Thomas Carlyle's *Sartor Resartus* (1833–34) and Jonathan Swift's *Tale of a Tub* (1704) we would say he had begun the gradual turn from the outer clothing of social status and literary form toward an exploration of existentialism and epistemology. This philosophical ground is well trodden in Beckett studies, with numerous analyses of his exploration of "the meaning of being" (Butler 1984) and his relationship with philosophy (Lane 2002). But what has not been addressed is his deliberate effort to craft an authorial persona by emphasizing specific, carefully selected aspects of his upbringing. His interest in this process is surely connected to the alternative career he was contemplating in 1933 as he edited the proofs for *More Pricks Than Kicks:* on December 6, 1933, he informed McGreevy he had mailed a set of proofs but was thinking of applying for a job in an advertising company in London and planned to ask his father's permission to do so (*Letters,* 171). His transference of this interest in advertising to his developing sense of himself as a writer is apparent from his treatment of "the Alba" and "the homespun Poet," characters in "A Wet Night."

The Alba gives us a clear idea about how Beckett was beginning to understand his function as a writer stuck in the trap between private feeling and public performance, between the inner self and the publicly advertised self. We meet her, "dressed insidiously up to the nines" (*GCE IV,* 113), with a "frontage abandoned in elegance" and a "mind . . . at prayer-stool" (114). While her mind engages in a "more anxious rite than sumptuous meditation," the Alba "gilds her option" in preparation to "be belle of the ball, gladly, gravely and carefully," crafting her image with such deliberate, businesslike care that "her appearance" becomes "a reality of preference" (114). All is art, craft, self-fashioning, advertising; her choices and preferences about how she represents herself become her outer "reality," her public persona. Inside, of course, is the part she uses to "delegate a portion of her attention with instructions to reorganize her features, hands, shoulders, back, outside in a word, the inside having been spiked" (114–15). In there, somewhere, is an authentic self, a self punctured by experience but defiant against burial or falsehood: "No me jodas en el suelo / Como si fuera una perra." This private self may be "anxious" but "She sings to herself, for her own pleasure" (115). In his analysis of Alba's mind as she dresses for success, Beckett finds the seed of a consciousness with the ability to detach itself from its social agency even as it deploys the fruits of this agency "without fear or favour" (115). For the Alba, the ideal self-advertisement is drawn from deep within but gives the impression of effortlessness.

A further clue to Beckett's developing persona can be seen in another character in "A Wet Night." "The homespun Poet" has "cropped" his hair, "plumping for the austerity of a rat's back" because he has "proclaimed himself in reaction to the nineties" (*GCE IV,* 118). Consciously framing himself as a writer "in reaction" to the previous generation of writers, the writers of the Irish Renaissance, he engages in a game of self-styling that emphasizes minimalist "austerity" over the showiness of the Celtic Twilight: "But the little that there was to do he had done, with a lotion he had he had given alertness to the stubble. Also he had changed his tie and turned his collar." He is "alone and unobserved" but he acts as though he has a public, pacing as he prepares to recite "his piece, d'occasion" (118). The homespun Poet plans to situate himself somewhere between the casual behavior of "an amateur" and the formal presentation of a "professional." He thus rehearses how to stand and deliver his poem, "Calvary by Night," working hard to give the impression of not working hard: "he had to have it pat in order not to have to say it pat" so as "to put across this strong composition and cause something of a flutter" (119). Given how Beckett would establish an international reputation as a man who preferred failure, and given the evidence we have already begun to present testifying to his ongoing effort to hide the hard work he did "behind-the-scenes" to establish this reputation, we must underscore the fact that in "A Wet Night" he created a character who consciously disguises the conscious effort he makes. The homespun Poet "encaptures us by failing once, twice, three times, and then, in a regular lather of volition, bringing it off." The joke in the name "homespun Poet" is in its reference to a spider spinning its web from its own internal excretions; its performance dramatizes "the spiritual evisceration of the performer" (119), turning the internal drama of self into a dramatic, but also physically detached, display of authorial control.

Both the Alba and the homespun Poet are driven by an urge to construct a public image by exploiting and then hiding the internal workings of their consciousness. Any conclusions we derive about an author's professional life by studying the creations of his imagination are, of course, suspect. However, the link between Beckett's life as a struggling writer and the homespun Poet is strengthened because Beckett had published "Calvary by Night" under his own name in *The European Caravan* in 1931. Beckett made a practice of explicitly crossing his own experiences with those of his characters. In *Dream* and *More Pricks Than Kicks* Belacqua was sufficiently close to Beckett that we can almost regard him as a surrogate. For example, when we meet him for the second time in "A Wet Night" Belacqua, the punk-poet, is described with the same phrase Beckett applied to himself in his October 18, 1932, letter to McGreevy—"dirty low-church Protestant" (*Letters,* 134; *GCE IV,* 129). In the story Belacqua has paused on his way to the Frica's "mauve salon" (130), sitting on the parapet of a bridge over the Grand Canal at Lower Baggot street. He has realized "walking through the rain was not enough, stepping out smartly, buttoned up to the chin, in the cold and wet, was an inadequate thing to be doing" (129). His expensive clothes, which include a "German shirt," a "reefer" (a close-knit woolen jacket designed for sailors), and a pair of "perfectly good boots" (137), offer too much protection from the elements, preventing "full value from the bitter nor'-wester that was blowing" (129). Belacqua's clothes represent the comfort and security offered by his class status, and they highlight the social privilege coloring the entire scene (just as the mature Beckett's expensive clothes call attention to his elite social status even as he poses on a pile of garbage in Bauer's "alley" photograph) (fig. 4); his shedding of these clothes suggests that his pursuit of independence drives him, on occasion, to purge the high-brow sensibility of his education, mimicking Beckett's ongoing efforts to manage the career-defining trappings of *his* social background. For Belacqua it is a temporary gesture rather than a lifestyle decision. Somehow, by "beating his bosom thus bared to the mean storm," Belacqua achieves a more adequate, "low-down" level of integrity (129). But it is the old story of the privileged using the fruits of their privilege to seek freedom from the trappings of privilege: only someone who can afford another pair would throw away his perfectly good boots. Tomorrow he will be well-heeled again. While he feels "sorry for what he had done" (it is not clear whether he feels ashamed for getting drunk, throwing up on the Garda's boots, exposing himself to the rain, or taking "leave of himself"), he is in no real danger (129). This remains true even after he has stripped himself in a gesture of bohemian defiance. Again his social position and agency are impermeable. Just as Beckett was protected by his social status when he drove recklessly around Dublin, once skidding his father's automobile onto the sidewalk within a few inches of a judge, with no consequences except a warning, so Belacqua is protected even when he vomits on a policeman.

The aesthetic "value" Belacqua gains by casting off his protective garments is represented by his increased poetic appreciation of his environment; he stares at the "Distant lights on a dirty night" of "trams hiccupping across the remote hump of Leeson Street Bridge" and proclaims "he loved them" (*Dream* 1992, 227). The importance of this scene on Baggot Bridge is apparent: Beckett retained the description in a lightly edited form when he turned an extract from *Dream of Fair to Middling Women* into "A Wet Night." Between the novel and the short story Beckett replaced "hiccupping" with "hiccups-o'-the wisp" (*GCE IV*, 129), underscoring the connection to low-church parables of spiritual revelation in which the subject deliberately experiences wretchedness to understand more fully the fatuity of manufactured lights and to purge himself of worldly sin: George Fox's seventeenth century trek to the storm-swept top of Pendle Hill in a suit made of leather is a useful context for a number of Beckett works exactly because it involves the shedding of sociocultural baggage in the interests of integrity (the shift from religious integrity to aesthetic integrity is, of course, crucial to the history of literature after Robert Burns and William Wordsworth). There are crucial differences between a man of Fox's stature, a man who created a movement, the Society of Friends, that continues to shape religious practice, and Beckett's Belacqua, a solitary Bohemian caught up in his own pursuit of self-understanding: Fox's revelation on Pendle Hill created a transformative theology while Belacqua's leaves him "wondering whence on earth could comfort spring" (129). Like Beckett at this point in his career, he has a lot of work to do before he can turn his critique of his environment into a source of comfort. After he has abandoned himself to the elements and to his most primal urges Belacqua dries himself with a "cambric pochette" (called a "Paris pochette" in *Dream* 1992); this reminds us of Belacqua and Beckett's status as well-traveled Euro-Irishmen. Then he drinks the bottle "at a single gulp" (130), plunging into the private debauchery allowed by his class position—even though he is on a public bridge, he remains unobserved until the policeman arrives. Conscious or not, the exotic handkerchief and reckless drinking reveal that Belacqua, like the authorial imagination that has produced him, is only a few steps down the road to the social and professional freedom he seeks. Beckett has a lot more bridges to cross before he will achieve an adequate level of authorial integrity, but he has begun to see the glimmerings of a viable professional persona.

"A Wet Night" underscores the strong sense of socioreligious agency behind the acts of contrition and self-surrender central to the work Beckett would write after 1945. Samuel Johnson, whose life and work he studied very closely in 1937, inspired Beckett to contemplate aesthetic applications of a religious vision of positive annihilation; as I have argued elsewhere, this gave Beckett the push he needed to develop a viable literary persona, a persona based on the idea that the best way forward is through a process of literary dismantling analogous to Derridean deconstruction (Dilks 2003). A deeper analysis of the bridge scene clarifies how his social agency began to translate into the kind of professional agency we will explore in chapter 3. Having thoroughly indulged himself on the way to the Frica's high-society cocktail party, Belacqua "is shocked . . . into something worse than sobriety" (*GCE IV,* 130) when he arrives but, threatened by "an abstract calamity," manages to respond "composedly" (131). He thus adjusts to circumstances, self-consciously managing his image by taking "a precautionary measure" as he "framed himself" to his best advantage (133). Belacqua thus engages in a form of careful self-representation equivalent to the displays of image construction by Alba and the homespun Poet. But his fate in the story is more complex, beginning with his observation, and somewhat surrealist interpretation, of the "seven phases" of a neon advertisement for Bovril (53), and ending with him throwing away his boots and crawling home, suffering from overconsumption with "such a belly-ache as he had never known" (137). He thus endures a quasi-religious journey from the world of commerce and the "faith jaundiced" (108) to a world of reckless charity and consumption-induced suffering. Again, this journey is the expression of a writer who overindulges himself in keeping with his social class but who then seeks to purge himself of commercial and social impurity through a series of acts of monastic self-deprivation.

The scene on Baggot Street Bridge in "A Wet Night" gestures toward the dominant aesthetic economy in Beckett's later novels, from *Murphy* to *The*

Unnamable, where characters expose themselves to a hostile environment even as they actively pursue a deeper, more comfortable level of consciousness. In other words, the bridge scene marks a moment in Beckett's career as a professional writer when he began to build an aesthetic program by tapping the ascetic, anticommercial part of his upbringing. It also marks a moment when he self-consciously analyzed the process through which a member of the Anglo-Irish elite, who was, however, ingrained with the consciousness of a "dirty low-church Protestant," could distinguish himself from his inherited cultural and social world. As the bridge scene and the party atmosphere at the "Casa Frica" suggest, part of this sociocultural milieu was hedonistic. But, as I have begun to suggest, this part was being displaced in 1929–34, as Beckett began a conscious effort to purge high-brow associations from his published work.

Given that "A Wet Night" deliberately parodies Joyce's "The Dead," especially in its closing description of the rain "that fell upon the bay, the littoral, the mountains and the plains, most notably upon the Central Bog it fell with a rather desolate uniformity" (*GCE IV,* 137), we can read the bridge scene as a sure sign Beckett had begun to resist and displace the "commodious vicus of recirculation" represented by Joyce. The Bovril advertisement brings Joyce's "skysign of advertisement" (Joyce 1939, 4) down to a more mundane level, replacing the bright beauty of snow with the murky inconvenience of mud. We should also read it as a sign he was entirely conscious of his situation, not only in relation to Joyce, but in relation to the marketplace: he deliberately distances himself from Joyce at the same time that he overtly reveals his interest in advertising, image making, and the ironies of literary posturing. While he admitted in the October 18, 1932, letter to McGreevy his inability to explain what his successful work accomplishes, he *had* begun to distinguish between writing associated with lies and decadence and the form of purgative writing he was attempting to create (*Letters,* 134). Beckett's grotesque language of poison, pus, and abscesses is familiar to us from early prose and poetry written "across the threshold of the gehenna of narratio recta" in *Dream of Fair to Middling Women* (Beckett 1992, 169) and with the "ink of pestilence" in "Enueg I" (*GCE IV,* 13). The letter thus anticipates developments more closely associated with the refined poetics of failure and uncertainty that would eventually distinguish him from Joyce and bring him fame. It is hard to give an adequate summary of such an important letter, but suffice it to say Beckett suggests McGreevy is one of the few people who might understand his uncontrolled and futile struggle to express himself and, further, McGreevy is one of the few who might appreciate his fight to destroy what gags him while he learns to accept failure and to embrace silence (*Letters,* 133–36). Seventeen years after he wrote the story, he would turn his stuttering effort to celebrate failure into a crucial component of his aesthetic—"There are many ways in which the thing I am trying in vain to say may be tried in vain to be said" (*GCE IV,* 562)—and twenty-four years later he would turn his revulsion at Joyce's self-enclosed, self-satisfied Jesuit poetry into a seminal statement about his difference from Joyce (Shenker 1956).

The scene on Baggot Street Bridge gives a very good idea of Beckett's nascent understanding of the relationship between aesthetics and ascetics. And the plot of "A Wet Night" anticipates the trajectory of a career designed to give the impression of an "appearance" specifically designed so it "might not provoke too much comment" (130). This impression is, of course, a lasting part of Beckett's legacy. Looking back at the December 6, 1933, letter to McGreevy, we note Beckett's confession that he has been inactive. We then note he reports he that has just sent off a batch of corrected proofs and has finished reading *Holy Living and Holy Dying* by Jeremy Taylor and Leibnitz (*Letters,* 171–72). As we shall see, this claim he was doing nothing often takes place in the context of descriptions of the immense and valuable work he accomplished in a short period of time: like his great mentor Samuel Johnson, Beckett was driven by a powerful work ethic and was never satisfied, even when his level of productivity was extremely high.

Social Acculturation

Brought up in a custom-built house in the upper-middle-class suburbs of Dublin by a fiercely independent, highly disciplined mother and a happy-go-lucky, entrepreneurial father, and introduced to the profession of writing by a number of well-positioned writers, publishers, and literary agents, Beckett had, by the time he was forty, absorbed personal, social, and professional skills sufficient to his survival and eventual prosperity in the literary marketplace between World War II and the collapse of the Soviet Union. As Vivian Mercier put it, "Beckett, like Malone, has sought unceasingly to divest himself of his identity by means of his art, but in the end he remains what he always was, an Irish gentleman of the professional classes, reared by a sporting father and an evangelical mother" (1977, 65). From birth until the age of twenty-two, he may have lived "like a Quaker" (Cronin 1996, 14; also see Bair 1990, 14, and Knowlson 1996, 25), but it was the Quakerism of those with cooks, housemaids, servants, and gardeners. He benefited from the upper-middle-class income of his wealthy, self-employed father and the social manners of an affluent mother. Free of the requirement to earn money for himself, he could depend on financial support from his family until he was at least thirty-one. On his father's side he was descended from wealthy silk weavers and builders, with a great-grandfather who owned factories and a grandfather who owned prized Dublin properties and won the contract to build the National Library and National Museum in 1885–91 (which later housed the Dail).

On his mother's side he was descended from landowners and land surveyors who had owned a mansion in Leixlip and a grain mill in Celbridge before a downturn in the 1880s forced them to sell up and move to the suburbs of Dublin. Between them, William Beckett and May Roe gave Samuel and Frank Beckett privileged access to education, society, and money together with a strict sense of manners and personal modesty. While Beckett's "obligation to express" and his obedience to the injunction "you must go on" are obvious extensions of the stern work ethic he inherited from his mother and her religious tradition, and while the asceticism he gravitated toward is clearly in line with the strict parsimony characteristic of the home that bred him and the puritanical nursing home he chose to die in, the drive to success came from a father who repeated the word "fight" three times on his deathbed (July 2, 1933 letter to McGreevy, *Letters,* 165). Until he moved permanently to France in late 1937, the struggling author used "Cooldrinagh," the family home, as a secure and comfortable retreat from which to mount an assault on the world of publishing. He ventured into the world of "crapulent dens," transforming them with his university-trained imagination into a "great major symphony of supply and demand, effect and cause, fulcrate on the middle C of the counter and waxing, as it proceeded, in the charming harmonies of blasphemy and broken glass and all the aliquots of fatigue and ebriety" (*GCE IV,* 104), but he could always return to the verbena bushes, bay windows, well-stocked fireplace, and waiter-served dinners; or if he wanted peace from his mother's "outbursts of temper" (Knowlson 1996, 26), he could make himself at home in a garret above the family offices in Clare Street, Dublin. And he could do so long after he had been supplied with sufficient resources to establish himself as an independent professional.

For example, in December 1935, when he was twenty-nine, he moved home to recover from pleurisy. He had just terminated the psychotherapy his mother had been paying for since September 1934 (she had provided two hundred pounds for him to attend a series of sessions at the Tavistock Clinic in London with Rupert Bion, a psychologist famed for his work with soldiers suffering from postwar trauma) when he told McGreevy, on January 16, 1936, that he was, like one of Virginia Woolf's advisees, settling in a room of his own and getting someone to build him some bookshelves (*Letters*, 299). Beckett's elite social class is evident: he was free to move back to the family home whenever he pleased and could recruit someone to build shelves on demand. In the period before he finally made a move to set up a permanent home in Paris in October 1937, he was afforded the financial freedom to take extended trips to Europe, to postpone and resign professional opportunities, to return to the comforts of home for extended periods, to spend a year in London attending to his mental health and, along the way, to forge an authorial image (not in the smithy, but in the bars, cafés, galleries, and salons of the soul as well as in the relative peace and quiet of various rooms of his own). In short, the living conditions he could take for granted gave him the security necessary to his growth into a writer with sufficient agency to achieve financial independence and international fame; along the way he was heavily subsidized by a generous supply of family money and assumed privilege. The conditions fertilizing his social agency were not, however, conducive to success in the market niche carved out by Beckett and his marketing managers in the postwar period; to be true to the image of a Left Bank writer with a reputation for a low-church level of integrity, he and his professional associates were obliged to develop strategies distancing him from his privileged upbringing and lifestyle.

Beckett's extensive command of European language and culture did not come cheap. He was, of course, educated at the best schools in Ireland, Portora Royal School in Enniskillen, County Fermanagh, and Trinity College Dublin. Both schools associate him with the Anglo-Irish elite pushed from power in 1921, and his rejection of Ireland in the 1930s must be seen as a rejection of the Irish Free State and of a theocratic nation in which his aversion to "Jesuitical poetry" was unlikely to make many friends. Beckett clearly had little interest in post-Independence Ireland; his travels between the age of twenty-three and thirty-two underscore his preference for European culture, giving a good sense of the elite context in which he developed the personal agency and cultural knowledge that are the basis of his career as a professional writer.

Between August 1926 and October 1937 he moved regularly between Dublin, London, and Paris, making extended excursions to Austria, Germany, and Italy. In August 1926 he took a leisurely bicycle tour of the Loire valley, and he spent his summer holidays in 1927 touring Florence and Venice; he was in Laxenburg, Austria, in October 1928, moving to Paris from November 1928 to September 1930, back to Dublin until March 1931, and then to Paris again for a few weeks in late March and April, ending with a trip to Kassel, Germany, in May and June 1931; in late June to the end of July 1931 he traveled in France with his brother, Frank, returning to Dublin through Paris and London in late July; he was in Dublin until December 20, 1931, when he went to Germany for a month or so and then to Paris from February until July 12, 1932, when he went to London for a few weeks. In August 1932 he was back in South Dublin, staying for an extended period until his move to London just after Christmas 1933. Then he stayed in London, with brief visits to Dublin, for almost two years, until just before Christmas 1935, when he returned to Dublin. In early October 1936 to April 1, 1937, he toured German cities, churches, museums, art studios, and private collections; then he lived in Dublin from April to mid-October 1937. In October 1937, backed with two hundred pounds a year inherited from his father but administered by his brother, he moved to Paris, living in hotels until he rented 6 Rue des Favorites in April 1938, where he would live with his permanent partner, Suzanne Dumesnil, until moving to a newly built apartment on the Boulevard St. Jacques after their marriage in Kent on March 24, 1961.

We can begin to understand how Beckett turned his talent into a viable living by taking into account the socioprofessional milieu that formed his self-assured personality before his first move to France in 1928, shaping his assumptions about professional writing in the years before his permanent emigration to France in late 1937 and establishing the foundation of the authorial persona he crafted in 1938 to 1950. The significance of this understanding becomes evident when we consider the recurrent indications in Beckett's oeuvre of his early socioeconomic context and the strong sense of personal agency it engendered. Beckett's self-sufficiency and confidence are apparent in his main characters: Murphy's stubborn refusal to compromise his idiosyncratic principles; Hamm's persistent enjoyment of his own storytelling voice in the face of what is "nearly finished"; Winnie's militant cheerfulness; the dogged determination of the climbers and searchers in *The Lost Ones;* the resilience of the woman in *Rockaby.* Beckett's creations do not go gently into the good night. And neither did he. Facing Joyce-beshadowed obscurity as he struggled to publish his second book, *Murphy,* in 1936 and 1937, Beckett plunged himself into a highly driven process of persona-building, using Samuel Johnson as a lever to vault himself into the new, post-Joycean kind of writing, setting himself up to become a viable professional writer.

Later we will explore how Beckett's professional agency expressed itself in his correspondence with Thomas McGreevy and George Reavey during the 1930s. But first we should conclude our construction of a general profile of the socioeconomics of Beckett's domestic milieu. Such a profile can be pieced together from the three main biographies (Bair, Cronin, and Knowlson) and from Vivian Mercier's *Beckett/Beckett* (1977), Lois Gordon's *World of Samuel Beckett, 1906–1945* (1996), and Eoin O'Brien's *Beckett Country* (1986). These sources describe Beckett as the strong-willed product of a wealthy, business-oriented environment with a strong work ethic; strict understandings of personal integrity, economic responsibility (including charity), and social decorum; and a deep sense of privacy, privilege, and independence. Mercier, for example, emphasizes his suburban life with neighbors who "were mainly well-to-do professional people, many of them Protestant, living in comfortable houses set in their own grounds" (1977, 28). Bair notes how "The furnishings" of his home were "no different from those in the home of any other prosperous Dublin businessman" (1990, 9). And O'Brien includes photographs testifying to an upbringing characterized by professionally landscaped gardens, private church pews, Georgian school buildings, formal outfits, a mix of aristocratic and entrepreneurial manners, and a dependence on cooks, cleaners, gardeners, and servants (1986). Cronin dwells on this background and shows how it sustained Beckett when he (ostensibly) struck out on his own, underlining how the legacy of two hundred pounds a year he received after his father's death in 1933 was on par with Flann O'Brien's very respectable civil service salary (1996, 196–97). Knowlson includes photographs clearly establishing the privileged character of Beckett's stock (126–29). And Gordon "proposes that Beckett was a gentle but heroic man with a reservoir of toughness and strength that enabled him to pursue both an altruistic bent and the need for personal and artistic fulfillment" (1996, 3).

While it may be true that "Samuel Beckett was a kind, modest man" who "avoided interviews, audiences, and, when it finally arrived, celebrity" (Gordon 1996, 5), it is also true his understanding of economic relations and personal ambition was cultivated in a home characterized by what Knowlson describes as "le grand style" (1996, 39). Modeled on his mother's upbringing in an Anglo-Irish "big house," his home environment moved to the rhythm of nannies and servants, strict decorum and formal manners. Letters were carried to the recipient on a silver tray; dinner involved elaborate table settings with knife-rests (of the sort Molloy claims not to recognize) and cloth napkins, finger bowls and multiple courses; the house was decorated with leopard skins and other trophies from colonial Africa; and play was dominated by the distinctly English customs of cricket, croquet, golf, rugby, and tennis (which is particularly noteworthy in the context of the Irish Nationalist commitment to Gaelic sports in the years leading to Independence, though it is less surprising when we remember Beckett went to high school in what became Northern Ireland). Social life involved garden parties and charity work, piano recitals and Sunday school, exclusive country clubs, frequent visits to first-class hotels, and close family ties with the resident of the region's original "big house," a local Irish-American celebrity called "Boss Croker" who raised race horses, including a winner of the English Derby. As Chris Ackerley and Stan Gontarski suggest when they describe Cooldrinagh, Beckett's big-house upbringing gave him the source material for the upper-middle-class lifestyle in *More Pricks Than Kicks* and *Watt.* It is the lifestyle rejected by Victor Krapp and Molloy and critiqued in *All That Fall* and *Happy Days.* There is evidence the young Beckett sought an escape from the trappings of this lifestyle by seeking what Bair identifies as a "Spartan simplicity and order" (1990, 20). But he was hardly invested, personally or professionally, in "the disintegration of Western bourgeois culture" (Gordon 1996, 5). While he rejected the specific material conditions of his upbringing, he retained not only the inner core of values created by those conditions but also a personalized version of many of its outer qualities.

Until 1930, with an academic career ahead of him and a family business as backup, Beckett lived in a material world of tailored jackets and hand-made ties, expensive cars and motorcycles (in the early days of these machines), thoroughbred dogs and tennis parties, custom-built housing and European travel and culture. When he went to school, he attended Elsner's academy, a kindergarten run by two German-born women. He moved on to the ominously named Earlsfort House in 1914, and then to Portora Royal School in Ulster in 1920, a privilege he shared with Oscar Wilde and a number of students who were to become major players in the British establishment, including some who became army generals. His hobbies were those of a typical upper-middle-class English public school boy (Bair suggests the members of his social circle referred to themselves as "West Britons," 1990, 26): he collected stamps from around the Empire; read a magazine called *The Union Jack;* competed at boxing, cricket, swimming and rugby; played billiards, snooker, bridge, and chess. As a student at Trinity College Dublin, where he went at the age of seventeen in October 1923, he rode a flashy AJS motorcycle and became notorious for riding "too fast for his own (and his passenger's) safety" (Knowlson 1996, 76). He had the upper-middle-class license to be reckless without long-term consequences: as already noted, when he drunkenly drove his father's car off the road and stopped within inches of Judge Eugene Sheehy, his only rebuke was a lecture on drinking and driving. Together with this social chutzpah came the overprivileged intellectual's license to satirize the world he grew up in. The futile lives described in *Dream of Fair to Middling Women* (1992) and *More Pricks Than Kicks* (1934) are characteristic of a world where a young buck could crash a car, lambaste his girlfriend, give away his last sixpence, waste his day traveling to and fro on a bus, throw away his best boots, and vomit on a policeman's shoes without suffering any significant loss. The nihilism of *Murphy* speaks of a world where unemployment is a mere inconvenience, where a young man can wear philosophical and theosophical systems as he would wear a tie or a scarf, and where suicide and madness are so thoroughly romanticized they become just play. Behind Belacqua and Murphy there is, of course, a well-groomed, well-nourished, highly cultured intellect, an apprentice craftsman with the money to tour Europe and explore different capital cities. The young man who produced these texts was a highly privileged scholar-socialite with access not only to exotic parties and expensive toys, but also to the high culture of expensive schooling, private language institutes, and elite libraries, theaters, and galleries. He also had relatively easy access to the carefully guarded secrets of a mental asylum in London and the inner circles of the publishing industry in Dublin, London, and Paris. While *Murphy* was being circulated among potential publishers, its author sat in foreign taverns writing desperate letters to his agent, George Reavey, in defense of a plot describing a character who struggles to decide which biscuit to eat and who is thrown into disarray by a chess game. While Reavey held meetings on his behalf, Beckett toured Europe, visited private art galleries, felt sorry for himself, wrote home for money whenever he needed it, and drank himself stupid.

Beckett's upbringing encouraged a casual but persistent attitude toward success, an attitude characterized by a turbo-driven, but private and guarded, ambition; by an outward modesty when in the company of personal and professional contacts; and by a public disregard for money. He certainly experienced ups and downs during his career as a writer, but his career was marked by steady progress from dependence on others to a situation in which he was able to provide financial and professional assistance to other creative writers. Further, as he achieved success he became vitally important to the professional lives of a wide range of academics and actors, directors and publishers, editors and artists. Along the way he remained free of the kind of patronage on which Joyce depended, and he steered clear of the celebrity events required of the previous generation of writers including Djuna Barnes, George Bernard Shaw, Gertrude Stein, and Oscar Wilde. He occasionally worked as a hack writer, translating and reviewing for money and, even after the success of *Godot,* contracting for commissions (especially for the BBC), but he was never entirely dependent on the sale of his writing because he was flush with inherited family money; in the early part of his career he came into contact with the dismal world of publishing described by George Gissing in *The New Grub Street* (1891) and George Orwell in *Keep The Aspidistra Flying* (1936), but he successfully skirted the worst aspects of this world, maintaining an aloof disdain for those, like Brendan Behan, who revealed their dependence on public acclaim. There were times before 1950 when he seriously considered full-time employment, but he managed to avoid the need for an extra-literary career of the kind pursued by T. S. Eliot, Flann O'Brien, C. P. Snow, and William Carlos Williams. He occasionally revealed political positions, writing against censorship, publicly supporting Steven Biko and Vaclev Havel, and backing a variety of humanitarian causes including Amnesty International and Oxfam, but he was almost entirely disengaged from the political embroilments that occupied and frequently dogged the professional lives of Kingsley Amis, Brendan Behan, Wyndham Lewis, Sean O'Casey, Ezra Pound, Virginia Woolf, and W. B. Yeats. When his American publisher, Grove Press, was attacked by anti-Castro demonstrators in July 1968 and was all but destroyed by feminist attacks in 1970, Beckett remained detached, continuing "to gain literary respectability" as Melvin Friedman put it in the introduction to *Samuel Beckett Now* (1970, 4), having nothing to do with those who braved the streets of Paris in May 1968. He liked a drink, but he avoided the self-destructiveness of Brendan Behan, Jack Kerouac, Hugh McDiarmiad, Sylvia Plath, and Dylan Thomas, using homeopathic remedies, moderate consumption, frequent exercise, and Mediterranean excursions to preserve his health. And he rubbed against the grain of cultural and social conventions, but he did so discreetly, avoiding the frenzy of media-driven scandalmongering that plagued Behan, Joyce,

D. H. Lawrence, Henry Miller, and, again, Oscar Wilde. He avoided the fuss by sauntering his way homeward after the Nobel announcement, but he was not driven into permanent hiding like Thomas Pynchon, Salman Rushdie, and J. D. Salinger.

In other words, Beckett's social agency allowed him to manage his professional life according to his own criteria, on his own terms. In order to craft this life he had to overcome a variety of social and intellectual pressures; he succeeded by living in a less fashionable part of Paris, by building a house in the country (with family money), and by surrounding himself with a loyal group of professional acquaintances. The association with Joyce was not the least of the pressures he had to overcome during the early stages of his career. But after his immersion in the work on Samuel Johnson in 1936–37, he took control of his authorial persona, crafting a mature public image designed to determine how academics, actors, directors, editors, producers, publishers, and reviewers presented him in the literary marketplace. The brilliance of this image, and one of the main reasons it is worth describing and analyzing is that, even as he controlled his authorial image by imposing strict rules on his private, personal, and public affairs, he conducted himself with charm and humility, humor and grace, becoming a model professional writer. His etiquette was unmatched: he was punctual, well-dressed, and confidential. He was prompt and courteous in writing "thank-you" notes: for example he wrote to Judith Schmidt, secretary at Grove, on October 6, 1959, expressing his gratitude for a bottle of Jameson's whiskey, apologizing for using the wrong name to refer to a Zippo lighter he wanted her to find for him, and thanking her for her work (SUL). He was loyal in his support of a number of writers, opening doors for Aidan Higgins, Nick Rawson, George Reavey, and Arland Ussher; on December 10, 1961, for example, he wrote to John Calder introducing Nick Rawson as a future star, asking his London-based publisher to help situate Rawson in the publishing industry (Lilly). In 1967 he was still writing in support of Rawson, allowing his praise for his poetry to be used in publicity materials (February 20, 1967, Lilly) and sponsoring him for an Arts Council grant in a note sent to Calder on March 15, 1967 (Lilly).

Beckett's courteous approach to professional relationships worked. And it continues to work; those he charmed continue to defend his public persona. Behaviors learned at his mother's dinner-table and his father's country club allowed Beckett to build and maintain a series of defensive, regulatory rings around himself. And these rings continue to function courtesy of the

Beckett estate and its agents (my own experience is not unique: even though they had worked out a contract with Beckett in 1985, courtesy of Beckett's deep respect for Martha Fehsenfeld, the editors of the *Letters* were delayed until 1999 and then spent almost seven years in "complex negotiations" with the Beckett estate [Fehsenfeld and Overbeck 2009, xv–xvi]). Having established these circles of protection, Beckett was able to control relationships between his private, personal, and public lives without seeming to do so, which put him in a position to ride the wave of literary fame while protecting himself from its more unpleasant "trappings." Because he conducted himself with such impeccable manners and such loyal generosity, he cultivated, and could count on, the full support of the various people who came into contact with each of the rings of defense he built around himself. Even those, like Billie Whitelaw, who suffered mental and physical pain as a result of his severe authorial and directorial discipline, praise him for his kind personality and charming demeanor. This intense precision is connected with the "artistic integrity" he learned from Joyce, but it is clear he learned the basics of this precision at home and from a wide group of people who helped him much more directly than Joyce during the years before he signed with Jérôme Lindon. It is also clear Beckett managed his professional life as a writer much better than did Joyce. Joyce may have given Beckett an artistic model to emulate, but his family and friends gave him material and pragmatic assistance and guidance; this assistance was much more beneficial as he transformed the social agency he had inherited into an authorial persona strong enough to sustain his career and maintain his legacy.

Literary Apprenticeship: The McGreevy Years

Given the kind of social and professional contacts and experience enabling his intellectual development and early literary experiments, we should not be surprised at Beckett's diligence in cultivating contacts in the publishing industry. While he would eventually establish an authorial persona as someone uninterested in a successful career as a writer, as someone who "has avoided every form of personal publicity" as Alec Reid put it (1971, 12), he began his career by taking advantage of any and all available resources. We have seen his concern in "Ding-Dong" with "the world of supply and demand" (*GCE IV*, 104) and must acknowledge his participation in Jolas and Joyce's efforts to sell "Work in Progress," noting his hands-on experience during his formative years with literary commerce and marketing. It is hard to imagine he was serious about a job in advertising, even though he follows up his idea about apprenticing himself to an advertising company by saying he had often thought about discussing a career in marketing with his father (*Letters*, 171). But he kept a lot of pokers in the fire and aggressively pursued any viable option.

Beckett's early sense of self-entitlement is evident from his experience at Trinity College Dublin, a university notorious as "the last bastion of English Protestant culture in Dublin" (Gordon 1996, 24): he successfully pursued the most competitive and lucrative scholarship available, a Foundation Scholarship. While he was enjoying this award, which gave him his first opportunity to move away from home into the city center because it came with a stipend, a cheap room, free food, and reduced tuition, he set his sights on another. With the help of his French professor, Thomas Rudmose-Brown ("Ruddy," aka "P.B." in "A Wet Night"), and a visiting "lecteur" from Paris in 1926–27, Alfred Peron (who would recruit Beckett into a cell of the French resistance in 1940–42), he pursued the appointment of exchange lecturer in English, representing TCD at the École Normale Supérieure in Paris (Peron's school). Again he was successful, taking up the position in fall 1928 after a one-year delay when his predecessor, Thomas McGreevy, parlayed a six-month stop-gap position into a further year. On his arrival in Paris Beckett built on his friendship with Peron, soon becoming part of a crowd of Irish expatriates including McGreevy (who had now turned the extra year into a full-time position and who would eventually change his name to MacGreevey to make it sound more "Irish"), Arthur Power, and Francis Stuart (who Beckett knew from Dublin and who would write a nostalgic obituary). Over the next decade Beckett would come into direct contact, in Paris, London, and Dublin, with some of the most important people in avant-garde publishing and the arts, including Richard Aldington, Sylvia Beach, Kay Boyle, Jacob Bronowski, Nancy Cunard, Georges Duthuit, Stuart Gilbert, Peggy Guggenheim, Eugene Jolas, James Joyce, Paul Leon, William Lowenfels, Desmond McCarthy, Samuel Putnam, Charles Prentice, Philippe Soupault, Edward Titus, and Jack Yeats. Along the way he would publish enough original works, translations, and other texts to establish a name for himself in Dublin, London, and Paris, and he would develop long-term friendships with a number of people who would act as his literary agents and advisors—George Reavey, Suzanne Dumesnil, Con Leventhal, Tom McGreevy, and Toni Clerkx. Alongside the image of Beckett as a version of the hapless character in *O Lucky Man!* (1973), Lindsay Anderson's film about a man damned to a life of strange adventures, we must place the image of a man who deliberately and diligently worked his way through the struggle from obscurity to fame, from failure to success.

As I have begun to suggest, Beckett's upper-middle-class, Euro-Irish upbringing firmly ingrained in him what his first biographer called an "old-world courtliness and consideration" (Bair 1990, x). In addition to training him in social manners requiring strict codes of dress and behavior (his publicity shots after 1951 rarely show him without a nicely tailored jacket), his upbringing established his attitudes toward authority; toward rules and conventions; toward the decorum associated with life in private, personal, and public spheres; toward intimate friends, business associates, and strangers. Most important, his upbringing firmly established the assumption that he would, like his father, become a self-employed professional with a protected private life and a carefully managed professional life. It took a while, but that is what he had become in the two decades before he posed for Jerry Bauer in a London alley.

Beckett flirted with institutional affiliations. In spring 1928 he taught at Campbell College, an elite public school on the outskirts of Belfast. In fall 1928 to spring 1930 he taught at the exclusive École Normale Supérieure in Paris for an exchange program organized through Trinity College Dublin. And in fall 1930 to the end of fall term 1931, he taught on site at Trinity College in Dublin. However, his intensely individualistic upbringing drove him to be as independent as possible: an undated letter written on a Friday in the summer of 1930 from the École Normale contemplates Tom McGreevy's offer for him to teach permanently at Trinity, explaining his dilemma over choosing whether or not to be tied down by a job when he knew rejection would cause pain to his family (*Letters,* 32). The prospect of an institutional commitment threatened Beckett's effort to find independence; the ingrained urge to achieve upper-middle-class respectability pressed him to choose loyalty over freedom, but the same urge also pressed him to seek respectability through self-employment. The moment he made the decision to resign from Trinity is historic in terms of Beckett's career as a professional writer because it is the moment he prioritized his own long-term professional agency over immediate domestic and institutional security: this biographical detail would be transformed into numerous literary scenes as his characters chose freedom over habit, uncertainty over expectation, subversion over convention. It was not an easy choice, and the decision to resign, made in January 1932, after he had worked at the prestigious job for four terms, left a lasting mark: Knowlson reports he still expressed regret in the 1980s about disappointing his father over the Trinity job; and his unprecedented decision to accept an honorary degree from Trinity in 1959 and his subsequent decision to make a substantial donation to the university's library may well have been in partial atonement.

Let's return to Beckett's beginnings as a professional writer. After making deliberate contact with the Joyce circle in early November 1928, Beckett maintained a regular, though often frustrating, connection with the publishing industry until the outbreak of World War II. True to the conventions of his upbringing, Beckett's introduction to Joyce was eased by a prior acquaintance. Beckett's uncle by marriage, Harry Sinclair, had visited the Joyce family in Paris in April 1926 (Ellmann 1982, 529). The undated letter to McGreevy already quoted describes a visit from Sinclair during which his uncle took him out for an expensive meal and a great bottle of wine, Chablis Moutonne 1926 (*Letters*, 31). In a subsequent letter from the same period Beckett promises McGreevy they, too, will share liberal amounts of the best wine in Paris (*Letters*, 36). McGreevy, Beckett's predecessor in the TCD post in Paris, also helped Beckett make contact with Joyce. A firm friend of both Nora and James Joyce since he had helped make hotel and chapel arrangements for an April 1926 visit to Paris by Nora's devout uncle, Michael Healy, McGreevy became a key advisor and confidant as Beckett worked out how to survive in the publishing industry, receiving more than 270 letters, cards, and other forms of correspondence from Beckett during the period from 1928 to 1966: well over 80 percent of these letters provide details of Beckett's professional life as a writer.

The Joyce connection cannot be overstated in terms of Beckett's commercial prospects because, apart from the obvious benefits of an association with the most famous writer in Europe, it gave access to Sylvia Beach (the editor of *Our Exagmination* and a key player in the preliminary stages of Beckett's relationship with Barney Rosset in May 1953), Eugene Jolas (who would publish Beckett texts with some regularity between 1929 and 1938), and Jack Kahane (the founding editor of Obelisk Press who would ask him, in 1938, to translate the Marquis de Sade and whose son would publish *Watt* in 1953). But Beckett's urge to social independence and his developing professional agency were too strong to allow an overdependence on Joyce and his circle. McGreevy became crucial to Beckett as he opened pathways away from Joyce's area of the literary marketplace. The Joyce/Jolas connection gave Beckett his first major publications in the June 1929 volume of *transition*, the short story "Assumption," and the essay on Joyce, "Dante

. . . Bruno . Vico . . Joyce." However, as he continued to associate himself with Joyce in the summer of 1930 by working on a French translation of the first part of the "Anna Livia Plurabelle" section of "Work in Progress," and while the Jolas connection allowed him to publish "For Future Reference in the June 1930 number of *Transition* (which had become a quarterly and now used a capital letter for its title), he worked to expand his professional address book, developing relationships in Paris and London with Richard Aldington, Nancy Cunard, Charles Prentice, Samuel Putnam, and Edward Titus. Closer to home, in Dublin, he cultivated relationships with Jack Yeats and Seamus O'Sullivan, publishing two parodic pieces in Sullivan's *TCD: A Miscellany:* "Che Sciagura" in November 1929 and "The Possessed" in March 1930.

When Aldington and Cunard awarded him the Hours Press Prize for his poem *Whoroscope,* which was submitted in the early hours of June 16, 1930, under pressure from McGreevy, Beckett gained his first stand-alone publication, a limited edition complete with ironic, explanatory footnotes. The Cunard prize also gave him his first publicity in the London press, a short notice in *Everyman* on July 3, 1930, describing how the poem would be published "almost immediately in an edition consisting of 100 signed and 300 unsigned copies at 5s. [shillings] and 1s. respectively." Beckett's joie de vivre is apparent not only from the process of composition of this poem, which involved numerous glasses of wine, but also from the manner of celebration. Like George Comstock in *Keep the Aspidistra Flying* (1936), Beckett immediately spent a large part of the ten pounds prize-money on a slap-up meal. He paid for Aldington, McGreevy, and Bridget Patmore to dine splendidly at the Cochon de Lait. But Beckett's work ethic was too deeply ingrained to let the joy of success scuttle a professional opportunity. Unlike Comstock, he turned the occasion to positive effect, using his evening with Aldington to develop a friendship with Cunard and her partner, Henry Crowder, opening the way for future publications. He went out with Aldington, Crowder, and Cunard on Bastille Day 1930. For this occasion he shared a poem, "From the Only Poet to a Shining Whore," written to be set to music and published as part of *Henry-Music;* a year later he worked on translations of surrealist poems for Cunard's *Negro Anthology* (in an October 9, 1931, letter to McGreevy, which is not included in *Letters,* he says he asked to be paid twenty-five pounds for his contribution; TCD, 20); on November 21, 1932, in another letter omitted from *Letters,* he noted Nancy Cunard's plan to engage him to translate Eluard and Breton (TCD,

38); and in January 1933 it was clear she had followed through because he was working for Cunard translating material from Congo and Madagascar (*Letters,* 149). Beckett kept contact with Cunard throughout the 1930s, tapping the wealthy heiress for commissioned translations until he began to develop long-term contacts in the French publishing industry after his move to Paris in 1937.

McGreevy's role was crucial. In opening the connection with Cunard he had given Beckett an important source of commissions for work in his capacity as a hack translator (September 8, 1935, *Letters,* 273). And the Aldington connection, bonded with drinks and fine food on the celebratory evening of June 16, 1930, and again a month later on July 14, led to Beckett's professional friendship with Charles Prentice. Prentice was a senior partner at Chatto and Windus in London and was the editor of Dolphin Books, a series of short studies of contemporary writers. Aldington passed along McGreevy's recommendation for Beckett to write a long essay on Proust along the same lines as the one McGreevy was already writing on Eliot. This eventually led to contracts for *Proust* (1931) and *More Pricks Than Kicks* (1934). Beckett's first letter to Thomas McGreevy in the Trinity College Dublin collection is undated: Knowlson speculates it was "probably" written in June 1930 while Fehsenfeld and Overbeck suggest it was "more likely" written in "Summer 1929" (*Letters,* 10–12). In any event, publishing was at the forefront of Beckett's mind. He sketches his first impressions after reading the first volume of *À la recherche du temps perdue* and goes on to describe it with scatological contempt, lamenting how long it will take him to read all sixteen volumes (*Letters,* 12). Opening with a nasty comment about an editor who had just returned his manuscript with insufficient postage, he goes on, in the next sentence, to express a sentiment characteristic of his irascible determination to become a professional writer on his own terms, free of any direct association with Joyce and his circle. He uses vitriolic prose to express his desperate desire to be published anywhere (except *Transition*) and asks McGreevy to give him contact informaticn for publishers (*Letters,* 11). His contempt for the industry is apparent. But even when all he can imagine are rags and garbage pails, he remains fully conscious of his dependence on the literary marketplace. This attitude is, of course, entirely in keeping with the attitude of an artist still soused in the romantic notion of the detached, nail-paring author, an artist who still wanted to succeed in the clean arena of commerce-free publishing but who knew he had to get his hands dirty if he wanted to make a name for himself.

From his correspondence with McGreevy there is more than a hint Beckett completed *Proust* out of a sense of professional and personal duty rather than any serious commitment to the novelist. We are struck, for example, by his disdain for the content of the book and by his repetition of the number of words he has been asked to write: his attitude is akin to a student writing an assignment rather than a scholar developing a compelling and necessary thesis. A July 7, 1930, letter explains the project is going incredibly slowly; he complains he can hardly imagine writing the necessary seventeen thousand words (*Letters,* 40). In an undated letter from late July 1930 in which he reports the Bastille night celebration with Cunard and Crowder, he again moans about his effort to get the project off the ground (*Letters,* 35). In late August he reveals a hard-edged disdain for the project, using scatological profanities to curse Proust and suggesting his book would be tedious. But he was determined to complete the project before he went on vacation (August 25, 1930, *Letters,* 43). Passing through London on his way to Dublin, he wrote from the Garlands Hotel in Pall Mall to say he had seen Prentice and was relieved to have given him the manuscript. Still, he felt it would be rejected as too casual and too derivative (September 17, 1930, *Letters,* 48).

Beckett's attitude toward academe at this stage in his life was made apparent in a satiric paper he read to TCD's Modern Languages Society on an invented French poet—Jean du Chas. Beckett told McGreevy he had written the poetry himself for his own amusement (November 14, 1930, *Letters,* 55). The paper, published as "Le Concentrisme" in *Disjecta* (1984b, 35–42), makes fun of the academic tendency to use newly discovered writers as the basis for new theories of art: Jean du Chas is perfect for pretentious scholarly writing because he has created an art "parfaitement intelligible et parfaitement inexplicable" (42). But Beckett's impatience with scholarly prose and the more formal aspects of his professional life as a writer should not make us think he was uninterested in the world of publishing. Indeed, despite his expressed disdain for publishers, including those like Seamus O'Sullivan, who agreed to publish his short story "Alba," he was preoccupied to the point of obsession with the effort to get published. His repeated notes of disdain and frustration are complemented by solid evidence of dogged persistence and celebrated success. For example, his irritation and dissatisfaction with the *Proust* manuscript did not prevent him from taking advantage of his connection with McGreevy to find out about Prentice: on October 5, 1930, he thanked Tom for giving him advice about a man who made top-level decisions at Chatto and Windus, adding that he still had not heard the editor's opinion about his manuscript (*Letters,* 49). This was barely two weeks after he handed it over and less than three weeks before contracts were signed. Beckett's keen, somewhat impatient attention to literary agents during his literary apprenticeship is suggested in a letter written on Garlands Hotel letterhead as he was passing through London in September 1930 (Fehsenfeld and Overbeck give a date of September 17 but do not give the full text). He was clearly thinking beyond Chatto and Windus to the American market, which was not covered by his contract, trying to work up the courage to see James B. Pinker, cursing himself for failing to follow through (TCD, 9). Pinker was a literary agent who did business between London and New York and had worked for Joyce in 1915-20. He had contacted Beckett earlier in 1930 offering a list of his clients in an effort to recruit Beckett, but Beckett was not impressed (*Letters,* 32). Impressed or not, in January 1931 he sent a copy of *Proust* to Pinker. Unfortunately he was too late; the Dolphin edition from Chatto and Windus was already scheduled for publication, precluding the possibility of an American contract (January 25, 1931, *Letters,* 61).

Within a month of handing the book to Prentice, Beckett had a contract for *Proust.* Signed on October 21, 1930, with the Dolphin department of Chatto and Windus, the contract provided an advance of twenty pounds and a royalty rate fixed at 10 percent (5 percent in the British colonies and dependencies). In exchange it gave Chatto first option on the publication of his next collection of essays or his next book of prose with a minimum of sixty thousand words. *Proust* was published in an edition of 3,000 copies in January 1931 and sold for two shillings. To earn his advance, Beckett would have had to sell 1,000 copies in the home market; total sales on March 31, 1937, added up to 593 copies, leaving a negative balance on his advance of six pounds, one shilling, and fourpence. Sales in 1931–34 totaled 492 copies, with 43 copies selling in 1934–35, 30 copies in 1935–36, and 28 copies in 1936–37 (Lilly). Although sales of *Proust* were hardly encouraging, Beckett worked hard in 1930–33 to take advantage of the commitment from Chatto to take an option on his second book, writing prose with concentrated, diligent, highly professional determination. And he did not do so just for himself. His desire to take advantage of contacts by helping his friends is evident from an undated letter from 1930 asking McGreevy if anything could be done to help his teacher at TCD, Thomas Rudmose-Brown, find a publisher for a book on Racine (*Letters,* 26).

When he was in Dublin working through the first year of a contract for three years at Trinity as a French lecturer, for which he would be paid two hundred pounds a year, increasing to three hundred and fifty by year three, Beckett continued to think his way through the game of professional publishing, using McGreevy as a sounding board and keeping in contact with a number of individuals who would become important to his developing career: George Reavey, Con Leventhal, Charles Prentice, and Samuel Putnam. He fulfilled his teaching obligations with the reassuring sense he would do the job for one year at the most: despite the setbacks and frustrations, he preferred the risky business of a freelance career in professional publishing to the institutional chains of university teaching. At this stage he was determined to boost his chances of success by maintaining existing options while making new contacts. In an October 5, 1930, letter from Cooldrinagh he told McGreevy about the efforts he was making to establish contact with people who could help him in the literary marketplace, including Jack Yeats and Lennox Robinson. Even though he was self-deprecating about his prospects and suggested he might not be sufficiently focused to succeed as a published author (*Letters,* 50), he worked hard to keep his name alive in literary circles. And although he claimed to be stuck in the paralyzing environment of Cooldrinagh and expressed his lack of interest in being published, he found the time and energy during the Christmas break to correct and return the proofs for *Proust* (January 6, 1931, TCD, 14). He also had a burst of energy during which he retyped *Proust* for Pinker (January 25, 1931, *Letters,* 61). A month later, and even as he cursed Pinker for turning him down, he wrote in a celebratory tone because *American Bookman* had requested a copy of *Proust.* Despite claiming he sent it along without much emotion, he cannot hide his delight. In the same free-flowing letter he asked McGreevy to remember him to the Aldingtons, reaffirming his connection with a man central to the avant-garde publishing industry (February 24, 1931, *Letters,* 67–71). As we have already noted, Beckett was like Samuel Johnson in his career-long tendency to lament his lack of work while producing at an incredible pace. Further, his letters prove his keen attention to the job of writing and the effort to publish.

With *Proust* slated for publication on March 5, 1931, the regular letters to McGreevy during this period suggest Beckett had turned his attention to commissioned translations and the effort to publish original poems. Five days after *Proust* was published he was in contact with Seamus O'Sullivan (the pen name of James Starkey), founding editor of the *Dublin Magazine,* to arrange a review of McGreevy's book on Eliot. He asked McGreevy to keep his name in circulation in Paris (March 11, 1931, *Letters,* 73). Even though he was suffering from pleurisy in late May, with colleagues at TCD picking up his teaching duties, he kept in contact with Joyce through Sylvia Beach, giving enthusiastic advice about the French translation of "Work in Progress." He also emphasized the priority he was giving to the review of McGreevy's book on Eliot and his work as a translator, insisting he was working industriously, if somewhat distractedly, on his short stories (May 29, 1931, *Letters*, 78–79).

At the same time, he was pushing the publication of his poetry, using his connection with Samuel Putnam to land four poems in *The European Caravan* (Bronowski 1931, 475–80): "Hell Crane to Starling," "Casket of Pralinen for a Daughter of a Dissipated Mandarin," "Text" [the poem, not the prose-poem], and "Yoke of Liberty." The headnote introduces him thus:

> S. B. Beckett is the most interesting of the younger Irish writers. He is a graduate of Trinity College, Dublin and has lectured at the École Normale Supérieure in Paris. He has a great knowledge of Romance literature, is a friend of Rudmose-Brown and of Joyce, and has adapted the Joyce method to his poetry with original results. His impulse is lyric, but has been deepened through this influence and the influence of Proust and the historic method. He has recently won the Hours Press prize with a poem *Whoroscope:* and has contributed to *transition* and *This Quarter,* and to the examination of Joyce's Work in Progress. (475)

The promotion of Beckett as "the most interesting of the younger Irish writers" in a headnote most likely written by Beckett and edited by Joseph Bronowski, gives a glimpse of Beckett's early understanding of himself as a writer: he is Irish, he is university trained and academically erudite, he is well connected, particularly with Joyce but also with a TCD professor, and he has developed an original literary method based on the influence of Proust. The relative influence of the two authors he cites is obvious: Proust is mentioned once; Joyce is mentioned three times.

Bronowski's introduction to the section on "England and Ireland" suggests Beckett's work is included in the volume because it is an example of "a direction given by Joyce" (436). This "direction," and the association it implies, is evident from the Joycean work he published, again as a result of his carefully nurtured relationship with Putnam, in *The New Review, An International Notebook for the Arts:* "Return to the Vestry" in August/October 1931, "Text" (the poem, reprinted from the *European Caravan*) in Winter 1931–32, and "Text" (the prose-poem that forms the paragraph on pages

82–83 of *Dream*) in April 1932. In addition to giving him a publishable style, the connection with Joyce facilitated the support of Jolas at *Transition,* who published "Calvary by Night" in March 1932 (it was included in *Dream* [1992, 213–14] and "A Wet Night," *GCE IV,* 118). But Beckett was persistent in his effort to break the association with Joyce. On his way back from a leisurely trip through the vineyards and cathedral towns of France with his brother in June and July 1931, he passed through Paris. Having attempted to make contact with Nancy Cunard, most likely to arrange further work as a translator, he went on to London, where he visited the Joyces, moaning about the lack of access to Joyce because of Nora and Lucia. He was more successful with his publisher, spending an evening with Charles Prentice on July 28, 1931, arranging to give him a copy of his latest short story, and proposing a new book on Dostoyevsky (though he admitted to McGreevy he was unlikely to complete such a project, *Letters,* 82). In October 1931 O'Sullivan finally published "Alba," and Beckett sent his poem "Yoke of Liberty" to *Everyman* (TCD, 20). In the same letter, dated October 9, 1931, he referred to the translations of "Surréalites inédits" he was doing for Cunard, wondering if the twenty-five pounds he had asked for might be excessive (TCD, 20).

Back teaching at TCD in fall 1931, he began to imagine that life as a professor, even if it were a life of incompetence, might be feasible (November 8, 1931, *Letters,* 94). At the same time he was contemplating his escape, imagining the prospect of a peaceful life, gazing at his own navel, with the occasional sexual and literary episode to liven things up (*Letters,* 87). In another undated letter from the same period, he seems to sit on the fence between academe and creative writing. On the one hand, he contemplates an academic book, noting the rise of Joyce's reputation in Dublin and wondering whether to capitalize on this rise by writing an extended prologue for "Work in Progress" or, perhaps, a book about its title. But on the other hand, in the same letter he admits he has made his decision to quit academe (*Letters,* 83). By December 20, 1931, any pretense he could endure the scholar's life had evaporated. Back at Cooldrinagh for the Christmas break he was secretly planning a prolonged trip to Germany (December 20, 1931, *Letters,* 99). He explains he had not yet resigned from TCD because he did not want to cut himself off from any opportunities, but he had clearly made his mind up to throw in the towel as far as university teaching was concerned. After spending Christmas in Germany, Beckett moved to the Hotel Trianon Palace, in a room adjoining McGreevy's. From that point on he was entirely devoted to the effort to succeed as a professional writer; as we have seen, he spent the next decade and a half exploring exactly what it means to be a writer, to represent oneself in narrative, to create a viable authorial persona.

Between February and June 1932 Beckett worked on *Dream of Fair to Middling Women* in the Paris hotel room. Along the way he also completed "Dante and the Lobster" and wrote a poem that helped repair his relationship with Joyce: "Home Olga" was written as a tribute for Bloomsday 1932. And he continued to develop an independent sense of professional agency. The significance of a postcard I have already referred to, written in June 1932 to Samuel Putnam, in which he vowed to get over James Joyce before he died (*Letters,* 108), becomes clear from the letters he would write to McGreevy on his way through London in July and August 1932. His concerted effort to take advantage of his contract with Chatto and Windus by submitting a novel had been interrupted by the May 7, 1932, assassination of France's President Paul Doumier by a Russian nationalist. The ensuing clampdown on foreigners forced Beckett, who lacked the necessary papers, to leave the hotel and, eventually, France. He forwarded *Dream* to Prentice from Paris before he raised the money to go to London. Unfortunately he clearly sent it prematurely: the book's raggedness, which reflects the unstable conditions under which it was started as well as the hurried way in which it was finished, suggests it would have benefited from a few more months of concentrated effort. But it also illustrates his full-on effort to take advantage of the two-book contract with Chatto and Windus. The letters he wrote McGreevy in the period between his arrival in London on July 13 to take up residence just off the Gray's Inn Road on Hampton Street and his arrival in Dublin to take up residence at Cooldrinagh, indicate his impatience in his post-TCD effort to establish himself as a financially viable writer. They also reveal his ongoing dependence on money from home to supplement his earnings as a hack writer. While he was able to raise the money for his journey from Paris to London by selling Edward Titus his translation of Rimbaud's "Le bateau ivre" for seven or eight hundred francs, on arriving in London he immediately collected ten pounds sent from home via Chatto and Windus. Just over a month later, on August 18, he reported he had been robbed of five pounds sent by his father, complaining he had no option except to wait for more money from home (*Letters,* 118). But the wait was too long. With no more money forthcoming to pay for food and lodging, and with his prospects for commissions and other jobs frustrated, he was forced to move home in late August 1932. John Pilling's assessment of this period in Beckett's career is on target, but it underestimates the young author's determination to succeed: "All Beckett's 'earnest endeavours' to write 'for myself' had come to nothing, or worse than nothing, since the two published extracts ["Sedendo et Quiesciendo" and "Text"] . . . had left him looking little more than a figure who had 'gone Joyce' because he was unable to do otherwise" (Pilling 1997, 57). Certainly he was frustrated, unable to sustain himself in London and unable to escape Joyce's grasp. At the same time, however, he had achieved *something*, demonstrating it was possible to make a living as a writer if he could increase his output and his rate of publication so as to create a favorable balance between earnings and expenses. Beckett was sufficiently privileged to be able to go home at the age of twenty-six to prepare himself for a new onslaught on the literary marketplace. By returning to the comfort of South Dublin's suburbia he could regroup without having to worry about every penny, every meal, every night of lodging; he could write without the pressure to earn a living, but he would remain focused on the effort to sell his work, achieving independence not only from Joyce but also from his parents through the products of his pen.

A letter to McGreevy on July 14, 1932, a month before he retreated to the domestic security of Dublin, indicates the importance of contacts in the publishing industry; after a bath and a nap at the Imperial Turkish Baths in Southampton Row, his first destination was the offices of Chatto and Windus, where he found ten pounds waiting for him together with a letter from Cissie Sinclair. While he obviously treated the publishing house as a postal address, he also took the opportunity to have a long meeting with Prentice, discussing *Dream of Fair to Middling Women*. The letter announces that he would be dining with Prentice the following Wednesday, noting the editor had expressed his interest in Beckett's poems, including "For Future Reference." But it also expresses pessimism about the possibility Chatto would accept *Dream* (July 14, 1932, TCD, 27). Undaunted, three weeks later, on August 4, 1932, Beckett explains his concerted effort to find a publisher for his novel and some poems, describing how he did the rounds carrying his manuscripts and a letter of introduction from McGreevy. While the letter reveals Beckett's desperate urge to get published, it also testifies to his growing frustration in the face of being rejected and ignored (*Letters,* 111–12).

The energy of Beckett's engagement with the world of publishing is partly driven, of course, by the need to make a living. Half-hearted about the possibility he might join his father's business in Dublin and disdainful of his brother's professional life, he was deeply aware of the difficulties involved in earning a living as a professional writer. But his persistence is clear. He is impatient for responses to his submissions, and he is impatient to overcome his writer's block. Writing has become his main source of satisfaction. Unfortunately it is not a reliable source of relief, and he is concerned his urge to write might have left him for good. While his frustration is alleviated by a self-deprecating humor and the possibility that one or more of his many potential publications might work out, his mood is darkened by frank expressions of futility and despair: toward the end of the letter he compares himself to a pest-infested vegetable. (August 4, 1932, *Letters,* 113).

In his next letter to McGreevy, written on August 18, 1932, from his temporary lodgings in Ampton Street just off Gray's Inn Road, Beckett describes a month spent prostrating himself in front of publishers and their agents and confesses his hard work has produced nothing exception rejection and dejection (*Letters,* 117–19). To a certain extent the letter situates Beckett in an obsequious position relative to the publishing industry; he notes which editors gave him a cigarette or a cup of tea and expresses disdain for an editor who resembles a TCD student. On the one hand, then, the letter shows his self-deprecating and hostile attitude toward those he wishes to impress. On the other hand, however, the letter also illustrates his diligent efforts to find favor with a publisher, any publisher. Clearly he has devoted many days to the job of cultivating productive contacts at the Hogarth Press, Grayson and Cape, *The Spectator, The New Statesman.* And he has also registered with an employment agency: Truman and Knightley sent him numerous notices of jobs throughout England plus one as an English teacher in Basel paying 275 francs a month for forty hours a week. Although these contacts had proven fruitless, leaving him both amused and despondent, there is a new determination in his attitude. From the earliest letters to McGreevy, he had expressed disdain for the publishing industry by punctuating descriptions of disappointments with variations of the phrase "Tant pis." And he does so here. But he also derides the younger Grayson and Mr. Ellis Roberts, engaging in the level of hostility typical of his response to rejections for more than a decade. Even though he represents himself as someone paralyzed by cowardice and worried his mother will be angry with him (remember we are discussing a man of twenty-six!), he is beginning to express the kind of independence we would expect of a man who successfully persisted in the face of the repeated rejections.

At the end of August, comfortably ensconced in the stately surroundings of Cooldrinagh, he told McGreevy his urge to write was returning

(TCD, 30). In September 1932 he settled down and began to produce sellable work. In his October 8, 1932, letter to McGreevy he noted he had sent off some translations and was looking forward to getting a check in the next few days. He also had good news about Gilbert publishing "Home Olga" in *Contempo* and Titus publishing "Dante and the Lobster" in *This Quarter.* It is also clear his novel, *Dream of Fair to Middling Women,* was in active circulation. True to the pattern we have begun to see, he had become bold in his relations with those he perceived as discourteous, writing nasty letters when publishers did not follow through with their promises (*Letters,* 128). At the same time, however, he acknowledged those who treated him with respect, applauding Edward Titus as a model of politeness in comparison with the rest of the industry. Even though he was sitting at home in Foxrock repulsed by the pervasive environment of stubborn sobriety and was still too insecure to brave the world without family support, he was self-confident enough to send a terse, bridge-burning letter to an important publisher, Grayson and Cape. Furthermore, he still trusted Nancy Cunard might bring him some work, and he had begun to wonder if Titus's public support might open some doors, giving him some leverage in Paris (*Letters,* 129).

From August 1932 to January 1934 Beckett settled into a relatively sedentary life in Dublin. Once it became clear, by May 1933, that *Dream* was not publishable in its current form, he set to the task of salvaging enough material to form the basis of his next book. Plus he continued to work on his poems. Letters to McGreevy during this period reveal he was composing and circulating early versions of poems eventually collected in *Echo's Bones,* and once Titus had rejected *Dream* he began to send out the short stories eventually collected in *More Pricks Than Kicks.* He also spent time contemplating aesthetics. In an October 18, 1932, letter parodying the very astute advice by Grayson Bros. to take a break from *Dream* and work on a more marketable book, he mourns the loss of writers like Homer, Dante, Racine, and Rimbeau who achieved a visceral and instinctive level of direct expression (*Letters,* 135). Earlier in the same letter he had distinguished between poems characterized by their indirectness and those with elemental authority: he used the French word for "optional" to describe many of his own poems, idealizing poetry with an ejaculatory effect (*Letters,* 134). He had, in other words, begun to imagine an aesthetic program designed to produce ecstasy rather than description, moving beyond entertaining stagecraft and trickery to the production of ecstatic purgations of the body and soul.

While it is clear he held on to the neo-Romantic artist's disdain for money, a disdain made possible by family prosperity, he continued to look for fee-paying work, tempering his idealistic aestheticism with a market-oriented pragmatism born of the urge to achieve independence on his own terms: he sought translations through Cunard and Titus; he shopped *Dream* to publishers, sending it to Titus in October 1932 (*Letters,* 138) and Gollancz in April 1933 (*Letters,* 155); and, perhaps seeking a way to get out of Foxrock while retaining the possibility he could continue to write for money, he looked for full-time employment, using a letter of introduction from Madame Redmond, a Frenchwoman he happened to meet in Dublin, to apply for a job at the *Daily Express* (*Letters,* 135–38). He also applied for a teaching job in Milan (January 5 1933, *Letters,* 149). Again we see a familiar pattern during this stage of his career: while he is deeply uncertain and often despondent, repeatedly claiming to be tired and unable to move, he is extraordinarily persistent and driven, including long poems with his letters to McGreevy, describing business meetings and his protracted efforts to publish through his carefully cultivated contacts, Nancy Cunard, Joseph Hone, Seamus O'Sullivan, Charles Prentice, George Reavey, Edward Titus, and Jack Yeats. He had decided to stay put, huddled against the cold, crafting a body of creative work he could eventually sell in his own name while taking advantage of the free orange juice at home (typed, undated, January 1933, TCD, 44); at the same time, however, he was restless, considering teaching jobs overseas, including one as a lecturer in French at Manchester University for three hundred pounds a year. We should assume he was joking when he claimed he had sold his vote (TCD, 45) but can conclude he was in earnest when he enlisted Charles Prentice and Jack Yeats to write letters of support for his application to work at the National Gallery, Trafalgar Square (October 9, 1933, *Letters,* 165–67).

The self-deprecatory but dutiful attitude Beckett assumed when he was working on *Proust* is again evident when he describes the writing he was doing for *More Pricks Than Kicks* in the spring and summer of 1933. Again he complains about the hard slog, explaining he had finished two short stories in the mode of Joyce's epiphanic structures in *Dubliners,* taking the edge off any appearance of well-being by claiming he did so without much enthusiasm, mainly to stave off boredom (May 13, 1933, *Letters,* 156–59). A few months later he would describe struggling to finish *Draff,* which became *More Pricks Than Kicks,* experiencing extreme pain as he sought a satisfactory ending, cursing the gut-wrenching drive to publish (November

1, 1933, TCD, 56). Again, we get the strong impression Beckett felt he was paying his dues, going through the motions of a profession defined in terms of publishing texts in exchange for a paycheck. He continued to expose himself to the hostility of publishers in a manner analogous to the ways Belacqua had exposed himself to the elements on Baggot Bridge, accepting the hard reality of publishing over the soft comforts of bourgeois cocktail parties and overstuffed settees. But despite all the moaning and groaning about finding it increasingly tough to write, and despite his belligerent, scatological jokes at the expense of Chatto, he sent a sixty-thousand-word manuscript to Prentice in late August or early September 1933 (*Letters,* 168). The material was, for Chatto and Windus, a definite improvement over *Dream:* as I have suggested, this is partly because it was less self-conscious and self-referential and was, thus, more suited to a relatively mainstream publisher. Produced in the well-fed comfort of Cooldrinagh and in the simple but quiet attic-cum-study above the family business in Clare Street, it was also much more "finished" than *Dream*. Despite his moaning and uncertainty he had pushed himself to complete a viable book. On October 3, 1933, Chatto followed through with the option in the *Proust* contract, agreeing to publish, paying Beckett twenty-five pounds less six pounds and five shillings advance on royalties. In the letter describing the deal Beckett explains how happy it made him to experience success in the marketplace (October 9, 1933, *Letters,* 166).

Published in spring 1934, the collection sold for seven shillings and sixpence. The contract gave Beckett a royalty rate of 10 percent for the first thousand copies (fourpence a copy in the colonies and dependencies), 15 percent for the next nine thousand copies, and 20 percent after ten thousand had sold. The reduction of six pounds and five shillings on his advance was because of Beckett's residence in Ireland: in the October 9 letter to McGreevy he suggests he could recover the amount by establishing English residency during the next six months (*Letters,* 167). Again, Chatto took the option on his next prose work above sixty thousand words (Lilly); in this case, however, they would refuse the next book submitted, *Murphy.*

In agreeing to publish *More Pricks Than Kicks,* Chatto and Windus displayed loyalty rather than business acumen: it would have been difficult for Charles Prentice to turn Beckett down after his regular visits for lunch, dinner, and a chat. They did, however, make the wise decision to print only 1,500 copies. Of the copies printed in April 1934, 452 copies had been distributed by September 30, 1934, reducing the balance to be paid off before Beckett would receive further royalties to thirteen pounds, three shillings, and seven-pence. Thereafter, sales dwindled considerably: 19 sold in September 1934 to March 31, 1935; 26 sold in April 1935 to the end of March 1936; and 4 sold in April 1936 to March 1937. When Chatto prepared the final account for the book on March 31, 1937, there was a further twelve pounds, seven shillings, and twopence to be covered before Beckett would have received money above his advance.

In short, in the apprenticeship of his career Beckett successfully turned his carefully cultivated, highly privileged social agency into a persistent, though anxiety-ridden, often ambivalent sense of professional agency. Despite his complaints and troubles, and despite repeated expressions of fatigue, despondency, and insecurity, he persisted in the effort to free himself from institutional bonds, using the safety and comfort of his family so he could make forays into the world of professional writing without any real risk. Along the way, he made contact with major players in the avant-garde publishing industry and landed some excellent publications. By the time *Echo's Bones and Other Precipitates* came out in December 1935 he had established a healthy résumé of professional credentials including two full-length books, one critical (*Proust*), the other creative (*More Pricks Than Kicks*); three short stories beyond those in *More Pricks* ("Assumption," "Sedendo et Quiesciendo," and "A Case in a Thousand"); one very short story ("Text"); an unpublished novel (*Dream of Fair to Middling Women*); the independently published, autographed collector's edition of *Whoroscope;* plus nine shorter poems ("Alba," "For Future Reference," "Text," "Hell Crane to Starling," "Return to the Vestry," "A Casket of Pralinen for a Daughter of a Dissipated Mandarin," "From the Only Poet to a Shining Whore," "Home Olga," and "Gnome"); a seminal essay on Joyce's "Work in Progress" ("Dante . . . Bruno . Vico . . Joyce"); two spoof essays ("Le Concentrisme" and "The Possessed"); a number of review articles (all written in 1934: "Schwabenstreich," "Proust in Pieces," "Humanistic Quietism," "Leishmann's Translation of Rilke's Poems," "Ex Cathezra," and "Recent Irish Poetry"); and a number of important translations of French poems by Breton, Crevel, Eluard, and Rimbeau and Italian poems by Commisso, Franchi, and Montale. In addition, he had worked with Joyce as he composed "Work in Progress" and had been central to the French translation of the first third of Joyce's "Anna Livia Plurabelle."

To put Beckett's December 1935 résumé in context: his list of publications was more than sufficient, in today's terms, to earn an assistant professor of modern languages at a major research university in the United States promotion with tenure and the rank of associate professor. In some institutions, the second book would get him promotion to full professor. It has become the norm in Beckett studies to describe him as having experienced "an unusually long apprenticeship" (Pilling 1997, 7), and this is certainly true, especially given what he would produce after his fortieth birthday. But what has been less prominent in accounts of Beckett's life and work is the space his social circumstances allowed for a prolonged period of professional development. The domestic and financial security provided by a loyal, if judgmental, family allowed him to experiment and explore in ways not available to the vast majority of his contemporaries, giving him, as it were, an extended period of adolescence. And he knew it. The poem "Gnome," published in the *Dublin Magazine* in summer 1934 communicates a self-conscious understanding of the level of indulgence he enjoyed well into his late twenties:

> Spend the years of learning squandering
> Courage for the years of wandering
> Through a world politely turning
> From the loutishness of learning

Obviously Beckett's "years of learning" overlapped with his "years of wandering." As Knowlson convincingly illustrates in his chapter "Germany: The Unknown Diaries, 1936–37," the six-month tour of Germany he went on three months after completing *Murphy* in June 1936 (he began *Murphy* on August 20, 1935, and told McGreevy he had completed the novel on June 27, 1936; he went to Germany on September 28, 1936, and left on April 1, 1937), provided material that would "remain etched indelibly in his mind for the rest of his life" (1996, 242). As we have seen, by December 1935 he had, however, developed the "courage" to dismiss not only those "politely turning" from him and his work, but also those who gave him the silent treatment in scornful protest at his loutish texts (December 31, 1935, TCD, 84). He had also developed a healthy network of professional supporters. Although this network was neither as devoted nor as trusted as those he would depend on after 1950, it allowed him to finish *Murphy* by retreating to a room of his own in Foxrock without losing contact with the publishing industry. By 1936 he had established himself sufficiently to travel for half a year (October 1936 through March 1937) and to immerse himself in Dublin's libraries for another half year (April through October 1937) without descending into obscurity. With the cooperation of Reavey and with Mary Manning as an outspoken defender of his cause, he was in a position to wander and learn while his next major publication, *Murphy,* did the rounds of British and American publishers.

3

Beckett's Professional Agency

The Reavey Years, 1932–1937

> Until he has freed himself from the mean influences about him—sodden enthusiasm and clever insinuation and every flattering influence of vanity and low ambition—no man is an artist at all.
>
> —James Joyce, "The Uncreated Conscience"

October 8, 1932, is a watershed day in Beckett's developing relationship with the literary marketplace because it marks the beginning of his professional correspondence with George Reavey (*Letters* 124–26). While it was slow to develop, this relationship would eventually put Beckett in a position to do the work that brought him international fame, adding two major publications to his résumé and giving him his first experience, after August 1936, of working with a professional literary agent devoted to his cause. In other words, Reavey is the bridge between Beckett's years as an apprentice and the years when he set himself up for literary success. He had known Reavey from his days at the École Normale Supérieure, first mentioning him in a summer 1930 letter to McGreevy describing Reavey in lukewarm terms but noting he had bought a new ribbon for Beckett's typewriter (*Letters,* 36). Beckett certainly had reservations about Reavey, and he would express these reservations even after the generous gift of a typewriter ribbon had been overshadowed by Reavey's Europa Press publication of *Echo's Bones and Other Precipitates* in December 1935 and his concerted effort, as Beckett's literary agent, to find a publisher for *Murphy* in 1936–1937. On October 14, 1937, Beckett told McGreevy why he had no intention of staying at the Reavey house, even for just one night (TCD, 140). This caution around Reavey is consistent with a feeling expressed in a letter to McGreevy written on the same day as his first missive to Reavey, October 8, 1932. He confirmed that he had received a letter from Reavey and gave the impression he was miffed by what he saw as Reavey's condescending reference to *Dream* and his patronizing promise of some work as a translator (*Letters,* 128). On the same day, however, we see clear evidence of Beckett's ability to finesse his tone with someone who might help him in the literary marketplace. He thanked Reavey for his letter and promised to send him a poem for his consideration. From the beginning of their relationship he engages Reavey as one poetic intellectual to another, joking in a way that assumes a shared aesthetic sensibility, using sophomoric bathroom humor to lambaste anyone who rejected his work (*Letters,* 125). Even as he seemed to dismiss Reavey's offer of help in the letter he wrote to McGreevy on the same day, the letter to Reavey makes a deliberate effort to develop comraderie with someone who could be of direct assistance in the business of publishing.

The return on Beckett's gesture to Reavey was not immediate. After October 1932, it would be more than three years before contact with Reavey brought a substantial publication, *Echo's Bones* (1935), and it would be even longer before Reavey would assume the position of Beckett's main literary agent. Eventually the Belfast-born Irishman would secure the 1938 Routledge publication of *Murphy.* In the meantime Beckett either acted for himself or continued to solicit assistance from the long list of friends and acquaintances we have already discussed. But October 8, 1932, is important because it marks the beginning of a professional relationship crucial to Beckett's career from 1935 until he signed with Bordas in December 1946. We cannot overemphasize the fact that it was a professional relationship rather than a personal friendship. Where the correspondence with McGreevy conveyed news about the business of publishing in the context of highly personal letters, the correspondence with Reavey is both intellectually playful *and* directive. He is ironic, but he also reveals a developing willingness to tell Reavey how to take care of business. In fall 1935, for example, he gives detailed and specific advice about where to send copies of *Echo's Bones* in London and Dublin, expressing his pleasure at the overall layout of the book, pointing out what he was doing to market the text actively (sending out numerous advertising brochures), suggesting a strategy for approaching Simon and Schuster in New York, and proposing whom to contact for the best chance of getting a well-placed review (*Letters,* 288–89). Beckett and Reavey would eventually become close, but the relationship took a long time to develop because it was based on affairs of business rather than the cultural ties linking him with McGreevy (McGreevy was from Dublin; Reavey grew up in Belfast). In other words, it was a professional liaison built over time, subject to the vicissitudes of the publishing industry, and entirely dependent on Reavey's effectiveness in securing publications; the relationship faded once Beckett relocated to Paris and found other agents who would enable him to achieve his literary ambitions.

There is some confusion about when Reavey began to act as Beckett's literary agent. In *Damned to Fame* Knowlson acknowledges Reavey "was seeking to place the book [*Murphy*]" while Beckett was in Germany, but he gives the impression Beckett only "offered the book to George Reavey to handle as his literary agent" after January 1937 (1996, 268). This is the first time Knowlson applies the phrase "literary agent" to Reavey. In his telling, Reavey became Beckett's agent after Chatto and Windus, on the authority of Harold Raymond, rejected *Murphy* a second time. However, Reavey's appointment book for 1937 suggests he was involved during the early stages of this failed transaction: a note for January 20, 1937, indicates he met Raymond at Chatto that day, presumably hearing the news about the rejection (HRHRC). It is safe to say Beckett and Reavey began their professional connection in October 1932 and put it on a solid footing during negotiations for the December 1935 Europa Press publication, but it was a number of months after *Echo's Bones* appeared in bookstores in early 1936 before Reavey became Beckett's main point of contact with the publishing industry. We can be more exact: a letter to McGreevy suggests he made the decision to enlist Reavey as his agent in early August 1936, seven weeks before he sailed for Germany on September 29, 1936, and six months before the January 1937 meeting with Raymond. In a rather exasperated tone he explains his reluctant intention to enlist Reavey as his sole literary agent (August 7, 1936, *Letters*, 365). In his next letter to McGreevy he explains his decision to take advantage of Reavey's services in the effort to find a publisher for *Murphy:* he already knew him and, consequently, would be spared extra work and worry (August 19, 1936, *Letters*, 367). If having someone to do the work of negotiating with publishers is taken as a defining characteristic of a professional writer, we can say Beckett entered a new stage of professionalism in early August 1936 (five months earlier than Knowlson suggests).

By understanding the developing relationship between Beckett and Reavey, we can begin to see how the deliberate efforts to publish translations and original work in 1929–32 gradually took on a more professional character in the period between 1932 and 1936. By the time he made his move to Paris in October 1937, Beckett was well positioned to enter the literary marketplace: he had an impressive résumé, an increasingly refined sense of his personal aesthetic, a good idea of how to situate himself as an author, a room of his own, enough contacts in the industry to find rent-paying commissions, a safety net of family money to support him through hard times, and an agent who would open new doors and negotiate contractual details. Back in October 1932, when he reached out to Reavey, his state of mind was like Belacqua's when he was stuck in a "Beethoven pause" in "Ding-Dong" or stalled on Baggot Street Bridge in "A Wet Night." His poems from the period are indicative of this mind-set, suggesting stagnation but also anticipating forward movement. Correspondence with both McGreevy and Reavey makes it clear he was actively working on the poems collected in *Echo's Bones and Other Precipitates* when he decided to drop academe in favor of professional writing. The poems in this volume demonstrate that Beckett was consciously working to expand from the limited marketability of his highly academic, novitiate writings to a style of writing with broader appeal. His poetry reveals the dilemma. By late fall 1932 he had sent Reavey drafts of "Enueg II" and "Sanies II." With the letter he sent McGreevy on October 18, 1932, Beckett enclosed a copy of "Serena II." In a number of the poems from this period bridges are a recurring theme, with "Enueg I," "Enueg II," "Serena I," and "Serena III" referencing specific bridges in Dublin and London. The overall effect of these "bridge" poems is, as "Enueg I" suggests, to situate the narrative voice in "skewered" and "fetid" stagnation, halted at points of crossing, contemplating "a dying barge" on a "stillborn evening" (*GCE IV*, 11–12). The poems can be read, then, as expressions of the author's feeling that he was, in effect, stuck on a bridge, contemplating the sights as he figures out how to give birth to a viable literary voice.

This expression of stultified frustration is evident in "Enueg II" where the "I" is

> sweating like Judas
> tired of dying
> tired of policemen
> feet in marmalade
> perspiring profusely
> heart in marmalade.
> (*GCE IV*, 14–15)

Significantly, the speaker of this poem is "lying on O'Connell Bridge" (15): he is unable to move from a position suspended above the River Liffey. The discourses of religion, politics, the law, and literature come together in a gummy, stagnant, confusing morass of scholarly erudition. But there is hope. While "Serena I" represented the "I" with his "breath held" like "a funnel hinged / for the obeisance to Tower Bridge," his life stuck in the involuntary contractions of "peristalsis" (22), "Serena II" describes a more vibrant movement between an earth "fat half dead" and an earth where "the rest is free-wheeling" (25). The dominant, repeated image of "this clonic earth" underscores the "see-saw" experience in the poem, with a character shifting between "this damfool twilight threshing in the brake" and "this crapulent hush" (25). While there is still a sense of being abandoned, motionless—"she took me up on a watershed . . . and left me"—there is also "a yo-heave-ho of able-bodied swans" as the earth "drops her young" (25). Stillborn stagnation and passive obeisance give way to an image of birth and the "dancing" of "the whales in Blacksod Bay" (25–26). While it is possible to interpret the name of the bay as one "hardly calculated to inspire confidence" (Harvey 1970, 94), we can also connect it with "eleutheria," freedom, through the smoke released by the burning of black sod and peat and through the dance of mammals with global access. Positioned on a "watershed," the speaker experiences the deflation of "the rubrics of a childhood" as the idea one can "behold Meath shining through a chink in the hills" is transformed into one of the "phantoms shuddering out of focus" so that "the fairy-tales of Meath ended" (24). The "watershed" is demystified, becoming a point where, "muzzling the cairn," the speaker, whose consciousness is crossed with that of a sleeping dog (again, see Harvey 1970, understands the alternating, "clonic" rhythm of give and take, stillness and movement, departure and return: "with whatever trust of panic we went out / with so much shall we return" (26). Ending with prayer, as does "Sanies II" ("Lord have mercy on us," [21]), "Serena II" projects a moment of relief from the "panic," potential relaxation as you

> say your prayers now and go to bed
> your prayers before the lamps start to sing behind the larches
> here at these knees of stone
> then to bye-bye on the bones.
>
> (*GCE IV*, 26)

As his relationship with Reavey developed, haltingly and cautiously, over the next five years, Beckett's attitude toward the publishing industry would vacillate between despair and hope, but he would keep on moving forward, building a sustainable reputation while keeping an idealistic eye on the light "shining through a chink in the hills" and a pragmatic eye on the "rout of tracks and streams fleeing to the sea" (*GCE IV,* 26). These glimpses of hope, which compel the narrator to "keep on the move / keep on the move" (28) despite "these knees of stone" (26), will eventually be distilled into a definitional characteristic of Beckett's oeuvre, quoted so often it has become a cliché of Beckett studies: "you must go on, I can't go on, I'll go on" (*GCE II,* 407). On the approach to his thirtieth birthday in 1936, Beckett's poetry speaks of an imagination coming to life; even though he "was not born Defoe" (*GCE IV,* 23), and apparently did not have the gift of journalistic, popular writing, the author was capable of making a living as a writer. But first he had to find a suitable style and method, and this required a shift in context. Like Joyce's Stephen Dedalus, who had to "fly the nets" in order to find a legitimate artistic voice, Beckett realized he had to escape not just "the Rock," the base on which he had always depended in Foxrock, but his own version of mother Ireland, the thinly disguised "she" in "Serena II." As Lawrence Harvey puts it, "The early years and the early loves are so many ties, bonds, and also fetters, to his Dublin home" (1970, 95). Ireland's embrace, personified in the context of Irish literature as the mother/lover image of Cathleen Ni Houlihan, is like a snare closing as its victim tries to escape. But escape is possible once one begins to follow "glimpses of hope," crossing bridges to more suitable contexts: just as Joyce's Stephen Dedalus could imagine freedom beyond the traps of family, nation, and religion, so Beckett's narrator could imagine when "the lamps start to sing behind the larches" (*GCE IV,* 26).

The five-year period 1932–37 is marked at its beginning by Beckett's first act of independence, his bold departure from the academic world of Trinity College, and it is marked at its end by his even more dramatic departure from Ireland. My overall argument is, of course, that we can see a deliberate pattern of professional development as Beckett put himself in a position to make a viable living as a writer. Reavey's role in this process is important exactly because it is transitional, giving the hardworking author a valuable point of contact with the publishing industry during a period when he needed public visibility but when he also needed prolonged bouts of domestic, scholarly, and creative seclusion. In many ways, his relationship with Reavey was focused on use and function, sometimes reaching a crude degree of opportunism. A November 4, 1932, letter to McGreevy is disdainful in its description of Reavey's plan to market Beckett's texts, but it also suggests his professional services might, one day, come in handy (*Letters,*

139). Two days later he sent a three-by-five postcard to Reavey asking for help placing a stack of poems with a publisher (November 6, 1932, *Letters,* 143). As I have suggested, the relationship was problematic from the beginning. Among other factors, Beckett had high professional expectations and Reavey could be frustratingly casual. After sending Reavey two poems—one of the two "Enueg" poems and "Sanies II"—probably with the letter he sent Reavey on November 6, 1932 (*Letters,* 143–44), Beckett impatiently reported to McGreevy that he had had no acknowledgment by November 21 (TCD, 38). It would be September 20, 1933, before Reavey's diary records a meeting with Georges Pelorson and "Sam Becket [*sic*]," recounting how Beckett "hurt a toe," wore overly narrow shoes, and was known for his dangerous driving. At this point Beckett remains a distant acquaintance. Reavey's notes are those of someone recording personal details about a professional client with a view to building a character sketch for a press packet: the distance is, of course, suggested by the fact that Reavey was still unsure how to spell Beckett's name.

There was little direct contact between Beckett and Reavey until spring 1934. In the meantime Reavey tried to professionalize himself by building an appointment book, listing contact information for publishers, writers, and editors. On June 16, 1934, we read the name "Sam Beckett," and on June 18, 1934, there is a record of a meeting with "Sam Beckett (and brother)"; a few months later, on November 13, he records a casual encounter "in Strand with reviewer," and the next day, November 14, he notes a meeting with "Sam Beckett at the Garrick" (HRHRC). We must be clear: at this stage Reavey was acting as a publisher, not an agent. When Beckett was back in London in late January 1935, after a month in Dublin, he continued to act as his own agent, telling McGreevy he had sent "Echo's Bones" (the short story) to Lovat Dickson, a Canadian publisher based in London. Beckett's keen attention to the publishing industry is evident from his suggestion the text might be more suitable for the *Evening Standard;* he also underscored his ongoing effort to find contacts who might get him work as a translator (January 29 1935, *Letters,* 243). Just over a week later he reported Dickson had returned the story and, again showing his resilience, noted he had immediately sent the story to *Life & Letters.* His impatience and insecurity is evident from his frustration at losing track of Charles Prentice and from his confession that he has lost the ability to face winter days outside (February 8, 1935, *Letters,* 247). Still, on March 10, 1935, he suggests that Reavey had begun to act in an expanded, more active role, establishing an office of his International Bureau in London and proposing work covering all aspects of a writer's job (*Letters,* 259). On March 29, 1935, Reavey's diary records a 5:30 meeting with Beckett. We can be fairly certain that this meeting addressed the deal referred to in a letter of April 26, 1935, when Beckett remarked that Percy Ussher offered his congratulations on the contract with Reavey's Europa Press and his success in securing Reavey's professional assistance (TCD, 74). This note points to Reavey's role as the publisher of *Echo's Bones* (the book appeared in December 1935 in a collector's edition of 327 copies, with 25 signed by Beckett). A further reference to Reavey's network of contacts in the publishing industry suggests Beckett had begun to imagine a public relations role for Reavey of the sort he would play after August 1936, especially when Beckett was in Germany from September 1936 to April 1937 (*Letters,* 260).

Beckett's work ethic during this period is evident. He moved to London in January 1934, living in Paulton's Square until August 2, 1934, then moving to Gertrude Street when he returned from a short visit to Dublin in September 1934. Even as he waited for proofs from Europa Press, he worked diligently on a number of other publishing projects. From his description of kite flying at the Round Pond in Kensington Gardens, it is clear he had begun working on the plot for *Murphy* (September 8, 1935, *Letters,* 274): Ackerley and Gontarski refer to a "holograph manuscript in six notebooks . . . dated 20 August 1935, suggesting he completed the novel in May 1936 and then worked on revisions in June" (2004, 387). Again, he is self-deprecating about his work, describing his endeavors as unfortunately trite, but he is also determined to push ahead and confesses he is so preoccupied with the job of writing he has no energy for anything else. His persistence in the face of emptiness and disintegration, which will later become one of the hallmarks of his aesthetic, is inspired by an image familiar to us from chapter 6 of *Murphy* contrasting the larger world of things with the smaller world of the imagination, in a place where the laws of supply and demand do not apply (*Letters,* 273–74). Beckett's search for a kind of writing expressing inner prayer indicates his effort to locate an aesthetic space outside the rules of the marketplace, a space appropriate to a writer who values the integrity of a lay preacher, a surplice over his day clothes. But his struggle to find freedom from mean commercial influences was saturated with a pragmatic appreciation that such freedom is only possible through hard work. In a letter postmarked September 23, 1935, and headed "Sunday" (which makes the date September 22), he explains in vivid detail how he is pushing himself forward despite thinking the material not only bad but boring (*Letters,* 277). Again, Beckett proceeds out of professional duty rather than personal interest, fighting his lack of interest in the project because he knows he must make a living.

The October 13, 1935, letter to Reavey to which we have already referred illustrates the keenness with which the twenty-nine-year-old author issued instructions about how to market *Echo's Bones;* it also suggests he was doing part of the work himself. In other words, Beckett did not yet trust Reavey to act as a fully fledged literary agent. He thanks Reavey for the advertising brochure for *Echo's Bones* and proposes a list of those who might receive the document; noting the efficacy of the brochures coming from Reavey, he also promises to distribute the advertising as the opportunity arises. The letter goes on to advise Reavey to contact Simon and Schuster in New York, offering them first refusal on *Echo's Bones,* suggesting how he might negotiate with them to turn an agreement on his prose into a contract for his poetry. Even though he finally defers to Reavey's professional expertise, he communicates his deep interest in the process of contract negotiations and expresses his satisfaction with the 20 percent royalty rate for *Echo's Bones and Other Precipitates* (*Letters,* 288). The disdainful tone for publishers evident in early characterizations of Chatto and Windus (the "C" replaced with an "S," an "n" added to "Shatto" and the "us" in "Windus" replaced with "up") and Hogarth Press, which he likened to a private mental institution in a letter sent to Reavey in October 1932 (*Letters,* 125), is absent from this letter. Instead we witness the more mature deliberations of someone with a keen understanding of the best ways to deal with booksellers and publishers. We have already seen Beckett's enthusiasm for marketing in an undated letter sent in December 1935 from Gertrude Street, London: he was full of advice about where to send the book for review and distribution; he was attentive to the packaging of the book; and he participated in the effort to earn as much money as possible from sales of the book. During the same period, back in Dublin, he described how he was organizing his life around the primary task of completing *Murphy.* That was not all. He was also working on an essay commissioned by Rudmose-Brown on Geulincx (January 9, 1936, *Letters,* 295) and was coming to terms with the anger created in his family by the collection of poems (December 31, 1935, TCD, 84). Even as he admitted that there had been no professional interest in the poems, and even as he acknowledged any reviews would likely be negative and sales poor (January 9, 1936; TCD, 85), he continued to put his emotional, intellectual, and physical energy into the task of building his life as a professional writer, establishing a room of his own with custom-built bookshelves, expressing his determination to finish the novel, waxing philosophical about the fate of *Echo's Bones* in the market. As I have suggested, in the years between 1932 and 1937 Beckett was at a watershed of the sort he describes in "Serena II"; my further contention is that he used his vantage point (which he could occupy somewhat comfortably because of his family's wealth and protectiveness) to plot and strategize, working out how to escape the debilitating silence, the "crapulent hush" of his domestic life at Cooldrinagh. In other words, he spent the five-year period before he made his permanent move to Paris professionalizing himself. Having a literary agent was, of course, part of this process, but so, too, was the role he developed for himself as an ongoing consultant and advisor on contracts, book covers, and advertising brochures. As we see in the June 29, 1966, letter to Beckett from John Calder, he would act as a consultant and advisor on the work done in his name until long after his fame was established (fig. 12).

In terms of the literary marketplace, Beckett's developing sense of himself as a professional is evident in his proactive use of a prospectus, in his savvy sense that it would be better for Reavey to petition prospective publishers, in his repeated offers of advice about publishing strategies, in his deferral to Reavey on the matter of negotiations with Simon and Schuster, and in his clear statement about the terms he would accept. He was still doing a lot of the work himself, but he was beginning to defer to a middleman. His professional attitude is further evident in his comments on the packaging of the book in the October 13, 1935, letter to Reavey: he aggressively intervenes to get Reavey to change the book cover from bright yellow to light tan (*Letters,* 288). I encourage any reader who doubts my thesis to consult this letter; it provides ample evidence of Beckett's engagement with his professional career, of his full awareness that hard work and well-placed contacts are necessary to literary success, and of the need to think carefully about packaging and distribution.

Of course, Beckett was a complex character. Even as he was beginning to defer to Reavey, he remained protective of his own interests, expressing disdain for a request to donate texts to the *European Quarterly,* a new journal that had contacted Reavey, because he would not allow his work to be published without the appropriate fee (September 1, 1935, TCD, 85). Behind this reaction is the continuing growth of a professional sensibility cautious about being used and increasingly, almost desperately, aware of his dependence on the literary marketplace as his one remaining option if he was to make a viable living (January 16, 1936, *Letters,* 300). This awareness is accompanied by his ongoing impatience with Reavey's overly casual approach to business: a February 6, 1936, letter to McGreevy expresses exasperation at the lack of news from Reavey and his failure to send free copies of the poetry book (*Letters,* 312). Part of Beckett's frustration may, of course, be because of the slow progress he was making with *Murphy.* In the same letter he tells McGreevy he was trying to gear himself up to write the last three chapters but was struggling, even though the work was a matter of mechanics (312). In March he would again tell McGreevy he had not heard from Reavey for many weeks, had heard absolutely nothing about *Echo's Bones,* and was at an impasse with his novel (March 5, 1936, *Letters,* 320). Even though he was out of contact with Reavey at this time and was thus more dependent on his own devices than usual, he vowed to do nothing in response to a request for texts by Mary Manning Howe, an old family friend who was working as an agent for Houghton Mifflin. Manning Howe had asked for Beckett's manuscripts and proposed he might apply to do some lectures in the United States, taking advantage of her father-in-law's job at Harvard (March 25, 1936, *Letters,* 324). His caution was based on his suspicion his old family friend was seeking to take advantage, situating herself as his US agent and thus earning commission.

At this point he was not ready to make the leap he would make six months later, when he enlisted Reavey as his literary agent and allowed Manning Howe to circulate the manuscript of *Murphy* in the United States. Manning Howe played a minor role in Beckett's career, giving him access to publishers in New York and Boston, but he never took her very seriously, suggesting she was a mere agitator and, on occasion, treating her with patronizing callousness. His disillusion with the profession of writing is apparent in the March 25 letter: he mentions he had written to Eisenstein to enquire about a job at the Moscow State Institute of Cinematography (324). As his thirtieth birthday approached in April 1936, he was still working hard to finish his novel and was becoming assertive once more about his status as a writer trying to make a professional living, telling McGreevy he was happy for *Transition* to publish poems from *Echo's Bones* providing they paid for the privilege (April 9, 1936, TCD, 93). Within the month he had roused himself with another "yo-heave-ho" (*GCE IV,* 23), persisting in his efforts to publish his work even when he was suffering from mental and/or physical debilitation. On May 2, 1936, he wrote an irascible, terse note to Reavey, asking what he had done about *Transition,* if he had heard anything from them, and when his poem was likely to appear. In the same short note he revealed he was paying close attention to the reception of his work, noting his responses to reviews in the Dublin press (*Letters,* 330–31). A few days later, on May 6, 1936, he firmly situated Reavey in an agent's role in relation to *Transition* magazine, scolding him for unclear communication about a business deal with Eugene Jolas: Reavey had initially given the impression that Jolas only wanted some poems, but now he was asking for a short prose piece in addition. Demonstrating the professional aplomb characteristic of his postwar career, Beckett quickly overcame his anger and offered to send a piece called "Censorship in the Saorstat." He did so on the strict condition they paid the going rate (332). This letter to Reavey also reflects Beckett's comfortable situation in the luxurious environment of Cooldrinagh: he could afford to turn down a commission to translate Eluard, taking the time to finish *Murphy* while he was enjoying the direct financial support of his family. More than two weeks later he was approaching the end of the book, telling McGreevy he had about two thousand words to write and was already making plans to find a publisher (May 23, 1936, *Letters,* 337). Finally, by June 9 he could tell McGreevy he had finished the first complete draft of the novel, imagining how much easier his life would be if he had someone to read the manuscript with an eye to consistency (340). On June 27 he was ready to send copies to McGreevy, Charles Prentice (who had retired in 1934), and Ian Parsons, the new editor at Chatto and Windus (345). He also had plans to send a copy to Simon and Schuster and was matter-of-fact in noting the likelihood Parsons would reject the novel as unpublishable.

As he was completing *Murphy,* Beckett got into a tussle with Reavey because his article on censorship arrived too late for *Transition.* Reavey claimed he had told Beckett the correct deadline; Beckett disagreed. But, more important, the author went on to question how Reavey had represented him in a prospectus for a collection of poems by Eluard. His keen sensitivity to how his public image was being crafted in the literary marketplace is readily apparent in his objections to the blurb on the book jacket, the description of him in the preface, and the association between his name and a book he deemed abominable (June 9, 1936, *Letters,* 340). Beckett's irritation with Reavey is an early sign of his deep and long-lasting concern with his public image, anticipating the level of control he would exert once his hard work had paid off and he had become an international celebrity. His annoyance was exacerbated by his belief too little was being done to publicize *Echo's Bones.* By June 27 Reavey had apologized and Beckett had begun to turn his attention from the poems to his effort to publish the novel; bypassing Reavey, he worked as a literary agent on his own behalf for four or five weeks after Chatto refused its option on the text. Instead he used McGreevy as a kind of informal editor, telling him in a July 7 letter he esteemed his advice above all others; in this letter he provides a detailed justification of the novel's plot and comments on the efforts he was making to find a publisher for his book both in Britain and in the United States (350–351).

By July 17, Parsons had rejected the manuscript and Beckett was planning to send the novel to Frere Reeves. A week later, on July 26, he complained there was still no news from Simon and Schuster. Within a month of finishing his second novel, Beckett's level of self-entitlement is apparent (*Letters,* 360). Failing to find a publisher after a mere four weeks, he begins to doubt the entire enterprise of professional writing, suggesting he did not want to spend his career writing books no one would read and that he didn't want to write anyway (362). This expression of impatience-inspired reluctance is particularly interesting because Beckett would eventually establish a professional reputation as someone with no interest in writing, who only wrote because he was obliged, who ostensibly preferred failure to success. On August 6 Reeves rejected the novel as unmarketable; Beckett complained to McGreevy that the reason given was entirely redundant because the only ground he could imagine for rejecting a manuscript was its prospect of commercial failure. Beckett's characterization of the letter suggests it echoed a report he received from Oliver Warner, a reader for Chatto, on July 2, 1936: Warner rejected the book because, much as he liked it personally, it was unlikely to make a profit. With the report came a note by Ian Parsons describing *Murphy* as "un-sellable" and Beckett as "a brilliant young man" who will never "have any more than an extremely limited public" (Knowlson 1996, 675).

Deeply concerned about the commercial prospects of his new work, and desperate to be published, he made the decision to hand it over to Reavey as his official agent, saving himself what he saw as the humiliating task of dealing directly with publishers (August 7 1936, *Letters,* 365). Again, this is a wonderful letter in light of the sustained personal relationships Beckett would develop with Jérôme Lindon, Barney Rosset, John Calder, and other publishers in the postwar period. Once he became successful, Beckett's direct relationship with publishers was no longer a humiliation; it was, indeed, to become a major element in the amplification and enhancement of his international celebrity. The difference was, of course, his ability to exert control over the publishers he enlisted. As we see from the period after the Nobel Prize was announced in October 1969, Beckett exerted careful control over his publishers when he acted to protect himself from unwanted aspects of his professional career.

In any event, by August 12, 1936, he was able to report sending *Murphy* to Reavey (367). Next month, Reavey's diary notes a "visit to Dublin" with the annotation "Sam: National Gal." (HRHRC). From Beckett's letter to McGreevy on Wednesday, September 9, we can conclude Beckett and Reavey met on Sunday, September 6. This letter reveals that, despite Reavey's efforts at increased familiarity, the relationship remained cordial and, from Beckett's point of view anyway, businesslike; the letter describes how hard he worked to keep Reavey at arm's length, avoiding spending too much time with him by putting him on a late train home (September 9, 1936, TCD, 107). Misgivings about Reavey's style and his reluctance to allow him to cross the line between the professional and the domestic sphere give an early indication of Beckett's ongoing effort to separate his life into carefully demarcated zones, allowing him to protect and control his private life and public legacy: he would only allow the lines between these zones to blur when he was certain he was in complete control. Just as Beckett's stage directions became unbendable, anyone daring to make directorial interpretations risking a legal challenge of the sort experienced by JoAnne Akalaitis and the American Repertory Theater over its production of *Endgame* in 1984 or the cancellation of performance rights experienced by Deborah Warner with her production of *Footfalls* in 1994 (Raymond 1994, 25), so Beckett's command of his public image became a matter of supreme control.

On September 29, 1936, Beckett sailed for Germany knowing his professional needs were being taken care of by proxy: the manuscript of his novel would remain in circulation through Reavey in London and Manning Howe in New York. While he was busy enhancing his cultural education by touring public and private art collections in Hamburg, Berlin, Naumburg, Dresden, and Munich, his career was being actively advanced. His close contact with Manning Howe and Reavey during this period is evident from his frequent and detailed updates on the status of *Murphy* and of the various poems being circulated in Dublin, London, and New York. Just over a week after getting to Hamburg he wrote about Simon and Schuster's rejection of *Murphy,* going on to express his avid interest in the book's journey from one publisher to the next (*Letters,* 376). In a manner anticipating his strategy when he traveled from Tunisia back to Paris in the months following the Nobel announcement, Beckett orchestrated his business affairs from a distance, writing postcards of the sort he sent Parsons on November 7, 1936 (379). For example, Reavey's business meetings with Dent on November 5 and December 6, 1936, were set up in response to letters from Hamburg; Beckett remained interested in their outcome, referring to these meetings in a letter to McGreevy on January 18, 1937 (431). Beckett's references to Hogarth Press and Nott suggest Reavey's meetings with Leonard Woolf on January 21 and Stanley Nott on Feb 25 also concerned Beckett's novel. The concerted effort to find a publisher for *Murphy,* with Beckett occasionally playing the role of whip-cracking taskmaster, and Reavey doing the rounds in London, is evident from a November 12, 1936, postcard from Hamburg in which he instructs his agent to force as much money out of the deal as possible. On November 13 he underlined how anxious he was for the book to be in print and acknowledged he would allow any cuts necessary to its publication (380). He was even prepared to sacrifice the organization of the book if it led to a contract. In pursuit of an agreement to publish his novel, Beckett instructed Reavey to use a three-pronged approach to commercial negotiation, advising him to express his indignation at any proposed changes, to hold the line where possible, but to remain open to suggestions so as to clinch the deal; he also advised Reavey to play one publisher against another, giving the impression the book might be published uncut in one market—the United States—so as to influence publishers in a different market—Britain (380–81).

Again, his keen attention to the ins and outs of the literary marketplace is undeniable. Just as he had been concerned about the cover of *Echo's Bones,* so now he made suggestions about the packaging of his novel, proposing a photograph to be used without a caption on the front cover. During the same period a letter to Mary Manning Howe reveals a facetious disdain for marketing, but it also provides evidence of Beckett's ongoing familiarity with the less savory tricks of the trade (Knowlson 1996, 231; November 14, 1936, *Letters,* 382–83). A month later, on December 13, 1936, writing from the Hotel Deutsche Traube in Berlin, his ongoing engagement with the effort to convince someone to sign a contract to publish *Murphy* led him to offer advice about ways to strategize, advising Reavey to play British publishers against Americans by giving each the impression the other was ready to make a deal (HRHRC). On Christmas Eve 1936 he joked about the compromises he was willing to make to get published, implying he would be willing to reduce the novel to its title and would change that if necessary (TCD, 111).

He was, however, deadly serious on December 27, 1936, when he exclaimed that his main interest was in getting the book published at any cost. In a letter Knowlson chooses to skip when he covers this period in his version of Beckett's biography (presumably because it reveals a level of desperation that does not fit with the image of a man "damned to fame"), Beckett proclaims himself ready to give up on an advance if it would help clinch a contract. He uses capital letters and emphatic repetition to emphasize his plea for action in getting the book in print. And again he writes with a level of assertiveness, indicating his keenness to do whatever was necessary to get published, giving Reavey permission to distort the truth if it would help leverage a deal (December 27, 1936, *Letters,* 405).

We can understand Beckett's increasingly desperate urge to publish *Murphy* in the context of his description of his dependence on monthly subsidies from home to support his travels (January 18, 1937, *Letters,* 428). He was, after all, approaching his thirty-first birthday. In this letter his embarrassment about continuing to receive checks from home is mitigated by evidence of his entrepreneurial skills: he mentions he has made the acquaintance of a bookseller's publicist at Ruhwoldt publishers. The publicist was Axel Kaun; the meeting would lead to a request, in June 1937, to translate Joachim Ringelnatz from German into English. When Beckett wrote to reject the offer he produced one of his more important statements about aesthetics, arguing for a specifically non-Joycean method (Beckett 1984b, 172).

Perhaps the budding author was running short of cash by February 23, 1937, because his assertiveness had, by that date, grown to a level of desperation we would not expect of the man who was to make a name for himself as a man "who loathed all forms of self-exposure or self-promotion" (Haynes and Knowlson 2003, 1). In a letter to Reavey he proposes they take advantage of Manning Howe's connections with Houghton Mifflin and the New York publishing industry while she is vulnerable because of her pregnancy. The note is doubly callous because in addition to exploiting the feelings of a family friend who he knows will set aside her own interests to help him, he indicates his intention to give Reavey, not Manning Howe, the rights to represent him in the United States (February 23, 1937, *Letters,* 454). In keeping with the image of Beckett as a flawlessly kind and sensitive man, we might dismiss this letter as the product of youth: but he was thirty years old at the time and had, as I have pointed out, already published a healthy list of essays, poems, and stories. He was old enough to know better. We should, then, read it as evidence of his overwhelming desire to publish. In the January 18 letter he had revealed to McGreevy his fear that Mrs. Susan Manning, Mary's mother, had her spies everywhere and acted as a conduit back to his own mother (428). It is undeniable that his occasional callousness as he struggled to make a name for himself can partly be explained by his effort to save face with his family and friends: he was determined not to arrive back home, after almost six months of family-supported travel, with *Murphy* sitting in yet another publisher's in-box; but he was also careful to mask his private feelings, expressing them in a letter to a trusted friend while, on the same day, writing a sweet, respectful letter to the very woman he sought to exploit (421–24).

We should not misrepresent the case. As his German trip went on, Beckett's attention was increasingly diverted from his efforts to publish *Murphy* to the art he was studying. While most letters from Germany make some mention of the effort to publish *Murphy,* they are increasingly dominated by detailed notes from his gallery visits. As Knowlson has demonstrated convincingly, Beckett was earnest in the translation of visual experiences into written texts. Typically he would first translate these experiences into words in long letters to McGreevy, Mary Manning Howe, and others; eventually he would use the imagery as a source of inspiration for his creative work. The gallery visits were, then, very important. But the frequent references to *Murphy* make it very clear his status as a professional writer was also crucial, forming a constant backdrop to his artistic explorations; after all, as far as his family was concerned the visit was worthwhile exactly because it promised to make Beckett more viable in the marketplace. A letter on February 16, 1937, turns to personal matters on page 4 after three tightly spaced pages devoted to the art museum in Dresden, particularly work by Giorgione, Raphael, and Vermeer; a private collection of modern art; and a performance of *The Marriage of Figaro* (see Knowlson 1996, 235). After discussing a letter from Brian Coffey, his improving health, and the death of Charles Prentice's father, he turns to his own inability to write. Finally, he turns to *Murphy,* lamenting its rejection by Dent and a long list of other publishers approached by Reavey during his absence, facing up to the prospect of going home without a book in production and without any immediate pay-off from his long, expensive trip to Germany (*Letters,* 447–48). We should not overlook Beckett's full awareness of his family's expectation that he would eventually benefit financially from his trip: he underscores this point. In any event, as the journey wound down, his increasingly desperate instructions to Reavey demonstrate his determination to avoid going home with nothing tangible to work on.

On March 7, 1937, he wrote a terse postcard from Munich saying it was time to let the book go to the one publisher who had expressed positive interest (458). And on March 20, again from Munich, he told Reavey he could do what he wanted with the book in Britain and the United States (467). Further proof of his increasing anxiety as he faced the prospect of returning home with no evidence of professional development is clear from the letter he wrote the next day to Mary Manning Howe, confessing he had written nothing for six months and saw little hope for employment at home except through his father's business, now being run by his brother, Frank. Without proof he had established a financially secure foothold in the publishing industry, he knew his family would pressure him to take a job, any job; and he knew his ultimate goal was to be self-employed. As he was getting ready to leave Germany at the end of March 1937 his prospects as a self-employed professional writer were not looking good.

Although he returned home embarrassed that his plans for his novel had foundered, Beckett's sense of professional agency was undaunted. On April 13, 1937, back in Dublin and settled into the garret room at the family's business offices at 6 Clare Street, he wrote to Reavey about the possibility of sending *Murphy* to Nelson Publishers in London for their Irish Writers series (*Letters,* 484); and the next day he brought Manning Howe back into the picture because she was, apparently, still shopping the book around to New York publishers, including Doubleday Doran and the Viking Press (April 14, 1937, *Letters,* 485). As we know from the July 9, 1937, letter to Axel Kaun, published in 1984 with Beckett's approval, the thirty-one-year-old writer was fully aware of the need to earn money, but he was intent on discovering his own aesthetic so he could make a living as a writer without seeming to pander to the reactions of his audience (Beckett 1984b, 171–72). In other words, he had begun to develop a strategy for making an independent living in the literary marketplace: a letter to McGreevy on April 20, 1937, suggests he was using Samuel Johnson as part of this strategy.

While he was, first and foremost, working on Johnson with the intention of writing a play about his love for Mrs. Thrale, Beckett's choice of subject reveals he also sought an artistic method engineered to put distance between himself and Joyce. In "Samuel Beckett's Samuel Johnson" (2003), an essay based on the three "Johnson notebooks" produced in the period between Beckett's return from Germany at the end of March 1937 and his departure for France at the beginning of October 1937, I argue that his work at Clare Street and the National Library marks a key transition in Beckett's development from a neo-Joycean writer to the writer who would become famous for creating a new, identifiably "Beckettian," way of writing. Back in July 1937, explaining why he refused to make a living by translating bad poets, Beckett makes it clear he sought an original way of doing things, a technique with no connection to Joyce's most recent work (1984b, 170–73). While this letter has typically, and rightly, been read for what it tells us about literature that sets out to subvert language distinct from Joyce's "apotheosis of the word," it can also be read as an indication of Beckett's determination, in 1937, to establish himself as a professional writer. We should not underestimate the fact that, at the exact period he was arguing for a new method, he was immersed in the life and work of Johnson, the man famous for saying "no-one but a blockhead wrote, except for money."

By September 1937 Beckett had decided his best option for authorial independence was to make a move to Paris. After a delay caused by the problem of raising the funds to make the trip and to survive in Paris (October 14, 1937, TCD, 140), he left Dublin on Saturday, October 16, 1937. As he entered this next phase of his career, Beckett accepted Joyce's prescription: "Until he has freed himself from the mean influences about him—sodden enthusiasm and clever insinuation and every flattering influence of vanity and low ambition—no man is an artist at all" (Joyce 1989, 71–72). As *Eleutheria* demonstrates, however, he knew such freedom is dependent on a safety net of acquaintances, casual, familial, and otherwise. His proximity to Joyce's career during the campaign to market the text that became *Finnegans Wake* (1939) taught him that any viable degree of artistic freedom is only possible with the support of a network of well-connected individuals prepared to take care of the more pragmatic aspects of life, including the commercial realities of the life of writing, while taking direction from the artist, the supreme commander. Beckett's complex, but ultimately successful, relationship with the literary marketplace is deeply rooted in his early ambivalence about the publishing industry: a deep, neo-Romantic commitment to the achievement of artistic independence and integrity is balanced by a Grub Street awareness of the dangers and pitfalls facing the successful artist. These dangers and pitfalls were exemplified by the circuslike public spectacle of Joyce's post-*Ulysses* life and were a central part of Beckett's personal experience in the period between 1932 and 1937. But he persisted.

Having participated in the process designed to sell Joyce's magnum opus, he knew the necessity of finding "pragmatic means to marshal [market] relations" (Rainey 1998, 170); having witnessed Joyce's professional life firsthand, he knew he had to have a plan. He thus developed strategies that would eventually allow him to succeed in the literary marketplace without being subjected to the public relations frenzy and the private turmoil that haunted Joyce and without hiding like Pynchon and Salinger. As his career developed, Beckett took control over his life as an artist by crafting a public image as someone uninterested in the fame he worked to achieve, crafting a personal voice marked for its integrity while he gathered and encouraged a network of professional acquaintances as they sold this "Beckettian" voice on the open market.

4

Deploying Positive Annihilation

Displacing Joyce, 1938–1945

> I can't see much sense in writing if you can't make any money out of it.
>
> —Orwell, *Aspidistra*

Protecting Beckett's Public Image

On February 20, 1938, Beckett wrote to George Reavey, his literary agent since August 1936, explaining his dilemma over a proposed commission to translate the Marquis de Sade's *Les 120 Journées de Sodome* for Jack Kahane at the Obelisk Press. After telling Reavey he desperately wanted to do the project and was satisfied with the offer of 150 francs per thousand words for approximately 150,000 words, he pointed to his main concern. The project might have a negative impact on his life as a professional writer. Flush with success at finding a publisher for *Murphy,* which had been contracted by Routledge on December 9, 1937, Beckett was nervous about jeopardizing his career. And, his doubts about Reavey temporarily set aside, he was reluctant to make a career move without Reavey's advice. He worried the project might adversely affect his long-term prospects in the literary marketplace in England (*Letters,* 604–5). A letter to McGreevy on February 21, 1938, describes the conditions of the proposed contract in a favorable light, embracing the importance of being able to write the preface because it would allow him to defend his decision to do the translation. From the letter it seems his defense goes as follows: while the book is undeniably obscene at first glance, it is certainly not pornography because it benefits from a brilliant structure; who could question a decision to translate a book with the same level of formal genius as *The Divine Comedy*? But he hesitates because he can't decide about the pragmatic consequences for his professional career. Again, his concern is that the association with a book regarded by many as indefensibly obscene might puncture his authorial balloon, leading not only to retrospective censorship and banning but also to even more problems getting published in the future (*Letters,* 607–8).

The Reavey letter is even more explicit about his concern over his reputation in the literary marketplace. The translation would have the advantage of bringing attention in desirable literary circles, getting Beckett's name known in a part of the literary marketplace where he might attract an audience, but it might hurt him by giving him a long-term reputation as a publicity seeker. Given his likely audience—readers raised on Joyce's aversion to any impression of commercial interests—that would be the kiss of death (February 20, 1938, *Letters,* 604). There can be no doubt Beckett was deeply concerned about his long-term prospects as a professional writer: at the same time he described himself as penniless (April 15, 1938, TCD, 160) after moving into an apartment with a rent of 400 francs a month, he turned down a commission that would have paid him 22,500 francs (fifty-six months' rent!). Obviously he decided his long-term professional career was more important than an immediate boost of desperately needed cash.

The February 20 letter is complemented by one he wrote to Reavey on January 12, 1938, from the Hôpital Broussais. As already noted, on December 9, 1937, Reavey's fifteen-month struggle on Beckett's behalf finally produced a contract to publish *Murphy:* the novel he had begun in August 1935 and finished in late June 1936 would be published by Routledge in March 1938. Correcting the proofs of *Murphy* while recovering from a near-fatal stabbing, Beckett contemplates how he might find an American publisher, but again he makes a decision to prioritize long-term benefits over short-term gains: he refused to use Joyce's influence. He was still trying to break the association and was confident the Routledge contract would, in any event, eventually lead to a US contract (January 13, 1938, *Letters,* 586). But he remained pragmatic in his approach to the marketplace: even as he sought to conceal and control his relationship with Joyce, he was writing an article in homage to Joyce for the *Nouvelle Revue Française.* Further, he had become Joyce's main proofreader for the manuscript that was to become *Finnegans Wake.* He concludes by asking Reavey to keep this news quiet because he was already burdened by the association and wanted to lessen its effects as much as possible (January 12, 1938, HRHRC). At the same time, however, he is careful not to burn bridges.

While the de Sade letters give a good sense of Beckett's active awareness of his public image at the beginning of his public transformation from a derivative, relatively marginal, modernist writer into a writer central to minimalist postmodernism, the changing ways in which he framed his relationship with Joyce give us a more extensive diachronic understanding. As we might expect, Beckett framed his relationship with Joyce differently at different stages in his career. Even as a blurb in *The European Caravan* in 1932 anchored his work to Joyce, he had vowed, in June 1932, to get over James Joyce (*Letters,* 108). As Ackerley and Gontarski suggest, "The Joyce Method" was, for Beckett, "as much exorcism as imitation" (Ackerley and Gontarski 2004, 287). Much of what he published before *Murphy* was part of this process of purgation, but finishing the novel in June 1936, going to Germany in spring 1937, immersing himself in the life and work of Samuel Johnson in spring and summer 1937, moving to Paris in October 1937, and contracting to publish *Murphy* in December 1937 had shifted his relationship with his erstwhile mentor. When he moved to Paris in October 1937, planning to make himself independent in all aspects of his life, he found himself dependent once more on Joyce and his friends. Again trying to establish himself without relying on his family, he found himself relying on familiar contacts. Despite any efforts he may have made to break the association, the ongoing connection with Joyce is apparent from Joyce's touching gestures of concern when Beckett was in the hospital after being stabbed in January 1938. Joyce paid for a private room and Nora showed up with a custard pie; when he moved into his new apartment in April 1938 Joyce donated furniture and bedding. Given that May Beckett made a special trip to Paris to see her son in the hospital, we can assume he was in a position to rebuff Joyce's help. He certainly knew, by January 1938, he could never become an independent author, a writer in his own right, if he continued to live and work in Joyce's shadow. But he had turned a corner. The trip to Germany, the success with *Murphy,* and the immersion in Johnson meant the association with Joyce no longer endangered his long-term professional reputation. Crucially, he wrote words to this exact effect in a January 5, 1938, letter to McGreevy (*Letters,* 581). In short, by January 1938 the association with Joyce was no longer a professional liability because he had begun to develop a viable aesthetic of his own.

Beckett's relationship with Joyce would, in fact, eventually become part of an effective marketing campaign. His American publisher, Grove Press, saw the advantage of the association when it developed the marketing plan for *Waiting for Godot* in 1953, describing Beckett as "Joyce's secretary." Beckett would later deny he served in this capacity (Gruen 1969), but Grove's early efforts to establish his name in the American market were eased by a close, but subservient, relationship with Joyce. In the early 1950s, when Rosset was building a core market for Beckett among the Greenwich Village set skeptical of "the establishment," it was an advantage to represent him in a secretarial role. Beatniks loved underdogs. But as the first glimmerings of success began to shine, the representation of the relationship would be revised, raising Beckett from the subservience of a "secretary" to the parity of a peer. By 1956, in the Shenker interview, he had effectively been elevated to the same level, his authorial persona defined through its difference from Joyce in terms of an equation of equalized opposites (on the one hand "omniscience" and "omnipotence"; on the other hand, "ignorance" and "impotence"). This way of framing the relationship between the two authors has been highly influential, not just defining how Joyce and Beckett function in the literary canon but also shaping understandings of the relationship between modernism and postmodernism. But for Beckett, it was too bifurcated. By 1969, after he had exceeded Joyce's international status by winning the Nobel Prize for Literature, the idea that they were opposites was too restricting, too neat in its identifications. Speaking with John Gruen he redefined his self-representation in relation to Joyce by casting it as a matter of "artistic integrity": "I was not influenced by his work, as many people have suggested. I can only say that Joyce had a moral effect on me—he made me realize artistic integrity" (Gruen 1969, 211).

Beckett's retrospective distillation of his understanding of Joyce's influence into a lesson about how to be a true artist pervades James Knowlson biography, and it remains one of the defining features of Beckett's legacy as an author: again, as Ackerley and Gontarski put it, "Joyce, SB insisted, had made him realize artistic integrity. From one uncompromising in such matters, this is the supreme accolade" (2004, 288). That the authors of this encyclopedic "companion" to Beckett quote from Beckett's post-Nobel conversation with John Gruen without citation is a sure sign Beckett's distilled version of his relationship with Joyce has become a received idea. Like many of the most frequent descriptions of Beckett and his work, the idea was initially expressed by Beckett himself. Seen as part of the pattern of his professional development, it reveals his sense of himself as an author who learned from Joyce in his early career, who became Joyce's equal, and who superseded Joyce when he was awarded an international prize Joyce never received.

As the de Sade letters suggest, the period between October 1937 and April 1938 was crucial for Beckett's prospects as a professional writer; the evidence suggests he spent a lot of energy worrying about these prospects, not only in terms of the association with Joyce, but also in terms of his more general public image. Before the Routledge contract for *Murphy,* he had told McGreevy he wanted to rid himself of the book wherever he could at any cost (December 22, 1936, *Letters,* 401), and he had told Reavey he would sign any contract offered, regardless of the terms, as long as he could get it published (December 27, 1936, *Letters,* 405). At that point he had been a desperate writer trying to extend his résumé by adding a novel. The two de Sade letters written immediately after the signing of the Routledge contract suggest he had grown up as a writer, becoming more conscious of the damaging effects of certain strategies and decisions and more aware of the need to cultivate associations that would get him noticed in certain circles, to reduce the appearance of associations that might drag him down, to establish a method and a network of his own, and to develop a viable authorial persona. To get to the next stage as an independent, professionally viable writer, Beckett needed to establish a name for himself without damaging his public image unnecessarily. Beckett's negotiations over the de Sade translation, his efforts to attract a particular audience, and his concern over his long-term reputation, came at the moment in his career when he had chosen independence over domestic security: his delay in making this life-changing trip from Dublin to Paris in late October 1937 was primarily financial, but he was determined to achieve independence regardless of the consequences. Beckett decided to throw himself completely into the business of making a living as a writer, overcoming a period at Cooldrinagh when he was feeling particularly sorry for himself (to Arland Ussher on June 15, 1937, HRHRC), and to immerse himself in a life where nothing was certain except his entire responsibility for what happened. Leaving the safe anchorage of home, he would either sink or swim. This was, anyway, the theory; the reality was that he had a lot of people he could turn to when the going got rough.

Jack B. Yeats played a vital role in Beckett's development as an independent artist. A living example of a writer and artist who had created a livelihood for himself without sacrificing control, without losing his private peace, Yeats lived a relatively quiet life, opening his studio in Fitzwilliam Square, Dublin, once a week to discuss paintings with those who were interested, but never allowing anyone to watch him paint and never allowing visits outside set times. Through Yeats, Beckett saw the possibility of achieving success without giving up control over one's private life and one's public image. Beckett had initiated contact with Yeats in January 1931, making private appointments on January 24 and January 31. They spent two intense and stimulating hours studying and discussing paintings (February 3, 1931, *Letters,* 65). In August 1932 he had used his acquaintance with Yeats to open the door to Wishart publishing company, publishers of *Sligo,* sending a packet of poems for their consideration (August 30, 1932, TCD, 30). Although he found the Saturday afternoon salons at Yeats's studio to be tedious (November 9, 1932, TCD, 35) because they attracted people he thought pretentious, Beckett continued to cultivate a personal relationship, trying to see Yeats on his own whenever possible. In October 1933 Yeats acted as a referee when Beckett applied for a job at the National Gallery, Trafalgar Square (October 9, 1933, *Letters,* 166–67). And even though he continued to loathe the atmosphere (August 18, 1934, TCD, 61), he went back to Yeats's open houses whenever he was in Ireland, expressing jubilation when a visit to the studio gave them an opportunity for private conversation. In the early summer of 1935, more than four years after they first met, Beckett remained reverential, reporting a distinction he made between aesthetic evocation and invocation as a way of revealing Yeats's sharp wit (May 15, 1935, TCD, 76).

Back in Dublin in 1936 after his extended stay in London, Beckett made a point of seeing Yeats regularly on Saturdays. In May 1936 he arranged to buy a painting, *Morning,* on an installment plan, borrowing ten pounds as the first payment and owing a further twenty pounds until August 1936, when he made the last payment (May 7, 1936, *Letters,* 333, and August 7, 1936, *Letters,* 366). Yeats obviously had a lot of respect for Beckett, and clearly there was trust and an intellectual resonance between them, but the relationship was professional rather than friendly, In response to paternal advice to walk five miles daily whether his problems were mental or physical, Beckett convinced himself their rather cold relationship was thawing and they were becoming good friends (August 7, 1936, *Letters,* 366), however, there is no sign they became anything more than acquaintances. Yeats would do what he could to help Beckett land a contract with Routledge in late 1937, but Beckett would subsequently report a rather icy comment by Yeats in August 1938: according to the letter, Yeats pointed out they had known each other for a long time and should, by now, have bonded, but the painter went on to say that the time meant little and the bond was equally inconsequential (August 5, 1938, *Letters,* 636). Even though Yeats remained standoffish, Beckett worked very hard to initiate and cultivate a relationship, using it to expand his circle of contacts beyond Joyce's Paris-based set. Perhaps most important were the professional conversations he had with Yeats, which helped him develop the vocabulary and attitude necessary to a literary career suffused with visual representation and interwoven with the careers of a number of visual artists (including Arikha, DuChamp, Etrog, Giacometti, Hayden, Le Wit, and the van Velde brothers).

Whether it was from the inspiration of Yeats or the excitement of having made a decision to "fly by those nets," following Joyce's Stephen Dedalus, who had decided to escape Ireland's traps of "nationality, language, religion" (1916, 203), Beckett was full of energy and enthusiasm when he passed through London in mid-October 1937 en route to Paris. While he was still uncertain where he might settle, and while his life until December 1945 would be characterized by instability and uncertainty, Beckett's relocation of his domestic base was a confidence-boosting leap of self-trust. As I have argued, the move was neither coincidental nor reckless. With the help of his family and friends, Beckett had been gathering the necessary resources since 1928. He arrived in Paris in the fall of 1937 armed with an impressive résumé, some great contacts in the publishing industry, the manuscript of a well-made novel in his suitcase, a safety net of family money (if not from his mother, from his brother), and the chutzpah of a man with a plan. When he met Reavey in London on his way to Paris he successfully communicated his enthusiasm, inspiring Reavey to renew his efforts as a literary agent. Reavey's appointment books from the time suggest there was a burst of activity on Beckett's behalf (HRHRC). First he records a series of meetings with Beckett, then a long list of meetings with potential publishers in October, November, and December 1937. A blue Lett's appointment book for 1937 records meeting "Sam from Dublin" on October 17, 1937. A week later, on October 24, he records "Sam—dinner"; then, on October 25, "12:00: Bozman Dent" and "5:45: Sam. din. Vic." Beckett continued on to Paris at the end of October, probably on the October 25–26 night train from Victoria; Reavey followed on October 29, meeting "Sam" for lunch in Paris on October 30. Then, back in London on November 8, Reavey lists "Gollancz" for a 3:30 appointment and "A + Unwin" for 5. On November 9 he met with Dent; on November 12 he lists another meeting with "Gollancz." Finally, on November 17 at 3, he lists a meeting with Routledge. This November 17 meeting predates a letter Jack Yeats sent to Routledge's T. M. Ragg on November 22, 1937, soliciting him either to "read Beckett's Ms" or to "give it to some very open minded reader": "A friend of mine, Sam Beckett, has the manuscript of a novel 'Murphy' which is to be submitted to your firm" (Knowlson 1996, 268). Even though it may not have been clear to Yeats himself, the evidence from the appointment books suggests Reavey enlisted Yeats's support for Beckett's book *after* he had already made contact with Routledge. The most likely scenario, then, is that Reavey made the initial contact with the publisher on November 17, with Yeats's letter of support arriving a few days later; Yeats's solid reputation at Routledge effectively tipped the scales in Beckett's favor. Beckett heard about the contract in a telegram from Reavey dated December 9, 1937. Reavey's hand in the agreement is clear from this telegram and from his appointment book for this date: "R. offer for *M* telephone Paris." The details of the Routledge contract are spelled out in a letter Beckett wrote Mary Manning Howe in December 1937 (some confusion has arisen over the date of this letter because at HRHRC it is enclosed with a letter dated December 13, 1936): the letter explains the details of the contract, twelve pounds and ten shillings on signing with an equal amount when the book was published; Routledge also took the option on Beckett's next two works of fiction (*Letters,* 569).

What is remarkable about this period in Beckett's professional life is his persistence in attaining a major book contract during a six-month period filled with major stress and trauma. In the summer of 1937, when he was working on his Johnson project at the National Library of Ireland and at Beckett and Medcalf on Clare Street, his domestic situation had been in crisis. With *Murphy* cold on his desk after almost a year, and with nothing substantial to show for the six-month excursion in Germany, he tested his mother's patience when he took an active role in a libel case between Harry Sinclair and Oliver Gogarty, embarrassing her with his apparent disregard for the inevitable public notoriety and ridicule in the Dublin press. As if that were not bad enough for his mother, on September 21 he had a crash in the family car and decided to go to court in pursuit of insurance money from the company covering the driver of the lorry he had tangled with. Perhaps he decided to follow his Dad's deathbed advice to survive at all costs by fighting, fighting, fighting; or perhaps he had already decided he was leaving Dublin permanently and felt he had nothing to lose. In any event, he decided to challenge the case in court.

Even though the judge lauded him as one of Ireland's finest writers, he rejected Beckett's plea and fined him one pound five shillings for dangerous driving. This ruling made the claim for an insurance payout a nonstarter. Sometime between the car crash and the court appearance, the series of increasingly heated arguments he had had with his mother since his return from Germany came to a head. On September 28 he described his relationship with his mother as dysfunctional to the point he could no longer sleep under the same roof until he could figure out a plan to emigrate (TCD, 137). It is not insignificant that he collapsed his need to free himself from mothers and their surrogates with his need to leave Ireland: he would cast off the baggage that came with family, nation, and past lovers. He had not yet made up his mind where to go, speculating on London but concluding he was better advised to try Paris because the economics were more feasible. He was prepared to try his hand, going into survival mode until the cards fell his way. It was not easy, but he needed independence more than he needed ease. And, again, the risk was reduced by the preparations he had made in the months and years before the move.

On October 1, with the Gogarty-Sinclair court date imminent, his mother went away for an unspecified period to an unspecified location; he took the opportunity to move back to Cooldrinagh to get his things organized for his departure, enjoying the luxurious home without the interference of his mother (October 6, 1937, *Letters*, 552–54). There is every indication in his letters from Cooldrinagh to McGreevy on September 28 and October 6 that he planned a long trip and saw the break with his mother as final. Now it had dawned on him that charity from his mother was well beyond the call of duty, he no longer expected subsidies or other direct support from home (553). This allowed him to pack his books and papers, preparing himself to face the world almost entirely on his own terms. He would continue to receive two hundred pounds a year paid by Frank as his legacy from his father, and he would soon find a life partner who would become indispensable to his economic and domestic life as a writer, but he would no longer treat Cooldrinagh as his home base. He was thirty-one.

In the context of his immediate prospects as a professional writer, the break from his mother was not exactly smart. He would be so unsettled for the next three months he could write very little; he would remain in the limbo of hotel living until he moved to Rue des Favorites in April 1938; his legal status was questionable, making regular work impossible; and, no longer in a position to write home when he needed injections of cash, he was desperately poor. Two weeks after he left Ireland he told McGreevy he was almost out of cash and did not know how he was going to survive another week (November 1, 1937, *Letters*, 557). A month later, on December 3, 1937, he told his friend he was thinking about getting a job but felt too unsettled. He could not convince himself to buy a work permit at the cost of two hundred francs plus stamps and five photographs (562–63).

His professional work as a writer was also stalled. The Johnson project he had been working on since he had returned from Germany was delayed until spring 1940. And he would not begin his next major project, *Watt,* until February 1941. In the meantime, he did some backsliding by going to Joyce for work. As already noted, in November and December 1937 he worked on proofs of "Work in Progress" at the rate of 250 francs for about fifteen hours work. Nonetheless, he also began to translate *Murphy* into French, beginning the translation soon after he was stabbed in January 1938 and laboring over it until spring 1940.

What is most remarkable, though, is that, unsettled as he was, he had the confidence to imagine a calmer future when he might be in a place of his own, debt-free and sufficiently organized to make an earnest assault on the literary marketplace. Further, he worked to achieve such a future, spending five months searching for an apartment suited to his needs as a professional writer, learning to live within his means without subsidies from home, and establishing legal residency and a work permit in France. Beckett's long-term commitment to the life of professional writing is evident from his ongoing interest in creating the best possible conditions for a productive career. In the short-term this confidence manifested itself as an effort to boost sales of *Murphy* by advising Reavey to ask the editor at Routledge to drop the price from eight shillings and sixpence to five shillings (*Letters,* 603). The depth of his commitment is underscored by his ongoing work on the proofs for *Murphy* during his hospital stay and his continued efforts to design the packaging of the book, telling McGreevy on January 12, three days after he was admitted, to ask Reavey if he had found the photograph he wanted to use as the cover (584). Beckett's idea to decorate the cover with a photograph of two apes playing chess did not work out, but his advice about pricing met with some success: the novel was published at seven shillings and sixpence, 12 percent less than the price originally intended. Read in the context of the advertising materials for *Murphy,* this interest in packaging and pricing gives us a glimpse of Beckett's involvement in the marketing of his texts. A letter of January 17, 1938, suggests these publicity materials were written by Reavey and shared with Beckett while he was working on the proofs; in the letter Beckett again reveals his concern about how his book would be packaged, checking to make sure the book would not be encumbered with a silly advertising blurb (587). His keen interest in the pricing and packaging of his work signals his engagement with publishing as a business and his investment in the development of a viable, sustainable public image.

Beckett's deliberate severance from "Mother Ireland" and his eventual displacement of the Joycean Molly with the Beckettian Molloy was part of a long-term strategy to establish himself as an author in his own right. But in the short-term, his Irishness and his connection to Joyce were essential to his prospects. The marketing materials developed by Reavey positioned him as an Irish writer whose "meaning is implicit and symbolic, never concrete." The Routledge "Order Form to Your Bookseller" was accompanied by 350 words describing the novel as a series of "ironic situations that only the Irish genius could conceive," its "style leavened with a Celtic waywardness which is as attractive as it is elusive." The blurb frames the text as a highly charged effort by a writer with an "abundant creative imagination" to escape from the dross materialism of social realism. Full of "spirit," "gusto," and "hilarity," the novel describes a character who "neglects or despises the criteria of the substantial world": "Hence he moves in the lower strata of society; he lives intermittently with a prostitute and her persuasions cannot move him to better his material prospects. He lives on the balance between the real charge for his lodgings and that which the landlady submits to his guardian who pays them" (MS 4065, RUL). In a shorter blurb in a catalog listing "new Routledge Fiction," *Murphy* is described as "displaying the characteristic waywardness and charm of the Irish" with a main character who "despises normal ambitions and conventions and lives in the lower strata of society" (MS 4065, RUL).

In an odd way, Beckett's emergence from the petty but debilitating concerns of the struggling author was facilitated by the chest wound he suffered in the early morning of January 7, 1938. Walking home from a restaurant with Alan and Belinda Duncan, Beckett was approached by a man on the avenue D'Orléans; Beckett refused a demand for money, an altercation ensued, and the man, a pimp named Prudent, pulled a knife. He stabbed Beckett in the chest, narrowly missing his heart, but puncturing the left lung. Prudent ran off and the Duncans called the police; Beckett had lost a lot of blood and was rushed, unconscious, to the nearest hospital, the Hôpital Broussais, rue Didot. After a night on the general ward at the Broussais, he was transferred to a private room and treated to the special attention of a Dr. Fontaine, where he would be well looked after until January 22. Joyce paid for the private room, donated a reading lamp, delivered flowers, and accompanied Nora when she brought puddings and motherly fussings. He was also treated to an emergency visit by his mother, brother, and sister-in-law: they flew from Ireland on January 9. This visit is important because it effected a reconciliation that would allow Beckett to take control of his relationship with his mother and Ireland. Even as the stabbing solidified his bond with Joyce and healed his relationship with his mother, the numerous visits from people including "Brian Coffey, Alfred and Mania Peron, Georges and Marcelle Pelorson, Peggy Guggenheim, and others he had not seen for years" (Knowlson 1996, 261) reminded him he was part of a complex social network of writers, publishers, and other Left-Bank dignitaries. Crucially, one of his visitors was an acquaintance from his first days in Paris, the woman who would become his life partner and a major contributor to his professional life, Suzanne Dumesnil. The attentions of such a diverse and well-connected group cannot have done any harm to his self-esteem, to his status in his family, and to his professional self-confidence. This is especially true because any visitor would see, on the table next to his hospital bed, the galleys of the novel he was proofing for Routledge.

The pain from the stabbing lasted for months, as his left lung slowly recovered its function; the affirmation that he had made the right decision to commit himself to professional writing was much more profound and long-lasting. On January 25, 1938, three days after he left the hospital, he told McGreevy a poem had written itself in English: this was "they come / different and the same" (*Letters,* 596) and was sent to *Ireland Today* before February 11 (note that the John Calder edition of *Collected Poems* says the poem was written in 1937 (Beckett 1977b, 175). This poem marks a new departure for Beckett's style, a style worthy of his new status as an independent writer; its blend of repetition and energy anticipates work he would do in 1946–50 and beyond. Knowlson is conservative in suggesting that he began writing original poems in French "as early as the beginning of April [1938]" (Knowlson 1996, 270); a letter sent to McGreevy at the beginning of April suggests he had already immersed himself in this effort. In January he had copied a poem for McGreevy written by King Charles IX, "Epitre a Ronsard," suggesting he was, in a minor way anyway, orienting himself toward writing in French before he was stabbed. A January 31, 1938, letter to Reavey includes typed copies of "Ascension," "La Mouche," and "Prière," but these are obviously misfiled and seem more likely to belong with a letter he sent McGreevy on June 15, 1938 (*Letters,* 601 and 632). These three poems indicate he had, by the summer of 1938, begun to produce original texts in French. But he was still developing his confidence: the French version of "Alba" published in March 1938 in *Soutés* was translated by Peron and, while he seems to have begun the job on his own, he was thinking about asking Peron to translate *Murphy*. Still, on April 3, 1938, he told McGreevy he couldn't imagine going back to English for his poetry (614); this establishes April 3, 1938, as the latest date for his shift to French, but it also suggests he had been gearing himself toward the use of French as a language of creation for some time.

Slowly but surely, things were beginning to improve. As he approached his thirty-second birthday Beckett was able to tell McGreevy that Routledge was satisfied with sales of *Murphy*. Two weeks later he had moved into his new apartment at 6 Rue des Favorites and, in the meantime, had written two poems in French, understating the truth by claiming they represented his only fruitful work since he arrived in Paris in October 1937 (April 22, 1938, *Letters*, 620). As he worked to establish his place in the indigenous publishing industry (rather than the English-language, expatriate-oriented industry dominated by *Transition* and Shakespeare and Company), Beckett made full use of contacts dating back to his days at TCD and the École Normale Supérieure: no sooner had he written his two poems than his old friend Alfred Peron agreed to publish one in *Soutés,* and his one-time student Georges Pelorson helped get a hearing for the other poem at *Voluntés.* But he was earning very little money and was almost destitute (620). True to his upbringing and his father's dying words, he continued to fight for survival, looking for a French publisher for *Murphy* and penning more poems in French. We might expect to see a surge in productivity after he moved into his apartment on April 15, 1938. And he certainly expressed his appreciation for the improvements in light and atmosphere (620). On May 12 he complained about producing nothing except a long poem in French and expressed disappointment about Gallimard's rejection of *Murphy* (TCD, 162), but he seems to have been producing considerable work in French because the June 15 letter suggests "Ascension," "La Mouche," and "Prière" were only the latest poems in a series (630).

While he gradually figured out how to work in French, Beckett adjusted his socioliterary life, developing much deeper connections with French colleagues at the expense of those in, or from, Dublin and London. This is most evident from the tapering off of his relationship with McGreevy, but it is also illustrated by his decreased interaction with Seamus O'Sullivan, Charles Prentice, George Reavey, and others he had relied on in 1932–37. Since 1930 he had sent an average of twenty letters a year to McGreevy, sometimes four or five a month. The only significant gaps came when they were living in the same neighborhood in Paris and, later, in London. But around the time he moved to the apartment on Rue des Favorites, there was a significant reduction. After sending three in April 1938, he sent one in May. In this letter he sounds a note that would become familiar throughout his career, apologizing for his lack of correspondence by blaming the constant interruptions to a peace he, ostensibly anyway, once enjoyed (May 26, 1938, *Letters,* 624). Three weeks later he wrote explaining how he would set aside his aversion to Ireland by visiting at least once a year while his mother lived (630). A month passed before he wrote a relatively short, 250-word letter on July 13, making arrangements to meet as he passed through London. A quick, 50-word note on August 1, 1938, making final arrangements for accommodation in London, missed its mark because McGreevy was away. A 1,000-word letter from Cooldrinagh at the beginning of his month-long visit to Dublin in August 1938 would be the last until a 250-word letter sent on April 11, 1939. Beckett was fully conscious of the break but was hard pressed to explain why they might have become estranged from one another (654–55).

In retrospect we can see the significance of this interruption in correspondence with the man who introduced Beckett to Joyce; who shared his intimate thoughts about personal, domestic, creative, and professional struggles; and who was his main sounding board for ideas about art, books, friendships, travel and, perhaps most important, the business of literature in the years before he launched a Paris-based career. Beckett's effort to revitalize the correspondence was heartfelt, and was followed by a 1,000-word letter on April 18, 1939, and another long letter on June 6, 1939. As the war approached, foreign correspondence obviously became difficult, and we should not read too much into the fact Beckett did not write to McGreevy until two months after the end of the European war, on August 6, 1945. But the sea change in Beckett's attitude meant the relationship with McGreevy would never be as intense as it had been before his permanent move to Paris. Beckett's affection for McGreevy would remain as constant as his definition of himself in relation to Joyce and Ireland, and he would refer to this old affection in his postwar letters, but a growing awareness of intellectual and aesthetic differences together with a pragmatic understanding that his home market was in Paris, not London or Dublin, made him increasingly hesitant to send his latest work and ideas to McGreevy.

Beckett was, of course, readjusting his sights. Since January 1938 he had written enough well-executed poems in French to seriously consider showing them to a master poet, Paul Eluard (June 15, 1938, *Letters,* 630). And he was, finally, beginning to equip his study. After picking up three crates of books from customs in late May or early June 1938, he prepared to build some bookshelves. But there is little sign he did much writing before he went home to Dublin in August. While there, his main experience was of profound and debilitating alienation. His inspiration, when he found it, came from the man who had already helped him sketch the contours of an independent authorial persona: Dr. Johnson (August 4, 1938, *Letters*, 637). As I have begun to suggest, the change in Beckett's relationship with McGreevy was part-and-parcel with the redefinition of himself as an author committed to indigenous French-Parisian literary and artistic culture; it was also a direct reflection of his new push to succeed by inventing a public image appropriate to his new lifestyle (this argument is worked out more fully in "Samuel Beckett's Samuel Johnson," Dilks 2003). The whole gallery of people who had helped Beckett in the 1930s including Reavey and McGreevy, Manning Howe and O'Sullivan, Parsons and Prentice, would have no significant role in this new lifestyle.

Beckett had to overcome the fact that the move to Paris put him in daily contact with the Joyce crowd; but the thirty-two-year-old was confident enough about his new approach to see Joyce when he felt like it without being overwhelmed. Working to define a literary program with little connection to Joyce's recent work (Beckett 1984b, 172), he could associate with Joyce without being enmeshed in his circle. Perhaps the most material evidence of this confidence is Beckett's decision to rent an apartment in an unfashionable part of town, well away from the often pretentious Left Bank (April 22, 1938, *Letters*, 619–20). With a place of his own situated well away from the entrenched scene, he could define personal and professional relationships on his own terms, developing the strategy of controlled public engagement and private retreat with which he would undergird his mature authorial image. In other words, Beckett immersed himself in "local" Parisian culture. While he would increasingly function as an anchor for other writers and visual artists, including English-speaking expatriates, he would do so on his own terms, building his professional life in a physical location that allowed him to engage and disengage at will. He could arrange to meet professional contacts in an international hotel close to his apartment; but he could also withdraw into a quiet, nonpretentious, light-filled, airy seventh-floor apartment.

Beckett's new level of professional aplomb is evident from the work he did to help Arland Ussher and Geer van Velde. Ussher was a friend from TCD who moved in the same circle as Con Leventhal (a trusted friend who would work as Beckett's personal secretary in the late 1960s and early 1970s). On April 6, 1938, while still at the Hotel Liberia, Beckett praised Ussher for his intense productivity, counseled him to be patient about getting things published, and assured him he had given him an introduction to George Reavey to act as a publishers' agent (HRHRC). In May he followed through with further efforts on Ussher's behalf (May 5, 1938, HRHRC, and *Letters,* 622). At the same time that he used his professional relationship with Reavey and others to help Ussher find a publisher, Beckett used his grand romance with Peggy Guggenheim (see Ackerley and Gontarski 2004, 239–40) to set up a May 1938 exhibition for van Velde in London at the Guggenheim Jeune Gallery. As a courtesy he also wrote a biographical blurb for the exhibition catalog and flew to London to support the show. He had met van Velde through Reavey soon after the move to Paris in October 1937, and they quickly formed a close friendship over chess, art, and alcohol; in June 1938, with Beckett in the driver's seat, Peggy and Beckett drove Geer and Lisl van Velde to the Côte d'Azur in Guggenheim's flashy Delage Sport. As we have seen from his relationship with Yeats, prior to 1937 Beckett had typically treated visual artists from the position of a somewhat awestruck student learning art appreciation; with Yeats, especially, Beckett's letters reveal a deep reverence for a master painter of international repute. But after 1938, with the benefit of five years of comprehensive study of art and art history, including intense correspondence and conversations with Yeats and McGreevy (who would become director of Dublin's National Gallery in 1950) and an extended period of note-taking in German galleries and museums (see chapter 10 of Knowlson's biography), his new relationships with artists were different. He was now a connoisseur with a refined eye, a respected voice, a small collection of his own, and, again, a network of important contacts in Britain, France, Germany, and Ireland. Most significantly, he was prepared to act as a booster for his friends and would do so on a number of occasions. The advertising blurb he wrote for Geer van Velde in 1938 was followed by blurbs for Geer and Bram van Velde in 1945, 1948, and 1949; in 1952 and 1960 he would write advertising copy for Henri Hayden; in 1961 he wrote the preface to a deluxe edition of Bram van Velde's work; and in 1966 he would write a blurb for Avigdor Arikha, translating it into English for an exhibition in 1967. As we will see when we consider Beckett's *livres d'artiste,* he would also support visual artists by collaborating with them on special, highly priced illustrated editions of his texts: Arikha would illustrate five different museum-quality editions of

Beckett texts; Hans Erhardt and Dellas Henke would each illustrate three; Edward Gorey and Leif Lage each did two; and other artists did one, including Geneviève Asse, Max Ernst, Sorel Etrog, Stanley Hayter, Jasper Johns, Louis le Brocquoy, Bram van Velde, and Sol le Wit.

Simply put, Beckett's reverential relationship with Yeats, which was still evident from "Hommage à Jack B. Yeats," an advertising blurb for a 1954 Paris exhibition that concludes "S'incliner simplement, émerveillé" (translated by James White as "Merely bow in wonder") (Beckett 1984b, 148–49), was displaced by more secure, more conversational relationships. Beckett may have remained a marginal literary figure until *En attendant Godot* hit the stage, but after his move to Paris in 1937 he quickly established himself as a key player in a new aesthetic movement.

Positive Purgation

For obvious reasons the war occupies an important place in Beckett's career. He was forced to move to avoid the occupying forces; he engaged in special operations for the Maquis; and he experienced the precarious life of a resident alien in an occupied country. At the same time he established a deep intimacy with Dumesnil, developing solid credentials as an antifascist Francophile, making himself a national hero for a nation other than the land of his birth—on March 30, 1945, he was awarded the Croix de Guerre by the French government. By the end of the war his ongoing pursuit of the profession of writer would be further transformed because, in addition to his other mentality-shifting, independence-building experiences, his erstwhile mentor would be four years dead.

By war's end Beckett was carrying a manuscript radically different in form and content from any he had produced before he quit Ireland in 1937. While the war period is crucial to our understanding of Beckett's ongoing relationship with the literary marketplace, we should recognize that the aesthetic transformation evidenced by *Watt* began to take place before his move to Paris. This transformation began when he sat in the National Library in Dublin reflecting on his gallery travels in Germany and studying Samuel Johnson: extensive doodling in the margins of the incomplete manuscript of "Human Wishes" suggests he had begun to think in intensely visual terms about his work and associated Johnson with this intensified visual imagination (Bryden 1992). We can accept the received representation of Beckett as an artist who experienced "a pivotal moment" in 1946 that "helped to change him and to transform his approach to his own writing" (Knowlson

1996, 318); we can accept Bair's description of this "vision" as part of his "realization that all his writing would henceforth begin from within himself" (1990, 350–51); we can also accept that this "revelation . . . transformed his whole outlook on writing" (Cronin 1996, 358). But we cannot accept that the revelation in 1946 was *the only* transformative moment in Beckett's career. Whether this imaginative shift took place in his mother's room (as Knowlson reports), on the end of Killiney Pier (as Cronin reports), on Dun Laoghaire Pier (as Bair reports), or elsewhere (for example, on a beach in Dieppe in 1938, in a study in Paris in 1947 during the composition of *Eleutheria* or, perhaps, ten years later when he was composing *Krapp's Last Tape*), we would insist he did the groundwork for an aesthetic focused on "the darkness of an inner world" (Knowlson 1996, 319) when he immersed himself in Johnson's "vision of positive annihilation" in 1937 (Dilks 2003, 285–87). In doing so, we challenge the received perception of Beckett as a passive receptacle when he engaged with "a whole zone of being that includes folly and failure, impotence and ignorance" (Knowlson 1996, 319).

As he would put it himself in 1956, he turned his attention to a realm of experience not previously "exploited" (Shenker 1956). He did so not just in response to "various crucial experiences in war-ravaged France" (Knowlson 1996, 318), not just as a "sudden" response to the buffetings of "a winter storm" (Bair 1990, 350), and not just in response to "a revelation, occurring on [his] 1946 trip to Ireland" (Cronin 1996, 358), but also in a deliberate, carefully planned effort to "exploit" previously unbroken ground so as to turn himself into a viable professional writer. In other words, in the poems he composed in French before and during the war, and in *Watt,* composed in the years after Joyce died, he figured out how to do what he had dedicated himself to accomplish in 1937, to become a viable professional writer. In sum, even if he had a career-defining vision when he was visiting Ireland in 1946, he had been readying himself for almost a decade. Between 1937 and 1946 he engaged in a conscious revision of his authorial persona, dismantling what he had inherited from Joyce and the other modernists so as to clear a space for a style and voice of his own. In other words, the "revelation" in 1946 was the culmination of an extended period of conscious analysis and preparation characterized by a number of transformative experiences: immersing himself in Johnson, leaving Ireland, settling in Paris, experiencing Nazi brutality, joining the Maquis, losing his primary literary mentor, going on the run, working in St. Lô, returning to postwar Paris, visiting Ireland after a six-year break.

One of Beckett's most important prewar decisions involved his long-term commitment to the woman who shares his grave. As he engaged in the sustained process of analysis that laid the foundations for his mature work, Dumesnil played an increasingly significant role. During the period when he wrote the work for which he would become famous, she became indispensable. Beckett would remain in contact with McGreevy and Reavey for the next three decades, but their role diminished as Dumesnil took over as his main source of personal and professional support. This support is evident from a solemn tribute he gave her in an interview with Knowlson in 1989:

> I owe everything to Suzanne. She hawked everything around trying to get someone to take all three books at the same time. That was a very pretentious thing for an unknown to want! She was the one who went to see the publishers while I used to sit in a café "twiddling my fingers" or whatever it is one twiddles. Sometimes she only got as far as leaving the manuscripts with the concierge; she didn't even see the publishers. It was the same with Roger Blin. She was the one who saw Blin and got him interested in *Godot* and *Eleutheria*. I kept out of the way. (1996, 340)

This tribute suggests Dumesnil played her most important role during an intense period in 1946–50 when Beckett was looking for a long-term publishing contract. But her crucial function in Beckett's professional life is, of course, much more comprehensive, going back to the prewar period and going far beyond the delivery of manuscripts and rehearsed speeches designed to enhance interest. Her first major contribution to Beckett's career came in 1938 and 1939 when she helped him settle into indigenous Paris. During previous visits Beckett had lived the life of a transient expatriate, but now he moved into the life of a permanent resident, renting an apartment, living with a national citizen, spending major holidays without going home. Even before he bought property in France in 1950, Beckett made a series of decisions in conjunction with Dumesnil to construct a settled domestic life, putting him in a situation to write without distractions and to establish a solid basis for a viable professional life. These decisions allowed him to settle in Paris and to hold things together through the devastations of World War II; it is impossible to say whether or not he would have been able to do so without Dumesnil, but we can say she exerted an inspiring and calming influence on his domestic, professional, and cultural lives.

Beckett knew war was imminent during the early summer of 1939. But this did not stop him pursuing his career. He had been invited to send something to Blainaid Salkeld for possible publication in a series devoted to poets from Dublin. He sent a four-line poem (June 6, 1939, *Letters*, 659). This was "Dieppe," which would eventually appear, as part of a series of twelve poems written in 1938 and 1939 (including "Ascension," "La Mouche," and "Prière") in *Les Temps Modernes* in November 1946. The poem substantiates the argument that the 1937 move to Paris had enabled him to begin producing texts with the easy flow of the prose for which he would eventually become famous; as I argue in "Samuel Beckett's Samuel Johnson" (Dilks 2003), this suggests that the "vision at last" described in *Krapp's Last Tape* (*GCE III*, 227) and associated by the main biographers with Beckett's return to Ireland after World War II (see Bair 1990, 350–51; Cronin 1996, 358–59; and Knowlson 1996, 318), is deeply connected with the prewar move to Paris (Dilks 2003). Most likely inspired by a walk on the beach as he waited for the Dieppe-Newhaven ferry in July 1938 (TCD, 164), the poem uses minimalist technique to capture a slight, yet profound shift in direction:

encore le dernier reflux
le galet mort
le demi-tour puis les pas
vers les vieilles lumières.

Beckett's translation, benefiting from the gerund and the constancy of the specific article ("the") is, in my opinion, even more elegant:

again the last ebb
the dead shingle
the turning then the steps
towards the lights of old.
(*GCE IV*, 37)

Beckett needed practice before he could achieve this Johnsonian balance of relaxation and control in more sustained texts. In the meantime he continued to establish a broad-based résumé as a French author. On February 28, 1939, he told Reavey he was making efforts to write and publish a series of short poems in French (*Letters*, 653). And by the end of the year he had already ground his way through most of the translation of *Murphy*, telling Reavey on December 6, 1939, that he had only four chapters to translate and expected to be finished in a month. He then expected to return to the Johnson project (*Letters*, 669). His work on "Human Wishes" had been suspended when he left Ireland in October 1937 and, without reference books until June 1938, he left the project dormant. We have already noted his renewed interest in Johnson during his Dublin trip in July 1938 and his work constructing bookshelves and a library in his new apartment, but his energy was already focused on his series of French poems and then on the translations of "Love and Lethe" and *Murphy.* On May 21, 1940, he would report a high level of productivity to Reavey, listing a piece he had written for *Paris Mondial* (which was canceled because of the imminent invasion of Paris) and his efforts on his Johnson play (HRHRC, see *Disjecta* [1984b] for a copy of the fragment he wrote at that time). He wrote this letter with German troops advancing on Paris and a week before the beginning of the evacuation of Allied troops from Dunkirk. Two days before Paris fell, Beckett and Dumesnil took a train south, arriving in Vichy on June 12. In his bag he carried his translation of *Murphy.*

The first stop in Vichy was the Hotel Beaujolais, where James and Nora were waiting for their son, Giorgio, before traveling to Zurich. There is every reason Beckett would want to see Joyce, and he benefited directly from what turned out to be their last meeting. Joyce gave him a letter of introduction to Valery Larbaud. This letter allowed him to borrow twenty thousand francs from Larbaud's wife, enough to fund the grueling four-hundred-kilometer journey to Arcachon. With an additional loan from Mary Reynolds, an American acquaintance in the Atlantic coastal resort west-southwest of Bordeaux, Beckett and Dumesnil were able to rent a beach house. They stayed in Arcachon until December 1940, returning to Paris once Beckett's papers were in order (Knowlson 1996, 274). Apart from an Irish passport establishing his official neutrality, Beckett needed a document to prove he had a legitimate reason to be in occupied France; otherwise he would be excluded from rationing and other services. Plus he risked deportation or worse. After he had made arrangements with his brother for regular payments of his legacy from his father's estate into a French bank, he arranged with Count Gerald O'Kelly de Gallagh for proper documentation. De Gallagh's note underscores the importance of neat identifications in times of war: "I, the undersigned, Minister Plenipotentiary and Special Counsellor at the Irish Legation, certify that Monsieur Samuel Beckett, an Irish citizen, 6 Rue des Favorites, Paris (15eme) exercises the profession of writer" (Knowlson 1996, 277). Without this official designation Beckett would never have been in a position to work for the Maquis through the British Expeditionary Force and would, most likely, have been forced to live in Ireland for the duration of the war. Beckett's notorious preference for France during wartime over Ireland during peace necessitated his acquiescence with a bureaucratic process of categorization. Because it defined him as an Irish citizen, a member of a neutral nation, and as a man with a profession—writing—the document allowed Beckett to settle back into Paris.

But a few weeks after he returned to Paris to resume his life as a professional writer, Beckett received shocking news: Joyce was dead. Despite being overshadowed by the rapidly expanding European war, and with the newspapers filled with stories about the blitz of London and the Battle of Britain, news of Joyce's death, in Zurich at 2:15 AM on January 13, 1941, traveled quickly. The story was given almost two full columns and a photograph on page 15 of the *New York Times* on Jan 13, 1941, and a half-column on the editorial page on January 14; in London his thousand-word obituary was sandwiched between an obituary for Miss Amy Johnson, who flew solo from Britain to Australia in 1931, and a tribute to Lord Baden-Powell, the man who founded the British Boy Scouts during the siege of Mafeking in 1899–1900.

Beckett was deeply aggrieved by the death of his friend and mentor; the two men had an incredibly intense relationship and a complex, empathetic understanding of each other's intellect and culture. Emotionally Joyce's death was devastating. But in terms of Beckett's professional life, Joyce's death was something of a relief: *Watt* is the expression of this relief. I have suggested that he had begun to make peace with Joyce when he moved to Paris in 1937, and that he had become less concerned about the association; but with Joyce still alive he could never fully control his life as a writer. He would always be known as a student of Joyce and would always be peripheral to Joyce's social circle. Long after he had vowed to get over Joyce in June 1932, Beckett continued to depend on Joyce and his friends; that dependence is evidenced by the work he did on the proofs of *Finnegans Wake* in 1937, by the publication of "Ooftish" and the review of "Intercessions by Denis Devlin" in *Transition* in April–May 1938, and by his use of Joyce and Joyce's contacts when he was stabbed, when he fled from Paris, and when he needed money. From this perspective, the novel Beckett began in February 1941, less than a month after Joyce's death, is crucial to our understanding of his life as a professional writer because it was produced during the period when he first experienced a sense of freedom from Joyce. In short, *Watt* gives us a clear sense of what happened during the period between the death of Joyce in January 1941 and "the siege in the room" that began in February 1946.

Beckett's characterization of the novel as a "stylistic exercise" (Knowlson 1996, 303) confirms Lawrence Harvey's point about *Watt:* even though the period during the war was "more or less a time of enforced artistic sterility" (1970, 222), the novel is an important link between Beckett's days as a latter-day modernist and his days as a movement-shaping postmodernist. It is his most experimental, most Sterne-like, novel with experimentation integral to its structure. And it is sufficiently self-conscious to reveal important details about Beckett's understanding of his vocation. During this crucial period, when there is a hiatus in Beckett's correspondence, *Watt* provides a bridge. For that reason, and despite the fact literary analysis is not our main interest, *Watt* is worth dwelling on. Because it is a "raw" experimental, transitional novel, it gives a good sense of how he understood his authorial position as he was making the transition between the approach that produced *Murphy* and the approach that brought him international fame.

The material circumstances experienced by Beckett during the composition of *Watt* are crucial to our understanding of the text as a bridge from the world of Joyce to the world of Beckett. Beckett's ongoing quest for freedom and his personal, professional, and cultural struggle against overly neat identifications was seriously challenged when he found himself living under the auspices of a German political system built on the definition and legislation of absolute categorical definitions: as we have seen, in order to survive materially in occupied France Beckett had to succumb to a set of neat categories. The decision to stay in France was not made lightly. After his six-month sojourn in Germany he knew exactly what he was dealing with. In an April 6, 1938, letter to Arland Ussher he had parodied Nazi idealizations of the perfect Aryan, joking about how the neat physical prescriptions were belied by Hitler's hair and the physique of other prominent Germans (HRHRC). Having agreed to live by the rules of this prescriptive system, Beckett knew he could only survive by developing strategies of resistance. His active subversion of German rule through his work with the Maquis was complemented by his active subversion of narrative mastery in his prose. The project he worked on throughout the war, the novel that became *Watt,* rebels against neat, self-sustaining, and delusional apparati even more thoroughly than *More Pricks Than Kicks* and *Murphy.*

Watt was begun in a hardcover notebook on February 11, 1941, while Beckett was settling into German-occupied Paris. He continued to work on it after September 1941, when he began moonlighting as a spy with "Gloria SMH" (he was recruited by Alfred Peron soon after Paul Leon was arrested).

By the time of the Allied bombing of Paris in March 1942 he had begun a second notebook, and he would return to it as the Nazis ratcheted up their anti-Semitic laws until the mass deportation of Jews from Paris in July and August 1942. After evacuating to Avignon and then Rousillon in September he began the third *Watt* notebook, continuing until the end of October; he then left it untouched for the winter. Between March and October 1943 his progress on the novel was sporadic as he worked for a living on a farm in Rousillon. Once the harvest was over in October 1943 he began a fourth notebook and would work steadily for the next fourteen months with interruptions when he participated in resistance activities in the spring and summer and when he moved back to Paris in October 1944. He completed a first final version in December 1944 and then began a further notebook (number five of six) in February 1945. By the time he traveled to Dublin via London on April 8, 1945, he had produced a typescript of the novel and would spend six weeks of relative tranquility at Cooldrinagh getting it ready for submission. He sent it to Routledge for consideration on May 25, 1945 (Pilling 2006, 94).

The unsettled conditions experienced during the composition of *Watt,* combined with an urge to positive annihilation and a more urgent struggle against sociopolitical categories, may explain the difference between a novel that plays with the philosophical idea of "a perpetual coming together and falling asunder of forms" (*GCE I,* 70) and a novel illustrating a process of deconstruction. The carefully plotted trajectory of *Murphy* is replaced by a disjointed, self-dismantling agglomeration. *Murphy*'s structure was sufficiently tight to allow the narrator to project forward and backward with a playful, but always controlling and often bored, narrative voice; *Watt* passes from one order of discourse to another, with radical shifts in narrative perspective, style, and voice. The self-confident social preening we saw in "A Wet Night," when Alba and the homespun Poet readied themselves for their audience at an upper-middle-class soirée, has become a more earnest and critical analysis of the ways in which narrative voices wear the clothing of language. And the self-confidence of the performer has been eroded; it as though he is suffering from a severe case of attention deficit disorder. Discrete sections function according to a stable pattern, but periodically, though unpredictably, there are abrupt shifts as the certainty of one narrative order collapses and another asserts itself, until it, too, collapses. In chapter 1, for example, there is stability for the first twenty-three pages, as Mr. Hackett and the Nixons interact. True to the discourse of social realism, they take

Watt's sudden appearance in their stride: they are intrigued and interested, but they soon return to their stilted, painfully decorous dialogue. The prescriptive codes available to these social realists prove inadequate to a character who will not be categorized, who represents an order of discourse they cannot handle; they retreat into the effort to apply neat categorizations, leaving Watt to move on. But the narrator leaves them and tags along with Watt. Just as Hackett and the Nixons try to encapsulate Watt, then give up, so with Mr. Spiro. His logical categories for coding experience prevail for the duration of the train journey, but they will not contain Watt, who drifts off into another realm of consciousness and then departs for another physical realm. Again the narrator leaves the analyst, tagging along with the analyzed, Watt. The narrator adjusts in response to each shift in context, trying to keep pace as the subject of analysis, the eternal question, eludes extant structures and forms, definitions and categories.

Besides the thread of continuity created by the presence of Watt, the only connection between the series of scenes constituting part 1 of the novel is the pervasive sense of economic relations. In this sense the opening chapter of *Watt* reveals Beckett's ongoing concern with the logic of authorship and the business of the literary marketplace; he is literally seeking a narrative voice adequate to his own situation as a writer who will, when the war is over, try again to sustain an economically viable professional career. Economic relations are apparent from the beginning through Watt's outstanding loan to "Goff" Nixon (*GCE I,* 180), through a conversation about the price of a tram ride (182–83), through the porter's exchange of milk cans up and down the platform (186), and through the newsagent's "warm nest of books and periodicals" (187). As Watt drifts on, finding himself opposite Mr. Spiro in a train compartment, he again falls into a situation contextualized by commerce: "I edit *Crux,* said Mr Spiro, the popular catholic monthly. We do not pay our contributors, but they benefit in other ways. Our advertisements are extraordinary" (189). Spiro frames his own "contribution to supplementary redemption" in terms of its "profit" (189) and goes on to explain his response to a series of questions from the "Author of The Chartered Accountant's Saturday Night" (190). As Spiro details what happens if "A rat, or other small animal, eats of a consecrated wafer," Watt drifts off into a world of "voices, singing, crying, stating, murmuring, things unintelligible, in his ear" (190). Watt's vacillation between the world of economic relations and the world of voices singing in his head is analogous to the pattern we have seen in Beckett's correspondence where he vacillates between statements revealing his intense investment in the business side of his literary affairs and statements suggesting he is only interested in what is going on inside his own skull.

As he travels from tram to train to road to kitchen, Watt experiences a series of episodes bearing witness to the omnipresence of economics. And he glides past them all with stoic imperviousness, equally indifferent to the members of every social class and every economic situation. The retired Mr. Hackett, the middle-class Nixons, and the aristocratic Lady McCann cross his path; they are interspersed with a working-class porter, a self-employed newsagent, and an intellectual editor/author: in all cases he proceeds unruffled, passively accepting whatever the world throws at him, whether a series of questions, a verbal insult, a riddle, or a rock (*GCE I,* 180–90). In the process of traversing the gamut of social classes with his lead character, Beckett traverses a range of stylistic options, dispensing with important aspects of his writerly context as effectively as Watt glides past a complex world of socioeconomic relations. By the time Watt is sitting in the kitchen playing his "little game" with the colors of the fire (198), Beckett has parodied and cast off Orwellian social realism, Eliotic poetics, the Proustian psychological novel, Joyce's socioreligious word games, and the Irish "big house" novel. It is as though he is clearing a space for a style of writing he can live with. After a process of systematic purgation, he arrives at a form of internalized monologue with the flow of Joyce's stream of consciousness in *Ulysses* but with a darker, more purgative application. Joyce's confessional application of the technique is displaced by a process of narrative dismantling. The style is both smoother and more comfortable than anything Beckett had written hitherto; as I have suggested, we recognize the process of purgation from "A Wet Night," especially in the way Belacqua strips himself in order to experience "the mean storm" (*GCE IV,* 129); but now there is a fluency making the catharsis more systematic, more purposeful. It is as though the process of thought and action attributed to Belacqua has been merged with the spirit of positive annihilation (borrowed and adapted from Samuel Johnson), creating what begins to function as a "Beckettian" principle of literary expression (Ricks 1993, 15–24).

The process I am describing deploys positive annihilation as an aesthetic principle designed to reduce presence. In *Watt* Beckett applies his vision of positive annihilation to the process of narrative dismantling, effectively eliminating a series of extant narrative options in the effort to craft a viable alternative with as much "un-presence" as possible. He thus inaugurates the process of dismantling he will continue in his postwar stories and novels, first in "La Fin, "Le Calmant," "Premiere amour," and "L'Expulsé," then in *Molloy, Malone meurt,* and *L'Innommable.* Once he had established a space for himself, carving a "Beckettian" niche in the literary marketplace, his network of friends and professional contacts helped him establish and disseminate his reputation as a self-dismantling author of self-dismantling prose and drama. Through strategies coupling him with his characters, these professional contacts helped Beckett establish the idea that he had, as an author, dismantled his connections with the material world, ridding himself of any concerns other than the actual work of creation, turning him into an icon of noncommercialized art (see fig. 8). Simply put, the lack of earthly possessions by Beckett's characters was transferred to Beckett himself, his publicity photographs representing him as though he had stepped out of one of his own plays or novels. Antimarketing became a logical way of marketing texts describing characters who seemed to have checked out from the commercial world. By extension the purgative method in his work and the nihilistic characters he created became part of the argument that he had no interest in publicity, self-promotion, success, fame, or money.

Two months after he chose to carry a piece of paper defining his origins and occupation so he could survive in occupied Paris, and less than a month after Joyce died, Beckett created a character who is introduced thus:

> Nationality, family, birthplace, confession, occupation, means of existence, distinctive signs, you cannot be in ignorance of all this.
>
> Utter ignorance, said Mr Nixon.
>
> He is not a native of the rocks, said Mr Hackett.
>
> I tell you nothing is known, cried Mr Nixon. Nothing.
>
> A silence followed these angry words, by Mr Hackett resented, by Mr Nixon repented. (*GCE I,* 184)

Early in a chapter dramatizing the displacement of category-driven forms of identification (aesthetic, personal, and social), Beckett underlines the deep-seated tension between self-righteous, category-driven social perception and a character that eludes categorical definition. Having weathered the storm of economic and conversational demands, and having turned the other cheek in response to verbal and physical abuse, Watt reaches the relative peace and quiet of his destination. He sits quietly in the kitchen, occupying himself by using his hat to play with the shifting light and dark between a lamp and a fireplace. As Watt prepares to await "the unsoiled light of the new day, of the new day at last, the day without precedent at last" (220), a gentleman appears, observes Watt, "goes away, without a word of explanation" (199), and returns to make "a short statement" (199). Delivered as a ten-thousand-word monologue with a couple of songs thrown in for good measure, and including a version of "Dieppe" ("on the dark shingle the turning for the last time again to the lights of the little town," [200]), Arsene's statement functions as both a prototype of the narrator/narrated style Beckett would perfect after the war *and* as a declaration of the timeliness of a style characterized by its elusiveness in response to neat categorical identifications.

While it is possible to see the language games he plays in chapter 3 of *Watt* as "Beckett's fullest deconstruction of language" (Albright 2003, 146), a much more important process of dismantling is demonstrated in chapter 1. As we have begun to see, each discrete section of the chapter parodies a stylistic option. Then, in a grand sweeping gesture, the first twenty-five hundred words of Arsene's statement redefine and reset the default, simultaneously articulating and deploying the method of positive annihilation: crucially, Arsene describes a moment of revelation anterior to Krapp's "vision at last": "For he knows he is in the right place, at last. And he knows he is the right man, at last . . . the fit is perfect" (*GCE I,* 200). In the context of my argument, "he" is Beckett the professional writer, an author who had struggled with the insecurities of being derivative and dependent, and who has now found an independent voice and a viable persona: "When in a word he will be in his midst at last, after so many tedious years spent clinging to the perimeter. . . . What a feeling of security!" (200). After years of "wandering" and "squandering," "turning" and "learning" ("Gnome," *GCE IV,* 9), the marginalized apprentice has found his voice and his vocation.

Watt certainly does not represent a complete separation from Beckett's earlier writing, but it is as though the voice speaking during the Arsene section has lain in wait, ready to emerge once all other available narrative options have been eliminated. Certainly, there are signs embedded in the first part of Arsene's statement suggesting Beckett saw himself entering a new authorial realm: "Having oscillated all his life between the torments of a superficial loitering and the horrors of a disinterested endeavour, he finds himself at last in a situation where to do nothing exclusively would be an act of the highest value, and significance" (*GCE I,* 201). Perhaps we should not overemphasize the date of the revelation: it took place on "a Tuesday afternoon, in the month of October" (201–2), in the month when, in 1937, Beckett severed his connection with his Irish home. And perhaps the pagination in the 1959 Grove edition is coincidental, with the preamble of Arsene's statement stretching from page 39 to page 45, in an odd parallel to the transitional years of the war. But we cannot overlook the fact Arsene frames "the nature of the work to be performed" as work done "chiefly, for himself, that he may abide, as he is, where he is, and that where he is may abide about him, as it is" (201); and we cannot avoid seeing Arsene's language as an anticipation of the language Beckett would use in "Three Dialogues with Georges Duthuit," written after he had produced the French versions of the texts for which he would become famous.

While Arsene's "short statement" is suffused with existentialism of the sort Beckett would be familiar with through his reading of Sartre's *Nausée* in 1938, it applies more immediately to Beckett's situation as a writer than Lance Butler suggests when he argues that Arsene's section "offers us a man who has become the man-God, the pour-soi-en-soi, who has connoted Absolute Knowledge" (Butler 1984, 199). Most immediately, the first part of Arsene's statement is about work more than it is about religion, philosophy, or any other abstraction. In other words, while it is perfectly feasible to interpret Arsene's words as evidence Beckett is gesturing toward "what is beyond the absolute, beyond God" (200), and while we might accept Richard Begam's argument that Watt is "a kind of phenomenological Christ, one who having suffered in the wilderness of Cartesian dualism, having borne the stigmata of fallen consciousness, now comes to a place of deliverance, even resurrection" (1996, 72), a more material, more immediate reading focuses on the actual scene taking place and notices the references to *work* and *exchange*. We are, after all, witnessing a shift change in the labor force: Erskine replaces Arsene upstairs; Watt replaces Erskine downstairs; Arsene leaves. The man they serve stays put. While Arsene waxes philosophical and reveals his familiarity with biblical discourse, the first pages of his statement anchor it to the job at hand. Terminology from business and work play a central role in the first part of the discourse: he describes "the appointments kept and the appointments broken," the new "premises," a debt "repaid, amply repaid," "the nature of the work to be performed" and its "exceptional fruitfulness," explaining how "he goes about his work, calm and glad" (*GCE I,* 200–201). As if to underline the secondary nature of philosophy, he tells us he experienced his revelation during "an instant of leisure" (202), dropping the subject because he has "information of a practical nature to impart, that is to say a debt to pay, or a score to settle" (204).

Of the four chapters in *Watt,* chapter 2 is the longest. It explores Watt's function in "Knott's establishment" (223), detailing his various duties and experiences with a "professional relation" (226). Throughout the chapter there is a self-consciousness about the materiality of language and writing, with Watt doing his utmost to find "semantic succour" by experimenting with words, "trying names on things, and on himself, almost as a woman hats" (234). Again we notice the commercial context, as words become commodities to be put on and off like hats in a haberdashery. The indifference Beckett had expressed in so many letters in the 1930s when he discussed writing projects has been transformed, through Watt, into an obsession with naming, "wrapping up safe in words the kitchen space, the extraordinary newel-lamp, the stairs that were never the same . . . and many other things in the house" (234). As the chapter goes on, it becomes clear naming is only one step in Watt's determined effort to organize the chaos of experience of "all that went on about him" (236). The chapter is a catalog of events baffling to Watt. At the same time, it is a record of his labor-intensive effort to describe, interpret, and "solve" (242) these events. When he has "turned little by little, a disturbance into words" and "had made a pillow of old words, for a head. Little by little, and not without labour" (262), he loses interest: "But when Watt had grasped, in its complexity, the mechanism of this arrangement . . . then it interested him no more" (262).

Just as the opening chapter uses and then drops a series of ways of describing experience, so chapter 2 works through and then drops a series of experiential problems, using "labour" to erase barriers to his positive progress. The narrative thus proceeds by disposing of the visit by the piano tuners (223–32); the preparation and delivery of Knott's food (237–40); the mechanism and support-system system for recycling leftover food (240–62); the system of bells and keys organizing movements around Knott's house (265–72); the description, interpretation, and ownership of a painting (272–74); the "period and distribution of service" (276); the pattern of croaking frogs (278–80); the schedule of visits by Mrs Gorman and Mr Graves (280–86); Watt's encounter with Mr. Knott (286–88); and a mysterious phone call (288). The narrator works his way, systematically and laboriously, through each of these events as each comes and then goes, "because all was a coming and a going" in "Mr Knott's establishment" (274). The plot thus functions like a production line in reverse, each part stripped from the product, to be dismantled and dumped in readiness for the dismantling and dumping of the next part. This process of dismantling made Beckett's postwar job as a professional writer possible because it cleared the decks, creating an opportunity for him to navigate a line of narrative enquiry that had previously been blocked.

Chapter 2 ends as Watt prepares to move to the first floor because he has been displaced on the ground floor by the arrival of Arthur. Erskine must now leave because he has been displaced by Watt. When Watt arrived, Erskine had been displaced from the ground floor and had displaced Arsene from the first floor. The production line continues, each "coming" leading to a shift in jobs, and each shift in jobs leading to a "going." Knott, the master, remains, but the narrative moves on. Chapter 3 skips to the scene of the storytelling, situating us in the place where Watt told "Sam" his "story" (345), in the place where he struggled with "the labour of composition" (295). Beckett moves the narrative to a metalevel, but he still posits writing as *labor.* In chapter 2 the narrator anticipates this move:

> I may . . . have left out some of the things Watt told me, though I was most careful to note down all at the time, in my little notebook. It is so difficult, with a long story like the story that Watt told, even when one is most careful to note down all at the time, in one's little notebook, not to leave our some of the things that were told, and not to foist in other things that were never told, never told at all. (270)

Again chapter 3 is, like chapter 2, a catalog of descriptions of incidents and explanations, but now we move more swimmingly from one episode to the next: it is as though, having dispensed with literary options in chapter 1 and existential and phenomenological problems in chapter 2, "Sam" has asserted his role as an active authorial agent and has freed the text from philosophical analysis, connecting its plot with less abstract, more material events. In other words, a concern with literary style in chapter 1 was displaced, in chapter 2, by a concern with philosophical issues and intellectual problem solving. Now these issues are displaced, in chapter 3, by a concern with material and mechanical problems. The fixing of a bridge, the feeding of rats, the description of Watt's voice, the geography of the garden and its fence: each of these discrete and important problems is given approximately three hundred words (as compared with approximately eight thousand words for the food-disposal problem in chapter 2). Not to put too fine a point on it, the author has become an authority, "Sam," and he uses his authority to deconstruct the author function. Because Watt's narrative has become a series of examples of how storytelling operates, Sam's narrative must respond by becoming a series of efforts to solve problems as they arise. In other words, the narrator, guided by a spirit of active dismantling (which functions as a literary interpretation and application of Johnson's religious vision of positive annihilation), explores a series of problems produced by the effort to tell a story.

Beckett's purgative progress toward an aesthetics of ignorance and impotence is evident from his subversion of all aspects of the linguistic and literary complex: as he had called into question the ability of Hackett and the Nixons to develop any substantial understanding of Watt's identity, and as he had cast doubt on Watt's perception and expression, so now he calls into question the ability of the narrator to develop an understanding of his subject *and* the ability of the author to complete his project. Watt's difficulty in distinguishing "between what happened and what did not happen, between what was and what was not" (270) is compounded by his struggle to find a set of linguistic and literary codes adequate to his experience at Knott's house. And his flawed perception and expression is further compounded by Sam confessing that much was lost in the transmission of the story: "Of this impetuous murmur much fell in vain on my imperfect hearing and understanding, and much by the rushing wind was carried away, and lost for ever" (295). The integrated problems of perception and expression, reception and representation (a problem Beckett was still exploring when he wrote *Catastrophe*) are framed most vividly in terms of a yin-yang relationship as the storyteller and the narrator, facing one another and walking in perfectly matched steps, pace up and down "between the fences" (301). It becomes evident from this episode in the garden that Beckett's understanding of the job of the writer was increasingly concerned with the material situation of the narrator both at the point when the details of the narration are gathered and at the point when the story is recorded. This concern gives shape to the experimental form of *Watt*, turning the novel into an extended analysis of how "the yarn was spun" (269). When they are walking back and forth between the fences, Watt and Sam are in physical proximity and synchronicity. But this intimacy between the speaker and the listener, which should create ideal conditions for clear communication, is counteracted by Watt's active effort to develop a linguistic system adequate to his experience.

Again the method is one of play and disposal as the narrative production line, operating according to the logic of positive annihilation, dismantles each option in turn. The narrative source, Watt, plays with ellipsis and euphony, reversing spelling, syntax, and sentence order, systematically shifting the order of discourse as he narrates his story. The narrative recorder, Sam, works to keep pace, decoding each formulation and classifying each discrete "phase" of Watt's linguistic devolution. As Sam adjusts to each new order of discourse—"But soon I grew used to these sounds, and then I understood as well as before" (repeated three times on pages 303–4 with a variant without the second clause repeated a further two times on page 304)—Watt changes the rules. As a result "Sam," the invented author, "missed I suspect much of great interest" (305). And this is not all: because of increasing deafness on his part, the narrator only "understood fully one half of what won its way past my tympan" (306). Beckett, at one step removed from Sam, thus builds incompleteness and unreliability into the relationship between the addressed and the addressee, making it clear that the narrative is built on deliberately obscure systems of communication. Each link in the chain of communication is rendered suspect; at the same time, however, the characters are clearly dependent on one another, neither Watt, nor Sam, nor Knott, nor Arsene having an existence apart from the others. Like the author who finally emerges from *Watt* with a viable literary approach in his grasp, the ostensible isolate, Watt, is materially dependent on a network of correspondents.

Self-conscious reference to the chain of communication would become a permanent feature of Beckett's narrative explorations after the war, remaining an explicit structuring principle in such late texts as *Ill-Seen Ill-Said* and *Worstward Ho.* In Beckett's newly forged understanding of the author function, the problematic equation of perception, expression, and interpretation is a central organizing principle. And it is always compounded by a revealed awareness of the fragility of linguistic and literary communication. As his career went on, Beckett continued to challenge the stability of the subject, the verb, and the object, exposing and interrogating the semantic structure of language in ways crucial to any definition of the shift from modernism to postmodernism and from structuralism to deconstruction (Derrida 1992, 61). *Watt* demonstrates that as Beckett experimented with different ways to deploy the aesthetics of positive annihilation in 1937–45 he increasingly applied himself to the process of untying the material conditions on which storytelling depends, dismantling the identity of the author-narrator to reveal the process of communication as a series of miscommunications and the process of identity formation as a series of disconnected, shifting identities without any stability of relationship. Intent on undercutting the authority of the author and the text, he deliberately exposed the series of steps separating the teller from the told, the narrator from the narrated, the author from the text, the text from the reader. Again, as we will see in our concluding chapter, *Catastrophe* brings these threads together into an intense illustration of Beckett's career-long exploration of the job of the professional writer as it interacts with the various mechanisms of production, distribution, and consumption.

Because eight years elapsed between the date in the summer of 1945 when Beckett did the finishing touches to *Watt* and June 1953, when it was finally published, we can assume the illegibilities and gaps in the manuscript are deliberate features designed to achieve an explicit effect. So, too, the "addenda" of "precious and illuminating material" left in note form at the end of the book because of "fatigue and disgust" (373). These features are the most obvious evidence of *Watt*'s function as a cusp text, expressing Beckett's effort to create a new narrative style using post-Joycean, postmodernist forms of representation. In his assessment of Beckett in the context of postmodernist culture, Steven Connor suggests "the most influential accounts of postmodernist fiction stress the prevalence of parodic 'metafiction,' or the exploration by literary texts of their own nature and status as fiction" (1989, 129). He goes on the argue, "Samuel Beckett's novels from *Molloy* onwards . . . require us to remain aware all the time of the process by which the fiction we are reading is coming painfully into being on the page" (129). This acute narrative self-awareness has its roots in the prewar work, but it entered a new phase after Beckett immersed himself in his Johnson project in 1937: he did not complete the project, abandoning the nascent play, "Human Wishes," after ten pages or so, but he *did* use a specific aspect of Johnson's character, the darker Johnson who exposed his inner turmoil in the "Prayers and Meditations" and elsewhere. Inspired by an intensely personal understanding of Johnson and by a keen urge to develop a post-Joycean style, Beckett developed an approach characterized by "positive annihilation," by an ongoing process of dismantling.

The period between 1938 and 1945 is, then, marked by an awkward but incomplete transition from the urge to structure in *Murphy* to the collapse into "indetermanence" (as Hassan [1967] calls it) expressed in the postwar novels. There is a residual yearning for structuring principles even as such principles are dismantled. That is why, even as he falls apart, Watt remains devoted to "the labour of composition," obsessively seeking models of understanding adequate to his experience (*GCE I,* 295). For his part, Sam laments "the confusion of his senses consequent on prolonged inanition" (309) and the problems arising from "a lack of method" (314). But as I have suggested, *Watt* is driven by the urge to clear a space for a new species of literary expression. Again, this is the space into which Beckett inserted himself as a viable professional writer in the years following a war responsible, in many respects, for the annihilation of modernist culture.

1. Advertisement for *Index on Censorship* used on posters throughout the London Underground in 1985. The advertisement was revived in 1990 for use on a T-shirt. Modified image and original text © *Index on Censorship,* London. Used with permission. Original photograph 1980 copyright John Minihan, used with permission.

2. Advertisement for *Evergreen Review*. Dated February 28, 1966. Barbarella © and ™ 2009 The Estate of Jean-Claude Forest. Beckett photograph courtesy of Lufti Ozkok and Sipa Press. Text of advertisement courtesy of Grove/Atlantic Inc. and the Grove Press Records, Special Collections Research Center, Syracuse University Library.

3. Beckett in his study signing a copy of the livre d'artiste edition of *Imagination Dead Imagine* for Sorel Etrog. Photograph by Roger Pic, 1977. Used with permission of the Photography Collection, Harry Ransom Humanities Research Center, the University of Texas at Austin.

4. The Nobel Laureate posing with garbage in an alley in 1973. Photograph © Jerry Bauer. Used with permission.

DAILY MAIL, Saturday, March 8, 1958

Beckett comes back to DEATH VALLEY

● At last fame catches up with the Godot man. But does he like it? As I spoke to him last night I wondered . . .

BECKETT
TO DECOMPOSE IS TO LIVE.

I WAS waiting for the man who wrote *Godot* to answer the telephone in the remote village 50 miles east of Paris where the international exchange had traced him.

In the early evening the Irish voice of Samuel Beckett, the mystery man of Left Bank literature, came through to the *Daily Mail* — but not to talk about himself.

"We'll have a drink together when you're next in Paris on duty, but I can't discuss my work," said the least-known major writer of the time, the translation of whose play *End Game* has just been banned in London by that dauntless joker the Lord Chamberlain after it had already had a London run in French.

Seldom photographed, never interviewed, Beckett, an attractive cordial man with the beaky, intense glower of a sparrowhawk has a deep revulsion against personal publicity.

Yet at last the work of this 52-year-old expatriate Dubliner, friend and secretary of James Joyce, is breaking through to a general public.

Brisk going

THIS week, after being excluded from Britain for years by threatened prosecution, two of his novels appear: *Malone Dies* (Calder, 10s. 6d.) and *Watt* (Olympia Press, Paris, issued here by Zwemmer Ltd., at 15s.).

As it normally takes at least a decade for any fresh European thought to tunnel under the 25 miles of the English Channel, this appears to be fairly brisk on the part of the British.

Actually his first novel, *Murphy*, was published here in 1938, when it was utterly ignored.

It was *Waiting for Godot*, the metaphysical horror comic which became the most argued-about play of 1956, that opened up the Beckett Death Valley to the tourists.

When you read these newly released, almost paragraphless novels the first thing that strikes you is, oddly enough, the slightly demodé flavour of their "experimental" form, and then you remember that Beckett is really a survivor, the last of those between-the-wars intellectual outlaws who used Paris as a wild Sherwood Forest.

Second, you are reduced to a state of near-paralysis by the remorseless similarity of everything Beckett produces.

Godot portrays two ragged derelicts in a state of ataxia, beyond the point of taking decisions, waiting in a blighted moon landscape for the salvation that they know will never arrive.

The hero of *Murphy* is roasted to death by an exploding gas-stove after hunting for sanctuary in a lunatic asylum.

In *End Game* the blind tyrant lives in a windowless cell with his parents in dustbins. *Molloy*, a crippled tramp on the road to nowhere, mumbles from his ditch: "To decompose is to live."

Malone Dies is the scribblings of a bed-ridden murderer lost in "molten gloom."

Watt, which for 10 years travelled in manuscript form around St. Germaine circles, is a nightmare excursion which ends with four bars of music, the threnody heard by Watt from that favourite lair, a ditch.

The pervading emotions are frustration, disgust, futility, and pessimism.

"Already a contemporary classic," claims the publisher of *Malone Dies*, "his work is coming to be recognised as worthy to stand beside that of Proust, Gide, and Joyce."

Bleak honesty

THAT, I think, is trying to boost a deliberately confined genius to unwarranted proportions. Yet genius he certainly does have.

If the long passages of pummelling boredom can be withstood, there are to be found a ferocious humour, an hypnotic poetry and an overall sense of undeviating bleak honesty.

Beckett has been until now an unhonoured genius. He has had to wait for fame with the fatalism with which his tramps waited for Godot.

As the overdue acknowledgment now swells to world scale I suspect that Beckett is shrinking back from it at a corresponding rate—retiring to his last ditch.

5. From the *Daily Mail,* March 8, 1958. The article illustrates how firmly entrenched Beckett's public image was by 1958. It represents Beckett as though he prefers failure to success, treating him as a character in one of his own plays or novels. Courtesy Associated Newspapers Ltd.

6. Beckett at the Closerie de Lilas, Paris with Sorel Etrog, Ayala and Samuel Zacks, and Francis Warner. Warner called the meeting to plan fund-raising and publicity for the Samuel Beckett Theatre at St. Peter's College, Oxford. *Daily Telegraph Supplement*, July 10, 1970. Published with permission of Francis Warner.

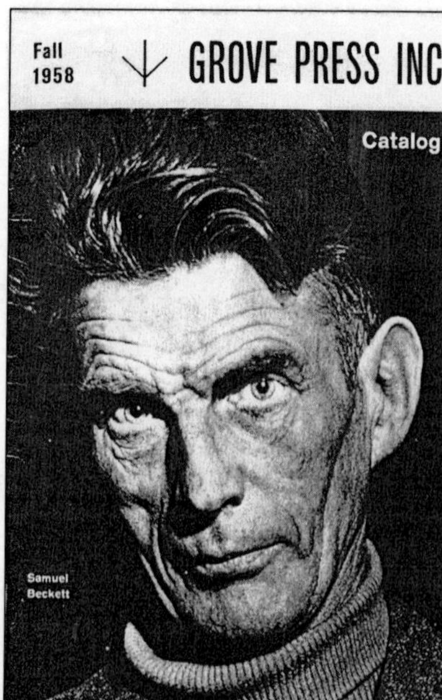

7. Cover of the fall 1958 Grove Press catalog. The photograph is by Brassai and is used courtesy of Corbis. The catalog cover is used with the permission of Grove/Atlantic Inc. and the Grove Press Records, Special Collections Research Center, Syracuse University Library.

8. The "floating head" photograph. Deliberately posed with a black background, Beckett wearing a black turtleneck, the photograph is the culmination of a series of head shots begun soon after Beckett signed with Lindon in 1951. Published with permission, John Haynes/Lebrecht Music & Arts Photo Library.

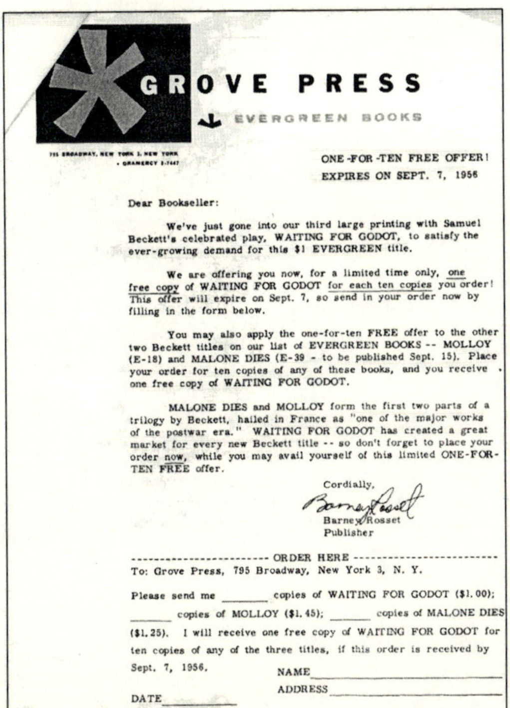

GROVE PRESS

EVERGREEN BOOKS

ONE-FOR-TEN FREE OFFER!
EXPIRES ON SEPT. 7, 1956

Dear Bookseller:

We've just gone into our third large printing with Samuel Beckett's celebrated play, WAITING FOR GODOT, to satisfy the ever-growing demand for this $1 EVERGREEN title.

We are offering you now, for a limited time only, one free copy of WAITING FOR GODOT for each ten copies you order! This offer will expire on Sept. 7, so send in your order now by filling in the form below.

You may also apply the one-for-ten FREE offer to the other two Beckett titles on our list of EVERGREEN BOOKS -- MOLLOY (E-18) and MALONE DIES (E-39 - to be published Sept. 15). Place your order for ten copies of any of these books, and you receive one free copy of WAITING FOR GODOT.

MALONE DIES and MOLLOY form the first two parts of a trilogy by Beckett, hailed in France as "one of the major works of the postwar era." WAITING FOR GODOT has created a great market for every new Beckett title -- so don't forget to place your order now, while you may avail yourself of this limited ONE-FOR-TEN FREE offer.

Cordially,
Barney Rosset
Barney Rosset
Publisher

------------------------ ORDER HERE ------------------------
To: Grove Press, 795 Broadway, New York 3, N. Y.

Please send me ______ copies of WAITING FOR GODOT ($1.00); ______ copies of MOLLOY ($1.45); ______ copies of MALONE DIES ($1.25). I will receive one free copy of WAITING FOR GODOT for ten copies of any of the three titles, if this order is received by Sept. 7, 1956.

NAME ______________________
ADDRESS ______________________
DATE __________

9. This promotional offer to booksellers for the Grove editions of *Godot, Malone Dies,* and *Molloy* gives a sense of Rosset's aggressive approach to the marketing of Beckett's texts in the United States. Used with permission of Grove/Atlantic Inc. and the Grove Press Records, Special Collections Research Center, Syracuse University Library.

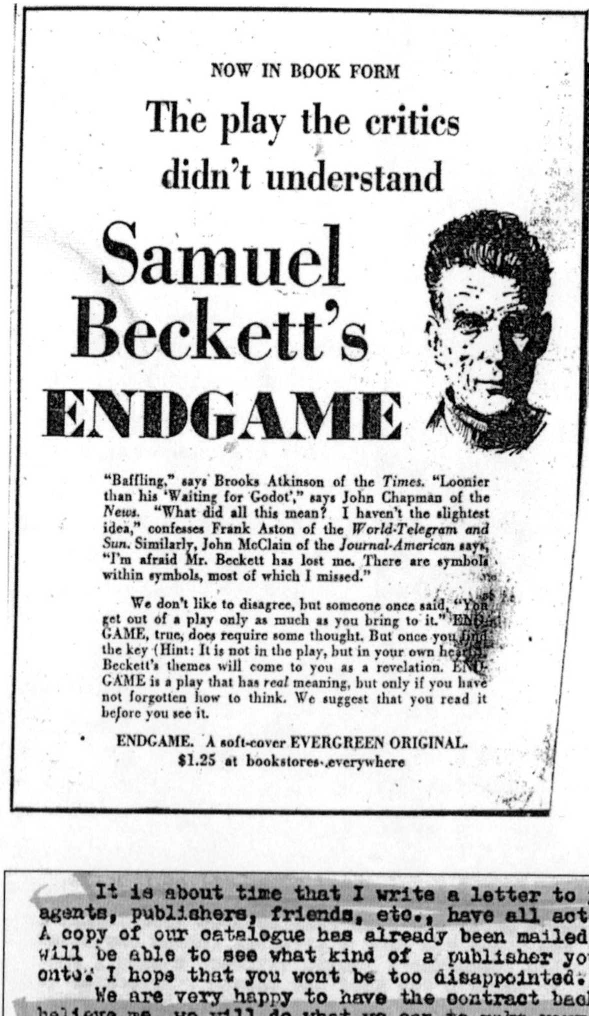

10. This advertisement, used in the *New York Times* and other newspapers in February 1958, appeals to anti-intellectual intellectuals. Text and image used courtesy of Grove/Atlantic Inc. and the Grove Press Records, Special Collections Research Center, Syracuse University Library.

It is about time that I write a letter to you - now that agents, publishers, friends, etc., have all acted as go-betweens. A copy of our catalogue has already been mailed to you, so you will be able to see what kind of a publisher you have been latched onto. I hope that you wont be too disappointed.

We are very happy to have the contract back from MINUIT, and believe me, we will do what we can to make your work known in this country.

Sylvia Beach is certainly the one you must blame for your future appearance on the Grove Press list. I went to see her with your work on my mind, and after she talked of you in beautiful words I immediately decided that what the Grove Press needed most in the world was Samuel Beckett. I told her that, and then she suggested that I make a specific offer. I certainly had not thought of that up to the very moment she took out a piece of paper and pencil and prepared to write down the terms.

11. Barney Rosset's first letter to Beckett on June 18, 1953, expresses his commitment to promote the author and clarifies the role of Sylvia Beach in making contact between Rosset and Beckett. Used with permission of Barney Rosset and the Grove Press Records, Special Collections Research Center, Syracuse University Library.

JMC/AM

Samuel Beckett, Esq.,
38, Bld. St.Jacques,
PARIS 14e.

29th June, 1966.

Dear Sam,

Thank you for your letter of the 21st July from Italy. I hope you are having good weather and able to swim a bit.

Very pleased with the news of the Nouvelles and Assez. I think we should leave Imagination Dead Imagine out of this one and put in the Three Nouvelles, From An Abandoned Work and Assez, and presuming that we can reprint in about two years, then collect them altogether with any other short work you have done in the meantime. Imagination is picking up a steady but not spectacular sale and we do have quite a lot.

You will be interested to hear that the 3 guinea special copies of Poems in English are now changing hands at 20 guineas a time between dealers. We have also sold quite a number of the How It Is recently in both the vellum and goatskin editions. By the end of the year we may be sold out of these and have them going up in value.

The specials of Imagination arenot yet bound due to technical difficulties.

My idea for the 'reader', subject to your approval, would be the following:-

1. the first Duthuit Dialogue.
2. one chapter of Murphy.
3. one chapter of Watt.
4. two extracts from Molloy (first part) and one from the second part.
5. extract from Malone Dies.
6. two extracts from The Unnamable.
7. an extract from Godot (subject to Faber's approval).
8. an extract from Endgame.
9. " " Embers.
10. Cascando (the poem).
11. one extract from How It Is.

not necessarily in that order, and I would like to include Dante and the Lobster if you would let me, which has already appeared in the Evergreen Review, but there is, however, no rush about this and I can discuss it with you the next time I come to Paris.

Bettina has just gone to Italy herself and is in Elba with the baby. She starts rehearsals on the 13th July for her Brecht which she is doing in Edinburgh and London, and immediately after rehearsals start for Lorca.

P.T.O.

12. Letter from John Calder to "Sam" dated June 29, 1966. The letter suggests Beckett's ongoing interest in his literary affairs during his vacations. It also shows Beckett's involvement in the production of Calder's collection, *A Samuel Beckett Reader* (1967). Used with permission of John Calder.

As for how the play is doing - I thought the Myerberg letter of May 1 would give you a good indication of it - anyway I am enclosing another copy. You will note that the total owed to the author's share (50% XXX to you, 40% Lindon, 10% me) comes to $2588.69 as of April 28th. I received my XXXXXXXXX $258.56 from Myerberg and I take it that your money was also sent off at the same time, but to whom I do not know - maybe Curtis Brown. The first full week grossed about $15000.00 , according to variety - the week the author's share came to XXX $1200.67, and the following week it grossed $16,000.00. This week is not represented on the Myerberg letter, nor the weeks which followed it, but it means that the author's share is running at well over $1000.00 a week, or more than $500.00 a week to you. This should continue as long as the play lasts, although of course it may tail off at the end. Does this clarify things for you. If it does not - ask questions, and if it does life the fog, tell me that too.

On the dollar Godot - we have sold over XXXX 6000 copies and a new printing of 5000 is due in today - we have unfilled orders for about 2000 copies, and I have ordered another 5000 printing to avoid another running out. Unfortunately all these royalty payments are supposed to go through that %$#"#$% Saunders. If you need mmney before the payments are due (in July), I will certainly advance you what you want.

We typed YELLOW out of your MORE PRICKS THAN KICKS and sold it to NEW WORLD WRITING for $128.00. I "neglected" to tell them that it had been published before until they were well hooked and so they said they would keep it even never before had they done such a thing. If it is all right with you I will deduct $28.00 from the price for our labor in typing XX the manuscript and our general all around ingenuity and zip on the $100.00 to you as soon as it enters our door. I also promised that Chatto and Windus did not own the story. If they should ever say they do , my head will be bloody.

13. This letter, dated May 18, 1956, expresses Rosset's excitement about the profits from the first New York run of *Godot* and from sales of the paperback version of the play. Used with permission of Barney Rosset and the Grove Press Records, Special Collections Research Center, Syracuse University Library.

July 3, 1956

Mr. Samuel Beckett
6 rue des Favorites
Paris, XV, France

Dear Sam:

According to reports received by me from Michael Myerberg the following sums are due you for the six week run:

$1474.40	week ending June 9, 1956
860.21	" " June 2, 1956
852.60	" " May 26, 1956
1137.22	" " May 19, 1956
2583.14	weeks ending May 12th and May 5, 1956
$6901.51	Total

I received a check for $656.39 covering everything due me through the last week of production, ending June 9th.

Best,

BR:js

Barney Rosset

14. A letter dated July 3, 1956, from Rosset to Beckett. Used with permission of Barney Rosset and the Grove Press Records, Special Collections Research Center, Syracuse University Library.

ROYALTY STATEMENT

Week Ending	Box Office Gross		5-7½-10% Author's Share	2½% Independent's share
5/5/56	$15,911.80		$1,266.18	$397.79
5/12/56	18,178.60		1,492.86	454.46
			$2,759.04	$852.25
Less balance of Royalty Advance				71.53
				$780.72
Due to Author			$2,759.04	
10% of Royalty due to author to be paid to Grove Press		$275.90		
Less payment made by Author to Grove Press on original Royalty advance		100.00		
Balance due Grove Press			175.90	
Balance due Author			$2,583.14	

Author	$2,583.14
Independent	780.72
Grove Press	175.90

15. This royalty statement accompanied the May 18, 1956, letter from Rosset to Beckett. It shows the profit Beckett made from *Godot* during the weeks before and after the Shenker interview was published in the *New York Times*. There is a 15 percent "bump" in box office profits. Used with permission of Barney Rosset and the Grove Press Records, Special Collections Research Center, Syracuse University Library.

5

A Room of His Own, 1945–1950

Hope is a knave befools us evermore,
Which till I lost no happiness was mine.
I strike from hell's to grave on heaven's door:
All hope abandon ye who enter in.

—Beckett's translation of a maxim by Sébastien Chamfort, *Collected Poems*

Capitalizing on the Ruins

Beckett's primary concern when he stopped off in London en route to Dublin after the fall of Berlin on May 9, 1945, was to find a publisher for *Watt;* even though he told his friends he wasn't particularly satisfied with the book and thought of it as a "joke," he would persist until the novel was published in 1953 (Harvey 1970, 222). While Ackerley and Gontarski suggest he "Finished manuscript of *Watt* on December 28," 1944 (2004, xxiii), we know from a May 10, 1945, letter to Gwynned Reavey that he was still working on the manuscript during his first postwar visit to Ireland in mid-May 1945: the letter describes his efforts to edit the book for publication (HRHRC). He sent the manuscript to T. M. Ragg at Routledge in late May 1945. In less than two weeks, on June 6, 1945, Ragg expressed his profound confusion in response to a manuscript he thought too erratic and unstructured to stand any chance of being published (Knowlson 1996, 311). But, true to the fighting spirit characteristic of his attitude since he moved to Paris, two weeks after the rejection Beckett was back in the saddle, as determined as ever to advance his career. He asked Reavey for professional advice about literary agents, specifically asking him to find agents who were young and energetic (June 20, 1945, HRHRC). The compulsion to publish *Watt* is apparent from Beckett's efforts to publish the novel *after* he had produced a major body of work in French and after he had secured the comprehensive professional services of Jérôme Lindon in 1951 (June 2,

1952, HRHRC). In 1953 he made the rather surprising decision to engage a group of young publishers—referred to as "the Merlin juveniles" in Beckett studies—to publish *Watt.* As we conclude our consideration of Beckett's professional life in the period before he became famous we must ask why Beckett was so keen to publish an unfinished, less than satisfactory text with an inexperienced company.

To me, his desire to publish the novel, despite his substantiated prediction that the inexperienced Merlin group at Olympia Press would make a mess of it, suggests he wished to call attention to the period in the development of his authorial persona between the death of Joyce and the end of German rule in Europe. If he had not published *Watt,* this period would have remained obscure. The pressure to earn money, which had motivated him in the years before the war and in its immediate aftermath, was no longer decisive by the time *Watt* came out in a bad edition in June 1953. As his April 16, 1953, letter to Manning Howe suggests (HRHRC), he was no longer desperate for money (though the letter makes explicit his desire to earn as much money as possible). There was, then, something special about *Watt,* about its place in the series of texts he had been producing since the early 1930s. Specifically, the novel established a decipherable context for his approach, allowing readers to trace his authorial development from the period when he was enmeshed in Joyce's approach to the period when he would become famous in his own right. *Watt* appeared six months after the breakthrough Paris production of *En attendant Godot,* a couple of weeks after he began to negotiate a long-term contract with Grove Press. This contract, drafted with Sylvia Beach in May 1953 and completed in June, enabled him to disseminate his public image in an international forum. *Watt* gave historical coherence to this image.

Even as Beckett plunged into his writing after the war, he kept an eye on the marketplace, making contact with Reavey as he passed through London in spring 1946. An entry in Reavey's diary on April 9, 1946, notes "Sam from Paris"; one for April 15 notes "Sam stays" (HRHRC). That business remained central to their relationship is evident from a letter Beckett wrote from Dublin on May 27, 1946, commenting on the manuscript's travels from publisher to publisher (HRHRC). Reavey's involvement in the effort to publish *Watt* is documented in his diary for June 15, 1946: "I. P. Watt—Cambridge." While Watt was acting as an official agent, Reavey negotiated on Beckett's behalf in England. Within a few days of this meeting, on June 19, 1946, Beckett wrote to Reavey agreeing to contribute something to

Documents, a Paris-based journal run by Georges Bataille and Carl Einstein, because he needed cash, indicating he wanted Reavey to act as his agent as he worked to publish *Watt* (HRHRC). On June 25, 1946, he wrote thanking Reavey for his efforts to find a publisher for the novel, flattering him by suggesting he was the one person who could get it in print. Over a year later, on August 15, 1947, he thanked Reavey once more for getting the manuscript in circulation, commenting that the driving force behind his effort to get it published was his need for money (HRHRC). Indeed, he suggests money is his only interest, echoing what he would tell Manning Howe in June 1953 about the first Broadway run of *Godot* (HRHRC). In an effort to boost the chances he would sell the manuscript to a publisher, Beckett continued to play the game of literary marketing behind the scenes: in the August 15, 1946, letter, trying to clinch a deal with Hodge, Beckett returned to the kinds of trickery he had counseled Reavey to use when he was trying to publish *Murphy* (HRHRC). He advises him to tell a white lie by saying Beckett was planning to return to English as a language of creation in the very near future. As he puts it in the letter, this possibility was extremely remote; but Beckett knew he could bait the hook with the prospect of future English-language publications. By November 18, 1946, Reavey had sent a letter announcing Hodge's rejection of *Watt*—in his reply Beckett claims he predicted as much, taking the news in his stride by turning toward his successes: he points out he has just completed a novella in French and has just published the French translation of *Murphy.* By December 1948 Beckett had had enough (HRHRC). On December 8 he asked Reavey to withdraw the manuscript from the publishers' circuit, returning the copy to him so he could take another look (HRHRC).

Although Beckett and Reavey stayed in touch until Reavey's death in 1971, Reavey's role as Beckett's literary agent was much reduced after the war. Like McGreevy's role as a trusted confidant, Reavey's part in Beckett's professional life had been compromised by Beckett's move to Paris; Reavey would have nothing to do with the publication of his books after the failed efforts with *Watt.* On December 15, 1946, Beckett wrote a note of professional farewell, thanking Reavey for everything he had done to help advance his professional career but informing him his services were no longer required when it came to future texts in French and English (HRHRC). Pierre Bordas had taken on the responsibility for his professional affairs and would function as his centralized business office, his literary agency, and his publisher (HRHRC). Bordas had contracted, in the first place, to publish a French translation of *Murphy*. It is thus clear that Reavey's involvement in Beckett's work would be restricted to those written in English before December 1946. And it is also clear Beckett understood the contract to mean Bordas would act as his agent on the English contract for *Murphy:* Beckett notes Routledge had paid him twenty pounds, less income tax, and he imagined he might be owed a little more money if the edition had sold out, as they seemed to indicate (HRHRC). Now, going into 1947, he assumed he could get Bordas to deal with Routledge, allowing him to write without worrying about contractual negotiations and the nitty-gritty business of the publishing industry. In case there was any doubt that Reavey's role was now secondary, and then tertiary, when Beckett made his move toward fame in the postwar period, a letter from February 21, 1959, responds to a request from Reavey for material not already covered by Beckett's American, British, and French contracts; he tells Reavey there is nothing available and nothing forthcoming, detailing his plan to withhold *Eleutheria* and *Mercier et Camier* (HRHRC).

Beckett's war was not over until December 1945, when he decided not to continue in his role as an interpreter and storekeeper for the Irish Red Cross in St. Lô, Normandy. Toward the end of his stint he told McGreevy he was beginning to feel trapped and needed to free himself soon if he were to make something of himself (December 21, 1945, TCD, 173). What he learned from the experience of the war and its aftermath is evident from "The Capital of the Ruins," an essay written and recorded for Radio Erin. It is dated June 10, 1946, but was not broadcast at the time and remained in the RTE vaults until 1983; it was first published in Eoin O'Brien's *Beckett Country* (1986, 333–37) and also appeared that year in John Calder's tribute for Beckett's eightieth birthday, *As No Other Dare Fail* (1986). After a journalistically succinct description of how "the Hospital of the Irish Red Cross in Saint-Lô" was set up, including details about its heating system, furniture, and "the number of in-patients," Beckett turns to "that smile at the human condition as little to be extinguished by bombs as to be broadened by the elixirs of Burroughes and Welcome" (Calder 1986, 73–74). As he moves toward his conclusion he notes that "'Provisional' is not the term it was, in this universe become provisional" (75); he thus provides a prosaic preface to a body of work punctuated by the word "perhaps." His conclusion is a sober reflection on the lessons learned: "those who were in Saint-Lô will come home realizing that they got at least as good as they gave, . . . a vision and sense of a time-honoured conception of humanity in ruins, and perhaps even an inkling of the terms in which our condition is to be thought again" (76).

In an unusually direct analysis of the problems of postwar reconstruction, Beckett reveals the extent to which he was in tune with the "provisional" spirit of the age: he would devote the rest of his life as a professional writer to the effort to express "perhaps even an inkling of the terms in which our condition is to be thought again."

After finishing his contractual obligations to the Irish Red Cross, completing a six-month term of civic duty helping to reconstruct St. Lô, Beckett settled into a writing routine he would sustain until January 1950, when he finished *L'Innommable*. His output was intense. Facilitated by Dumesnil and initially supported by his contract with Bordas, this routine was wonderfully conducive to his professional well-being; in less than nine months he managed to write an important short story, "La Fin," and an equally important novella, *Mercier et Camier*. Begun on February 17, 1946, "Suite" was published in July 1946 as "La Fin" in *Les Temps modernes*, edited by Simone de Beauvoir and Sartre. While "La Fin" was being edited in May 1946, he wrote "The Capital of the Ruins." The groove he was in is evident: even though a controversy erupted over the publication of the short story (de Beauvoir refused to publish the second half of the story, claiming Beckett had submitted the first half as a complete work), Beckett had already begun *Mercier et Camier* before the first part of "La Fin" was published. Nothing could derail him: he wrote during his trips to Ireland and he wrote during his vacations with Suzanne. Between July 5 and October 3, 1946, he devoted his energies to the completion of his first long prose text in French and, before the year was out, wrote three further stories in French at the rate of one per month, "L'Expulsé" in October, "Premiere amour" in November, and "Le Calmant" in December. Further, on and off through 1946 he reworked his French translation of *Murphy* and, in December 1946, signed a contract for its publication.

As we gauge how Beckett established a prominent place in the French literary marketplace, thus opening the way to America, Britain and the Commonwealth, and Europe and beyond, it is tempting to ask who discovered Beckett. James Knowlson is unequivocal: "the real credit for discovering Beckett as a French writer must go to the young débutant publisher Jérôme Lindon" (342). In doing so, he rightly removes Tom McGreevy, George Reavey, and Pierre Bordas from the top of the list. But perhaps he overstates the case. We have already seen how Beckett's relationship with McGreevy tailed off after the move to Paris, but we should not underestimate his importance as a sounding board in the lead-up to the move. And, while

Reavey's role as a literary agent was vastly reduced in the postwar period, his work on *Echo's Bones* and *Murphy* helped prepare Beckett for the new phase in his career, giving him the confidence to commit himself to life as a professional writer. Pierre Bordas failed to follow through with a long-term commitment, but his decision to publish *Murphy* at Editions Nouvelles Françaises in December 1946 gave Beckett a boost at exactly the right time. In the context of the constrained publishing industry in the wake of World War II, Bordas's commitment to a non-French author was bold. Any Paris-based printers and publishers who did not actively collaborate with the occupying forces suffered heavily from Gestapo destructiveness; those who did collaborate suffered from reprisals after the occupation. Few managed to walk the line between collaboration and resistance. Machinery and intact buildings of the necessary size were in short supply and thus expensive; so, too, were the basic materials of publishing—electricity, labor, paper, ink, glue, metal, printers' tools, photographic plates. Even though it was short-lived, the Bordas contract gave Beckett the freedom and the confidence to write what would turn out to be his career-defining work.

On January 4, 1948, he told McGreevy he had written himself to exhaustion, producing four novellas, two novels, and a play in less than two years. He lamented that the texts were falling on stony ground as far as publishers were concerned, but he was undeterred, devoting every waking moment to his job (TCD, 178). Seventeen months after he signed with Bordas, he wrote a further letter to McGreevy, echoing the line at the beginning of the second paragraph in *Molloy* by suggesting he was beginning to understand what he was doing and what he would do for the next decade. In the context of my argument about Beckett's understanding of himself as a professional writer, this letter is crucial because it clearly frames his writing in terms of work and getting a specific job accomplished, avoiding translations and teaching so he can focus on his own creative output, following his urge to write because he finally understands his own perspective as a writer (March 18 1948, TCD, 179). At this point he was actively writing *Malone meurt*. The reluctance, indifference, boredom, frustration, and desperation accompanying the creation of *Proust, More Pricks Than Kicks,* and *Murphy* have been transformed into a spirit of positive creativity he could envision as a ten-year vocation. He admits it is a strange feeling, but he senses he is making positive progress. He is optimistic about *Eleutheria* and can imagine it will eventually be produced on stage. The language of reluctance and desperation would return in subsequent letters, but Beckett could now project sufficient courage and energy to accomplish a clear mission. In this same letter he exclaims, with some amusement, that the French translation of *Murphy* had sold six copies. Again, this fact does not slow him down: optimism is apparent in the next sentence when he points to a very friendly appraisal in the French press. He is supremely self-confident, identifying the problem with sales of the French *Murphy* as a marketing failure rather than a failure of his novel, complaining at Bordas's unwillingness to do the basic job of a publicist by sending copies to reviewers (March 18, 1948, TCD, 179). In any event, Bordas lost faith in Beckett when it became apparent that the print run of 3,000 was selling very badly indeed: for the record, a total of 285 copies were sold up to May 1951. Bordas gave Beckett an advance of ten thousand francs for *Mercier et Camier* in January 1947 but did not follow through with publication; in January 1948 Bordas declined his option on *Molloy*, allowing Jacoba van Velde, aka Toni Clerkx, to shop it around as she saw fit (January 13, 1948, RUL)

The relief expressed in the December 15, 1946, letter to Reavey was, then, short lived; but the long-term effect on Beckett's professional career was indispensable. It is impossible to say what would have happened without the Bordas contract, and it is certain that George Reavey, Georges Duthuit, Roger Blin, Jérôme Lindon, Barney Rosset, and, to a lesser extent, John Calder, should each take some credit for "discovering" Beckett. But Bordas's contribution remains crucial. Between October 1946 and January 1948, the dates during which he was covered by the Bordas contract, Beckett successfully transformed the authorial persona he had invented with Samuel Johnson's help before his move to Paris into a series of marketable texts.

While it would be 1950 before the Minuit contract set him on the road to financial security, Beckett had already established a name for himself, in Paris anyway, in Georges Duthuit's reincarnation of *Transition*. In 1948 Duthuit, who had bought the name from Eugene Jolas in 1947, published French and English versions of "Trois Poemes/Three Poems." The poems are "my way is in the sand flowing"; "what would I do without this world faceless incurious"; and "I would like my love to die"; they are identical to the versions in *Collected Poems 1930–1978* and *The Grove Centenary Edition* with the exception of the last line of the last poem, which appears in *Transition 1948* as "pleurant la seule qui m'ait aimé / mourning the first and last to love me (96–97) and in *GCE IV* as "mourning her who thought she loved me" (41). *Transition* volume 5 in 1949 carried the essay Ruby Cohn would reprint in *Disjecta* as "Three Dialogues with Georges Duthuit" (Beckett 1984b, 138–45). In *Transition 1949* the piece followed an essay by

André Du Bouchet called "Three Exhibitions: Masson—Tal Coat—Miró" (89–95) and was accompanied by a series of reproductions of paintings by Masson, Miró, and Tal Coat; the volume includes six reproductions by Bram van Velde spanning 1929–49. As already noted, Beckett's essay appeared as "Three Dialogues: Tal Coat—Masson—Bram van Velde" (97–103). In this original publication it appeared with an appendix of "Some Sayings of Bram van Velde" (104), including the aestheticist mantra "Art conceived as a profession, what an abomination!" (104). In 1950 Duthuit published "Two Fragments" in *Transition,* volume 6, the first from Beckett's English translation of *Molloy* (from "I left the shelter of the doorway . . ." to "Egypt without bounds, without infant, without mother," *GCE II,* 59–61), the second constituting the entire first paragraph of the English version of *Malone Dies* (*GCE II,* 173–74).

Beckett's appearance in Duthuit's revamped version of *Transition* in 1948–50 associated his name with prominent French authors including Artaud, Bataille, Breton, Genet, Gide, Jouve, Malraux, Ponge, and Sartre. Beckett was beginning to get himself noticed in France by publishing texts using the experimental literary voice he had developed in Arsene's section of *Watt.* As we have seen, this voice emerged from the dismantling of a ragged assortment of narrative options. By the time Bordas baulked at *Molloy* (written in May to December 1947 and submitted in January 1948), Beckett was firmly ensconced in his situation as a full-time creative writer; he had written "La Fin," "Le Calmant," "Suite," and "Premiere amour," using the short story genre as a manageable and publishable venue in which to deploy his voice and persona, and he had written *Eleutheria* and *Mercier et Camier,* working out a dramatic, dialogue-based version of the style that would allow him to write *En attendant Godot* in October 1948 to January 1949. By the time Bordas officially pulled the plug, Beckett had completed *Molloy,* famously projecting his next two major projects at the beginning of the second paragraph (*GCE II,* 4). By the time he published *Molloy* it had become the antepenultimate novel in the series; in the January 4, 1948, letter to McGreevy he suggested *Molloy* was the penultimate text, the second to last in the series started with *Murphy* (TCD, 178). *Malone meurt* (written January to September 1948) was the logical continuation in the process of positive annihilation; and this process was to continue with *L'Innommable* (written February 1949 to June 1950).

The work produced during the intense period of creativity in 1946–50 has dominated discussions of Beckett's entire oeuvre. Called his "greatest creative period" by Cronin (1996, 358), this phase produced the texts for which Beckett would become internationally famous over the next two decades. It is why the attitude Beckett displayed toward the publishing industry in 1946–50 has shaped perceptions of his overall attitude toward commercial publishing. Bair, for example, suggests his "recalcitrance" and his "refusal to do anything to promote his book"—*Watt* in 1951—is linked to a "need for privacy . . . so obsessive that he could never allow himself to be put into a situation where strangers would have the right to invade it" (1990, 360). Beckett's need for privacy during a specific period of intense productivity has, then, been transformed into an unbending characteristic used to describe his entire career. Bair works hard to plant the idea the attitude displayed during this five-year stage was the result of a permanent quality rather than a pragmatic response to immediate circumstances. She tells us that, in the face of Suzanne's being "reluctant to see him closet himself away while nothing was being done to place finished work," Beckett was "adamant . . . and refused to do anything himself. He had admitted long ago that he hated to deal with publishers, and was only too happy to turn his affairs over to friends who enjoyed commercial interchange" (367). As we have seen, his ability to withdraw was made possible by the hard work, determination, and planning he had engaged in during the 1930s, particularly in 1936–39, when he was systematic in researching visual art (in Germany) and an authorial persona (through Johnson), and when he devoted himself to the establishment of a secure milieu in Paris, complete with a private study and a trusted domestic partner. From now on he could depend on a growing circle of intimate friends and professional acquaintances to advance his career, and, behind the scenes, he could continue to fight his way to commercial success.

Dumesnil's Crucial Role

Although it is premature to suggest Beckett's literary affairs were centralized after December 1946, his connection with the business of literary marketing changed radically during the period between 1946 and 1950. Bordas gave Beckett an advance of ten thousand francs, but lagging sales of the French edition of *Murphy* soured the relationship, and the rejection of *Mercier et Camier* sounded its death knell. Still, as the Reavey letter from December 1946 suggests, the contract gave Beckett a sense, however fleeting, of what it feels like to be a writer with a long-term contract for all future work in French and English (including translations) (Knowlson 1996, 328). Even though it did not work out as planned, the Bordas contract confirmed Beckett's status as a viable professional writer; a commitment beyond a single text when he felt he was working according to a definite ten-year plan was clearly exhilarating, and it allowed him to put distance between himself and his prewar contacts. This process was facilitated by Dumesnil's increased personal commitment to the job of making money out of Beckett's creative writing, a task fueled by the tedium of the other jobs they both did to eke out a living in postwar Paris. With Reavey's days as Beckett's primary literary agent done and dusted, and with Bordas playing a significant but relatively passive role, Beckett was dependent on Dumesnil for personal and professional support. In short, once Bordas dropped Beckett, declining the option on *Mercier et Camier* in 1947 and refusing *Molloy* in January 1948, Dumesnil became Beckett's informal literary agent. From January 1948 to October 1950, while Beckett wrote two long novels and his first major play, she was not only his constant, trusted confidante and companion, helping him as he developed a fluent voice as a French author, but she also functioned as an agent, traipsing around Paris hand-delivering manuscripts to potential publishers.

Beckett and Dumesnil are intermingled in death: he followed her to the grave within six months of her death in July 1989 and, as he wished, his body lies beside hers in the Cimetière du Montparnasse. This postdeath intermingling reinforces the intricate weaving of their lives. Dumesnil was instrumental in helping transform Beckett from a struggling writer desperate to be published at almost any price into a writer famous for his indifference to money and success. Perhaps Dumesnil's most important, most sustained and sustaining contribution to Beckett's career as a writer is the environment of domestic stability and personal privacy she helped create. This environment was particularly difficult to achieve in the years immediately following World War II, when every social transaction was complicated by wartime damage and the process of recovery. Much has been made of Beckett's description of their budding relationship on April 18, 1939, because he used the word "dispassionately" (TCD, 168). This has led Bair to characterize her, rather disdainfully, as a "surrogate mother" who "devoted her life to filling his every need, from providing food and doing laundry to acting as his literary agent and even, for a short time, financial provider" (1990, 281). Bair certainly describes roles Dumesnil played in her life with Beckett, but her characterization is misleading, making it seem as though Dumesnil were little more than a matronly maid-servant. She was, in fact, a highly intelligent, well-respected woman and an author in her own right. Dumesnil published a teaching text, *Musique Jeux* (1935) and contributed a decent short story, "F—," to *Transition 1948*. Knowlson and Cronin are more accurate than Bair when, respectively, they point to "the thoughtful, calm, caring side of Suzanne" (Knowlson 1996, 271–72) and "Suzanne's humanizing, calming and reassuring effect" (Cronin 1996, 300). Less focused on Beckett's need for a mollycoddling mother, Knowlson and Cronin characterize Dumesnil as a steady, decent, trustworthy friend who provided intellectual companionship along with her more mundane contributions.

As I have begun to suggest, this more complex description of Dumesnil's role in Beckett domestic and professional life gains credence in light of events in 1939 to 1945. Beckett's famous commitment to France at war over Ireland at peace was carefully thought out in the lead-up to Germany's invasion of Poland, and it is directly connected with his commitment to Dumesnil: he knew a return to Ireland would derail his efforts to achieve independence, and he knew he could survive wartime France with Dumesnil at his side. On April 18, 1939, he told McGreevy he planned to serve in France if there were a war, invoking Dumesnil as a key factor. Having begun the letter by saying he had just turned thirty-three and was wondering if the remaining years would be any better than those already gone, he mentions Dumesnil and implies she has brought a significant improvement to his perception of life (*Letters*, 655–57). Again, the effort to determine why Beckett chose to commit himself to France is as quixotic as the effort to determine why he began writing in French in 1938. But in light of his apparent indifference about his destination when he decided to leave Ireland for good in September 1937, his absolute commitment to France in April 1939 surely reflects considerations other than national allegiance. After all, the thrust of his public life and professional work is decidedly transnational: during the war he would work for a cell of the French underground organized by the British Intelligence service; after it, he would work for the Irish Red Cross rebuilding a town in Brittany; his first publishing contracts after the war were with French companies, Bordas and Les Editions de Minuit, but by the mid-1950s his negotiations involved companies in England, Germany, Italy, Ireland, Spain, and the United States, and his language of creation would, after 1955, shift from English to French and back, with the occasional text written in German. First publications and premieres occurred in England, France, Germany, and the United States. Throughout, his two most consistent commitments were to his career as a writer and to Suzanne Georgette Anna Deschevaux-Dumesnil.

Because of the closeness of Beckett and Dumesnil there is no correspondence or any other direct record of what she did to promote his work, but we can be certain she was much more important to his professional life than Bair suggests when she describes their domestic relationship: "she began to sew to augment their meager income" and "she catered to all his comforts, seeing that he had food, clean laundry and linen" (1990, 357). We get a sense of Dumesnil's professional role when Bair describes her as "his agent," noting that "In the fall [of 1947] she took *Eleutheria* from Clerkx and followed it through the remainder of its peregrinations until Beckett withdrew it from consideration. It was Suzanne who tried to persuade Bordas to bring out *Mercier et Camier*. . . . On a more mundane level, it was Suzanne who called for and returned the translations" (367). Mundane or not, Dumesnil's work was crucial. By Bair's account she took the script of *Godot* to "commercial producers" and then to Blin (398). Bair's mention of commerce reminds us that, to date, all but a few discussions of Beckett's connection with commerce have been put in the context of his nonchalance toward publicity and publishers. One notable exception is Stephen Brown's "Fail Better! Samuel Beckett's Secrets of Business and Branding Success" in the March–April 2006 issue of *Business Horizons*. Brown argues that

> despite his anti-business reputation, Samuel Beckett is a perfect role model for our paradoxical times. His "fail better" philosophy is very much in keeping with today's creativity-driven, hyper-competitive, warp-speed world of fads, fashions, and here-today-gone-tomorrow consumer crazes. This article argues that, in a world where every organization is customer oriented and every executive is au fait with best textbook practice, Beckett's idiosyncratic esthetic encapsulates several salient secrets of business and branding success. (2006, 161)

Brown's argument marks a unique departure from the received understanding of Beckett's relationship with business and marketing. More typical is Bair's description of his attitude toward Dumesnil's effort to find a producer for *Godot:* "When [Dumesnil] asked Beckett if she should take the script to Blin, he shrugged nonchalantly" (1990, 398). This color commentary, describing a gesture that would only have been seen by Dumesnil, parallels Bair's description of her "stricken" face when she received the phone call about his Nobel award (604); it imposes a received understanding of Beckett's authorial image onto a private scene. It is just as unlikely Dumesnil would have described Beckett's gesture to anyone as he would have been to describe "a stricken look on her face." Bair's earlier statement, "he hated to deal with publishers and was only too happy to turn his affairs over to friends who enjoyed commercial interchange; as for himself, he preferred privacy" (367), is part of the same received understanding. As we have begun to see, the facts complicate this largely unquestioned public image: in the 1930s Beckett had a full calendar of appointments with publishers; in 1951–85 he sat for a series of professional photo sessions; in the same period he engaged in extensive and protracted correspondence with Jérôme Lindon, Barney Rosset, and other professional acquaintances; throughout, he was willing to assist in decisions about the packaging of trade editions and the production of limited editions and *livres d'artiste,* often making direct interventions in public representations of himself and his work (as is suggested by Calder's request for Beckett's "approval" in fig. 12).

Dumesnil's contribution was, then, personal and professional, giving Beckett the luxury to ignore what Bair calls the "mundane" aspects of life. Or, rather, by taking care of the domestic economy while giving him quiet advice about French idiom and hawking his literary efforts around the city, Dumesnil allowed Beckett to concentrate on the production and refinement of the raw material necessary to his long-term prospects as a professional writer. While the population of Paris was dealing with the disruptions and uncertainties inherent in a society recovering from a devastating war and a prolonged occupation, Dumesnil made it possible for Beckett to settle into the routines of his profession. After he finished his work at St. Lô in December 1945, and after a trip to see his mother and brother in Ireland, Beckett returned to the apartment on the Rue des Favorites he had shared with Dumesnil since 1939. For the next five years he would engage in what a number of people have referred to as "The Siege in the Room": Bair cites Maurice Sinclair, John Montague, and Jack MacGowran as sources for the title of her chapter; this suggests to me that the phrase comes from Beckett, making it another piece of circumstantial evidence pointing to his self-fashioning (1990, 687). Knowlson is original in calling the period "A Frenzy of Writing" (1996, 323). Throughout, Dumesnil would provide financial, domestic, and professional support: as Beckett wrote to McGreevy on January 4, 1948, it was impossible for him to survive on his small allowance from home, but he had no interest in tutoring students or doing translations. During this period, the two of them were almost entirely dependent on Beckett's inheritance and Suzanne's income from piano lessons and dressmaking (TCD, 175).

When she was not earning money by sewing clothes or giving piano lessons, and when she was not soothing Beckett during his moments of frustration, providing homeopathic remedies for his various bodily ailments, or giving casual advice about his use of French (Mania Péron eventually became Beckett's official source of advice on French usage), Dumesnil was shopping for bargains and waiting in lines for bread, vegetables, and other basic household commodities. It is likely she was also responsible for finding the commodities essential to Beckett's trade: paper and ink, typewriter ribbons and carbon paper. These supplies were in desperately short supply well into the 1950s. This important work of domestic, social, and professional sustenance was Dumesnil's most persistent contribution to his professional career after the war; in short, her hard work and conscientious planning allowed Beckett to continue writing with few distractions in the most severe material circumstances. For example, on November 24, 1947, he described his awful living conditions, noting how his marginal status made every transaction doubly difficult, but he went on to brag that he had just completed the manuscript of another book, *Molloy* (TCD, 174). By this point, Dumesnil had begun to play a role even more directly supportive of Beckett's professional life. Clearly, Beckett and Dumesnil understood each other so profoundly that he craved her company. In a letter Beckett wrote to MacGreevy on August 19, 1945, Beckett suggests the strength of their bond, revealing the extent to which he associated her with the tranquility necessary for composition, wishing he could have stayed home with her instead of being stuck in St. Lô (TCD, 172). In May 1946 Toni Clerkx made a hash of negotiations with *Les Temps modernes* over the publication of "Suite" (which became "La Fin" and, later, "The End"). Beckett turned to Dumesnil. From May 1946 until the end of October 1946, she promoted his texts by carrying them around Paris, walking them from one publishing office to another, doing her utmost to sell his work.

Dumesnil's first success came in 1946, when she convinced Bordas to publish the French *Murphy* (Nov 24, 1947, TCD, 174); when Bordas lost interest, declining to publish the second text she gave him, *Mercier et Camier,* she went back to work. While Clerkx remained active, corresponding with Bordas about potential publications, it is clear Dumesnil did the legwork, especially after Bordas rejected *Molloy* in January 1948, effectively dropping Beckett. She persisted until October 1950, getting manuscripts in the hands of a number of editors and publishers including Robert Carlier, Max-Pol Fouchet, A. C. Gervais, Maurice Nadeau, and Tristan Tzara: these important players in the world of Paris publishing would have been familiar with Beckett's name through his association with Joyce and through his recent publications in *Transition;* they provided vital links to the indigenous publishing industry. At the same time, Dumesnil shopped the texts of *Eleutheria* and *En attendant Godot,* arranging the March 1950 meeting between Beckett and Roger Blin and, thus, setting up the January 3, 1953, premiere of *Godot* at the Théâtre de Babylone. A few months after the meeting with Blin, Carlier passed the manuscript of *Molloy* on to Georges Lambrichs at Les Editions de Minuit. Lambrichs passed it along to Jérôme Lindon. The day after Lindon first saw the manuscript, reading it on the Metro on the way home and almost losing the manuscript in a gust of wind at a station (a detail repeated so often it has become part of Beckett's received mystique because it underscores the part played by chance), Dumesnil sat in the office at Minuit to discuss terms for publishing *Molloy, Malone meurt,* and *L'Innommable.* Dumesnil had set up the deal but she was obviously out of her depth; at the next meeting she was accompanied by Toni Clerkx. Lindon had already drawn up the contracts, and Dumesnil took them back to Beckett, presumably passing along Clerkx's professional advice. Contracts were signed on November 15, 1950. Beckett's career was officially launched and, while Blin and Lindon must be credited with the vision to appreciate Beckett's potential, neither would have had the chance to develop this appreciation had it not been for Dumesnil.

We can develop a fuller appreciation of Dumesnil's contribution to Beckett's professional career by contemplating her social position: she was a well-respected musician from an upper-middle-class background who had risked her life to help liberate France. Beckett's name in Paris before the war was, of course, associated with the expatriate circle surrounding Joyce, Shakespeare and Company, *Transition,* and other English-language publications; he was part of a transient immigrant group with tenuous connections to indigenous French culture. His only work translating a text into French, the first part of Joyce's "Anna Livia Plurabelle," had been as part of a team, and his participation had been displaced by writers with deeper connections to French culture (Paul Leon, Adrienne Monnier, Philippe Soupault). While his work with the Maquis had certainly given him street credibility, and anyone who knew he had been awarded the Croix de Guerre would have taken notice, he was essentially unknown in French literary circles when he settled back into Paris life in 1946, which explains why he reconnected with *Transition,* still a predominantly English-language journal even though it was now edited by a Frenchman, Georges Duthuit. Again, we should not underestimate the professional benefits gained from Beckett's visits to the offices of Duthuit because he came into contact with an important network of French writers, but neither should we overlook the distinct advantages to be gained when the person delivering his manuscripts was well connected, well respected, and French.

Dumesnil's role as an intermediary between Beckett's private and professional lives was relatively short-lived because, largely as a result of her work, first Bordas, then Minuit, Grove, and Calder and Boyars stepped in to manage his literary affairs. Along the way, again as a result of her efforts, Roger Blin became one of Beckett's greatest champions. But the way she played the role underscores the fact that he achieved international fame and commercial success because others were prepared to advocate his cause while allowing him to remain in the background, making it possible for him to maintain his apparent indifference to fame and money even as he achieved both. I am not interested in second guessing whether or not Beckett would have become internationally known and financially secure were it not for Tom McGreevy, James Joyce, George Reavey, Pierre Bordas, Toni Clerkx, and, most important, Suzanne Dumesnil. Nor am I proposing he would have remained an obscure Joycean were it not for Jérôme Lindon, Barney Rosset, and John Calder. But these nine names form an important narrative backdrop to Beckett's literary career. Without McGreevy's letter of introduction, Beckett would have been very unlikely to have met Joyce in 1929, Nancy Cunard and Richard Aldington in 1930, and Charles Prentice in 1931; these contacts led to his first publications in *transition*, the publication of *Whoroscope*, and the contract with Chatto and Windus for *Proust* and *More Pricks Than Kicks*. Reavey published *Echo's Bones* and found a publisher for *Murphy;* Bordas gave Beckett a window of opportunity in which he could function as a professional writer; Clerkx arranged for the publication of Beckett's first publications after World War II; and, as I have suggested, Dumesnil did the legwork to initiate the first production of *Godot* and the publication of *Molloy, Malone meurt,* and *L'Innommable*. The stage was set for Beckett's career to take off once his work was in the hands of Lindon, Rosset, and Calder.

6

Relaxing into Fame

Contracts and Agreements, 1950–1956

> Moins d'un mois après la parution de son premiere roman, la critique unanime salue l'apparition d'un grand écrivain français.
>
> —Editions de Minuit advertisement, 1951

> Believe me, we will do what we can to make your work known in this country.
>
> —Rosset to Beckett, June 18, 1953

Five Steps to Sustainable Fame

Beckett's postwar rise to fame took place in five main stages, moving him from a position of dependence on prewar acquaintances who were keen but not always competent, mainly Clerkx, Dumesnil, McGreevy, and Reavey, to a much more comfortable situation in which he was surrounded by a network of trusted, highly capable professionals who would do their utmost to make his work known. Between 1946 and 1956 he built a viable career as a professional writer, making agreements and signing contracts sufficient and substantial enough to sustain him and Dumesnil for life and his beneficiaries for generations to come. By the end of this period, with the fifth stage of development, he would prove the sustainability of the success of *Godot* by writing subsequent marketable texts. More important, perhaps, during this period he deployed strategies for engaging with the literary marketplace compatible with his private needs, his personal situation (with friends and family), and his authorial persona. Beckett's correspondence during the period attests to an ongoing struggle with physical and mental tiredness, personal commitments to Dumesnil and others, an increasingly complex set of contractual obligations, and a pressing need to find peace to write new work. By fall 1953 he was finally reaping what he had sown, spending mornings translating *Molloy* into English with Patrick Bowles, getting ready to work on the German translation of *Molloy,* and spending afternoons and evenings, sometimes as late as midnight, helping with rehearsals for *Godot*. He was, however, a persistent complainer: he moaned about the contracts cramping his style and his custom-built country retreat causing too much trouble (September 27, 1953, TCD, 188).

As his international reputation blossomed, Beckett's personal and professional lives became increasingly complicated, threatening to end his career before it had properly begun. Again and again he lamented his inability to find time and peace to write, telling McGreevy he was exhausted, debilitated, and suffering from profound writer's block (December 14, 1953, TCD, 190). But, as we might expect of a man with solid experience in the publishing industry, including intimate knowledge of Joyce's days as Europe's most celebrated writer and over twenty-four years as an active author with solid contacts in four major cities, he gradually figured out a careful, deliberate balance between his personal and professional needs. By November 1955 he was telling McGreevy he had decided to adjust to a healthier lifestyle by making major changes (November 6, 1955, TCD, 197). A week before *Godot* opened on Broadway in April 1956, he explained why no one should pay attention to his attitude toward his work and why he was not equipped for a long-term career in the writer's profession (April 10, 1956, TCD, 198); by that point he had, however, already worked out a relationship with the literary marketplace allowing him to continue producing marketable work until a few months before he died.

In the midst of a proliferation of conflicts and misunderstandings, as agents, publishers, and producers divvied up the rights to his work, and even as he continued to complain about exhaustion and despondency, Beckett managed to establish a position of supreme control protecting his ability to write, preserving his influence over the layout of his published books and the performance of his plays, putting him at the center of a network of market-oriented professionals who would act in his interest. He was so effective in achieving control over his life and work that his agents and representatives continue to protect and preserve his authorized legacy as we begin the third decade after his death. Periodically Beckett would issue a statement about what he was, or was not, prepared to do in his capacity as an author; without exception, his publishers did his bidding, giving him whatever privacy he demanded, protecting him from the public spotlight except as he chose. The house in Ussy, bought with the inheritance from his mother's estate, was crucial to his new way of living. As he adjusted his lifestyle to accommodate the demands of a successful career, his early complaints about the custom-built house in the country gave way to a deep appreciation for an isolated retreat away from the people and conversations in Paris (November 27, 1957, TCD, 209). The cottage, typically used to affirm the idea that Beckett was uninterested in the trappings of fame, is a material manifestation of the level of control Beckett exerted over his professional life.

A clear sense of Beckett's path to fame is crucial to our understanding of how he adjusted his private, personal, and professional lives to achieve sustained success in the literary marketplace without seeming to compromise his private space. First, the Bordas contract and the scattering of publications in French journals in 1946–50 gave him confidence and established his name among the Left Bank literati, but in these days before the publicity from *Godot,* the French version of *Murphy* sold as badly as the English version, and Bordas could not afford to honor its commitment. While he probably regretted the decision, Bordas can hardly be faulted for leaving Beckett in limbo. Without a solid contract for future work Beckett remained a hack writer, doing the literary equivalent of piecework. True to his pattern, he fell back on his old contacts, sending material to the revamped version of *Transition*—called *Transition Forty-Eight* in 1948, *Transition Forty-Nine* in 1949, and so on—with Georges Duthuit editing and Jolas on the advisory board. As I have suggested, publication in *Transition* now had a certain cachet among French writers: "the only English-language review entirely devoted to contemporary French writing" (Ackerley and Gontarski 2004, 158), the journal was the most effective way in the postwar period to associate his name with the best contemporary writers in French including Artaud, Bataille, Genet, Mallarmé, Malraux, and Sartre. This association set him up for the second major development in his postwar career: as noted above, in the spring of 1950, Roger Blin committed himself to a production of *Godot.* When he was contacted by Dumesnil, Blin had already heard of Beckett through Tristran Tzara and one of the advisory editors at *Transition,* Max-Pol Fouchet (in both cases owing to Dumesnil's efforts). A few months later, on November 15, 1950, Jérôme Lindon signed him up at Les Editions de Minuit (again because of Dumesnil). These commitments from Blin and Lindon enlarged Beckett's audience and gave him a solid professional presence in Paris; on February 17, 1952, Blin recorded a segment from *Godot* for Club d'Essai de Radio, boosting interest in Beckett, stimulating sales of *Molloy* (published in an edition of three thousand copies by Les Editions de Minuit on March 15, 1951, with fifty deluxe copies and five hundred signed for "Les Amis des Editions de Minuit") and *Malone meurt* (published in an edition of three thousand copies on October 8, 1951 with fifty deluxe copies) and preparing the ground for the forthcoming stage production of the play.

The third phase of Beckett's rise to international fame was inaugurated by the January 5, 1953, opening of *En attendant Godot* at the Théâtre de Babylone: the buzz from Blin's minimalist production was enough to sustain 400 performances. Audiences were relatively small, capacity at the Babylone being 230, but the length of the run gave the play time to make a mark. Articles by such prominent writers as Bataille, Blanzat, Fouchet, and Nadeau (all familiar with Beckett through the social network centered on the offices of Duthuit's *Transition*) helped establish Beckett as a leader of the Paris-based avant-garde, bringing significantly increased attention to the novels. The first edition of *Godot* (2,500 paperback copies were printed on October 17, 1952, selling for 360 old francs—around a dollar) was soon exhausted; for the record, by 1964 Les Editions de Minuit had sold forty-five thousand copies. Beckett's name was thus firmly established in the French marketplace years before he gained a firm foothold in Britain and the United States. As Lindon recalled in an October 11, 1954, letter to Grove Press, "La sortie du livre a provoqué la publication d'une centaine de critiques environ" (The book [*Godot*] provoked the publication of around a hundred reviews). The Babylone production created the energy for what must be seen as a fourth phase of development: always on the lookout for authors who might make the crossover from the European scene and sensing that the Left Bank had produced a new phenomenon, a score of English-language publishers approached Lindon. In June 1953, Barney Rosset of Grove Press pushed his way to the front of the pack and reached an agreement to publish an English translation of *Godot* and, subsequently, English translations of the novels: Grove's contract with Les Editions de Minuit was initiated by Sylvia Beach and negotiated through a New York agent (acting for Lindon), Marion Saunders (fig. 11). This led to the first US productions of *Godot* in 1956 and opened the door to the marketplace beyond Europe.

With his first step to fame, Beckett benefited from the space provided by the Bordas contract; with his second step, Blin and Lindon put him in a position to consolidate his status as an important writer in French *and* English; his third step, the production of *Godot* at the Théâtre de Babylone, established him as a Left Bank celebrity. The fourth step happened when Rosset came onboard, opening the way to English-language productions of the play and inaugurating a three-year period of expansion in his reputation.

This phase culminated with the New York production of *Waiting for Godot* in April 1956. Shortly after the first Babylone run ended in summer 1953, Blin revived the play with the same cast. In fall 1953 he took the play on a tour of Switzerland, Italy, and Germany, expanding Beckett's audience across Europe, so that, by January 1954, Beckett's European reputation as an exciting new playwright was firmly established. Then Peter Hall directed an English-language version in London (31 performances at the New Arts Theatre beginning August 3, 1955, followed by 226 performances at the Criterion beginning September 3, 1955); Alan Simpson put the play on in Dublin and environs (a nineteen-week run beginning October 28, 1955, at the Pike, followed by a week at the Gate beginning March 12, 1956, and an eight-week tour until June 17, 1956); Alan Schneider directed the American premiere in Miami (ten days beginning January 3, 1956); and Herbert Berghoff took over for the New York production (six weeks beginning April 19, 1956). By the time Pamela Lyon, acting for John Calder, wrote to Beckett on November 8, 1956, to inquire about the possibility of publishing his books in English (Lilly), Beckett was well on his way to international fame. The only question that remained at the end of 1956 was whether or not he was a one-hit wonder: could he build on the success of *Godot* with subsequent work? The fifth step to international fame would come when Beckett was able to produce work demonstrating he had staying power.

As previously noted, Beckett had become financially secure as a result of the generous family inheritance received on his mother's death in October 1950; in addition, he now began to earn significant royalties from his work, particularly in the United States under Rosset's command (figs. 13, 14, and 15). For example, from May 1956 until he was awarded the Nobel Prize for Literature in October 1969 (becoming the first Irish writer to receive the award since Bernard Shaw in 1925), Beckett earned an average of five thousand dollars per year solely from sales of the American paperback edition of *Godot* (by comparison, his average income from the sales of the French edition was significantly less than one thousand dollars per year). During the same period he earned at least fifteen hundred dollars a year from American professional and amateur performances of *Godot* and received regular, though smaller, checks from royalties for *Endgame, Krapp's Last Tape, Happy Days,* and the other twelve scripts published and/or performed between 1956 and 1970. Much has been made of the fact that Beckett's estate was not exactly flush when he died in 1989; an *Evening Standard* article, "Not Pozzo money," reports that "The mystery surrounding Samuel Beckett's finances has taken a twist today with the publication of his will amounting to a mere £15,375." The article quotes Mary Bryden, then an associate researcher at the Samuel Beckett Library in Reading: "He was never very interested in money" (May 22, 1991).

Ignoring the more obvious conclusion to be drawn about an estate that continues to sustain the lives of Beckett's descendants—that it was managed with an impeccable understanding of tax law and the rules of inheritance—we might suggest, instead, that after 1950 Beckett could afford not to be "very interested in money." We might remind ourselves of letters he wrote to Reavey on June 19, 1946, and August 15, 1947, enthusing over the prospect of earning money, going so far as to say he didn't care where he was published because all he wanted was money (HRHRC). And lest we dismiss this economic interest as a consequence of conditions immediately after the war, we can recall his April 16, 1953, letter to Susan Manning gloating over how much money the New York production of *Godot* had earned during its first one hundred performances, expressing his keen hope and interest in making a lot more money (HRHRC). And, again, we might note his April 9, 1956, letter to McGreevy reporting the New York opening of *Godot,* commenting that his *only* concern was how many dollars it would earn (TCD, 198). This series of letters remains unpublished. The parts referring to his interest in money are unquoted or downplayed in the current biographies and, for some unexplained reason, censored in this one. Presumably Beckett's avid concern with financial profit runs counter to the image the Beckett estate is invested in protecting. In any event, to verify what I am arguing you must either go to the various archives I consulted, paying photocopying and other costs for the privilege of perusing Beckett's correspondence, or you can do what I did with the McGreevy letters, pay a fee and receive a microfilmed copy (in 2005, Edward Beckett authorized me to purchase a copy of the McGreevy correspondence from Trinity College Dublin for one hundred pounds; the Beckett estate subsequently banned me from using any of this material, *whether previously published or unpublished,* in this book). In any event, Beckett's money-focused comments fade after the success in New York; this is, I would argue, evidence of the luxury of financial indifference rather than any intrinsic lack of interest in money. As Beckett relaxed into his role as a thriving professional writer, his attitude toward money also became more relaxed; the May 18, 1956, "Yoicks Yoicks" letter from Barney Rosset gives an excellent sense of the euphoria accompanying Beckett's success in the marketplace (Fig. 13).

To focus on Beckett's interest in making money is not to treat him as a "charlatan" (Bair 1990, ix). Neither does it detract from his status as one of the twentieth century's most important authors. Rather it is to accept him as a product of his social background, of an upbringing with a high priority on economic independence and the ability to move freely without worrying about money; as Deasy put it in *Ulysses,* describing the English of South Dublin, the "proudest boast" is to say "I paid my way" (Joyce 1934, 30). Beckett was not like Deasy, but after 1950 he could share Deasy's "rich delight" at being financially independent (31). In any event, to focus on the fact that Beckett's estate in England and Wales was only worth £15,375 when he died is to ignore the value of his apartment in Paris and his property in Ussy, his capital assets in Ireland, his ongoing royalty payments from across the globe, the immense profits his estate continues to generate from his work (not only from royalties but also from the sale of manuscripts, correspondence, permissions, etc.), and his sale of thousands of pounds worth of manuscripts in the 1950s and 1960s and his tax-deductible donation of millions of pounds worth of manuscripts and other artifacts to Reading University Library between 1972 and his death in 1989. It is also to ignore that, after 1953, he lived a celebrity lifestyle, staying in five-star hotels; taking long, regular vacations of four weeks, six weeks, two months; retreating to the privacy of his custom-built house at Ussy or (after 1961) his specially designed apartment on a major boulevard in Paris; carefully orchestrating his contacts with the media; and exerting tight control over his work.

Throughout, he depended on a trusted network of dependents, many of them professionals in the literary marketplace, to protect his private life and his public image. When he wanted money he simply wrote to his publishers. On November 27, 1968, for example, he requested the deposit of two thousand dollars into a bank in Funchal, Madeira, to keep him going for a vacation he had decided to extend; the following year, when he was in Tunisia during the Nobel "catastrophe," he requested a deposit of five thousand dollars (SUL). In sum, the received idea he had no interest in money or fame distorts his life and legacy. It does so because it occludes his successful effort to make a living from his writing, deliberately downplaying his love of cigars, fine whiskey, expensive wine and haute cuisine in order to protect his authorial persona as someone more comfortable in an alley with garbage or crammed into the corner of a sparsely furnished room (fig. 4). In reality, he was a man with a highly marketable signature, an iconographic face, a constant stream of royalty checks, and a highly productive, privileged and protected lifestyle. Again, Beckett's posing for Jerry Bauer sitting on garbage in an alley, wearing expensive clothes, masquerading as a "tramp," is a sure sign he was entirely conscious that "Samuel Beckett" was a product of self-fashioning and the deliberate marketing of a specific public image. It is also, I sincerely believe, a sign he wanted us to know he knew.

Blin, Lindon, and a House of His Own

As suggested in chapter 5, Beckett's ability to achieve a long-term career as a professional writer was largely the result of efforts by Dumesnil to give him access to, and sustainable credibility in, the post–World War II Parisian literary marketplace. In March 1950 she had initiated contact with Roger Blin and had opened the way to the contract with Lindon. Together with the Editions de Minuit contract to publish *Molloy* and *Malone meurt,* the Blin agreement to produce *Godot* gave a solid foundation for a lifelong, prosperous career. The first month of discussions with Blin were handled by Dumesnil as Blin considered whether to go with the more traditional big-cast, split-stage production of *Eleutheria* or the more radical, though more manageable, *Godot.* After deciding to go with the minimalist play, Blin met Beckett in April 1950 to lay out his plans. It would be almost three years before the January 3, 1953, stage premiere; in the meantime, Blin lobbied on Beckett's behalf, raising money from private subscriptions and a government grant (five hundred thousand old francs from the Ministry of Education, roughly equivalent to fourteen hundred dollars at a time when the average American earned thirty-five hundred dollars a year), attempting productions at the Théâtre des Noctambules in Fall 1950 and the Théâtre de Poche in July 1952. The February 17, 1952, radio transmission of a short version of the play organized by Blin was prefaced by Beckett's introduction:

> I don't know who Godot is. I don't even know (above all don't know) if he exists. And I don't know if they believe in him or not—those two who are waiting for him. . . . All that I knew I showed. It's not much, but it's enough for me, by a wide margin. I'll even say that I would have been satisfied with less. (Knowlson and Knowlson 2006, 126)

This "taster" production stimulated sufficient interest to make the stage version feasible, setting the tone for critical reception, establishing a precedent for less direct media strategies Beckett would use repeatedly after 1956 (fig. 12). A sampling of the reviews published during the four hundred performances at the Théâtre de Babylone, suggests the success of Beckett's approach and the impact *Godot* made on a literary establishment that took notice because Beckett had already made an impression in Paris, and because Blin and Lindon gave him "must-see" credibility. The audience showed up in modest but steady numbers, and the reviews came in a heart-warming flow. Sylvain Zegel's January 7, 1953, review in *Libération* made a bold claim: "Paris has just recognized in Samuel Beckett one of today's best playwrights." On January 16 Jacques Audiberti wrote for *Arts-Spectacle:* the play is "a perfect work that deserves a triumph." On January 27, also in *Art-Spectacle,* Jean Anouilh wrote, "*Godot* is a masterpiece" (Cohn 1967). In the February 1953 issue of Georges Bataille's *Critique,* Alain Robbe-Grillet heralded the play as a fundamental statement of existential truth: "Beckett's play was 'the most banal, the least audacious expression imaginable' of the human state, the state of simply 'being there'" (Cronin 1996, 423).

When Beckett signed with Lindon on November 15, 1950, the commitment was "to publish all three with 'all due speed, as soon as possible'" (Bair 1990, 408). Lindon paid an advance of twenty-five thousand old francs for *Molloy* (this was about seventy dollars in 1950 and was a very modest fee; the average weekly wage in the United States in 1950 was sixty-two dollars). The novel was published in a first edition of three thousand copies (*Les Temps modernes* had issued a substantial extract from the novel in September 1950 and an English-language "Extract from *Molloy*" would appear in the spring 1954 issue of *Paris Review*). *Malone meurt* followed in 1951 in a printing of three thousand. On October 17, 1952, anticipating the premiere scheduled at the Theatre de Poche, Lindon published *Godot* in an edition of twenty-five hundred copies. On July 15, 1953, he published three thousand copies of *L'Innommable* (to Beckett's horror, an advance extract, "Mahood," appeared in the February 1953 issue of *Nouvelle Revue Française* with a section excised [Ackerley and Gontarski 2004, 320]). This ongoing flurry of publications was intensified by the upcoming publication of *Watt* by Olympia Press under the imprint of Editions Merlin on August 31, 1953.

A December 11, 1950, letter to Reavey provides a detailed account of his new professional situation since he had been released by Bordas and had signed with Editions de Minuit to publish the three novels he had written since the war (HRHRC). As I have suggested, Beckett's decision to sign with Lindon is important because it marks a sea change in his relationship with the literary marketplace, altering his perception of publishing as an industry and markedly changing the circumstances under which he worked. From that point on, everything he considered worthy of publication would be published, and he was to retain almost total control over the editing and production process. Bair, inclined to indulge in amateur psychoanalysis, explains Beckett's long-standing "problems" with publishing in terms of a "complicated relationship with his mother" that caused a "necessary self-defense" and an urge to "remain elusive" so as to maintain his "mental stability" (1990, 408). I have to differ. I am more inclined to see his laid-back approach as a perfectly understandable reaction to a history of rejections and broken promises. The long struggle to publish *More Pricks Than Kicks* and *Murphy,* and the ongoing effort to publish *Watt,* had given him extensive experience with the more cutthroat side of the publishing industry. Even those who had given him contracts, Chatto and Windus, Routledge, and Bordas, had proven to be fair-weather friends, pulling out when the financial going got tough. His "refusal to see Lindon" was only temporary and is not, I would suggest, evidence "he was absolutely incapable of acting in his own interest" (Bair 1990, 408); it is, instead, evidence of an astute pragmatism born of long experience. He was understandably reluctant to expend energy on potentially futile negotiations, and he was legitimately concerned his work might be unmarketable and thus bad news for a small business like Les Editions de Minuit. Another reason enters the equation: he had the luxury of being able to stay in the background while others, in this case Dumesnil and Clerkx, acted on his behalf.

Beckett decided to enter into direct correspondence with Lindon partly because his only other option in 1950 was to continue as a hack writer: while Lindon was hooked by Beckett's manuscript as soon as he read it, it is unlikely he would have committed his limited resources to Beckett without a personal connection. It was a good decision for a man who, having spent over a decade trying to break into the mainstream publishing industry, understandably preferred upstart companies like Cunard's Hours Press and Reavey's Europa Press, which had treated him with respect by allowing him to create limited edition, autographed copies. There is another reason Beckett was open to Lindon's offer. It is very likely Beckett knew Minuit had been set up in 1942 by Pierre de Lescure to publish Resistance pamphlets during the occupation. Most famously, de Lescure had published *Le Silence de la mer* by Vercors, a book widely regarded as a symbol of anti-Nazism and a standard text for anyone connected with the Maquis. Lindon bought into the company in 1948 and became managing director. He gained some notoriety in the Latin Quarter by publishing a new generation of authors including Georges Bataille and Maurice Blanchot. Lindon's youth (which was one of the prerequisites Beckett listed when he asked Reavey to help him find a new literary agent on June 20, 1945 [HRHRC]), his connection with avant-garde writers, and the association with the Resistance, were all positive factors for Beckett. While the newness of the publishing house clearly caused Beckett some anxiety because he was afraid *Molloy* would sink like a stone, meeting the same fate as his previous full-length publications and forcing Lindon into bankruptcy, the opportunity gave him a fresh start in the publishing industry. Crucially, the connection with Minuit meant Beckett was free of any association with Joyce and with the publishing houses that had been the bane of his life until 1950; his decision to go with Lindon, like his later decisions to go with Rosset and Calder, must be seen, then, as part of a deliberate strategy to associate himself with a new generation of "alternative" publishing houses, giving him a fresh start and, crucially, a high level of control. A major advantage was that the companies he signed with were relatively small and were thus able to concentrate their efforts on his work, giving him uninterrupted attention when he demanded it, always deferring to his requests and instructions. It is not just that Calder, Lindon, and Rosset were important to Beckett; it is also that Beckett was one of the main pillars on which these three men built their publishing careers.

As I argued in the introduction, Beckett's authorial image would evolve over the next two decades into an aestheticized, otherworldly persona, making him seem inseparable from the solipsistic characters he created. Unfortunately, this persona would also make him seem much less savvy about the business of publishing than he really was. This image of a man caught up in his creative work so thoroughly that he abandoned his texts as soon as they were finished is captured most vividly in Deirdre Bair's rather creative account of how Beckett (or was it Watt himself?) delivered the manuscript of *Watt* to Richard Seaver in 1952 at the literary quarterly *Merlin:*

> Seaver was in his room when someone knocked at the door. He opened it to find a very tall man peering myopically at him through round-rimmed glasses. A bundle of manuscript bound in a makeshift hopsacking cover was thrust into his arms, and the man, without a word, turned abruptly and plunged down the stairs through the gloom and clutter of the antiques-cum-junk in the shop below. When Seaver removed the hopsacking, he found the entire manuscript of *Watt.* (Bair 1990, 432)

Setting the scene so the author appears anonymously and unannounced, silently arriving and abruptly leaving, plunging his way through the "gloom and clutter" of used goods, Bair recounts a story passed along by a man, Seaver, who helped define Beckett's public image in the early 1950s. Consistent with a pattern familiar in biographical accounts of Beckett, the narrative deliberately blurs Beckett with a character from his own novel, giving the impression of absolute public indifference on the author's part. Seaver's account, reported by Bair in a way designed to blur him with his literary creations, represents Beckett as a figure of mystery, as disengaged from the world of literary commerce as a rolled carpet, as though he were a man who would dump his work with the same attitude as he would dump an old vacuum cleaner (let's recall he had carried this manuscript across France on numerous journeys working on it whenever he could during some of the most difficult times in his life: he was clearly very attached to *Watt*). Seaver and Bair frame Beckett's appearance at the publishing house in the same terms Beckett used to frame Watt's appearance in *Watt.* The emphasis on Beckett's myopic eyes and the "hopsacking cover" sustains the image of a writer with tunnel vision, a writer so bound up in his own private aesthetic vision he has little interest in its material or public form. The effort is to create a consistent image of Beckett as a thoroughly disengaged, noncommercial artist; but, again, it is an image out of synch with the life of a writer who had, from his earliest days, enlisted the active support of numerous figures in the publishing industry, who would soon begin to enjoy the financial success of *Godot,* whose sustained effort to craft a viable authorial persona was beginning to gain purchase by turning him into a cultural icon, and who was still trying to publish *Watt* after he had already written a much more concentrated body of work.

As we have seen, in reality Beckett engaged the world of commerce with his eyes wide open, enlisting and manipulating agents and publishers as he saw fit, involving himself in the business of marketing brochures and book covers, focusing on the bottom dollar and staying tuned to the details of contracts and agreements, but such an attitude was out of step with the characters and the worlds he represented in his texts. For their part, his publishers ensured he would not suffer from the dissonance between the life he lived in private and the life he represented on the page and the stage.

The marketing of Beckett's postwar image began when he signed with Minuit. As Cronin puts it, while Minuit was hardly likely to provide "big hype," the new contract represented a "small quantitative leap from the world of the man alone, in whom nobody is interested, into the world of organized and organization-backed promotion which makes the individual a property to be expanded and developed" (1996, 411). Quietly, but surely, Jérôme Lindon built a market for Beckett's texts. He hailed the publication of *Molloy* as "Le Plus Grand Événement Littéraire de L'Après-Guerre" (The biggest postwar literary event). In an advertisement in the Paris press in 1951, Lindon claimed, "Moins d'un mois après la parution de son premiere roman, la critique unanime salue l'apparition d'un grand écrivain français" (Less than a month after the publication of his first novel, criticism unanimously salutes the appearance of a great French writer). As a result of this publicity, the more amateurish, once indispensable contributions of Reavey, Dumesnil, and Clerkx were displaced. However, during this period Beckett was still being advertised and sold in a relatively small market. After June 1953, with the success of the Paris *Godot* as a crucial marketing device, Barney Rosset *did* provide the "big hype," systematically transforming Beckett's authorial persona by developing a coordinated marketing campaign designed to sell as many books as possible. Initially this campaign targeted beatnik intellectuals, university professors, and Americans who looked to Europe for "culture" (see figs. 2, 7, and 9).

As is often the case when someone moves into the public spotlight and becomes the subject of "hype," Beckett was unsettled. His early reaction to his developing fame is apparent in an October 1951 letter to Susan Manning. Writing to a personal friend with deep connections to the social group of his upbringing, he counterbalances his confession about not producing any work and being more interested in growing carrots than in his vocation with an account of his blossoming prospects. *Malone meurt* was about to be published and a second extract from *Watt* was due to appear in *Irish Writing* (HRHRC). The idea that he was more interested in gardening than literature is odd in the context of a letter with so much information about his literary affairs. But at the same time as it obeys the self-effacing decorum of his socioeconomic class, it also gives an insight into his new situation, ensuring that those who might have been disappointed by his earlier struggles were now apprised of his recent success (as he had suggested in a letter written when he was worrying about the publication of *Murphy,* he knew Susan Manning would spread the word about his prospects in the south Dublin neighborhood of his upbringing). While the October 1951 letter expresses some anxiety about developments in his professional career, it also illustrates a new-found ability to relax; a newly discovered author with extensive experience of, and obvious interest in, the publishing industry, he knew he could focus on immediate concerns (carrots), leaving the business of book publication and stage production, advertising and promotion, to the professionals.

Beckett was clearly relieved to move to a new phase of his career: as he put it to Reavey on June 2, 1952, he could rely on Lindon to take care of everything connected with his professional life (HRHRC). The French *Godot* launched Beckett internationally, first across Europe and then in Britain and the Commonwealth and the United States. It is most significant that it helped him secure the services of the American publishing industry under the entrepreneurial guidance of Barney Rosset, an aggressive business mogul who was brimming with ideas about ways to turn Beckett into an international phenomenon (see figs. 2 and 9). Beckett's relaxed attitude as he entered the most intense period of his evolution into a successful professional writer was facilitated by those who stepped forward to market his texts while disseminating a complementary authorial image, but it was also possible because he had recently achieved financial independence as a result of his mother's death. As we have already noted, more than a year before Blin's production of *Godot* produced any income, he made plans for a two-room, custom-built house in Ussy-sur-Marne, a comfortable twenty-five-mile train ride from Paris. Again, the connection between Beckett's professional life and the economic security given him by his family should not be underestimated. Because he sometimes referred to the house as "the house that Godot built," Bair concluded he "used the income from *Godot* to pay for the property" (1990, 418). This notion is clearly erroneous because his plans for the house date from the six months immediately following the death of his mother in August 1950, well over two years before the Paris premiere of *Godot*. May Beckett left an undisputed estate of two thousand pounds together with her life interest in the estate of her husband. William Beckett's estate, which was mainly invested in housing in Dublin, had been valued at thirty thousand pounds in the 1930s (Cronin 1996, 408). With only his brother, Frank, to share the estate, Beckett was flush: as Cronin puts it, "For Sam the days of monetary hardship were over" (408). Although he had struggled like everyone else in Europe during the postwar period, he was independently wealthy before he began to earn a substantial income from his writing.

On December 23, 1951, Beckett wrote to Susan Manning about his plans to build a house of his own at Ussy (HRHRC). Although he was panicked by the low-church fear of owning property, and although it took him a while to adjust to the difficulties incumbent on a homeowner, his

Cooldrinagh-influenced upbringing prevailed, and by 1953 the house at Ussy was fully habitable and was becoming a regular part of the rhythm of Beckett's life and work. It was an ideal retreat for a professional writer. The "spartan simplicity" (Knowlson 1996, 351) and "barrack-like tidiness and simplicity" (Cronin 1996, 416) are what we would expect of a retreat specially designed for the job of writing. With built-in bookshelves; an oak desk; basic amenities for cooking, heating, and sleeping; a comfortable outside seating area; and a sizable plot of land (making it a perfect place for Beckett to go for long spells of physical work [August 6, 1960, SUL]), Beckett's country cottage functions as a material sign of his independence and security as a professional writer, as a writer who could express disinterest in the commercial side of his craft because he truly had no need for the money. It also both connects him to, and separates him from, his Irish context. Built by a builder local to Ussy using "rough designs" sketched with his brother's expert help (Frank had been head of the family construction business in Dublin since 1933), the house is reminiscent of "the plain, Irish slated cottages which were built around the turn of the century, with a long central room, a tiny kitchen and bathroom" (Cronin 1996, 414). Built with inherited money, with the deliberate purpose of facilitating his career, the house put Beckett in a position to move between the city and the country in a way that recalls his father's movements between the remote suburbs of Foxrock and the city of Dublin (a movement with an obvious influence on the plot of his most Irish play, *All That Fall*). In sum, the house in Ussy gave Beckett a sanctuary in support of, and in homage to, his life as a professional writer, putting him in a better position to regulate interactions between work and play, friends and business associates, private and public life.

From then on, Beckett would run his private, personal, and professional lives according to a careful plan, retreating to Ussy or a quiet resort in southern Europe or northern Africa when "the big world where Quid pro quo was cried" became too much (*GCE I*, 6). Whenever he felt the urge he stepped forward to control productions of his plays, flying across Europe at will, retreating when he felt like it, going public when he chose, delegating as he saw fit. Selected individuals were invited into his inner sanctuaries, visiting the cottage in Ussy and his apartment in Paris (the short list includes Kay Boyle, Ruby Cohn, Lawrence Harvey, Joseph Hayden, James Knowlson, and Barney Rosset); a second tier were afforded public meetings in Paris at such places as the Café Depart, the PLM, Le Petit Café, and the Falstaff. Occasionally he invited photographers, journalists, and/or academics for one-on-one meetings, again carefully regulating any public record of how he looked and what he said, telling them to leave their cameras and notepads at home, losing his temper when confronted with opportunistic photographers. Beckett did not fear publicity; he feared unauthorized publicity.

In short, after 1953 Beckett positioned himself so he could exert tight control over all private and public aspects of his career, exerting a level of control without parallel and, apparently, without end. Beckett's correspondence continued to reveal his almost obsessive interest in his role as a professional writer. But now his network of intimate professional contacts became much more extensive and comprehensive. As his letters to Tom McGreevy and George Reavey petered out, his letters and cards to business acquaintances including actors, booksellers, directors, publishers, scholars, and writers multiplied; his English-language correspondents include Kay Boyle, John Calder, Aidan Higgins, Mary Manning Howe, Mary Hutchinson, John Kobler, A. J. (Con) Leventhal, Jack and Gloria MacGowran, Susan Manning, John Montague, Barney Rosset (and other Grove employees, especially Judith Schmidt), Jake Schwartz, and Arland Ussher. Rarely do these letters and cards omit reference to texts he is directing, editing, translating, or writing; when no text is directly mentioned, the correspondence typically refers to contractual problems, royalties, his workload, and/or his frustrations as a writer. From his letters we develop a sense of a writer who was deeply immersed in his professional business, with a fluid, constantly negotiated relationship between his private, personal, and public lives. Again, the Beckett estate's refusal to allow me to quote directly from any Beckett correspondence, published or unpublished, further substantiates the argument that Beckett's authorial persona and ongoing legacy are the product of media management by those who stand to make the most profit from the protection of this persona and legacy. The resistance to a thesis that is solidly based on words written in Beckett's hand is, as far as I can tell, based on a fear that this thesis might undermine Beckett's saintlike image as an artist who stood above commercial concerns and had no interest in a successful career. In the absence of any explanation from those who control Beckett's estate, all I can say in response is that there is overwhelming evidence, much of which I have been forced to censor from my manuscript, to demonstrate Beckett's long-standing habit of inviting and/or precluding professional contact according to his own needs and wishes, quietly consulting and guiding a network of trusted friends as they conducted his public affairs in his name, negotiating all aspects of the interface between himself and the literary marketplace.

The network Beckett built is sincere and determined in its protection and celebration of his image as a pure artist, as an exceptional author who stands head and shoulders above the crowd exactly because he represents a fundamental opposition to commercialism and publicity (see fig. 8). In this representation, which goes hand-in-hand with the idea he was "damned to fame," it is crucial that he is "distinguished by his public silence" (Brater 1986, 13). As Alec Reid put it in a Grove Press book published in 1968 to boost Beckett's reputation and then reissued in 1971 to capitalize on the Nobel Prize award, "Throughout his life, quietly but uncompromisingly, Beckett has avoided every form of personal publicity. He is naturally reticent, unassertive, with a deep respect for the privacy of others, and a considerable impatience with the spurious, impersonal world of press parties, public relations and the rest" (1971, 12). As I've argued, part of the reason for this characterization is the tendency to emphasize the conditions he endured (and enjoyed) during the four-year period following World War II; as a consequence it has become taboo in Beckett studies to quote and analyze direct evidence illustrating his engagement with the marketplace and his enjoyment of his fame and money (see fig. 6). Because he was able to focus on his work for four intense years, from 1946 to 1950, and because the work he produced during this period established his characteristic style in the marketplace, the "siege in the room" has become emblematic, displacing the facts. Again, the ubiquity of this phrase, and of the phrases used to claim that Beckett "avoided every form of personal publicity," suggest a coordinated strategy. There are those in Beckett studies who treasure the idea of Beckett sitting in his study chiseling away at his work with the concentration of Benvenuto Cellini, his aesthetic concentration making him oblivious to the cries of the marketplace. But it is undeniable that in 1929–50 he and various acquaintances hawked his wares like those of any other writer, meeting and cultivating every available contact, using every trick in the book to publish his work; it is also beyond question that after 1950 he encouraged and facilitated publicity for his work, setting new standards for dignity and professionalism in the business of literary marketing but, nevertheless, participating in this business with keen attention and unflagging interest (see figs. 3, 6, and 12).

As I argued in the introduction, the series of publicity photographs from the 1951 "passport" image to the Minihan hotel room "studies," including the trend-setting head shot by Brassai (fig. 7), the carefully posed Bauer shots with garbage (fig. 4), and the classic "floating head" portrait by Haynes (fig. 8), provide sufficient evidence to raise questions about Richard Seaver's assumption Beckett "would cringe" at the description of his life's work as a "career" (Beckett 1976, xxxviii). Even as he speculates on Beckett's discomfort with the idea of a "career," Seaver describes Beckett as a consummate professional, noting how he was driven by "the dedication, the single-mindedness necessary to realize, against all odds, one's artistic potential" (xxiii). Proof of this devotion to careful self-presentation is given in Seaver's description of the manuscript of *Watt,* first published in an edition of 1,125 copies in August 1953 by Merlin, a journal-cum-publisher with an editorial collective made up of Seaver, Patrick Bowles, Charles Hatcher, Jane Lougee, Christopher Logue, and Alexander Trocchi. The contract gave Beckett 50,000 francs, the equivalent of $100; the ordinary edition of 1,100 numbered copies sold for 850 francs; the special edition of twenty-five signed copies on deluxe paper sold for 2,500 francs each. Seaver writes, "As is always the case with Beckett manuscripts, *Watt* was in impeccable condition. As we proofread it, we found virtually nothing even to query, much less to change" (xvii). This is, of course, an odd thing to say about an edition "riddled with errors" (Ackerley and Gontarski 2004, 628) and about a novel deliberately left unfinished, marked with question-marks, notes about an "illegible ms.," and accompanied by an "addenda" of material left out because of "fatigue and disgust." It is also an odd thing to say about a text that, for all its importance as a transitional, experimental novel, could have done with a more aggressive editorial eye, with an eye less inclined to interpret *anything* Beckett did as a sign of artistic integrity: even the most devout Beckett aficionado must admit the repetitions and tricks characteristic of *Watt* are somewhat tedious, pushed much further than is necessary to their apparent purpose. *Watt* is an important novel because of its place in Beckett's canon, but it is not a great piece of literature.

Perhaps as important as Olympia Press's publication of a novel revealing Beckett's experimental approach to the construction of a viable narrative persona is the press's youthful devotion to his cause. After 1957, Rosset's *Evergreen Review* would ratchet up the hype in terms of the marketing of Beckett's work by giving him newsstand visibility and accessibility, enhancing his credibility among a new niche in the literary market, the beat generation and their peers, specifically selling his work to "intellectuals," including those in charge of college book orders (figs. 2, 9, and 10). Roy Kuhlman covers and bold advertising strategies were designed to appeal to the twenty-somethings, making Beckett's texts ideal for university-level literature courses. But the Merlin collective did it first. *Merlin,* one of the many English-language journals that had sprung up in Paris in the early 1950s as the economics of publishing settled down in the aftermath of the war, must be credited with attempting to do for Beckett what *Transition* had done for Joyce in 1927–38. In the second, fall 1952, issue, *Merlin* published an enthusiastic essay by Seaver, confirming what he would later describe as its "pro-Beckett stance" (xviii). With few exceptions, subsequent issues carried poems, stories, and excerpts from Beckett's novels. And continuing the context-building achieved through publication in Duthuit's version of *Transition,* but with the specific purpose of putting Beckett front and center, the journal associated Beckett with the most fashionable authors in the business, William Burroughs, J. P. Donleavy, Vladimir Nabokov, Pauline Reage, John-Paul Sartre. Patrick Bowles and Richard Seaver, two of the "Merlin juveniles" (Knowlson 1996, 355) would become an important part of Beckett's debut on the world stage, writing favorable reviews (without acknowledging their relationship with Beckett) and helping translate his postwar texts, including "La Fin" (Seaver) and *Molloy* (Bowles). Barney Rosset was much better positioned to boost Beckett's name and would hire Bowles to help translate *Molloy* and Richard Seaver to help build Grove Press, but the individuals in the Olympia/Merlin collective were the first to treat Beckett like a star, boosting his name and image, helping put him on "must-read" lists at the historical moment when he was poised for the great leap forward from Left Bank fashionability to Euro-American celebrity.

Building Trust, Selling Cheap: Grove Press

In the months following the January 5, 1953, opening of *En attendant Godot* at the 230-seat Théâtre de Babylone, English and American publishers swamped Beckett with offers for English language versions of his texts. Beckett, scalded by their rejection of *Murphy* and *Watt,* refused offers by established houses. Consistent with his commitment to Les Editions de Minuit in 1950 and his later decision to sign with Calder and Boyars in 1956, he went with a relatively new and small company recently taken over by Barney Rosset, the ambitious son of a Chicago banking family and a former documentary filmmaker in the Signal Corps. A brief history of Grove Press allows us to appreciate how the association boosted Beckett's position in the literary marketplace (Gontarski 2000). Rosset bought the press for three thousand dollars in 1951, immediately dedicating himself to the publication of limited runs of books intended for esoteric and eclectic audiences, developing a "new formula for fiction publishing" ("Advance-Guard"

1953). As *Newsweek* suggested in "Advance-Guard Advance," a feature dedicated to the press in March 1953, the list comprised "highbrow books." Although the company had "no intention of making each unit pay its own way," allowing the publication of books with appeal to a small, cultlike audience akin to the coteries targeted by magazines like *Transition* and publishing houses like Hogarth Press, it quickly became clear that a large number of small-market titles would be possible because of a small number of controversial, large-market titles by such writers as Jack Kerouac, D. H. Lawrence, and Henry Miller. Rosset made up for lack of experience in the publishing industry by keeping overheads low and adopting a "Heinz 57 Varieties" approach: as reported in *Newsweek,* his hope was that "an overall sale for all his books" would be "large enough to keep the firm going." His ace in the hole was, however, his publication of sensational works with mass-market sales: Rosset's main sideline became the publication of politically controversial texts and the republication of out-of-print pornographic novels and, in the case of *I Am Curious (Yellow)*, the distribution of a scandalous film.

Rosset, a graduate of the New School for Social Research, officially took over from John Balcomb and Robert Phelps in 1952. At that time, Grove had only published three books, all reprints: Melville's *The Confidence Man* (1949), *The Verse in English of Richard Crashaw* (1950), and *Selected Writings of the Ingenious Mrs. Aphra Behn* (1950). Rosset immediately set out to turn Grove Press into an industry-leading outfit. When they signed Beckett, Rosset's company had four full-time staff: Rosset, Don Allen (an editor), Loly Eckert (the German-born secretary who married Rosset in September 1953—she was replaced in 1956 by Judith Schmidt, who became Beckett's main liaison at Grove), and John Gruen ("Head of Publicity and Promotion Department"). In these early days they were housed in the dining room of a converted ground-floor apartment in Greenwich Village. Rosset had studied avant-garde magazines and publishing houses at college and was familiar with *Transition,* edited by his fellow American, Eugene Jolas. On April 27, 1953, a letter sent to booksellers by John Gruen (the man who would write a feature article on Beckett for *Vogue* magazine in December 1969, omitting any mention of his previous job as a booster for Beckett's press) makes it clear that innovation, based on a "new formula," was part of the company's philosophy from the beginning. Covering the six-week period since Gruen became Grove's "publicity man," the letter calls attention to the positive press in response to Grove's second season under Rosset's control: "in these short weeks so many wonderful reviews have been coming our way that I can hardly keep up with my ideas for them" (Grove History, 1951–53, SUL). Gruen was clearly doing his job, thinking of ways to exploit any attention to the company by transforming it into major publicity: he is able to list "lead reviews" of *Count d'Orgel* by Raymond Radiguet in the *New Yorker* and *Time* magazine, quoting directly from an article in the *New York Review of Books.* He also reports that "the same week *Newsweek* had a story and a photograph about Grove Press itself," referring to a front-page article on *The Collected Poems of Edwin Muir* in the *NYT Book Review* (April 5, 1953) and enclosing a copy of the *Book Review*'s article on Giovanni Verga's *House by the Medlar Tree.* In conclusion he writes, "I think you will agree with me that things are happening at Grove Press and, when you read our books, I think you will see why." In a postscript he identifies *The Palm Wine Drunkard* by Amos Tutuola as "the 'big' book of our Fall list."

The letter is effective as a marketing tool because it uses Gruen's personal position as a new employee at Grove to promote the Press. The casual tone ("Please feel free to call me," "I can hardly keep up," and "Just a hint") disguises a concerted effort to call attention to "these accolades," to show how effective Grove has been in promoting its product, and to advertise three existing and one forthcoming title. As if to underline Grove's status as a small press on a level with the specialty booksellers likely to stock its books, the letterhead lists the company's five employees, the four mentioned above plus Evans Herman (a part-time assistant). Even as it developed into a multimillion-dollar business on the strength of a list of pornographic and politically controversial titles in the 1960s, the small press image would remain crucial to Grove's marketing strategy; it is, of course, an image well-suited to Beckett's persona as a noncommercial author.

Between 1953 and 1969 Grove Press would become America's most successful avant-garde press, grabbing headlines by publishing unexpurgated versions of Roger Casement's *Black Diaries* (1959), D. H. Lawrence's *Lady Chatterley's Lover* (1959), Henry Miller's *Tropic of Cancer* (1961), Edgar Snow's *Red Star over China* (1961), Frank Harris's *My Life and Loves* (1963), and the anonymous *My Secret Life* (1966). Rosset's biggest money-spinner was, however, *I Am Curious (Yellow),* which earned over six million dollars in distribution fees in 1969 (Gontarski 2000, 8). As he noted in an article about the press published in the *Clarksdale Press Register* on February 19, 1955, Rosset made a point of soliciting a wide range of texts, "international and local and backwards and forwards in time" (2), "advancing the international aspect of the Grove Press program" by sponsoring a one-thousand-dollar contest "for manuscripts to be submitted by citizens of India." By the time Rosset signed Beckett in June 1953, the press had issued an eclectic list of over forty original titles in addition to special editions of Jane Austen, George Eliot, and Anthony Trollope; by 1958, Grove's original titles included 150 hardbacks and 120 paperbacks, including four bestsellers by Beckett (*Endgame, Waiting for Godot, Molloy,* and *Malone Dies*); by 1962, propelled by a lucrative scandal and a high-profile court case involving the 1959 release of *Lady Chatterley's Lover,* the list filled a ten-page catalog with over six hundred titles (the twelve by Beckett now included *Happy Days, Krapp's Last Tape, Murphy, Poems in English, Proust, The Unnamable, Watt,* and *Three Novels*).

This rapid expansion gives some idea of Rosset's aggressive approach to the industry: his development of a cheap line of paperbacks under the Evergreen Books imprint, his use of Evergreen Records and the *Evergreen Review* to boost sales and to galvanize a youth movement, his direct marketing to college professors, and his willingness to publish politically and sexually transgressive texts, suggest his trend-setting role as an innovator driven by his devotion to free speech and the allure of commercial success. By 1958, Rosset could boast that his journal, *Evergreen Review,* was "the fastest growing, most vigorous literary magazine in America today" (SUL). For more than fifteen years the risks paid handsome dividends. Rosset's bold strategies worked very well until 1969, when the company achieved its peak value of seventeen million dollars. But Rosset overreached. His absolute commitment to freedom of speech and his aggressive marketing strategies eventually backfired, bringing adverse publicity and a retaliatory bomb attack on the Grove Press offices on July 26, 1968. The wrath he incited when he published pro-Castro texts and featured a photograph of Che Guevara on the front cover of *Evergreen Review* was exacerbated by a feminist-led, antipornography protest by his own employees beginning with a sit-down strike on April 13, 1970. Interestingly, the temporary shutdown was initiated on Beckett's birthday, presumably by women who knew the importance of the first major celebration of Beckett's birth after Rosset's lead author had won the Nobel Prize. Despite the ongoing increase in Beckett's success as a moneymaker, it was all downhill for Rosset and Grove Press after 1970: he could not overcome the debt burden from his decision to build a modern office block just prior to the company's financial meltdown. Ann Getty and Lord Weidenfeld led a corporate takeover in 1984, buying Grove for two million dollars, then forcing Rosset out in 1985. Rosset had had a good run, and Samuel Beckett was one of the main beneficiaries.

Rosset's tactics in the period between 1953 and 1970 had a major impact on the transformation of Beckett into an internationally renowned star. In the process, Beckett became Rosset's "best example" of "writing . . . termed avant-garde" (*Clarksdale Press Register* 1955, 2) and his most reliable source of income, providing a steady flow of royalties and profits for thirty years: for example, Rosset's 10 percent share of the author's allocation for English-language stage productions of *Godot* gave him an average of $150 per year between 1955 and 1969. If we add the profits from the eleven Beckett titles he had published by 1962 (a number rising to thirty-two titles by 1981 plus a sixteen-volume collected set), and include the share from translation rights of performances, Rosset's financial benefit from Beckett's work was substantial, averaging well over $2,000 a year for thirty years and increasing from one year to the next. In the early years these profits from Beckett's work were crucial to Rosset's expansion, giving him a reliable source of income so he could take legal risks by publishing banned and controversial, and ultimately highly profitable, texts by authors such as Henry Miller and D. H. Lawrence. For his part, Beckett's indebtedness is clear: after the new owners of Grove fired Rosset in 1985, he gave Rosset a text to help launch a new publishing venture, North Star Line. *Stirrings Still* (1988), the last major publication by Beckett before his death, is dedicated to Barney Rosset.

As with Merlin and Minuit, Grove Press associated Beckett with an upstart publishing house. As the rapid growth of the catalog suggests, Grove gave Beckett access to a greatly expanded market and made him part of a literary movement that would shape the Euro-American avant-garde in the decades after World War II. Militantly proactive, Rosset's publishing house made Beckett its lead author, featuring his face and name on its catalogs, in its letters to booksellers and professors, in its advertising and marketing campaigns, and on the covers of the *Evergreen Review* (see figs. 2, 7, and 9).

Beckett's gratitude is evident from a letter to Rosset on August 18, 1958, in which he acknowledges receipt of the 1958 catalog with the Brassai portrait as its cover, expressing his embarrassment at being featured so prominently and his profound gratitude for being honored so highly by someone he regarded as a true friend (SUL 20). Grove went further for Beckett than for any other writer on its list, organizing a series of events to publicize his work, projecting and protecting his image as an author with no interest in publicity while doing everything they could to "give interest in Beckett an additional boost"

(November 30, 1953, SUL 27). As the publicity department at the press did everything it could to "get Beckett known," Rosset enlisted the support of Bowles and Lindon, sending them requests for publicity materials in almost identical letters dated November 10 and November 11, 1953, respectively. He received "the material you asked for" from Bowles in a letter dated November 18, 1953. In a subsequent letter on November 24, 1953, Lindon promised further publicity materials "par courrier séparé un colis" (by separate post a package) ("Molloy," SUL 27). The publicity packet included the passport-style photograph attributed—dubiously—to Gisèle Freund (Bair 1990, 412; Cronin 1996, 411), photocopies of French reviews, original photographs of the Babylone production of *Godot,* and biographical material. From the outset, Rosset's commitment to Beckett was focused on the effort to "make a good impression in the American stores" (Dec 7, 1953, SUL 27).

Expanding what Merlin had begun to do for Beckett in Europe, Grove established Beckett's place in the American literary marketplace by associating him with such authors as Antonin Artaud, Kay Cicellis, Jean Genet, Allen Ginsberg, Eugene Ionesco, Jack Kerouac, Vernon Lee, Alain Robbe-Grillet, John-Paul Sartre, and Amos Tutuola (all published by Grove Press and *Evergreen Review*). Rosset thus amplified the strategy of the Merlin editorial board to establish Beckett as a key player in the postwar counterculture. This antiestablishment culture of beatniks and dropouts was gaining pace in the 1950s, becoming a driving force in the 1960s: it associated Beckett with "alternative" literature, turning him into a leading figure in "the underground" (fig. 2). Again, Beckett's leading role was evident from the appearance of his photograph and/or name again and again on the covers of *Evergreen Review* and the Grove Press catalog; almost every issue carried his work and very often his work was advertised in a prominent place; a constant stream of advertising materials and news releases promoted his texts with special offers for those who ordered his books in bulk (figs. 7 and 9). By 1958 Beckett's *Endgame, Waiting for Godot, Molloy,* and *Malone Dies* would share the "Evergreen Books Bestseller List" with Kerouac's *Subterraneans,* Dostoevsky's *House of the Dead,* de Beauvoir's *Marquis de Sade,* Cocteau's *Opium,* del Castillo's *Discovery and Conquest of Mexico,* and Fromm's *Forgotten Language.*

When Grove published the English translation of *The Unnamable* in September 1958, the book was marketed to booksellers at the American Booksellers Association conference with a "buy ten, get one free" offer. Announcing the publication of Beckett's novel as "the literary event of the season!" the ABA convention "Free Gift Certificate" promotes Beckett's novel alongside Alain Robbe-Grillet's *Voyeur* and Pieyre de Mandiargues's *Girl Beneath the Skin*. A note on the back of the certificate thanks booksellers "for making our experiment a success," explaining:

> Last Spring we announced our experiment with original fiction in paperbacks. We said then we didn't know if it would work, but we felt we should try it to evolve a new formula for fiction publishing. With five big printings of Jack Kerouac's *The Subterraneans* now off the press in three short months, you and we have proved the point—and sold a lot of books into the bargain. Original fiction *does* sell in paperbacks!

We are reminded that the "dollar paperback" of *Godot* earned Beckett an average of five thousand dollars per year from 1956 to 1970: by 2006 it had sold 2.5 million copies (Prial 2006, 2). And we are reminded that a major part of its success was on college campuses. In a 1955 note addressed to "Dear College Teacher," Grove pushed "inexpensive texts to be used for courses in modern European and comparative literature," listing *Waiting for Godot, Molloy,* and *Malone Dies* in an "Examination copy offer" as texts adopted "in some of the leading universities and colleges" (SUL). One consequence of this major push on university campuses was to fuel the growth of the Beckett industry in academe as professors turned classroom explanations into career-defining articles and books.

The history of Grove became entwined with the history of Beckett's relationship with the literary marketplace in May 1953 when Rosset tracked Beckett down by going through Sylvia Beach at Shakespeare and Company: Rosset's recollection in 2006 bypasses Beach, suggesting it was Richard Seaver, then an editor at Merlin, who acted as the liaison between Rosset and Lindon; but it is very clear from a letter Rosset wrote in 1953 that Beach, the American who shares with Eugene Jolas the prestige of being the first to publish Beckett, acted as a booster for Beckett. As Rosset put it in his first letter to Beckett on June 18, 1953:

> Sylvia Beach is certainly the one you must blame for your future appearance on the Grove Press list. I went to see her with your work on my mind, and after she talked of you in beautiful words, I immediately decided that what the Grove Press needed most in the world was Samuel Beckett. I told her that, and then she suggested that I make a specific offer. I certainly had not thought of that up to the very moment she took out a piece of paper and pencil and prepared to write down the terms. (SUL 20, fig. 11)

Beach had written Rosset a note on May 25, 1953:

> I saw Mr Samuel Beckett, and learned from him that everything had already been arranged through his agent in New York [Saunders]—apparently the contract was signed, and there was nothing left for me to do but to congratulate him on having such nice publishers, and to bring him your greetings. And I congratulate you on having secured Beckett. (SUL 20)

This note leaves open the possibility that Beach had expected to participate in contract negotiations and was, perhaps, a little disconcerted Beckett was already committed to an agent and a publisher, leaving her without an official role. As the occasion of Rosset's letter suggests, more than three weeks of negotiations took place after Beach's May 25 letter. A draft of the contract was drawn up in New York on May 26 by Saunders, acting as the US literary agent for Minuit: the cover letter for this draft is on letterhead for "Marion Saunders: Literary Agency," and it is signed, on behalf of Lindon, by Georges Borchardt. The long-term consequence of this arrangement is seen in the 1970 statement of royalty percentages for *Samuel Beckett: Collected Works* when it was published in a "reg. edition @ 59.50" and a "limited edition @ 125.00." Under "GP-640," the stock code for the English translation of *Waiting for Godot,* 2.125 percent is allocated to Beckett, 6.375 percent to Les Editions de Minuit, and 1.5 percent is assigned to the estate of M. Saunders. The May 26, 1953, cover letter for the draft of the *Godot* contract, annotated in pencil in the Grove office, also fixes the date by which Rosset had agreed to publish English translations of *Malone meurt* and *Molloy.* Priority was given to *Godot,* but terms for the novels were under active discussion. After inviting revisions to the *Godot* contract, Saunders informs Rosset that, for the two novels, "we intend to follow the contract for *En Attendant Godot* as a whole, inserting of course the proper royalty terms and the arrangement for subsidiary rights." The Grove annotation responds to a question by Saunders, "Do you intend to do *Malone Meurt* first and *Molloy* second, or vice versa?" with the handwritten note "vice versa." In response to a second question, "Is the $800 advance to be applied to book number one, or to be divided $400 for *Malone* and $400 for *Molloy*?" the note indicates "divided." A June 1, 1953, letter from Ephraim London, Rosset's New York lawyer, indicates some "serious objections to the Saunders contract." He goes on to recommend three main revisions: (1) a change in the clause pertaining to dates of delivery of a "publishable ms." recommending that, "if possible, payment of advance should be made on receipt"; (2) a change in how Rosset signs—"Suggest you sign as 'owner,' not as 'president'" and "designate the publisher as 'Barney Rosset, doing business as Grove Press'"; and (3) advising against shortcuts in the contracts for the novels, "I think it is better if two agreements are drawn." If Rosset had taken London's advice about how he signed his name, the 1985 takeover would not have deprived him of the right to continue publishing Beckett's texts because "Barney Rosset, owner of Grove Press" would have continued to own the contracts: as it was, when Getty and Weidenfeld bought Grove Press in 1984, Rosset was cut out of every contract he had signed as "Barney Rosset, Grove Press" or "on behalf of Grove Press."

In any event, the *Molloy* contract followed the one for *Godot,* but Rosset stalled on the contracts for the translations of *Malone meurt* and *L'Innommable:* these contracts, drawn up on November 15, 1954, and March 9, 1956, respectively, cut out the agent and are signed, "For and on behalf of Grove Press" (SUL 20). When the *Malone meurt* agreement was drawn up, it conformed to Saunders's May 1953 proposal that the *Godot* contract become the model for the contracts for the English translations of the novels, but there were two significant changes: Bowles was dropped and Saunders was no longer a party to the agreements. Saunders would continue to receive a share of *Godot* royalties, but Rosset was astute enough to cut her out of subsequent contracts. The *Malone* contract, signed by Rosset on November 29 and by Beckett on December 9, 1954, is on Grove Press letterhead and is titled thus: "Memorandum of agreement between Samuel Beckett, 6 rue des Favorites, Paris XVeme, France and Grove Press, 795 Broadway, New York 3, N.Y. USA, covering the English translation of *Malone meurt*" (SUL 20). Rosset, on behalf of Grove, had managed to cut out two "middlemen" (a translator and an agent) in one swift move. This agreement significantly increased Beckett's and Rosset's shares of the profits.

A final agreement concerning the translation of *Godot* was drawn up on June 2, 1953. Unfortunately this agreement is missing from the Grove editorial files (it was probably in a briefcase with the *Molloy* contract and other papers Rosset left on a train from New York to East Hampton in June 1954 [June 8, 1954, SUL 20]), but its contents are summarized in a June 18, 1953, "Memorandum of agreement between Samuel Beckett, c/o Les Editions de Minuit, 7 rue Bernard-palissy, Paris VI, France (represented by Marion Saunders, Literary Agency) and Grove Press, 795 Broadway, New York, N.Y., covering the English translation of *En Attendant Godot.*" In exchange for full ownership of Beckett's translation of the play, so that "any book publisher, magazine publisher, play, radio, movie, or television producer, etc., in any country, wanting to use that translation, will have to apply to Grove Press for permission," the contract gave Beckett an advance of "$150 (one hundred fifty dollars) plus a royalty of two and one half percent on the published price of all copies sold of Grove Press's regular trade edition."

Beckett's extensive, regular, detailed correspondence with Rosset challenges the received idea that he "hated to deal with publishers" (Bair 1990, 367), suggesting the relationship he developed was based on deep trust and direct engagement and underscoring his intense interest in the public fate of his work. In his first letter directly to Beckett on June 18 1953, Rosset begins, "It is about time that I write a letter to you—now that agents, publishers, friends, etc. have all acted as go-betweens." He goes on to assure Beckett "we will do what we can to make your work known in this country." And he gives some sense why he opposes the proposal to "publish the first act in advance of book publication": it "might really serve to take a little of the edge off the book publication. . . . *En Attendant Godot* should burst upon us as an entity" (SUL 20). On June 25, 1953, Beckett replied with the first of many long letters (five hundred words plus) sent to Rosset during a professional relationship lasting until 1989. Among other things he expressed his appreciation for Rosset's perspective on the advisability of publishing act one of *Godot* in *Merlin* and concluded with his gratitude for Rosset's risk in committing to his work. He expressed a heartfelt wish that they would, through their professional partnership, benefit from the winds of success (SUL 20).

We should not be surprised by Beckett's interest in furthering the success of his published texts; nor should we be surprised at his willingness to deal directly with the first English-language publisher committed to the publication of his work. But, given his public image, we *are* surprised. From the biographies we would not expect a letter of the sort Beckett sent Rosset on July 5, 1953, in which he describes the delay of a package he had put together for Mr. Oram [who had the New York rights to performances of *Godot* until November 1, 1953] containing the first act of *Godot* and copies of press reviews. If Beckett "loathed all forms of self-promotion," why did he send a parcel of press clippings he knew would be used for publicity purposes in New York? Like Estragon and Vladimir he could have done nothing; like Pynchon or Salinger he could have said "no."

As we might expect once we set aside the received idea Beckett loathed all forms of self-promotion, Beckett was more than happy to help Rosset publish and market English-language versions of his books. A letter from Beckett on July 18, 1953, tells Rosset he had found a translator for *Molloy,* Patrick Bowles. The letter also suggests Beckett's full awareness of the importance of an honest relationship between author and publisher. In the June 25 letter he had checked to make sure Rosset knew he was taking on a writer who violated literary conventions and was not going to compromise on matters of form. He returned to this point on July 18, insisting he would only make changes necessitated by the process of translation between languages and asking for Rosset's assurance he was willing to publish the resulting texts. He concluded by underscoring the importance of an unequivocal, clear understanding between publisher, translator, and author before the job began (1953, SUL 20). Concise and precise, Beckett uses his considerable experience in the literary marketplace together with the self-confidence of his South Dublin social class to identify and assert the key aspects of the publishing industry from his point of view: he, the author, retains complete authorial control; the publisher prints whatever he sends.

Given his prewar experience with the publishing industry, he knew very well he was privileged to claim this authority: no established publishing house would give a relatively untested author the freedom and control Grove gave Beckett. By being so clear, he set the stage for a healthy professional relationship grounded in personal trust. The foundation of the relationship was the assumption that Beckett was always right. Certainly Beckett is irascible, ornery even, but he makes the business agreement crystal clear, giving Rosset an exact understanding of how he understands their professional relationship. The effect was to solicit from his new publisher an important assurance: "By all means, the translation should be done with only those modifications required by the change from one language to another. If an insurmountable obstacle is to appear, let it first appear" (July 31, 1953, SUL).

On August 4, 1953, Rosset had just received the Merlin printing of *Watt* from Marion Saunders's agency and writes, "Dear Mr Beckett, I am putting aside WATT, which I received this morning, to write this letter. Fifty pages poured over me and I will inundate myself again as soon as possible." Having set himself up as an avid reader, Rosset puts on his publisher's hat, expressing dismay over the poor quality of the French edition: "One irritation did jut out at me and that is the lack of good proof reading in the pages I went through. . . . To find one word deliberately distorted and the next botched by the type-setter can spoil the tone so easily. Also it is a shame that the type-face used is so scrubby and ugly. Good writing can also look well without losing any of its intrinsic value" (August 4, 1953, SUL). He goes on to suggest how the title page and "the reverse of the title-page" should be printed to indicate copyright information and proposes "The books should be sold to us at cost by Merlin and the profit to you and them (whatever your arrangement with them is) will come out of royalties on which we will make a small advance." This level of detail was, perhaps, too much for Beckett, but it had a positive effect from Rosset's point of view. In his response on September 1, 1953, Beckett clarified his position vis-à-vis Merlin. He acknowledged his deep satisfaction that a book turned down by a long list of London-based publishers has finally been published, going on to confirm his delight at the prospect of a well-made American edition. Finally, claiming an incompetence belied by his clarity concerning publishing arrangements, he gave Rosset authority to negotiate with Merlin on his behalf. In effect, he gave Rosset free rein to negotiate the deal as he saw fit (SUL 20).

The relationship with Rosset was extremely important, but it is just one of the many trusting relationships with a range of professionals that define Beckett's relationship with the literary marketplace after 1953. We have already listed many of those who assisted Beckett as he built the foundations of his career. Over the next phase of his career he would add many important professional acquaintances to his address book, including directors (Walter Asmus, Herbert Blau, Roger Blin, Alan Schneider), personnel in radio and television (Barbara Bray, Martin Esslin, Mary Hutchinson, Donald McWhinnie), actors (Barry McGovern, Jack MacGowran, Patrick Magee, Billie Whitelaw), photographers (Jerry Bauer, John Haynes, John Minihan, Lufti Ozkok), reviewers and editors (Patrick Bowles, Mel Gussow, Harold Hobson, Con Leventhal, Richard Seaver), academics (Kay Boyle, Ruby Cohn, Lawrence Harvey, Hugh Kenner, James Knowlson), booksellers (Jake Schwartz, Henry Wenning), and various other characters associated with the business of literature (Pamela Mitchell, Judith Schmidt).

In the case of Rosset we have the advantage that the Grove Press editorial files at Syracuse University allow us to study the development of what is best described as an intimate business partnership. From Rosset's first letter in June to their first meeting in September 1953, they address each other as "Mr Beckett" and "Mr Rosset." After September 1953, when they met during Rosset's honeymoon (a fact suggesting they shared a common tendency to merge domestic and professional activities), Rosset began a letter "Dear Samuel Beckett" (October 19, 1953). In response to this letter, on October 27, 1953, Beckett makes a bold move toward familiarity by addressing the letter with even more intimacy and by including direct and fond reference to Rosset's new wife, Loly. Four months after their first contact, Beckett's faith in Rosset became explicit when he registered his appreciation for Rosset's extreme hard work in ensuring the success of *Godot* in New York, acknowledging that the 1 percent royalty payment for Rosset's work publishing and publicizing the play was nominal to the point of being derisory.

Beckett's famous avoidance of performances after the rehearsal stage (Bair 1990, 483–84; Knowlson 1996, 359 and 392) must be qualified by noting his great pleasure in attending a number of evenings during the first run of the Paris production of *Godot.* Almost nine months after its premiere he continued to enjoy the play's ongoing ability to create controversy, displaying great amusement in an October 27 letter to Rosset by recounting an episode when a heckler was forcibly ejected from the Théâtre de Babylone. By November Beckett was writing letters to his dearest Loly, moving easily between professional and private details, treating Loly Rosset with the same degree of trust as he had established with her husband. In a letter dated November 20, 1953, he shared professional and personal thoughts with an equal degree of blunt candor. After expressing his distinct pleasure with Grove's decision to publish *Godot* in the spring, he confirmed his agreement with a release date before the first English language performance. He detailed the status of the *Molloy* translation and provided information about the final performance of the Paris production of *Godot,* which ended its run on November 8, 1953. Further, he noted the play was now on tour in Germany and embraced any resistance it might meet. He truly enjoyed the impact *Godot* had on audiences. Finally he observed how much he liked *The Catcher in the Rye* by Salinger. Even though the letter contains statements indicating that Beckett was despondent, the details of the letter reveal he is switched on, his mind actively connecting different aspects of his private and professional worlds. The wide range of subjects he addresses in a letter sent within six months of his first contact with Rosset gives a good sense of the deep trust, engagement, and intimacy that would characterize a relationship responsible for well over 30 percent of Beckett's income for the duration of his career.

During the 1930s this mix of emotional confession, personal interest, and professional information was, in the main, reserved for letters to friends, particularly Mary Manning Howe and Tom McGreevy. At that stage in his career, publishers were a loathsome necessity and, as we have seen, were to be courted, parodied, and manipulated with equal alacrity.

But after the success of *Godot* in Paris, Beckett's days of courtship, parody, and manipulation were over. He reserved some jabs for the inexperienced team at Merlin, and he would remain honest in digging at *New World Writing*'s montage of extracts from *Molloy* and *Malone meurt* and the poor standards of book production in France. But with Lindon, Rosset, and later John Calder, he was always very respectful and friendly. We have already noted Beckett's active involvement in the choice of translator for *Molloy* and his direct assistance in establishing Grove's editorial policy toward what might be considered violations of form. On December 14, 1953, he also gave his advice and opinions about the layout and cover art for the Grove edition of *Godot,* typing out exactly how he would like to see it on the published page and recommending the exact photograph used for the cover. This extremely important letter provides solid evidence of Beckett's direct contribution to the materiality of the published text, underscoring his deep engagement with the literary marketplace and his commitment to the commercial success of his work.

Beckett begins the letter by objecting to Rosset's design for his edition of *Godot* on the grounds that it is confusing and misleading, creating too much variety on the page. He argues the proposed design is visually terrible, giving the impression some characters are more important than others. What we notice is the gentleness and confidence of the tone and the precise attention to detail. With great delicacy he rejects his American publisher's first two choices and proposes some very specific solutions. While he assents to Rosset's plan to use a capital letter to introduce each line of speech as relevant, "V." representing "Vladimir," "E." representing "Estragon" and so on, he makes clear his preference for the full name to be used, either in a column down the left-hand margin or in the center of the page with the text beneath. He insists this repetition of names would underscore the rhythm of repetition in the text: to illustrate, he types five lines with the full names centered and the text beneath. After all this, he proposes a different design based on the layout used in the Minuit edition with the full name in a repetitive pattern down the left-hand side (December 24, 1953, SUL 20). The Grove first edition uses a layout very close to Beckett's preferred design, modifying the Minuit composition by separating the column of names from the column of text to give an impression of greater symmetry. This design, modified slightly through the omission of colons, is used in the four-volume *Grove Centenary Edition* published in 2006. Beckett thus had a shaping influence on the layout of the definitive US edition of his most important work.

Beckett's irascibility and assertiveness when it came to publishing techniques is apparent from his annoyance at the fragmented excerpts from *Molloy* published in *New World Writing* in April 1954 alongside an explanatory and effusive review by a longtime friend of Beckett's from Dublin, Niall Montgomery, "No Symbols Where None Intended": Beckett objects to the heavy-handed slashing of his text, likening it to an ulcerated stomach. A few months earlier his close attention to the materiality of the published text had been further demonstrated by his proactive role in identifying the photograph used for the front cover of Rosset's edition of *Godot*. In the December 14, 1953, letter he calls attention to still photographs taken during the performance in Krefeld, pointing to one that captures the scene at the end of act one where Vladimir pulls Estragon toward the side of the stage. In his eyes the photograph encapsulates the play and makes a great front cover for the book. He promises to track it down and put Rosset in contact with the photographer, amending the typewritten letter with a handwritten note giving the exact mailing address of a company called Foto Dönitz on Winertzhof in Krefeld (SUL). Beckett thus takes a decisive hand in the packaging and design of the book that would, over the next fifteen years, earn him well over seventy-five thousand dollars and put him on the road to a Nobel laureateship. In a follow-up letter of December 29, 1953, Beckett expresses his deep gratitude to Grove for their agreement on the composition of the play and gives specific advice about how to set the stage directions, recommending they follow the neat and simple format used in the manuscript. But, showing his trust in the company, he also accepts their freedom to do something else if they could see ways to improve his design. When the jacket was put together using the photograph Beckett had selected, he sent a note to the designer, Mr. Turner, thanking him, praising the Dönitz photo on the front cover, acknowledging that the smaller details he had questioned were not important. Again we are impressed by Beckett's clear ideas about the packaging of the text, by his delight at how the book looks, by his easy professionalism, by his deference to his professional accomplices, and by his attention to the entire production process.

A July 13, 1953, letter from Rosset to Beckett gives a good sense of the easygoing manner behind their highly successful business relationship: "As to the translation of the novels, I am naturally disappointed to hear that you prefer not to undertake translation of the novels yourself. I can well see your point, however, and it would seem a little sad to attempt to take off that much time to go back over your own book but I hope that you will change your mind" (SUL). Rosset makes his preference known, but he does so in a chatty tone, underscoring his sensitivity to Beckett's mood. He makes it his job to weigh the benefits of a translation by the original author against the delay incurred in the production of new work. And he works to calm Beckett's anxiety: "As to the obscenities within the books, my suggestion is that we do not worry about that until it becomes necessary. Sometimes things like that have a way of solving themselves" (July 13, 1953, SUL). Casual as he was in his dealings with the author, Rosset was an astute businessman. When the publication date for *Molloy* approached, he consulted attorney Ephraim London about words "that might be considered objectionable" (June 8, 1955, SUL), engaging legal counsel as he had during contract negotiations for *Godot* and the first two novels. But in correspondence with Beckett he focuses on cultural linguistics, revealing his sharp sense of Beckett's universalist aesthetics and demonstrating remarkable savvy in negotiating with a man ostensibly resistant to compromise. Having raised a question about words "such as skivvy and cutty" (in *Godot*) that would "give the writing a most definite British stamp" (August 4, 1953, SUL), he writes, "That is perfectly all right if it is the effect you desire. If you are desirous of a little more vagueness as to where the scene is set it would be better to use substitutes which are of common usage both here and in Britain." Again, in the context of Beckett's famous resistance to any changes in his texts because his main principle was "artistic integrity," this approach to the issue of potential obscenities is little short of brilliant. It appeals to Beckett's prior acceptance of revisions necessitated by the change from French to English and, thus, opens the possibility for compromise on an issue Beckett had initially said he had no intention of negotiating (June 25, 1953, SUL). On September 1, 1953, Beckett deferred to Rosset by agreeing to change any words not familiar to an American audience, asking his publisher to identify any such words (SUL).

Rosset's diplomatic skill in engaging Beckett in the complexities of the literary marketplace and in the creation of a more marketable text is also apparent in the August 4 letter. Wearing the hat of a professional publisher preparing a text for a specific market, Rosset proposes that the American edition of *Watt* "should be printed on good paper and put in a binding up to American standards"; in his response on September 1, 1953, Beckett expresses his extreme pleasure at the prospect of a high-quality American edition. While Beckett did not respond immediately to Rosset's commitment to "keep the price of the book [*Watt*] at the lowest possible figure and give it a fighting chance to get sold," on October 18, 1954, he told Rosset he was in total agreement with the plan to reduce the cover price of the book as much as possible (SUL). The letters from autumn 1954 give a good sense of Beckett's level of engagement with the business side of his career.

Beckett spent three months in Killiney in the summer of 1954 to help during his brother's final illness (Frank died tragically young on September 13, 1954, two months after his fifty-second birthday). While there, he received a letter from his American publisher asking for information about the English performing rights to *Godot,* the translation of *Molloy,* and the Merlin edition of the novel (August 18, 1954, SUL 20). By return of post, Beckett describes his slow progress revising the translation of *Molloy,* going into microscopic detail about his current publishing situation (August 21, 1954, SUL 20). Even though, true to habit, he claims to be disconnected from every aspect of his work, his prompt response reveals deep engagement with his business affairs. Distracted by a gut-wrenching family crisis and almost five hundred miles away from his office, he devotes most of the letter to a detailed description of the shenanigans over the forthcoming production of *Godot* in London, explaining the situation with Alec Guinness and putting Rosset in contact with Donald Albery. He goes on to advise Rosset to get a contract in writing from Merlin to assure the simultaneous publication of the Merlin and Grove editions of *Molloy* (August 21, 1954, SUL 20). Beckett's proactive role during this period is obvious and undeniable: on his way back to Paris after his brother's funeral, he stopped off to chat with Albery and Peter Glenville, his London producers, managing to squeeze in a business meeting with Sir Ralph Richardson to answer questions about *Godot.* Apparently Richardson wanted detailed biographical information on Pozzo (October 18, 1954, SUL 20). In the letter Beckett explains the serious consideration he gave to withdrawing the contract for Glenville and Albery to produce the play in London unless they put the play on stage by February 1955 (six months after the contract was issued). He further notes he has made progress with the translation of *Malone* and is agreeable to a contract for the translation based on the one given to Patrick Bowles. Finally he confesses he has written a nasty letter to Alexander Trocchi complaining about the bowdlerization of his work in *Merlin.* It is not just that we see ample evidence of professional engagement at a time when there were great demands on his personal life. It is also that his interventions in his business affairs are incredibly detailed, forthright, and, on occasion, aggressive.

By fall 1954 Beckett was so trusting of Rosset that, having made the decision to drop Bowles as a co-translator, he was ready to accept a contract to translate *Malone Dies* even though he was not entirely comfortable with its terms. He admits in the letter that he was willing to do so because he was indebted to Rosset for becoming his conduit into the American literary marketplace (October 18, 1954, SUL). Again Beckett makes his views known, but he is willing to defer to Rosset out of respect for the publisher's long-term commitment and professional expertise. Beckett's ongoing engagement with the publishing industry is, once again, explicit in the cover note he sent with the *Malone* contract on December 7, 1954. Remarkably business-like in its tone and content, the letter employs the discourse of commercial exchange and contract law, using terms like "herewith," "duly," and "ultimatum." Functioning as a cover letter for the signed copy of his contract for *Malone,* the note specifies his agreement to control the release of his final page proofs preventing Maurice Girodias at Olympia Press from publishing in advance of the Grove edition. He again intervenes in the actual production process by advising Rosset to use an independent printer to set the type, despite the expense. In conclusion he notes his aggressive stance on the London contract for *Godot,* again using legalese to explain why he is ready to withdraw Albery and Glenville's rights, claiming their deposit as a forfeit for not fulfilling their end of the deal (SUL 1). Beckett's direct treatment of the nitty-gritty of the publishing industry demonstrates his willingness to set the tone for how publishing decisions should be made; when necessary he was prepared to offer advice about the printing process and, when pushed, would issue an ultimatum to ensure adherence to contractual obligations.

With secure contracts for publications in French and English, and with *Godot* attracting attention throughout Europe, Beckett's life as a professional writer became increasingly complex and demanding. But with over twenty years experience under his belt, he was up to the task. Beckett's professionalism during this period is complemented by his keen interest in the various productions of *Godot* across Europe. In February 1955 he notes that the Blin production in Arnhem, Holland, was to begin on March 5 or 6, telling Rosset he had just received a stack of reviews from Rome, mostly positive: in this letter he laments receiving a letter from Leo Kerz of the New Repertory Theatre asking for the rights to produce an eight-week run on Broadway with Buster Keaton, Marlon Brando, Wally Cox, and Fred Allen: he expresses deep sorrow at being forced to turn Kerz down because he was still under contract with Albery and Greenville to produce the premiere of

Godot in London. He could not bring himself to break his agreement with the London producers by allowing a prior English-language production in New York (February 11, 1955, SUL 20). Again we note his diligence in understanding and honoring his contractual obligations and his detailed-oriented participation in the entire process.

A letter he sent Howard Turner the day before *Godot*'s London opening on August 3, 1955, demonstrates a profound level of ongoing engagement with the business of production rights in the United Kingdom and United States. The letter also reveals his deep concern about being cut out of the production process. Delving into the details of the Albery-Glenville contract, he specifically laments the impact of the postponements in London on a New York premiere and expresses anxiety about the Arts Theatre production. In his opinion, the producers had been too standoffish throughout: he complains they had neither apprised him of their plans nor asked him his ideas, changing their minds frequently about the actors, the stage set, and the overall shape of the production but never consulting him at any stage. In the letter he acknowledges that the financial deal, five hundred pounds as an advance against royalties, gave them the right to ignore him, but he still laments their lack of contact (August 2, 1955, SUL 1). His pessimism about the London production is directly associated with the offhandedness of those involved and his feeling of disconnection from the process. He had, perhaps, been spoiled by the Blin production because it gave him complete freedom to attend rehearsals, chat with the actors and director, tinker with the script, make general recommendations about the staging of the play, and help design the set. As we have seen from Beckett's contract negotiations with Rosset, he preferred a situation in which the strictly professional terms of a working relationship and the ultimate authority of the author were mixed with heavy doses of casual "give-and-take."

The move to a West End theater with a London-based attitude about business upped the level of formality, increasing the level of prestige but decreasing the level of authorial involvement. For better or worse, the London stage is a highly professionalized space, with entrenched procedures for casting, set design, and rehearsals: a new writer could not just walk in and make a casual contribution to rehearsals and other aspects of the production without disrupting the well-oiled machinery of West End theatrical culture. This was a privilege to be earned over time. It would be ten years before Beckett's name was sufficiently established to allow him to cross the line between authorship and production in West End versions of his plays. By 1964, when he helped George Devine produce *Play* at the Old Vic, Beckett would be in a position to exert more direct influence; in the meantime he had to make do with a March 22, 1955, agreement giving him, through Lindon and Rosset, the right to ensure the play was produced according to the terms of the author's contract. This agreement gave him influence but no rights regarding casting, stage design, blocking, pacing, and other crucial decisions. The script and stage directions could not be changed without Beckett's consent, but everything else was in the hands of the director and producer.

A major long-term effect of Beckett's limited contractual rights over the London production of *Godot* was his impotence when it came to the US rights. On October 3, 1955, Albery contracted with Michael Myerberg to present *Waiting for Godot* on Broadway and, subsequently, in the United States of America, again limiting Beckett's rights to those "provided for in the author's contract." This contract allocated an author's share of 5 percent on box-office receipts up to $5,000, 7.5 percent on receipts from $5,000 to $8,000, and 10 percent on receipts above $8,000, adding "a managerial over-riding profit royalty of 2.5% throughout" to be paid to Albery's "Independent Plays" ("Godot Play Production," SUL). The contract required Myerberg to pay "$1000 on account of the royalties on the box office receipts" for a three-month option to produce the play on Broadway, and a further $1,000 for a nine-month extension in the event he had not exercised his right within three months. The $2,000 Myerberg paid was not "returnable in any case." Again, having sold the rights to his work, Beckett had given up on any possibility he could participate in its production: he had no say until the rights reverted to him. In the meantime negotiations were out of his hands and had to be sorted among Albery, Myerberg, and Rosset (SUL). When he signed the initial contract with Albery's Donmar Productions (a subsidiary of Independent Plays, which was in charge of the New Theatre on St. Martin's Lane, London), Beckett knew little about the theater business and was willing to defer to a professional company that *did* know the business. Beckett's serious misgivings about Albery's production and the attitude of the West End theater industry were salved by his respect for Albery's understanding of the industry and the audience in London (October 18, 1954, SUL). On the one hand he was frustrated by his lack of control over the production: a week after the London opening, he wrote disdainfully to MacGreevy about the English production mincing his play to pieces, imposing difficulties and problems on a play he regarded as straightforward (August 11, 1955, TCD, 196). He explained how he had thrown up his hands, deciding to withdraw. But on the other hand, he was excited by the play's success: on August 25, 1955, he wrote to Rosset with news about the extension of the run at the Arts Theatre and the rumor that the play might be transferred to a larger theater; and on October 26, 1955, he reported a conversation with Harold Hobson, the London-based theater critic. Beckett was clearly excited by Hobson's news about the play's success at the box office. Again, Beckett's expression of nonparticipation and fatigue must be seen in light of his keen attention to the ups and downs of the production. He may have withdrawn to Paris, but he made up for his physical distance by maintaining regular contact in extensive written correspondence.

When the English translation of *Godot* first opened in London in August 1955, Beckett's major business dealings were organized through Lindon in Paris and Rosset in New York. Duthuit's revamped version of *Transition* had stopped publishing in 1953 and, with the exception of agreements with Merlin/Olympia for *Watt,* interaction with Roger Blin as he toured Europe with *Godot,* and the occasional deal with the Irish journals *Envoy* and *New Irish Writing,* his professional life was relatively manageable. But the success of *Godot* in London began seriously to complicate matters. Business contracts began to pile up as his agreement with Lindon for the French rights was supplemented by separate contracts covering rights to perform, translate, and publish in the major European countries (Italy, Germany, Holland, Spain), as well as Britain, France, Ireland, and the United States. By the end of 1955 his contracts for *Godot* included the following "welter of contracts and quasi-contracts" (as Rosset called it in a letter to Beckett on January 11, 1956): Albery's Donmar Productions held the English-language performance rights; through Faber, Curtis Brown held the British publication rights; Marion Saunders was acting as the New York agent for Les Editions de Minuit; on his own behalf, Michael Myerberg held the American performance rights; through Minuit, Lindon continued to hold a stake in the global publishing rights; and, through Grove, Barney Rosset held rights to the English translation of the play (for English-language publications and performances in any country other than Britain and Ireland). In short, Beckett's position in the literary marketplace had become immensely complicated.

The stresses and strains emerging from these agreements and cross-agreements in the run-up to the productions of *Godot* in England and the United States were particularly distracting (December 17, 1955, SUL). The main source of trouble was Albery's sale of the American production rights to Myerberg; because Albery and Myerberg, apparently with Lindon's knowledge, bypassed Grove, Rosset felt compelled to call attention to the translation contract. Specifically, he asserted his right "to enforce" the "agreement with Lindon whereby I get 10% of gross received, to be taken out of Lindon's share" (October 25, 1955, SUL 20). By return of post, Beckett assured Rosset he could depend on him to protect his ownership of the translation of *Godot* and could be confident he would continue to receive his share of the royalties for the translation. Beckett's assurance was bolstered by a letter from Lindon, dated October 28, 1955. Rosset summarized Lindon's agreement in a letter to Beckett: "10 percent of gross revenues received from the English production will be put to our account" and "all will be harmonious between us" so long as the agreement is kept and "the cost of revision is [not] used as a way of depriving us of our agreed upon share of the proceeds" (SUL 32). This latter point refers to a niggling misunderstanding about the difference between the scripts used in London and New York (the Faber and Faber edition of *Godot* differs in a number of ways from the Grove edition because the London edition was censored by the Lord Chamberlain; see Ackerley and Gontarski 2004, 620–21). Lindon demanded payment from Rosset for alterations to the translation; Rosset refused. This particular problem was settled relatively quickly, with the agreement that Rosset owned rights to all versions in English, regardless of any revisions to the script.

With Beckett and Lindon's support, Rosset proceeded to request written agreements from Albery and Myerberg. The ensuing confusion led Rosset to send Beckett a letter reporting "an extremely annoying procedure": Myerberg referred the request to Albery, and Albery sent it to Saunders, resulting in a demand from Saunders for payment for "all the work she was going through" (December 6, 1955, SUL 20). On the same day Beckett sent a cable from London imploring Rosset to desist from blocking the US production and assuring him he would be fully compensated with the appropriate percentage for his rights to the translation (December 6, 1955, SUL 32). In a subsequent letter Beckett confirmed the agreement and acknowledged he should be blamed for creating the problem by failing to mention the translation agreement when he contracted with Albery (December 17, 1955, SUL 32). Rosset and Curtis Brown (Albery's London agent) agreed Beckett should not be held responsible for business deals, agreeing it was Lindon's job to make Albery aware of Rosset's interests: "Beckett himself would certainly hate the thought that anyone might suffer through his singular incapacity for business" (December 12, 1955, SUL 32).

This complicated matter was finally cleared up to the satisfaction of all parties on January 10, 1956, when Curtis Brown sent a cable accepting Rosset's terms. A January 13, 1956, letter from Kitty Black at Curtis Brown explains,

> As Mr Curtis Brown cabled you, we have had an official letter from Jérôme Lindon asking us to pay you ten percent of all monies so far received on behalf of Samuel Beckett, both from the London and New York productions. . . . The royalties paid to the time of writing, less agent's commission, total £1,796.10.9. The sum we shall apply to send to you, therefore is £179.13.1, and once Bank of England permission has been granted, a monthly cheque can be forwarded as required. (SUL 32)

Because Myerberg's contract was subsidiary to the contract with Albery, it was now absolutely clear Grove would receive 10 percent of the author's share of all English-language productions of the play. In return, Rosset gave Curtis Brown permission to "authorize all future productions of the play, both by amateurs and professionals, without reference to me," noting he did not "include this to cover the United States" (January 17, 1956, SUL). We have already noted the telegrams, letters, and conversations testifying to Beckett's direct interventions in the contract dispute. It is also worth underscoring that he directly initiated the resolution by instructing Lindon to ask Curtis Brown to make provision for direct payments of the 10 percent royalty rate owed to Rosset from Albery's box-office receipts and to settle any arrears immediately (January 6, 1956 [wrongly dated January 6, 1955], SUL 1).

With Beckett's position stated so clearly and insistently, Myerberg finally fell into line: on May 1, 1956, he sent Rosset the first of a series of royalty payments, in this case representing 10 percent of the author's share of the Miami production and the first two weeks in New York ($1,292.85 to Beckett; $258.57 to Rosset; $1,034.28 to Lindon; see fig. 15). This was, as Meyerberg put it, "In accordance with instructions from Mr Donald Albery, Independent Plays Limited and Les Editions de Minuit" (SUL 31). Once bitten, Beckett precluded any problems over the Pike production in Ireland by sending Alan Simpson a personal note clarifying his agreement with Rosset and stipulating the payment of 10 percent of the author's share from all English-language productions of *Godot* (January 6, 1956, SUL 1). This proactive strategy worked: on July 4, 1956, Simpson sent Rosset a check for nineteen pounds and three shillings plus a comprehensive statement of accounts from the nineteen-week run at the Pike, the week at the Gate, and the three-week tour of various halls across Ireland (Carlow, Clonmel, Cork, Drogheda, Dundalk, Dun Laoghaire, Navan, and Waterford).

As Beckett's intervention in this contract dispute demonstrates, the relationship between Beckett and Rosset was completely solid by the time *Godot* had its American premiere in January 1956. Despite misunderstandings and the occasional disagreement, they had developed a bond based on mutual trust and honesty. This point is supported by a paragraph in a letter from January 6, 1956, in which he defers to Rosset's calculation of what he is due from the translation of *Malone* and asks for the balance of whatever Rosset deems payable to his account. Beckett's ongoing engagement with the packaging of his books is also illustrated by this letter; he thanks Rosset for sending him a copy of the cover of the paperback *Godot* and expresses his wish to name Harold Hobson in the blurb as an acknowledgment of his help in stimulating box-office sales in London (SUL 1). This close, market-focused relationship between Beckett and Rosset was reinforced by the deal Lindon and Rosset had worked out for the translations of *Godot* and *Molloy* and by their full collaboration in the marketing of Beckett's work. Back in August the American publisher had written to tell Beckett "Your work is attracting attention here and I feel certain that some day your merit will gain its place" (August 18, 1954, SUL 20). With *Godot* off the presses in June 1954, ready to be launched in autumn, and with Beckett finishing the English translation of *Molloy*, Howard Turner, the new publicity manager at Grove, wrote to Lindon on October 6, 1954, requesting "copies of any reviews which you may have of the edition you brought out two years ago" explaining, "these would be of great assistance to us in preparing catalogue and other promotional material" (SUL 27). Less than a week later, on October 11, Lindon sent "l'affiche jointe, que nous avons publiée un mois après la sortie de livre" (the advertisement, which we published a month after the book came out) plus articles by Bataille and Jean Blanzat (SUL 27). Lindon also included a list of eleven pithy quotations from French reviews of *Molloy, Malone meurt,* and *En attendant Godot.* Beckett's professional affairs were, then, being pushed forward with great expediency across international borders. Once more, we should note Beckett's direct participation in this commerce from the beginning: back in July 1953 he had included press clippings covering the Paris production when he mailed his translation of *Godot;* quotations from this material were used to advertise the play in London and New York (fig. 10).

By fall 1955, *Molloy* was in bookstores in New York, and Rosset began to receive inquiries from London-based publishers "concerning the publication of MOLLOY in England." Noting "the performance of the play has excited a great deal of interest," he wrote,

> I am very happy to see the bubbling up of interest and my strong feeling is that your work is going to be more and more known as time goes by. There definitely is an underground of interest here, the kind of interest that slowly generates steam and has a lasting effect. GODOT has definitely been picking up in sales the past few weeks and I also attribute this to the London production. (October 20, 1955, SUL)

Often Beckett let others take care of his business affairs, but we misunderstand his relationship with the literary marketplace if we ignore his interest in increased sales. For example, a November 12, 1955, letter to Rosset explains his belief that the less expensive edition soon to be released in New York would sell very well on bookstands in England and Ireland (SUL 1). During this period Beckett was actively working out a strategy for dealing with a business situation with definite aesthetic and economic benefits and also with personal and creative drawbacks; his professional career had begun to take on a life of its own, getting in the way of his ability to focus on his private life and his creative work. On September 13, 1955, in a letter enclosing more press clippings of reviews of his work, he told Rosset he was very happy with the high quality of the printing and presentation of *Molloy.* But he went on to complain about being swamped with literary affairs in France, apologizing for the delay this caused with his translation of *Malone Dies* (SUL 20). In September 1955 Olympia issued its edition of *Molloy;* at the same time, Minuit was preparing the November 1955 publication of *Nouvelles et textes pour rien.*

Together with the increased media attention brought by the transfer of *Godot* from the New Arts Theatre to the much larger Criterion Theatre, and with the upcoming Pike production in Dublin, Beckett's fall 1955 schedule was under serious pressure. It appears he added to his busy professional commitments during this intense period by frequenting the Closerie de Lilas, the Falstaff, and other bars in Montparnasse, developing important social/professional relationships with Avigdor Arikha and Joan Mitchell, among others. The process he was going through in the effort to control his professional life is evident from the November 12, 1955, letter to Rosset. Explaining why it is unlikely he would accept Myerberg's offer to make an expenses-paid trip to New York to help with *Godot,* he begins to sketch out the terms under which he might assist: he would need a clearly defined role ensuring he was not in the way and was not at cross-purposes with the director, and he would need guaranteed protection from interviews and questions. At the same time he is sensitive to the demands a producer was likely to put on him, especially a producer who had paid his expenses, and was aware that his terms might be too stringent (SUL 1). By November 20, Beckett had begun to imagine a way of participating in the New York production by providing his insights from a distance and being excused from the interview circuit (SUL 20). On November 26 he met the director of the American premiere of *Godot,* Alan Schneider, in Paris and traveled with him to London to see *Godot* at the Criterion. Beckett clearly knew the American production of his play promised to open a new avenue in the literary marketplace, and he knew his participation, whether direct or remote, had the potential to be immensely helpful in creating a box-office success.

Whether or not the London production was "all wrong," as Beckett is reported to have told Schneider, Albery's production, under the direction of Peter Hall, was hugely successful. Despite being the first English-language run of an almost unknown writer's first play, it was truly a hit. This brings us full square against one of the most resilient myths about Beckett's relationship with the literary marketplace: the failure of the early productions of *Godot.* The received narrative tells us the early productions were met with "waves of hostility," as Peter Bull (Pozzo) put it in his memoirs (quoted in Bair 1990 and Knowlson 1996), so that "soon a noisy exodus began" (Cronin 1996, 447). "Without exception, the popular press dismissed it as rubbish" (Bair 1990, 453), so that "the English production seemed conspicuously to have failed" (Knowlson 1996, 374). These descriptions apply to the first few performances in London and would apply to the first American production in Miami, provoking Beckett to refer to the production in Miami as a disaster. But they distort the truth.

Beckett's pessimism about the prospects for Albery's version of *Godot* in the West End was almost immediately overshadowed by its immense success. All three biographers credit reviews by Harold Hobson and Kenneth Tynan with a dramatic turn in the tide (Cronin 1996, 448), that "transformed the play, more or less overnight, into the rage of London" (Knowlson 374); the effect was to "reverse public opinion" and to "start audiences streaming into the theater" (Bair 1990, 453). The real story, then, is that after a few days the play became a box-office sensation, embraced by London's "alternative crowd" and heralded as "insidiously exciting" by Harold Hobson (who would contribute a decade later to Calder's birthday celebration, *Beckett at*

Sixty). Furthermore, adding to the argument we have already begun to make about Beckett's involvement with his work when it went out into the commercial world, the evidence demonstrates Beckett was intensely interested in the production from beginning to end.

In a way directly connected with the tendency to downplay the extent to which Beckett engaged with the literary marketplace, there has been a tendency to overplay the failure of the early performances of *Godot.* These supposed failures have, indeed, become as much a part of Beckett's authorial persona as his ostensible lack of interest in the commercial success of his work. On the Left Bank, at a theater with 230 seats, *En attendant Godot* attracted a steady, if sometimes rambunctious, audience for more than four hundred performances, becoming the center of conversation in fashionable circles exactly because it offended mainstream audiences: at the heart of the play's success was a coterie of the sort soon to be cultivated as the target audience in New York. Fully aware of what had happened in Paris, and capitalizing on the media reaction to the Miami production, Myerberg would advertise the play by appealing directly to "70,000 bona fide intellectuals" interested in a play "which flouts every concept of conventional theatrical entertainment" (as Arthur Gelb put it in "Wanted: Intellects," an article reporting an interview with Myerberg on the front page of section 2 of the *New York Times* on April 15, 1956). Like the first run at the Babylone in Paris, the London production quickly attracted a sizable audience, especially after Hobson described it as "bewildering . . . exasperating . . . insidiously exciting" (*Times,* August 7, 1955) and Kenneth Tynan wrote how the play "pricked and stimulated my own nervous system," and "forced [me] to re-examine the rules which have hitherto governed the drama" (*Observer,* August 7, 1955). In a paradox central to Beckett's life as a professional writer, the notoriety of a "disastrous" play, famous for emptying theaters, quickly attracted a "cult" audience (as Tynan wrote in a second article on August 14, 1955): Albery and Glenville's London production of the play was so successful it had to be moved to a larger theater, the Criterion, after a month. In short, the myth of failure transformed the play into a box-office success. Failure was already becoming a central component of the marketing of Beckett's work (see fig. 10).

The complexity of Beckett's engagement with the literary marketplace during this phase of his career is evident from a letter he sent Barney Rosset on February 22, 1956 (SUL). I had hoped to quote the letter in full because, in a relatively short burst of prose, it covers a range of business issues current in the first six months of 1956, when he finally began to make serious profits from his work. The letter recommits to inexpensive paperbacks of the sort responsible for Grove's explosive growth from a tiny concern in 1953 into a leading publishing house in 1958. Noting he had revised parts of *Malone Dies* when editing it for *Irish Writing*, he apologizes for the extra edits. On the subject of *Waiting for Godot* he expresses his keen interest in receiving a copy of the one-dollar edition; reports the rapid sales of the scrambled Faber edition; points out the lack of news from Albery, Schneider, or Meyerberg about plans for the play after the Miami production; describes his plan to meet Kitty Black to discuss the matter; gives news of the one hundredth performance at the Pike Theatre in Dublin; and concludes by reporting the London producers are trying to engage with the tourist trade. Further, he indicates he has finished a draft of the play that would become *Fin de partie* and is struggling with the translation of *L'Innommable*. Touching base with what is going on in England, Ireland, and the United States, the letter reveals Beckett's active and enthusiastic engagement with a wide range of business affairs, including behind-the-scenes planning for the English-language version of *Godot* and the development of a popular audience through cheap editions and tourism. The letter testifies to his personal contact with Dublin-based publishing and anticipates direct correspondence with the producers of *Godot* in England and America as well as with the proposed director of the play on Broadway. The visit he refers to from Kitty Black of Curtis Brown Limited suggests ongoing and direct involvement in negotiations over the contract for West End and Broadway productions of *Godot*. The status report on his creative endeavors gives Rosset news he had been waiting for since the translation of *Malone Dies* arrived on his desk in the first few days of December 1955. And the news about the longevity of *Godot* in Dublin and the expansion of its audience in London indicates more than a little interest in the commercial success of his work.

The Miami production effectively stimulated sales of *Godot:* by March 8, 1956, Rosset could report that there was "much commotion and pleasantly so, milling around *Godot*" and that the "Paper bound edition [published in January 1956 to coincide with the Miami production] has already sold 1900 copies, in its brief weeks of existence, while the hardbound has more or less run its course at 800" (March 8, 1956, SUL 1). This movement in the direction of blockbuster commercial success gathered speed when the New York production began on April 19, 1956, at the 805-seat John Golden Theater on 45th Street between Broadway and Eighth Avenue. From Myerberg's point of view the New York run "was extremely well received and the box office was more than satisfactory" (June 8, 1956, SUL 1). While Myerberg's collaboration with Independent Plays "returned less than half of the capital invested," Myerberg was resolute that the "good deal of money I spent on publicity . . . far beyond the potential of the cast" was a worthwhile investment because "We have been turning away hundreds of people for the last few days." On May 1, 1956, Michael Myerberg sent Rosset 10 percent of the author's royalties from two weeks in Miami and two weeks in New York. The author's share from a production still described as "the Miami fiasco" (Ackerley and Gontarski 2004, 621), accumulated on a sliding scale starting at 5 percent, then 7.5 percent, then 10 percent of the box office receipts, was $2,585.69 (Beckett received 50 percent of this amount, Lindon 40 percent, Rosset 10 percent). From this point on, Beckett would earn 5 percent of the box office receipts for American productions of *Godot,* another 4 percent going to Les Editions des Minuit, and 1 percent going to Grove. We have already noted the spike in sales of tickets to the New York production during the week ending May 12, following the May 6 publication of "Moody Man of Letters" (Shenker 1956). The gross at the box office was more than $2,000 higher than the preceding and following weeks and was only outdone by the final week (fig. 15). This is partly because of Myerberg's management. Rosset explained to Beckett on May 18 that "[t]his business of extension ad nauseam is merely a coy Myerberg trick to make people rush to the box office." We have no evidence of any complaint from Beckett about the rush. Au contraire.

Before the noninterview with Shenker appeared, New York's *Variety* published a snippet on May 2, 1956, showing *Godot* took in $10,000 at the box office during its first four performances at the Golden Theater (*Variety* 1956). Under the contract with Myerberg, Beckett received 5 percent of the gross box office receipts to $5,000, 7.5 percent on the next $3,000, and 10 percent on anything over $8,000. With ticket prices at $5.75 and $4.60, the potential gross was approximately $4,000 per performance. Of the $10,000 grossed in the first, short, week of April 19–21, and the first full-week of April 22–28, Beckett's share was 50 percent of "the entire author's royalty of $1,979.61 (again, the amounts, $778.92 for the week ending April 21, 1956, and $1,200.67 for the week ending April 28, were to be split 50 percent to Beckett, 40 percent to Les Editions de Minuit, and 10 percent to Grove). Added to the amounts due from the weeks ending January 7 and January 14, 1956, in Miami, which gave a total author's share of $673.71 and $153.17

respectively, this gave Beckett $1,293 from the Miami production and the first two weeks of the New York production. Myerberg's royalty statements for the week ending May 5, 1956, show that there was a box office gross of $15,911.80, with $1,266.18 owed to the author. For the week ending May 12, after the Shenker article was published, the gross rose to $18,178.60, with $1,492.86 owed to the author. In this second two-week period, once Grove took its 10 percent cut of $275.90, minus an original royalty advance of $100 (which Myerberg omitted to withhold from the first check to Rosset for $258.56), Beckett earned $2,583.14. In subsequent weeks the author's share after Grove's 10 percent had been deducted was $1,137.22, $852.60, $860.21, and $1,474.40 respectively. From the Miami production and the eight-week New York run from April 19, 1956, to June 9, 1956, Independent Plays, Donald Albery's company (which had been granted performance rights by Donmar Productions), earned close to $3,000. This left slightly more than $8,370 to be sent to Les Editions de Minuit and just above $1,000 to Grove. Once Minuit took its 40 percent share, Beckett was left with $5,022.

That was not all. The paperback was selling fast. On June 8, 1956, Myerberg informed Beckett, "We have sold almost 3,000 copies of the play [*Waiting for Godot*] at our performance." We know from a letter Rosset sent Beckett on March 26, 1956, that the Grove paperback edition had sold well over 2,000 copies in the weeks since it was published. By May 18 he was able to report he had "sold over 6000 copies" with "unfulfilled orders for about 2000 copies." Rosset goes on to report, "a new printing of 5000 is due in today" and "I have ordered another 5000 printing to avoid running out." In the first six months of sales of Grove's hardback version of the play, from June 1954 to January 1955, a total of 238 copies had sold. Another 64 sold between January 31 and July 31, 1955 (royalty statements dated October 15, 1954, and March 21, 1955, sent to Saunders's agency, SUL 30). As already noted, by March 1956 "the hardbound" had "more or less run its course at 800," with the final 163 copies selling during the first part of the period covered by a royalty statement sent to the Saunders agency on June 30, 1956. In the first half of 1956 the $1.00 Grove paperback sold 12,297 copies; in July 1 to December 31, 1956, it would sell a further 5,741 copies. There is some confusion about the royalty owed to Beckett because the memorandum of agreement dated June 18, 1953, indicates a "royalty of 2.5% on the published price of all copies sold of Grove Press's regular trade edition," but the royalty statement for July 1, 1956, through December 31, 1956, is clear: "Royalty accrued @ 10% of our list price $1.00." This statement seems to adjust the previous period's statement, crediting the author's account with $1,212.78 from the previous period (which would represent 7.5 percent for the first 3,000 copies of the hardback and paperback combined plus 10 percent of sales above 3,000 for the paperback for the period) and $573.89 for the period to December 31 (almost exactly 10 percent of the sales for this period).

Although the June 18 agreement names a royalty figure of 2.5 percent "for the ownership of this translation," and this figure appears on a June 30, 1956, royalty statement, a separate note indicates "Marion Saunders Literary Agency" should be paid "7.5% of list price of $4.75 on first 3000 copies and 10% thereafter." Subsequent royalty statements, including the one for the period ending June 30, 1957, are unequivocal in allocating 10 percent for the paperback and 7.5 percent for the hardback. Going back to the period of the Miami and New York productions of the play, Grove's accounts tell us the actual check sent to "Beckett, c/o Saunders" was $1,212.67 in August 1956 and $573.89 in January 1957. With 15 percent of the total author amount going to Saunders, sales of *Godot* in the six-month period including the Miami production and the New York production gave Beckett $1,030; the following accounting period gave him $487.81. In January 1956 Beckett had received 50 percent of the fee Myerberg paid to continue his option on the play, which gave Beckett $500 to be deducted from his "share in the profits" (Contract of October 3, 1955, SUL). In the period between January and June 1956, Beckett received approximately $6,234 in earnings from American productions of *Godot* and American sales of Grove's two editions of the play. In addition, Grove sold the translation of *Godot* to Faber and Faber in March 1956 for $150, giving Beckett a cut of $75.

The dollars Beckett earned in the first six months of 1956 do not, of course, constitute his entire income for the period. *Godot* opened at the Arts Theatre on August 3, 1955, moved to the larger Criterion on September 12, 1955, and remained there, playing to capacity audiences, until May 1956. A note sent to Rosset by Curtis Brown on January 13, 1956, indicates, "The royalties paid to the time of writing, less agent's commission, total £1,796.10.9" (50 percent to Beckett, 10 percent to Rosset, 40 percent to Lindon). This accounting represents the amount for the first five months of the play, allowing us to deduce that Beckett's share for the remaining four months of the London run was approximately £800. To this amount we must add Beckett's share of the £172.7.3 sent to Lindon from the Pike Theatre Club in Ireland. The play was performed at the Pike in Dublin from October

29, 1955, to March 1956, moving to the Gate Theatre in March, then touring as noted above, ending at the Gas Company Theatre in Dun Laoghaire on June 17, 1956, earning Beckett approximately 103 Irish pounds. Finally we should add any income from the Faber edition of *Godot* published in March 1956. For the first six months of 1956, Beckett received a minimum of £1,000 plus $6,734 for English-language productions of *Waiting for Godot* in America, England, and Ireland. Beyond this, we also know he was due $100 from the contract with *Theatre Arts* magazine to publish *Godot* in August 1956, $100 for the sale of "Yellow" to *New World Writing* in May 1956, and an advance of $150 on the March 9, 1956, contract to translate *L'Innommable* for Grove: a May 22, 1956, letter from Rosset indicates they "sent off a check or cheque yesterday directly to Lindon [look, no agents] for the sum of $400 as an advance for 'L'Inno'" (SUL). As for the hardbound *Molloy,* which had sold 576 copies by February 17, 1956, he was still working off his advance of $150.

In sum, between January and June 1956 Beckett earned well above $7,000 plus £1,000 in England, Ireland, and the United States. At a rate of $2.80 per pound, his income for the first six months of 1956 approached $10,000 or, to put it in a currency he could spend on the streets of Paris, 3.5 million French francs. If he had, indeed, gone to New York in 1956, Beckett could have used his money to buy tickets for himself and thirteen friends, round-trip in first-class cabins on the SS *America* (at $700 per person). If he had traveled alone he could have put a 50 percent down payment on a fully equipped, brand new four-bedroom house in New Jersey (at $17,990 in Lawrence Brook). While there he could have flown eighty or so friends to Miami and back on Eastern Air Lines (at $50.50 each way during the day on a "World-famous Constellation"). Or he could have bought one hundred friends in Paris a top-of-the line Columbia "3-speed Automatic, High-Fidelity portable" record player at $85 per unit. Or, if he'd been thinking about *Krapp's Last Tape* he could have bought seventy Pentron high-fidelity portable tape recorders at $127 each. Profiting immensely from his association with Beckett, Barney Rosset could well afford the gift of such a tape recorder, given to Beckett in 1957.

We have already seen Beckett's keen participation in the business of publicity photography. We have also noted that an author reputed to be "naturally reticent" and "unassertive" engaged in a series of interviews with journalists and scholars, participating in the creation of some of the most influential readings of his work. As the money came in, creating "One success after another . . . [i]n Europe" (as Rosset wrote on February 15, 1955 [SUL]) and creating spendable income, Beckett's status among those who supported him came into conflict with his own assessment of himself. Beckett had become an actively transformative influence, but he projected the idea that he was entirely passive, ignorant of everything but the urge to write.

In his memoir, *Entrances: An American Director's Journey,* Schneider describes his first meeting with Beckett, during the fall 1955 London production of *Godot* after it had moved to the Criterion: "When I met Sam, I wanted primarily to latch onto anything that might help make *Godot* a success on Broadway. When I left him, I wanted nothing more than to please him. I came with respect and trepidation; I left with a greater measure of devotion than I have ever felt for a writer whose work I was translating to the stage" (1987, 225). Schneider's "devotion" to Beckett would be matched over the years by numerous professionals in the theater, in publishing, in broadcasting, in the media, and in academe.

As we saw in his obituaries, Beckett was a very charismatic man who inspired long-lasting loyalty, allowing him to maintain his public image as someone only interested in failure, ignorance, and impotence without sacrificing the fruits of success. A January 11, 1956, letter to Schneider, written during the Miami production of *Godot* and published during the first New York run of *Endgame* in March 1958, is a favorite source for those loyal to the ideas Beckett had little interest in success and failure on the public level and that he preferred failure. We have already seen how the Miami production set Beckett up for a campaign using the perceived failure of the American premiere to create a market for his work. But what is most interesting about this "I prefer failure" letter is that it was published in the *Village Voice* on March 19, 1958: it was part of the publicity designed to expand the audience for Schneider's production of *Endgame.* As the blurb introducing the series of letters to Schneider suggests, the play was "now a hit at the Cherry Lane." Despite the claim that Beckett was reluctant about the publication of these letters, it is very obvious that the decision to publish Beckett's correspondence in the *Voice* was part of a long-term marketing strategy designed to associate Beckett with an aesthetic defined in terms of failure. With the assistance of a director who had now become a devoted spokesman in the United States, Beckett thus participated not only in the publicity campaign for *Endgame* but also in the construction and dissemination of his own public image.

7

Selling Beckett as an Unknown Celebrity, 1956–1969

> Despite popular legend Beckett was never a recluse; he may have been a hermit in his head but he had a very active, sporadically controlled, social life; his friends a world-wide network of sentinels of his privacy.
>
> —Lennon, "Evenings with Sam"

Building a Post-*Godot* Legacy

Beckett began a new phase of writing roughly a year after the opening of Roger Blin's Babylone production of *Godot* on January 5, 1953, eventually finding his way out of the creative impasse he had been in since he completed *L'Innommable* on January 5, 1950. The intense period of creativity following the war fizzled as he focused his energies on supervising the building of a writer's retreat, assisting with the Blin production of *Godot*, and responding to the ensuing surge of public interest. The lack of new work is largely explained by his involvement in the business of creating the conditions most conducive to a life of writing and publishing. While the death of his mother and the building of the house in Ussy were distractions, the main barriers to new work came from his professional obligations as he helped transform a series of manuscripts into publishable texts, viable productions, and sustainable contracts. A quick summary of his publication record in 1951–53 suggests why his creative endeavors took a backseat. On March 10, 1951, Minuit published a run of three thousand copies of *Molloy* along with fifty deluxe and five hundred signed copies; they followed later in the year with three thousand copies of *Malone meurt,* again publishing fifty deluxe editions. On October 17, 1952, Minuit put out an edition of twenty-five hundred copies of *En attendant Godot.* After the January 1953 premiere of the play, Lindon followed with *L'Innommable,* issuing three thousand copies with fifty deluxe versions on July 18, 1953. As already noted, immediately after *Godot* put

Beckett on the road to fame, Richard Seaver of Merlin Press contacted him to arrange for Maurice Girodias, son of Jack Kahane, to publish *Watt* in an Olympia edition (it appeared on August 31, 1953). In the meantime, Beckett arranged for the publication of extracts from *Watt* in *Envoy* in January 1950, in *Irish Writing* in December 1951, in *Merlin* in winter 1952–53, and in *Irish Writing* in March 1953. He also published translated excerpts from *Molloy* and *Malone meurt* in *Transition* 6 (1950) and a translated extract from *Molloy* in *Merlin* in autumn 1953. Then, when Grove signed him in June 1953, he committed to the translation of *Molloy* (with Patrick Bowles). Later he would commit to being the sole translator for *Malone meurt* and *L'Innommable,* beginning a process that would occupy him until June 1958, when he sent Rosset the completed translation of *The Unnamable.* There is no better evidence of Beckett's drive to fame than the fact that in the midst of all this activity he continued to work, in 1950 and 1951, on the pieces eventually published as *Texts for Nothing* and, at the same time, produced at least four still unpublished, "abandoned" texts (see Ackerley and Gontarski 2006, 560–61 and Cohn 2001 202–7). Even as he adjusted himself to the success of Blin's *Godot,* he published three new texts: "Trois textes pour rien" were published in *Lettres Nouvelles* in May 1953.

The commitment to produce German and English translations of *Waiting for Godot* and his three novels put a serious dent in his ability to create new work, but these texts gave him access to the global marketplace, contributing significantly to his long-term prospects. There is no doubt he was slowed down by business affairs but, determined to extend his career beyond *Godot,* he was persistent. First conceived in spring 1954, completed in June 1956, and staged in April 1957, *Fin de partie* would prove he was more than a strange, barely known hermit who had produced one successful play. However, it did not come easily. A detailed account of his three-year struggle to produce a new play provides clear evidence of his determination to sustain his career as a professional writer beyond the success of one work. Bogged down in nihilistic prose in 1950–52, he was completely consumed with translating his work from French to English in 1953. Toward the end of 1953 he told McGreevy he had exhausted his creative well, but he equivocated, saying he was stuck but might be able to write for the theater (December 14, 1953, TCD). By February 11, 1954, he was struggling to write something new, describing a scene from the early stages of his second major play. He still gave the impression he was almost finished with his ability to write (SUL 20), and a year later he was making little progress because he was compiling a book out of the first three stories he wrote in French together with the prose (which became *Texts for Nothing*) produced in the wake of *L'Innommable.* At the same time he was translating *Malone* for Grove Press and was continuing to revise the play he had first mentioned back in February 1954: a solitary man crawling in a rock corridor had become two characters living in a sterile world (February 11, 1955, SUL 20). On March 27, 1955, he described going back to the drawing board with his play. However, he still found time to work on the translation of *Malone* and could report excellent progress in a letter to McGreevy on June 5, 1955 (SUL 20). Finally, on February 22, 1956, he was able to declare the completion of a first final draft of a new play and the beginning of work on the translation of *L'Innommable.*

Beckett's struggle to produce new work seems to have eased around the time the New York production hit its stride. On May 2, 1956, he wrote Barney and Loly a letter full of news: a London bookstore had bought thirty of *Echo's Bones* for the equivalent of thirty dollars or so; Nancy Cunard was managing to sell her copies of *Whoroscope* for one pound each; he was on the verge of signing a contract to publish *Godot* in Japan; and the Italian edition of *Godot* was well on its way to publication (SUL 1). His ebullience is understandable. Editors across Europe and Asia were vying for contracts to capitalize on his current success and future prospects. This international interest had direct consequences on his pre-*Godot* texts, validating a period in his life when his efforts to cultivate an audience had fallen on stony ground. Name recognition meant early texts had jumped in value; *Watt* was selling in two editions, one from Olympia, one from Grove; within a few months Grove would reissue both *Murphy* and *Proust.* We can well imagine the boost of confidence propelling him to finish *Fin de partie* in June 1956. He also had the incentive of a professional commission. The organizers of a festival in Marseille had asked him for new work. In addition to being swamped with professional activities connected with the success of *Godot,* he was overwhelmed with the effort to produce a play and a mime for the Festival d'Avant-Garde in August. Finally, on June 21, 1956, he was able to inform Alan Schneider he had completed a new one-act play with a projected running time of about ninety minutes (Ackerley and Gontarski 2004, 196). Even though both *Fin de partie* and *Actes sans paroles* were completed before the Marseille Festival, there was insufficient time for rehearsals (July 30, 1956, TCD, 200). His professional frustration is apparent in a July 4, 1956, letter to Nancy Cunard: he expresses exasperation at the disorganization and unprofessionalism of the organizers, concluding it would be a mistake to participate. He subsequently withdrew the play from the festival. But he did not sit on his hands. He now had a complete play manuscript on his desk, and he took the opportunity to shop it around until he found a venue at the Théâtre de l'Oeuvre, scheduled to open in February 1957. When that fell through, he committed to an April 1957 premiere in French at the London Court Theatre as part of a celebratory "French Fortnight" organized by the Union Française des Industriels Exportatrices. This is just one of many examples of Beckett's resourcefulness in turning manuscripts into public texts.

The shenanigans over Beckett's first post-*Godot* play seem to give validity to his claim that he was unqualified to be a professional writer (April 10, 1956, TCD, 198); when he made this claim a week before *Godot* opened on Broadway, there was no certainty he had established a reputation sufficient to sustain a viable career. Incompetence, bad planning, and a reluctance to appear in public made it seem as though he would retain his status as an amateur writer. He seemed incapable of producing texts on demand and, although he had experienced a modicum of fame in Europe, he was overwhelmed by the effort to turn his first play into a long-term success. By the time he made the decision about withdrawing *Fin de partie* from the Marseille Festival, however, he had begun to earn serious money in the United States and was being heralded around the world as a revolutionary new writer. His context had, in other words, changed radically in the months following his April 10, 1956, letter to McGreevy. This leads me to conclude that his decision to withdraw the play was a reflection of high professional standards. Like his decision to refuse the highly lucrative contract to translate the Marquis de Sade for Jack Kahane in 1938, it was a matter of sacrificing short-term gain to protect his long-term reputation.

Beckett's letters from the period after the Broadway premiere of *Godot* suggest he was keen to keep his business affairs clear and above board and was happy to capitalize on his fame by signing copies of *Whoroscope* (1930). In a letter to Cunard on September 23, 1956, he invited her to increase the value of her stock by sending them to him for his autograph. A few months after he claimed not to be a professional writer, he made the highly professional decision to augment the market value of his texts by attaching his increasingly valuable signature. And he also made an important breakthrough.

On September 27, 1956, he sent the script of *All That Fall* to the BBC Third Programme in good time for it to be aired on January 13 and 19, 1957. As I argued in "Voices Out of the Air: Freedom, Death, and Constraint in

All That Fall" (Dilks 1998), the play is important for many reasons, not least its explicit Irish setting and its direct engagement with relationships between private, personal, and public experience. But for the argument of this book, the January 13, 1957, airing of Beckett's first radio play is significant because it was the first performance of a new work after the success of *Godot*. There can be no question it was a commissioned job. That is clear from a letter he wrote to Aidan Higgins on July 6, 1956, stating he had been asked to supply the British Broadcasting Corporation with a play for the Third Programme (HRHRC). And it is confirmed by a letter he wrote to McGreevy on November 23, 1956, explaining what a great time he had working with the BBC (January 30, 1957, TCD, 202). Two months later he wrote to Higgins boasting about the great success of *All That Fall* on BBC Radio and was happy to admit he was already thinking about working with them again, probably on a project to include music by his nephew, John Beckett (March 4, 1957, HRHRC). Beckett's openness to planning sessions with John Morris of the Third Programme, and the long-term relationships he developed with Barbara Bray, Martin Esslin, and Donald McWhinnie suggest he was comfortable in the BBC's formal corporate environment, with its decorous treatment of authors, its carefully written contracts, and its high-quality productions. He had experienced a hectic year and had, in the process, shifted his authorial status to a level of professionalism in keeping with one of Britain's stodgiest institutions.

As discussed above, negotiations over dramatic rights to the English-language *Godot* were creating excessive stress and exhaustion. Adding to the strain, *Godot* had come out in a bowdlerized edition from Faber as a result of interference by the Lord Chamberlain (February 22, 1956, SUL). Further, publication of the novels had been beset by difficulties over copyright laws (March 15, 1956, SUL) and the threat of legal censorship (April 7, 1956, SUL). Beckett's fame had brought an avalanche of letters, invitations, and other disruptions. Preparations for the Marseille Festival had damaged his peace and confidence (May 16, 1956, SUL). The subsequent effort to find a venue for *Fin de partie* underscored the problem of working in an amateur environment with people who did not plan for proper casting, rehearsals, and the other aspects of literary commerce. It was, then, a welcome relief to work with an organization that negotiated in good faith, crafted clear contracts, and produced his work without undue hassle and aggravation. By November 1956 the writer who once pounded London's pavement is search of contracts for *Dream of Fair to Middling Women, More Pricks Than Kicks,* and *Murphy* had achieved long-term commitments from key players in the main centers of English-language publishing, London and New York. His contract with John Calder for the publication of "the complete trilogy, in one volume" seriously bolstered his professional footing in Britain: by the end of 1956 he had dependable outlets for his plays (with Faber and Faber), for his prose (with Calder), and for his media texts (with the BBC).

On November 22, 1957, he would admit to Ethna McCarthy that he was spending occasional bouts in Paris trying to do a month's worth of business in a few days. He also told her he fantasized about calling it a day and giving up on his blossoming career because it was too much trouble (HRHRC). On October 28, 1959, he commented to Con Leventhal it would be a lot easier if he could treat writing as a profession, again implying he was most comfortable thinking of himself as an amateur and could easily do something else instead (HRHRC). But as a commissioned BBC author with contracts in Britain, France, Germany, Italy, Japan, the United States, and beyond, he could no longer legitimately deny his professional status. Indeed, his involvement in the business of literature was rapidly entering yet another phase. With the successful negotiation and completion of the *All That Fall* commission, he opened the door for a long-term relationship with one of Britain's most prestigious organizations. In the immediate future he would complete a series of commissions for the BBC including *Embers* (first aired on June 24, 1959), *Words and Music* (first aired on November 13, 1962), and the television play *Eh Joe* (first aired on BBC 2 on July 4, 1966). Coming soon after he accepted an honorary doctorate from Trinity College in July 1959, *Embers* earned him his first major prize, the Prix D'Italia, in September 1959. The prizes were not the least of it. Even though he continued to consider such prize-winning work not to be his best (to Higgins on March 24, 1959, HRHRC), royalties began to come in from all directions. On October 5, 1960, he acknowledged he had recently calculated that US royalties were now paying above 30 percent of his annual income; he thanked his lucky stars for the various checks flowing in from around the world, underlining the fact that they added up to a nice tidy sum (October 5, 1960, HRHRC).

Without access to every royalty statement sent to Beckett and every tax return he completed, we can only estimate his annual income. But based on the records at Grove, and assuming Beckett was correct in thinking the Grove income represented 30 percent of his total income, we can calculate he earned well over $30,000 in 1960 and had increased his annual income to over $50,000 by the time he won the Nobel Prize in 1969. To put this in perspective, the average annual income in the United States in 1969 was $8,540. Based on figures from the United States census, this average had risen to $52,029 in 2008, allowing us to calculate that Beckett's income in 1969 was the equivalent, in today's figures, of at least $300,000 a year.

Un Célèbre Inconnu

Between 1956 and 1989 Beckett managed to retain his reputation as an amateur even as he achieved worldwide recognition and an income on par with the wealthiest two percent of people in the wealthiest nation on earth. Somehow he became an internationally successful professional writer with the reputation of "un célèbre inconnu," and he became a model of how to achieve public fame without sacrificing one's private life. From this perspective Beckett's career is truly remarkable because he applied the same degree of control over his public image as he exerted over his stage directions.

The idea that he was an unknown celebrity hit the magazine stalls in Paris in February 1957, and it would become his main selling proposition (see fig. 2). Anticipating the production of *Fin de partie* at the Théâtre de l'Oeuvre in Paris, Madeleine Chapsal coined the phrase in a biographical sketch published alongside an extract from the Editions de Minuit text of the play (1957). Even though the Théâtre de l'Oeuvre backed out and the first production of the play in French was at the Royal Court Theatre in London on April 3, 1957, Chapsal's representation of Beckett as an amateur gained traction. It was, after all, in complete concert with Beckett's preferred representation of himself. Chapsal describes him as "secret et volontairement inconnu" and quotes him as saying, "L'auteur, ça n'est pas intéressant" (1957, 26). The paradox inherent in the tension between Beckett's reputation for secrecy and his engagement with literary marketing is apparent in the use of a full-page photograph (by Charpentier) on the front page of the magazine, together with an additional photograph in the middle of a page-long biography. The claim that he is "secret and voluntarily unknown" and the quotation from Beckett, "the author is never interesting," are odd in the context of an article designed to promote interest in Beckett and his latest work by showing "une parenté entre l'homme et l'écrivain" ("a kinship between the man and the writer). The premise of the article is, in fact, that the author's life *is* interesting because it helps us understand his work. Indeed, the article proposes a direct parallel between Beckett and his texts, implying we can understand what he wrote if we understand the man. Chapsal's stated purpose is to help him attain the fame he deserves: "Samuel Beckett est un homme grand, sec et droit" ("Samuel Beckett is, beyond doubt, a great man"). Beckett was, then, inserted into the French marketplace in 1957 as an unknown celebrity who preferred gardening to writing (Chapsal 1957). As we saw in the Kyncl article, and as we see in the biographies, the obituaries, and throughout Beckett studies, this representation is repeated as though it has the validity of a sacred truth.

Fortunately some people have applied common sense to the situation. Steven Connor, for example, has suggested, "if Beckett really counted as close friends all those who hint deliciously at close and continuous intimacy with him, then the most celebrated literary recluse of the twentieth century would have a social diary to rival Nancy Mitford's" (1988, 195). On the one hand, he is a man famous for his aversion to fame and the media; on the other, a surfeit of evidence demonstrates the existence of "a freemasonry of the great man's friends" (Lennon 1990). At the center is a man celebrated as a heroic, humble, generous figure, around him an extensive, loyal, protective network of professional friends and devotees. The problem for the writers celebrating Beckett's life in the days after his death was this: even though "The most obvious personal feature of the late Samuel Beckett was his profound dislike for publicity that would intrude on his privacy," Beckett was famous enough to compete with news about the fall of Ceauçescu's regime in Romania. The print given to stories about his life and the sheer range of photographs to which the editors had access demonstrate that his private life was part and parcel of his public function and international celebrity (Kyncl 1989). Ostensibly "unknown," his face had been iconographic and his life legendary for over thirty years. We need only compare the tributes to Beckett when he died in December 1989 with the tributes to J. D. Salinger when he died in January 2010 to see the difference between a man reputed to be averse to "the trappings of fame" and a man who really was averse to these trappings: Beckett's friends and acquaintances, business partners and professional contacts flooded the newspapers with anecdotes, articles, interviews, and photographs; Salinger's death was met with a few short pieces recounting the few publicly known facts about his life, with two or three different photographs showing up in the media.

As Kyncl's article illustrates, the tension between Beckett's ostensible aversion to fame and his prophetlike status must, somehow, be explained. For Kyncl, the explanation is in the realm of the absurd; for me, it is in the realm of literary marketing, requiring close attention to the variety of promotional events organized in his name by the "sentinels of his privacy"

(Lennon 1990), challenging us to explain why so many of those who were close to Beckett repeat not just the same ideas, but the same words when they represent his relationship with publicity and the marketplace.

Limited Editions and Livres d'artiste

As we have noted, the marketing of Beckett's work took off after he contracted with Les Editions de Minuit in 1950 and, especially, when he signed with Grove Press in 1953. In addition to advertising in mass distribution newspapers and magazines, Lindon used limited editions to stimulate sales: the first edition of *Molloy* was printed in a deluxe edition of fifty plus five hundred signed for "Les Amis des Editions de Minuit"; the first edition of *Malone meurt* included fifty deluxe signed copies; and, again, *L'Innommable* "été tirée a cinquante exemplaires sur vélin supérieur numérotés de 1 a 50" (copyright page: "fifty copies published in superior vellum numbered 1 to 50," RUL). Again, this technique was part and parcel of modernist aestheticism with its roots in Keatsian romanticism. Marked with the author's signature and other indications of the personal presence of the writer and/or the bookmaker, the book, as a book, is transformed into something other than an item of mechanical reproduction: it becomes an individualized artifact marked with evidence of the author's physical presence. As Connor suggests, "Personal contact with Beckett is clearly a valued commodity. . . . If one cannot be in the presence of the celebrated Beckettian voice, for example, then the physical presence of his equally famous handwriting may be an acceptable substitute" (1988, 196). Connor goes on to analyze the "absurd and rather sinister" problem of "manuscript fetishism" in which handwritten archival materials "attain the status of an icon, or holy relic" (198). A related form of fetishistic infatuation happens, of course, with the author's signature. Because Beckett refused book-signing appearances and lectures, interviews and public explanations of his work, his signature, image, and interpretive statements became more valuable than they would have been had he acted like almost every other writer in the twentieth century.

The printing of signed special editions was a favored practice of modernist publishers, and Beckett benefited from the practice from the beginning of his career. The Hours Press edition of *Whoroscope* in 1930 appeared as one hundred signed copies with two hundred unsigned (as noted above, when Nancy Cunard contacted Beckett after the success of *Godot* in London, he agreed to sign the remaining copies so she could sell them for the optimum price). Reavey's October 1935 edition of *Echo's Bones and Other Precipitates* by Europa Press was released in a print run "limited to 325 copies, of which 25 on Normandy vellum are signed by the author and numbered I to XXV (6 shillings or 25 francs)." The run also included "250 copies numbered 1 to 250 (3 shillings or 12 francs)," plus "50 copies marked Hors commerce" (advertising/subscription form, HRHRC). Favored by smaller presses because it allows them to compensate for the higher per-book price necessitated by smaller print runs, the limited edition approach was well suited to a budding writer making a name among a coterie audience. It was especially suited to a writer who chose to avoid the media. As public demand grew, his publishers fended off demands for him "to speak or read to an . . . audience" by sending, at Beckett's request, a series of generic refusals in his name—"Mr Beckett does not do any lecturing, or public reading" (May 24, 1965, SUL 1). His publishers took on the responsibility of answering casual enquiries from admirers: "Mr Beckett receives a great many letters, and it would be impossible for him to answer all of them. I, and other people, answer many of his letters for him. Please understand that if he answered all his mail, he would have no time left for his work" (October 1, 1965, SUL 34). He was, in Peter Lennon's view, protected by "sentinels": they answered his letters and respected his careful use of the telephone as a screening device. As a result Beckett's handwriting became a valuable commodity: the cards he sent to his closest professional acquaintances telling them the specific hour of the day when he would answer the phone have become valuable artifacts; John Calder auctioned thirty-six such cards for over 10,000 English pounds in 1990; in December 2006, a large box of letters to Henri and Josette Hayden sold at Sotheby's for 360,000 euros; and in July 2007, seventeen letters and seventy-seven postcards sent to Beckett's aunt Peggy Beckett and his uncle James sold for 57,600 English pounds. In some cases, individual recipients have published facsimiles to reinforce the legitimacy of a given publication (see Lennon 1990; Minihan 1996). Simply put, because he exerted tight control over his public appearances, his signature, notes in his handwriting, and any statements he made about his work became especially valuable.

Because Beckett did not participate in standard publishing industry practice in the postwar period, refusing to go on the bookstore and college circuit, his publishers arranged for him to sign "limited edition sheets" designed to be bound into published texts. The technique was used by Grove for *Murphy* and *Proust* in 1957 and became standard practice for the next thirty years. Grove's *Malone Dies* (1956) was published in two editions, an Evergreen book plus "a hard bound limited edition of 500 copies" (copyright page); and the Grove edition of *Watt* included 7,500 copies in paperback, 1,000 in cloth, a "specially bound limited edition of 100 numbered copies" and "a specially bound and signed edition of 26 copies lettered A through Z and 4 copies, hors commerce, numbered 1 through 4" (copyright page). Not to be outdone, when John Calder published *How It Is* in 1964, it included "100 copies on hand made paper bound in vellum marked A1 to A100 signed by the author (hors commerce); 100 copies on hand made paper bound in Morocco marked B1 to B100 signed by the author (hors commerce) and 4,000 copies of a hardbound trade edition" (copyright page). Even though Ackerley and Gontarski complain that this edition of *How It Is* "reflected the commercialism that would bedevil SB's texts" (2004, 259), it is clear Calder was simply continuing a practice Beckett had participated in with keen enthusiasm for many years. He had, after all, been very efficient in returning the "250 Limited Editions sheets" for *Proust* and *Murphy* sent to him on January 30, 1957. Judith Schmidt acknowledged their return a week later in a letter dated February 7, 1957: "Thanks for getting the Limited Editions sheets back to us so quickly" (SUL 1). As Breon Mitchell and Lois Overbeck's *Word and Image: Samuel Beckett and the Visual Text* (1999) demonstrates, it is a practice he would escalate after 1964.

The sheer number of limited edition "livres d'artiste" produced with Beckett's direct collaboration during his years of fame suggests his enthusiasm for museum quality and collectors editions of his texts. The Editions de Minuit printing of *Nouvelles et textes pour rien* (1958) with six reproductions of signed pen-and-ink drawings by Avigdor Arikha, published in an edition of two thousand numbered copies, was followed by four further editions with art by Arikha. In the case of *The North* (an early excerpt from *The Lost Ones*) published by John Kolber's Enitharmon Press, London in 1972 (137 numbered copies) and *Au loin un oiseau* published by Double Elephant Press, New York in 1973 (90 numbered copies, plus 30 hors commerce copies), the texts were signed by Beckett. Other notable livres d'artiste include John Calder's 1979 printing of *Imagination Dead Imagine* with twenty-four original lithographs by Sorel Etrog (60 numbered copies signed by Beckett, plus 10 hors commerce); Gotham Book Mart's 1976 edition of *All Strange Away* (200 copies signed by Beckett; 26 hors commerce), which followed Gotham's 1968 edition of *Beginning to End: A Selection of the Works of Samuel Beckett* (300 numbered copies and 26 lettered copies signed by Beckett) with illustrations by Edward Gorey; and the Iowa City Center for the Book's editions of *Waiting for Godot* (1976, 40 copies, 7 signed by Beckett) and *Company* (1983, nine proof copies signed by the author, printer, and artist plus 52 additional numbered copies) with etchings by Dellas Henke. Further notable artists' texts include the 1976 printing of three hundred copies of *Foirades/Fizzles* with etchings by Jasper Johns, signed by Beckett and the artist; the 1984 Overbrook Press edition of *The Lost Ones* (250 numbered copies, signed by Beckett); the 1987 Yves Rivieres Editeur and Les Editions de Minuit version of *Texte pour rien* with lithographs by Bram van Velde (75 copies signed by Beckett, 10 copies hors commerce); and the John Calder/Blue Moon edition of *Stirrings Still* with lithographs by Louis Brocquoy (1989, 226 copies signed by Beckett and the artist). The production of these expensive editions allowed Beckett to develop a very special relationship with the literary marketplace, each unique text gaining value from his reputation for silence and secrecy, absence and anonymity.

Handmade and specially bound versions of Beckett's books function as a logical extension of the proposal that Beckett was fundamentally committed to artistic integrity, to a set of basic aesthetic principles inherited from an era before the age of mechanical and photographic reproduction when, as Walter Benjamin puts it, "the unique value of the 'authentic' work of art" has "its basis in ritual" and "[t]he secular cult of beauty" (1968, 224). William Morris and, later, the Bloomsbury group, helped establish the modern tradition of manually reproduced, limited editions situated in a graduated zone between a unique work of art such as the Book of Kells and a mass-produced literary text. The rules of supply and demand determine the value of each copy of a given text (see Rainey 1998). Handcrafted specially bound and illustrated books are developed as an aesthetic response to the increased emphasis on mass production and, as Stephen Enniss and Lois Overbeck put it in their essay in *Word and Image: Samuel Beckett and the Visual Text*, these texts are "created rare" (Mitchell and Overbeck 1999, 6). Obviously they gain value from this rarity, becoming collectors' texts and museum texts; coveted by those interested in the author, by those interested in the artist, and by those interested in the history of literary texts as printed artifacts, they attract the attention of rare books sellers and investors. Advertised and sold to the highest bidder, they become investors' texts and library texts held by research institutions dependent, by definition, on otherwise inaccessible material for their very existence.

As you might imagine, these texts are expensive, which makes it even more intriguing that Beckett would collaborate in the creation of livres d'artiste from fragments and drafts of "finished" texts he had already published in trade editions: examples include *L'Image* (from *Comment c'est*), *The North* (from *The Lost Ones*), *L'Issue* and *Sejour* (from *Le Dépeupler*), and *Trial Proofs of Foirades/Fizzles.* Beckett was, in fact, more than willing to recycle texts; because of its title, the most amusing example is *From an Abandoned Work.* Before being broadcast on the BBC Third Programme in 1957, the text had appeared in 1956 in *Trinity News.* Subsequently it appeared in *Evergreen Review* in 1957, in a Faber edition in 1958, in *No's Knife* in 1967, in a Manus Presse trilingual edition in 1969, in *Breath and Other Shorts* in 1971, in *First Love and Other Shorts* in 1974, and in *Six Residua* in 1978. Since then it has been republished many times and is included in the Grove Centenary Edition of Beckett's collected works (in volume 4). This commercial exploitation of an "abandoned" text surely redefines the word "abandoned," challenging us to rethink how we respond to the persistence with which Beckett published "disjecta," "fizzles," "residua," and other material giving the impression of professional disinterest. Again, Beckett's career is studded with examples of the commercial advantage gained from his supposed disinterest.

A detailed look at the New Overbrook Press edition of *The Lost Ones* gives a good example of the development of an artist's text, demonstrating Beckett's ongoing involvement in the production of a highly professional and marketable text and illustrating how Beckett's museum-quality texts were packaged and marketed. The Overbrook text, carefully edited by Beckett, stands as the definitive version of the prose piece. Initially published in 1970 by Les Editions de Minuit as *Le Dépeupleur* in an edition of 10,000 copies with 399 special numbered copies designed to celebrate the Nobel award, the text was translated into English for publication in 1972. John Calder and Grove Press released it in a limited edition of 100 copies and, following the precedent established in 1965 when Calder released *Imagination Dead Imagine* in a hors commerce edition of 100 numbered and signed copies at the same time as the text appeared in the *Sunday Times* on November 7, 1965 (it was reprinted in *Evergreen Review* in February 1966 and in a 1966 trade edition from Calder), the limited edition text was followed immediately with a printing in the *New York Times* (December 16, 1972). With the exception of an *Evergreen Review* version published in 1973, English versions of *The Lost Ones* are dogged by errors related to the architectural dimensions of the "cylinder" (Ackerley and Gontarski 2004, 326): a structure intended to have a surface area of twelve million square centimeters was described with eighty thousand, turning a habitation for humanoids into a dollhouse. Beckett took the opportunity offered by Charles Altschul to correct these errors and make other changes during the development of a handmade, limited edition version of the text.

Altschul, the founding owner of the New Overbrook Press, printed Beckett's text as his inaugural publication because it was a good opportunity to revive "a family printing tradition which goes back to his 17th-century ancestors in Prague" (*Los Angeles Herald Examiner,* April 11, 1984) by printing a text by a commercially viable author. In the article he is quoted as saying "Beckett was not actually my first choice." A recent graduate of Yale, Altschul was an eager entrepreneur who created rarity value by limiting the edition to 250 copies and 60 artist's proofs with the proofs signed by Charles Klabunde and each copy signed by Beckett. He worked to gain media attention by giving private showings to journalists in advance of publication, stimulating demand by pricing it at $1,750 from April 13 to June 15, 1984, and $2,000 thereafter, and he maintained interest in the limited run by sending publicity packets to a select list of prospective buyers. Altschul used publicity materials describing the book as "A limited folio edition signed by the author Samuel Beckett and illustrated with etchings by master printmaker Charles Klabunde" (MS 2754, RUL), and he sent out a marketing letter:

> Critics, connoisseurs, art and rare book dealers alike have been unanimous in acclaiming this lovingly-crafted work as a collector's item of rare beauty. Copies have been acquired by prominent collectors, libraries and museums throughout the world, including the Bibliotheque Nationale, the Library of Congress and the British Museum. (October 1, 1984, to Dr. Pilling from Charles Altschul, RUL)

Explaining that "*The Lost Ones* is currently available in Europe for $2,600," the letter uses the generic buy-it-while-you-can trick of marketing: "I hope you will have an opportunity to acquire a copy of the folio for your personal collection before the edition is sold out." As supporting material, the letter includes the *Los Angeles Herald Examiner* article by Digby Diehl and a brochure situating the book in the context of "a long-standing tradition for fine publications of distinguished quality and value" (RUL). Two pages of the brochure present two large, carefully arranged photographs, reinforcing the different kinds of professional craftsmanship used to make the book. The photographs situate the text on a print-shop desk: one places the copyright page, with Beckett's signature clearly legible, beneath a presentation box for the book, a slug case, and one of Klabunde's artist's proofs ("The Way Out," number 56); the other puts a fragment of Beckett's text beneath the prints (page 23 of the Overbrook edition; *GCE IV*, page 397, line 29, to page 398, line 5), and includes two additional Klabunde prints and miscellaneous typesetting instruments. In the body of the brochure the emphasis on the text as a commercial artifact continues. While some effort is made to explain that *The Lost Ones* is important because it was the first prose text after Beckett's Nobel Prize and because "Beckett's lost people" are "a mirror of our own existence," and while the brochure claims Beckett's "alterations . . . make it the definitive version of his work," the bulk of the brochure is designed to bolster Klabunde and Altschul's credentials and to enhance the aesthetic and financial value of the text. Again, the key is in the balance between professional and artistic integrity. Three long paragraphs describe Klabunde's "worldwide critical acclaim," his association with "prominent museums and private collections throughout the world," and his "superb artistry." The longest paragraph in the brochure explains Altschul's credentials and ambitions; the second longest details how "The finest materials and techniques were used to make this presentation of Beckett's prose masterpiece a distinguished addition to any fine collection."

The New Overbrook Press edition was designed as a rare collector's item selling for thousands of dollars (in 2010 the going rate for a copy of the 1984 edition hovered around five thousand dollars). Altschul's enterprise depended for its success on the cachet associated with Beckett's name and image, his signature and face, and, of course, his status as a Nobel laureate. Another way of putting this is to say Altschul chose Beckett because he was a marketable commodity with a track record of selling livres d'artiste. Endorsed by Beckett, with photographic evidence of his direct involvement featured in the advertising materials, the young entrepreneur exploited Beckett's cultural status and his literary genius to create a valuable artifact that functions as a "cultural icon" (Mitchell and Overbeck 1999, 13). In terms of the most basic principle of the literary marketplace, the investment value of the artifact is directly proportional to the quality and rarity of the text multiplied by the status of the author: despite the claims about it being "definitive," the Overbrook edition of *The Lost Ones* is more important as an artifact than as a written document. As Breon Mitchell suggests in "Image and Imagination: Samuel Beckett and the Livre d'Artiste," there were times when "the writing" was not Beckett's main priority: "Although we know of no case in which Beckett requested or suggested that one of his texts be illustrated, such special editions were clearly in complete accord with Beckett's own continuing interest in the visual arts, his personal friendships, and his constant generosity" (Mitchell and Overbeck 1999, 12).

Beckett's interest in the visual arts and, more specifically, in connections between printmaking, graphic design, and his own areas of the literary arts, made him willing to support the production of special editions of his texts. Personal friendships with Avigdor Arikha, Sorel Etrog, Bram van Velde, and other artists also played a part in his enthusiasm. A further explanation of his enthusiasm for livres d'artiste involves his desire to support professional acquaintances who had, through their devotion to his work, become part of his intimate inner circle. His involvement in special autographed editions throughout his career illustrates his willingness to support the publishers who helped make his career so successful. This is evident because a number of the livres d'artiste were specifically designed to earn extra money for John Calder, Jérôme Lindon, and Barney Rosset. The best example is the edition of *Stirrings Still* (1988) illustrated by the Irish painter Louis Le Brocquy. The text was dedicated to Barney Rosset and published for one thousand pounds in London by John Calder and two thousand dollars in New York by Rosset's new publishing company, Blue Moon Books. Limited to two hundred copies, all signed by Beckett and Le Brocquy, the book specifically exploits Beckett's iconographic face, featuring a lithographic portrait on its frontispiece and an eighteen-carat gold stamp of a stylized side profile of Beckett's face on its linen cover. The paper was deckle-edged Velin de Rives, and the book was quarter-bound in parchment with eight additional lithographs. In 2006 Whyte's auction house in Dublin sold a copy for thirty-four hundred euros (around $4,300).

Beckett's interest in artists' texts and his loyalty to professional acquaintances merged with his participation in events designed to promote his work with the release of *Beginning to End: A Selection of the Works of Samuel Beckett* in 1968 and the subsequent publication of a special artist's edition of the previously unpublished *All Strange Away* in 1976 (*All Strange Away* would appear in Knowlson's *Journal of Beckett Studies* 3 in summer 1978 before being published by Calder in 1979 and Grove in 1981, as part of *Rockaby and Other Short Pieces*). Both texts are illustrated by Edward Gorey and issued by Gotham Book Mart, New York. The first of these books marks the culmination of a long collaboration between Beckett and Jack MacGowran on one-man shows pieced together from excerpts from Beckett's prose and drama: after he worked with MacGowran on the BBC version of *All That Fall* in 1957, the two developed a close professional relationship and personal friendship. This relationship is true to the pattern of Beckett's interaction with actors and directors he identified as sympathetic interpreters of his work. Over the years Beckett developed extraordinarily close relationships with a number of theater professionals including the directors Walter Asmus, George Devine, and Alan Schneider and the actors Patrick Magee, Barry McGovern, and Billie Whitelaw. He specifically wrote *Krapp's Last Tape* (aka "the Magee Monologue") for Magee in 1958; worked with McGovern on a monologue first produced in 1985 using excerpts from *Three Novels* ("I'll Go On"); and wrote *Not I, Footfalls,* and *Rockaby* specifically for Whitelaw. In the case of MacGowran, they began working together in 1961 on a script in response to a suggestion by Donald McWhinnie, assistant head of BBC Radio Drama, making a first presentation of "End of Day," with McWhinnie directing and MacGowran acting. The first performance was at a Tostal in Dublin on October 5, 1962. Beckett gave advice during the read-through of "An entertainment from the works of Samuel Beckett" for the follow-up performance of *End of Day* in London and then, uncharacteristically, attended the first night at the New Arts Theatre on October 16, 1962. By all accounts he remained in constant contact with MacGowran as he perfected a show designed as an author-directed strategy to stimulate interest in his prose texts and poems. Although he was uncharacteristic in making a public appearance to support the project, the strategy was typical of Beckett: again, instead of doing the bookstore and college lecture circuit himself, he arranged for a trained actor to present his prose and poetry on stage. His success with this method of boosting interest in his work was such that Billie Whitelaw and others would dedicate themselves to the task as a sort of sacred mission, continuing lectures and readings "in the spirit of Beckett" long after Beckett died (Foxrock Foundation 1990).

In 1963 MacGowran was asked to develop a revival of his one-man Beckett celebration in America with Alan Schneider directing; again, Beckett's participation is evident from his letters of encouragement and support. As we should expect from the professional approach Beckett developed in the wake of the problems with rights to *Godot,* he remained extremely attentive to contractual issues. For example, a letter dated July 4, 1963, encouraged MacGowran to accept the offer from Schneider and himself, noting his preference for author-directed collaboration on the spoken parts. Taking into account Barney Rosset's US rights to the English translation of *Godot* under a contract negotiated almost a decade previously, Beckett underscored the need to solicit Rosset's approval (HRHRC). Less professional than Beckett preferred, MacGowran tried the author's patience by planning a program in Dublin without heeding Beckett's preference for his work not to be performed in Ireland (he had held to this position since the censorship of Sean O'Casey's work in 1959), but personal friendship overcame professional principle and Beckett gave the go-ahead. Beckett could not resist making a suggested change to the program, asking MacGowran to avoid Lucky's monologue on the grounds it needed context to make any sense, but he gave MacGowran free rein to choose another passage as a replacement (September 12, 1965, HRHRC). In the same letter he also approved MacGowran's plan to exhibit the autographed copy of a notebook at an October 1965 presentation of the one-man show in Dublin; the notebook contains an early draft of *Fin de partie,* early versions of the *Molloy* translation into English, two unpublished short stories, and a ten-line fragment of an unpublished text called "Godot." Beckett had given this manuscript to Tara MacGowran three months earlier, on her first birthday, with the personal inscription, "with love from Sam Paris June 1965"; in 1995 it was valued at one hundred thousand pounds (*Times* July 12, 1995). The strong relationship between author and actor is evident from the advice Beckett gave in a letter dated February 6, 1966. Listing the poems he thinks MacGowran should use from *Echo's Bones* for a forthcoming BBC program organized by Martin Esslin, Beckett promises to join MacGowran in London for the studio recording (HRHRC). Beckett participated directly in rehearsals and the final take when the BBC *Monitor* program recorded "End of Day" in February 1964, collaborating with MacGowran during a visit to London to work on the premiere of *Play.* It is worth noting that in this period Beckett emerged as an author-director. By 1964 he was sufficiently established to be fully accepted in the BBC's corridors of power: they gave him freedom to choose his own actors, orchestrate the set design and costuming, and take as much control over direction as he chose.

The work Beckett did to support MacGowran eventually led to a commercial release of the recording of the 1964 BBC session by Claddagh Records in February 1967. They pressed a twelve-inch vinyl record of MacGowran and Beckett's script, called *MacGowran Speaking Beckett.* That was not the end of his commercial involvement in MacGowran's interests. Beckett's response to his friend's death in January 1973 provides ample evidence to support Breon Mitchell's claim about the connection between the livres d'artiste and Beckett's generosity to personal friends. Further, it provides evidence he remained keenly aware of the business implications of his publishing decisions. The second book illustrated by Gorey was published in 1976, at Beckett's instigation, to raise money for Gloria and Tara MacGowran, Jack MacGowran's beneficiaries. In June 1973 Beckett offered Andreas Brown of Gotham Book Mart in New York a text written in 1964 when he was struggling to write *Imagination Dead Imagine,* and he specifically stipulated any profits from a book eventually known as *All Strange Away* should be directed to the MacGowran family through a charitable trust set up for the purpose (June 27, 1973, HRHRC). Beckett also paid close attention to contractual details concerning the text, making clear no deal could be made unless Grove Press and John Calder agreed. He further required the contract to include a provision returning the rights to Calder, Grove, Minuit, and his other standard publishers on a particular date (June 27, 1973, HRHRC). Brown received confirmation of such an agreement on August 7, 1973, and by October had secured permission from John Calder. In the meantime Brown approached Gorey to provide illustrations (September 6, 1973, HRHRC). After some delay, which provoked Beckett's threat to withdraw permission (April 8, 1975, HRHRC), the author finally received the galley proofs on March 12, 1976. On May 12, 1976, he received the title pages to be signed and inscribed for binding into the text. And on April 11, 1977, he received a copy of the book. He promptly wrote to Brown acknowledging receipt of a text he regarded as gorgeous, offering his deep gratitude and best wishes (April 12, 1977, HRHRC).

Put in the context of Beckett's relationship with Jake Schwartz and Henry Wenning, collectors and dealers in rare books, Beckett's collaborations with Gotham Book Mart and Jack MacGowran are part of a consistent pattern. This pattern developed rapidly in the years after the Broadway production of *Godot* in 1956. We have already addressed some of the events and exhibits organized in Beckett's honor between 1956 and 1972 (see chapter 1). We will consider these in more detail, focusing on the boost to his status afforded by the celebrations of his sixtieth birthday in 1965–67 and the long-lasting effect of the Samuel Beckett Exhibition in 1971. In many ways the sixtieth birthday celebrations consolidated Beckett's international fame and the 1971 exhibition consolidated his legacy. The effects of these celebrations and the exhibition continue to be felt now that we have commemorated the fortieth anniversary of Beckett's Nobel award and have entered the third decade after his death.

But before we turn to these important events we should note Beckett's direct participation in the process that made his handwriting marketable.

Schwartz, an entrepreneurial opportunist by anyone's standards, contacted Beckett shortly after *Godot*'s Broadway premiere offering to buy any available manuscripts or typescripts. Beckett trusted the man. For the next three years they were in close contact. Beckett profited modestly from the sale of his drafts and notes; for his part, Schwartz profited wildly, buying very low and selling very high. On May 5, 1956, Beckett thanked Schwartz for a healthy check and promised to keep in touch (HRHRC). A few months later he sent Schwartz a fair copy of *Waiting for Godot* and assured him he would root around in his papers for the corrected typescript of *All That Fall* (January 13, 1957, HRHRC). On March 25, 1958, he sent the three notebooks constituting the manuscript of the translation of *L'Innommable,* including in the packet four versions of *Krapp's Last Tape* in typescript (HRHRC). He followed on August 10, 1958, with the corrected manuscript of the English version of *The Unnamable* and promised to send a signed copy of the Minuit limited edition of *Nouvelles et textes pour rien* illustrated by Avigdor Arikha (August 10, 1958, HRHRC). Much of this material is now at the Harry Ransom Humanities Research Center, which began to build its collection in 1957 and now rivals Reading University as the main depository of Beckett archives; Beckett's relationship with Schwartz opened the door to this important development.

However, Beckett's trust in Schwartz evaporated in 1961. An American dealer in rare books, Henry Wenning, informed him about the huge profits being made at his own expense (Bair 1990, 534). Even though Beckett would, from now on, refer to Schwartz as "the Great Extractor," making a wry joke about his occupation as a dentist and the immense profits he made in 1956–61, there can be no question the process through which Beckett's extremely valuable papers entered the marketplace was in full swing. There can also be no question about Beckett's cooperation in getting the process going in the period between 1956 and 1961. Furthermore, while his experience with Schwartz may have been a rude awakening, his connection with the market in rare books and manuscripts would continue unabated until he decided to set up his own archive through James Knowlson in 1971. Beginning in 1961, Wenning became his "official agent" (Bair 1990, 534). In other words, Beckett now had a conduit through which he could disseminate artifacts to the various archives in Europe and the United States. A July 29, 1964, letter from Judith Schmidt of Grove Press to Wenning makes it clear Beckett gave his American publisher permission to put the collector in contact with anyone interested in original manuscripts (SUL

20). And a June 6, 1967, letter from Beckett to Wenning reveals that he continued to forward manuscripts to the collector as he reached the peak of his fame in the late 1960s: he told Wenning he had asked Judith Schmidt to forward manuscripts of *Molloy, Malone Dies,* and *The Unnamable,* humbly suggesting they might not be worth much but acknowledging they might be interesting to somebody (WUL). An August 12, 1967, letter makes it clear that the author kept Wenning apprised as he dredged his files for marketable items: he told Wenning he was planning to sell a manuscript in support of the South African National Congress, admitting the edits and revisions made the text almost unreadable but justifying his decision because it was a good cause. His professional connection with Wenning was such that he felt obliged not only to tell him about the deal but also to defend his decision (WUL).

As we have already seen, Beckett was happy to turn his trunk manuscripts into published texts or archival resources, and he was not averse to product "stretching," turning different versions of the same text into discrete consumer artifacts. He occasionally released two or three stages of the same project as separate publications and often released the same text in different collections and publications, thus earning multiple royalty checks for different manifestations of the same text. Subsequently he would empty his back files and earn a few extra checks by passing along notebooks, manuscripts, and edited typescripts, giving collectors and archivists the opportunity to own a set representing the germination, revision, production, and publication of any given work. As he did so, he fueled the development of special collections at a number of universities in the United States including the University of Texas, Austin; Indiana University in Bloomington; the University of North Carolina at Chapel Hill; Dartmouth College in New Hampshire; and Washington University in St. Louis. He helped establish important collections at Trinity College Dublin and Reading University. Early notes and drafts, working copies, proofs and galleys, and hand-corrected published versions, performance texts, production notebooks, and signed first editions all became valuable items to be sold on the open market or to be gifted to professional friends and acquaintances (for example, in March 2010 Bloomsbury Auctions, New York, sold a signed first edition of the 1952 Les Editions de Minuit paperback of *En attendant Godot* for nine thousand dollars; as a comparison, unsigned copies of the first edition of the Minuit paperback, which was printed in a run of twenty-five hundred, were sold for three to four thousand dollars in 2010).

Often the texts Beckett donated found their way to the marketplace: the Cambridge and Grove series of the "The Theatrical Notebooks of Samuel Beckett," edited by James Knowlson, are good examples of this process. By including facsimiles in Beckett's own hand, including the "many changes, corrections, additions, and cuts" he made when he directed the plays "in Berlin, Paris, and London," the editors "provide a unique insight into [Beckett's] way of envisaging his own plays" (see the advertising blurb for the series at http://www.groveatlantic.com/grove/bin/wc.dll?groveproc~genauth~56~2513~DESC). Again, the fact there is a market in Beckett's theatrical production notebooks gives us a sense of Beckett's unique relationship with the literary marketplace: because he was famously absent, any sign of his presence as a writer has become a marketable commodity. While the complete boxed set of the "Grove Centenary Edition" sells for one hundred dollars in hardback, the single volume of the *Waiting for Godot Theatrical Notebook* sells for seventy-five dollars; the complete set of "Theatrical Notebooks" published to date costs over three hundred dollars. The mark-up is largely the result of the added authenticity and presence created by evidence of Beckett's living hand.

The Beckett Archive and the Beckett Theatre

Beckett's deliberate construction of an authorized archive is evident from his direct contributions to the library at the University of Reading. Competing in size and importance with the Beckett and Carlton Lake collections at the Harry Ransom Humanities Research Center in Austin, Texas, and enhanced through a reciprocal relationship with Washington University in St. Louis, the Beckett International Foundation at Reading University was established by Beckett himself and is directed by his authorized biographer, James Knowlson, the man who also oversees the editing of Beckett's theatrical notebooks. The archive also benefits from the direct support of Les Editions de Minuit and the estate of Jérôme Lindon. Stocked with "over 600 manuscript, typescript, and photocopied typescript items of original Beckett material, including manuscript drafts, annotated copies and corrected copies" (see BIF Web site), the collection is worth millions of dollars and remains indispensable to the work of anyone who has any hope of establishing a name as a Beckett scholar. As the description on the Beckett International Foundation Web site points out, "The Foundation is uniquely fortunate in that almost all of its manuscript resources were donated by Samuel Beckett himself, some of them being inscribed by the author to this effect. Others have been donated by Beckett's family and friends, by publishers and researchers." The library is distinct exactly because the archive was set up by Beckett and because the core of its collection was gifted by Beckett. As Knowlson wrote in his obituary for *The Independent* on December 27, 1989:

> Reading, my own university, has benefited enormously from Beckett's generosity. Until 1971, when a Beckett Exhibition was organized there, most of his manuscripts had, like those of so many other twentieth-century writers, been acquired by a number of American universities. Once Beckett knew that we too were aiming to establish a major collection, he began to donate regularly manuscripts, books, even paintings that he owned. Almost everything that he wrote in the past two decades is to be found there in manuscript and typescript form, often in both English and French versions. (19)

John Pilling, also a professor at Reading University, echoes Knowlson in an article for *Catalyst,* a magazine based in Reading, by arguing that "The future of the Foundation depends upon corporate acts of generosity comparable with the exceptional kindness that permitted it to come into being, best epitomized by Beckett's typically modest refusal of an honorary degree in recognition of his gesture" (Pilling 1990).

Apart from being established by Beckett himself through direct contact with the library's director (rather than through the mediation of agents and auction houses), the Beckett archive at Reading is also distinct because its patrons and supporters include Beckett's three main publishers—Calder, Lindon, and Rosset—plus a number of individuals who are directly invested in the preservation of Beckett's legacy. In most cases the major donors were Beckett's business acquaintances; it is little surprise they came to understand Beckett's legacy from Beckett's point of view and remain some of the keenest defenders of this legacy, specifically as it exempts Beckett from any interest in the marketplace. Beyond his publishers the best examples are Martin Esslin, Jocelyn Herbert, Elmar Tophoven, and Billie Whitelaw, all close, working, professional allies deeply invested in the preservation of a particular "Beckettian" vision and legacy.

Perhaps most significantly, we cannot ignore James Knowlson's role as Beckett's chosen curator and "authorized" biographer. In a tradition including Patrick Bowles, Ruby Cohn, Lawrence Harvey, Con Leventhal, and Richard Seaver, Knowlson became an influential voice in Beckett studies, lending his support to Beckett's efforts to control the public transmission of his private and personal affairs. Crucially, his biography perpetuates Beckett's reputation as an author disinterested in public fame, averse to success, and immune to the influence of money and the marketplace. Knowlson's scholarly integrity is beyond question, but the library at Reading and the exclusive, pen-in-hand interviews Beckett gave in support of his authorized biography must be seen as extensions of a long-standing effort on Beckett's part to shape public reception of his life and work through the agency of a respected *and loyal* intermediary. The very fact that Beckett established an intimate relationship with the overseer of the most valuable texts associated with his life and work is evidence enough of his wish to control his legacy in ways comparable to the ways in which he tried to control productions of his plays. We cannot fault the employees of the Beckett International Foundation or any other institution for enjoying the opportunity to be associated with such desirable materials and to be at a center for the international network of Beckett scholars. But in the case of the Beckett library at Reading it is difficult to disentangle Beckett's relationship with Knowlson from the ongoing effort to perpetuate a particular authorial image: as we have seen, his biography of Beckett is seriously flawed because its emphasis on an aesthetic model of understanding leads to neglect of important aspects of Beckett's professional life. Knowlson gave his "generous support" to "The Foxrock Foundation," with its deliberate and explicit mission to protect Beckett's public image with Beckett's "blessing," and he wrote a biography protecting and preserving the romantic idea that Beckett was "damned to fame."

The time is long overdue for us to connect the dots, recognizing the ways in which Beckett himself established the guidelines used to define his authorial persona and to perpetuate his legacy. Given the resistance to my thesis in the inner circles of Beckett studies, particularly in the United Kingdom, it is also worth underscoring examples demonstrating Beckett's deliberate efforts to highlight his complicity in the process. As we have seen, the modified Minihan photograph used in the advertisement for *Index on Censorship* is a key example (see fig. 1). So, too, are the Pic photograph of Beckett signing a copy of *Imagination Dead Imagine* and the Bauer photograph of Beckett sitting on garbage (figs. 3 and 4). But perhaps the most telling example is the play we analyze in our conclusion, *Catastrophe*.

Before we turn from the livres d'artiste to fuller consideration of the events leading to the creation of Reading University's Samuel Beckett archive in 1971 and the Beckett International Foundation in 1988, we should consider the Sorel Etrog version of *Imagination Dead Imagine* (1979) because in addition to being one of the finest artist's editions of a Beckett text, it also connects Beckett's keen interest in professional craftsmanship with the fame-building process. This process would culminate with the Nobel Prize award in 1969 and would be extended through Beckett's eleventh-hour collaboration with his authorized biographer. As already noted, Beckett invited a photographer, Roger Pic, to document, and thus to authenticate, the historic moment when he inscribed this museum-quality text with an autographed dedication to the artist. In itself, this invitation indicates a desire to reveal the author's direct participation in book signing and marketing. As the title page tells us, the prose text first appeared as *Imagination morte imaginez* in 1965 and in an English translation from Calder and Boyars, also in 1965. It also appeared in Grove's *No's Knife* in 1967 and *Six Residua* in 1978. The book Beckett signed while posing for Roger Pic in 1979 "was designed and illustrated by Sorel Etrog between 1969 and 1977 and has ten original prints on Arches paper and a portrait of Samuel Beckett." It appeared in an edition of "fifty copies numbered 1–50" and "ten copies hors commerce I–X. All signed by the author and artist" (copyright page, RUL). The moment documented in the photograph thus represents the culmination of a decade of planning beginning before the Nobel award.

Interestingly, a photograph taken five months before the Nobel announcement at the Closerie de Lilas in Montparnasse on May 19, 1969, documents part of the planning process (fig. 6), linking the livre d'artiste of *Imagination Dead Imagine* with Francis Warner's plans to build the Samuel Beckett Theatre at St. Peter's College, Oxford. This theater project deserves attention, not only because it has been neglected by Beckett's main biographers but because it reveals another aspect of Beckett's direct participation in tributes to his life and work and in the process of promotion and publicity preceding the Nobel award.

A fellow and tutor in English and Anglo-Irish Literature at the college, and a friend of Beckett's since 1962, Warner initiated plans for "a workshop for one of the really great dramatists of our time" in 1967, building on the enthusiasm generated by the events and publications celebrating the sixtieth anniversary of Beckett's birth. That Beckett was honored by, and in support of, the project is clear from the June 1, 1967, letter we have already mentioned. This letter is unequivocal in granting Beckett's full support for Warner's project. Richard Whittaker's report in the *Irish Times* on March 10, 1970, quotes this letter of support, going on to suggest Beckett had "undertaken to produce a play in the first season that the theatre is open." With

Beckett's authorization in hand, Warner asked his college (a Christian foundation) to allow him to raise money (initially £70,000) to "build the theatre, offset performing losses and open a bursary to help young playwrights." He was given the green light by St. Peter's in January 1968 (Ezard 1970). By the time the photograph was taken at the Closerie de Lilas, Warner had been campaigning for over two years and had raised over £25,000, including a promise of "one thousand pounds a year for five years" from Barney Rosset (April 11, 1968, SUL 34). Beckett's most overtly entrepreneurial publisher knew a good business prospect when he saw one. Confirmed in an exchange of letters between Warner and Grove on April 18, April 23, and April 24, 1969, the proposed amount of $2,400 per annum promised to earn Rosset a steady flow of "new scripts" for publication by Grove. In the meantime, Warner gained the support of Calder, Lindon, and Charles Monteith (the Faber and Faber executive who had secured the firm's rights to British and Commonwealth publications of Beckett's plays), as well as Beckett's bibliographer, John Fletcher, and his preferred director, Alan Schneider. He also managed to persuade Henry Moore to provide a sculpture for the entranceway and Buckminster Fuller to donate his services as the architect; further, he had put on a number of fund-raising events including "a series of pump-priming banquets in New York (presided over by the English poet W. H. Auden) which raised £12,000" (SUL 34).

The occasion for the dinner at the Closerie de Lilas was a May 20, 1969, conference during which Fuller presented his architectural plans to Beckett, Sir Alec Cairncross, Al Latner (a potential donor), Herbert Marshall, Harold Pinter, Ayala Zacks, and Samuel Zacks; the plan was to design a submarine-like bubble made of ferro-cement suspended underneath the college quad. It would seat 250. Its projected cost increased almost exponentially: the figure of £40,000 for the building reported in the Oxford-based newspaper *The Isis* on November 1, 1967 (Hodson), had risen to £70,000 by May 1968 (Blake). By February 1970 the building cost was reported as £170,000 (O'Donovan). Above these escalating costs, the theater also needed funds for overheads, a figure increasing from £70,000 in November 1967 to £180,000 in May 1970. In response to this escalation, Warner extended his list of potential donors: the first £5,000 from Richard Burton was supplemented by Edward Heath (leader of Britain's Conservative Party) and a number of dignitaries including Edmund Blunden, Benjamin Britten, Christopher Fry, Graham Greene, Robert Lowell, John Osborne, Harold Pinter, Peter Ustinov, and Arnold Wesker. As Anthony Holden of the *Financial Times* reported in February 1970, Warner's "personal commitment to the scheme [had] an evangelical air" and involved "a good deal of furious travel" including "a world poetry-reading tour to raise further funds" (Holden 1970). The effectiveness of Warner's efforts to persuade and enlist donors is very impressive: in May 1968 he managed to solicit an undisclosed but "very generous donation" from Prince Charles (*Daily Mail* 1968). He also gained the support of the Labour Party's Minister of Arts, the Right Honorable Jennie Lee, MP, quoting a message from her in the official, limited edition program for the March 1970 fund-raiser: "I am sure that an experimental theatre of this kind could be of great value to young playwrights everywhere and I wish the project every success" (Warner 1970).

The May 1969 photograph at the Closerie de Lilas shows Beckett at a table with Mr. and Mrs. Zacks, Warner, and Sorel Etrog (fig. 6). Etrog had already begun work on the special edition of *Imagination Dead Imagine* intended to raise additional money for the theater. The dinner makes Beckett's direct involvement absolutely clear: while Warner was buzzing around the world raising funds for the theater, Beckett was home in Paris, ready to wine and dine potential donors, offering support as needed, but keeping his head down so as to preserve his reputation as a man uninterested in such public tributes. As it happens, on this particular occasion he helped woo one of the main donors to the capital campaign; the next day, Zacks, a Canadian businessman, would donate £70,000 to the project (the donation was announced publicly in Oxford on March 8, 1970). During the next eight years Etrog would work on the illustrated, collectors' edition of *Imagination Dead Imagine,* and Warner would continue his "evangelical" effort to sell the idea to potential donors. The May 1969 gathering suggests Beckett was on the verge of a new level of public recognition; this recognition would come less than five months later in the form of the Nobel Prize for Literature. A benefit night held at the Oxford Playhouse on March 8, 1970, reminds us that his name had extraordinary cachet in the literary marketplace: he was successful in raising money with a minimum number of public appearances (researchers may dig up further evidence, but for now, so far as I can tell, the only public event captured on film was the night at the Closerie de Lilas).

More typically, Beckett's name was used to raise money without his physical presence. For example, his attendance at a March 1970 "Celebrity Gala in Aid of the Oxford Samuel Beckett Theatre Appeal" would be evoked through a brochure containing "two original portraits of Mr Beckett by Avigdor Arikha" (Warner 1970). This "Celebrity Gala" included contributions by Lawrence Harvey, Richard Ireland (who replaced Richard Harris), Patrick Magee, Siobhan McKenna, Wolf Mankowitz, and Huw Wheldon. The first part of the evening was structured by Warner, with five showings of *Breath* interspersed with a performance of Yeats's Purgatory (Magee as "Old Man") and sections dedicated to Beckett's relationship with "Paris and Joyce" (McKenna as Molly Bloom), his life during World War II, and his biography from "Godot to Nobel." According to the *Financial Times* report on March 9, 1970, the first part of the evening featured "a biographical synthesis of extracts from the work of Beckett and his friends" and "two complete performances of Beckett's play *Come and Go*" (Holden 1970). In part two a screening of *Film* was followed by an "Open Discussion under the chairmanship of Huw Wheldon on Samuel Beckett's achievement," concluding with "a Public Announcement" of the Zacks's donation and the award of Fuller's honorary fellowship at St. Peter's. While the evening itself raised less than two thousand pounds, it spurred Harvey and Mankowitz to negotiate for "first options on a quota of future new plays at the theatre"; they eventually donated one hundred thousand pounds for the privilege (Ezard 1970).

By 1979, when Beckett invited Roger Pic into his study to witness the signing and inscription of the artist's edition of *Imagination Dead Imagine*, Warner had passed the fund-raising efforts to a charitable trust, the Oxford Samuel Beckett Theatre Trust. Formed in 1976, this charity continues its commitment, through an award inaugurated in 2003, "to help the development of emerging practitioners in the field of experimental theatre and, in general, to encourage the new generation of creative artists," promising that "Bold and innovative projects will be favoured" (http://www.osbttrust.com).

Evenings "with" Beckett

The events organized to raise money for the Samuel Beckett Theatre prepared the ground for the Samuel Beckett exhibition held at Reading University (May to July 1971), the Institute of Contemporary Arts in London (August to September 1971), and the University of East Anglia, Norwich (October to December 1971). As already indicated, this exhibition was organized with Beckett's full support, and it functions as a graphic demonstration of the effectiveness with which Beckett's friends and supporters collaborated to promote his name and fame. The use of A. J. "Con" Leventhal as a keynote speaker and as the writer of the foreword for the catalog is, perhaps, the most convincing evidence of the direct connection between Beckett and the exhibition.

A friend of Beckett's since they were students together at Trinity College Dublin before Beckett had published a word, Leventhal had worked for the author as a public relations secretary in the 1960s. Instrumental in the doctor in litteris award given to Beckett by Trinity College Dublin in July 1959, and the likeliest person to have written the citation (which repeated the mantra asserting Beckett "cares little for the outward emblems of fame"), Leventhal resigned his post at TCD in July 1963 to take on the job of managing Beckett's literary affairs. A series of letters written by Beckett to Leventhal in February to April 1963 reveals the work the author did to help Leventhal make the move from Dublin to Paris, making clear he paid for the move and paid Leventhal a salary (the Leventhal letters are in their own collection at HRHRC). On February 27 Beckett went into detail about living arrangements and what he could pay, using his estimate of past and future income to calculate an offer of sixty pounds a month (about seven hundred francs). He sweetened the deal by offering to pay costs associated with settling in Paris. On March 19 he explained the pros and cons of a third-floor apartment versus one on the fifth floor, explaining how the higher apartment would get more light and had a better view. Just over a week later, on March 27, Beckett agreed to sign the lease agreement for the fifth-floor apartment and promised to sort out furniture and utensils for the bedroom and kitchen. On April 18 he assured Leventhal he was paying the rent to hold the flat and was working on stocking the place with linens. Finally, on April 30, 1963, he offered to pay Leventhal's fare and, perhaps joking about his protracted endeavors to make sure Leventhal was comfortable, said he would make sure the bed was soft enough.

After Beckett set him up with a modest apartment on the Boulevard du Montparnasse, an address he would keep until well into the 1970s, Leventhal quickly established himself as Beckett's personal secretary and public relations contact, "dealing with correspondence and shielding him from an intrusive public" (Ackerley and Gontarski 2004, 319). He would, for example, play a crucial role in setting up the exhibition in England in 1971, answering Knowlson's enquiries about publishers' terms and other contractual issues (October 27, 1970, RUL), passing along Beckett's agreement to autograph one hundred copies of the catalog (November 4, 1970, RUL), writing the foreword for the limited-edition catalog, and attending the exhibition as Beckett's personal representative. He was, in effect, Beckett's press officer, paid seven hundred francs a month to mediate between Beckett and the various agents and agencies who made his professional life possible. As we have seen from Beckett's use of literary agents in the years before he became internationally famous, the role Leventhal played is entirely consistent with Beckett's previous career. But Leventhal was on an entirely different level than any previous agent: he was, to Beckett, thoroughly trustworthy, sharing his education and interests so completely he was qualified to assume his job at Trinity when Beckett resigned in 1931. Leventhal was thoroughly dedicated to the advancement of Beckett's career during the years when Beckett's fame expanded to the point that he became one of the best-known Nobel laureates of the twentieth century.

In 1953, when fame became likely, Beckett made the decision not to do public readings of his work and not to allow note-taking interviews. These restrictions tied the hands of his publishers and producers, but it also gave them a unique selling proposition: Beckett became "the unknown celebrity." This proposition would only work, however, if they came up with a way of making Beckett present in the literary marketplace without compromising his reputation as someone opposed to, and untouched by, literary marketing. Like Honda, he was the product that sells itself. And, also like Honda, he needed a marketing strategy designed to advertise this feature. Beckett's various marketing agents responded by organizing "evenings with Beckett," hiring actors to read from his work and inviting scholars to provide biographical and intellectual contexts. In the absence of the author himself, Beckett's publishers provided surrogates. Often these surrogates were actors Beckett had directed in his plays, such as Jack MacGowran, Patrick Magee, and Billie Whitelaw, or they were his long-time friends, as with Leventhal. When they were on stage, speaking with the authority bestowed on them by "Sam," each would repeat the three Beckettian commandments: Beckett does not engage in self-promotion; Beckett has no desire to be famous; Beckett has no interest in money.

This strategy began in 1955 with evenings planned to boost interest in the London premiere of *Godot.* Albery and Glenville organized a series of public meetings at the Arts Theatre after the play moved to the Criterion on September 12, 1955. On October 3, 1955, for example, there was a "public inquiry" asking the question, "Is Waiting for Godot Good Entertainment?" The promise of the evening was to "Resolve the Problem / Do We—or Don't We / Wait for Godot." After the play moved to Dublin on October 28, 1955, Leventhal took the stage at the Pike Theatre to engage in a post-play conversation and to issue author-approved proclamations (*Irish Times,* February 6, 1956). Like many interpretive statements issued since 1955,

Leventhal's remarks were delivered as though "told by Sam"; fifteen years later he would repeat the performance, again speaking for "Sam," taking the microphone to address the audience at the 1971 exhibition in Reading. Beckett's awareness of these events is apparent from a letter he sent Leventhal on February 27, 1956, expressing his amusement in response to Leventhal's report about the debate at the Pike (HRHRC). These events were just the beginning of a series designed to publicize Beckett's work without Beckett having to go public.

True to his more aggressive, entrepreneurial style, Barney Rosset organized a much more ambitious event in New York in October 1956. Dedicated to "The Poetry and Prose of Samuel Beckett," Rosset's promotional tribute took place at six thirty on Tuesday, October 23, 1956, at the Poetry Center at the 92nd and Lexington YM-YWHA. Rosset greeted those willing to pay two dollars for readings by Alvin Epstein and Albert Dekker with a description of Beckett's rise from "obscurity" in the years since 1953; Epstein played Lucky in the New York *Godot* and Dekker was a movie actor who had, most recently, performed in *East of Eden* (1955) and *Kiss Me Deadly* (1955). Rosset went on to explain, "Tonight we will not read from *Godot* but we will go back into Beckett's earlier work along with the more recent," the purpose being to "establish the background from which *Godot* came" and to show that the other writing can "also stand on its own merits as interesting and good work" ("Y program about Beckett," SUL 33). In the press release, which describes Rosset as "Mr Beckett's publisher and personal friend," drama editors were assured "Mr Beckett has personally selected the works for this presentation." The clear intention is to underscore Beckett's approval of a program carefully orchestrated to capitalize on the fame produced by *Godot* while stimulating interest in his prose texts. The event was fast on the heels of the September 1956 publication of *Malone Dies* and only a few days before the opening of Myerberg's November 1956 New York production of *Godot:* as we might expect, Rosset uses his introduction to plug the Grove editions of *Godot* and *Molloy,* but he does not include readings from these already well-advertised texts. It was, of course, entirely appropriate to end an evening of Beckett readings with the first page and a half of *Malone Dies* because it allowed Dekker to end the evening with the sentence "Enough for this evening."

An August 30, 1956, letter from Beckett to Rosset proves Beckett was directly involved in planning the promotional evening. His proposal was to present a roughly chronological sequence from "Dante and the Lobster" to *Texts for Nothing,* including the first few pages of *Proust,* the "Murphy's Mind" chapter from *Murphy,* "Enueg I" from *Echo's Bones,* the final few sentences from the end of the first part of *Molloy,* the first few pages of *Malone Dies,* and the first few pages of chapter 3 of *Watt.* He also suggested the inclusion of passages in French from *L'Innommable* (on the assumption Roger Blin was to record a section especially for the evening) or, failing that, three French poems and "From an Abandoned Work." Interestingly, it seems Beckett's tentative plan had been to provide a recording of his own reading of *Textes pour rien* as a conclusion. The letter makes it clear Beckett gave free rein: he annotated the list of suggested readings with a note saying that Rosset could do what he wanted (SUL 33). Given a rough plan, but also given the freedom to revise as he saw fit, Rosset chose to market *The Unnamable* and *Malone Dies.* The former was forthcoming, a "work still in progress insofar as the English version is concerned," and the latter was fresh off Grove's presses on September 15, 1956. Marketing took precedence.

The program shows Rosset's deliberate, author-sanctioned intention to make commercial hay out of the evening. "Backtracking just slightly" so as to "conclude the program by a short reading from the opening pages of *Malone Dies,*" Rosset whetted appetites for Beckett's prose work by providing what can only be called a biographical celebration. While there is no record to prove books were on sale at the reading, we can assume Rosset provided a table selling the newly printed paperback of *Malone Dies* at $1.25 a copy and the "500-copy Limited Edition, bound in cloth, at $5.00" (Grove Press News Release, SUL). Presumably he also sold copies of *Waiting for Godot* and *Molloy.* The program narrative, approved by Beckett in September 1956, describes a first stage of growth from the status of a "divine amateur" to the status of "a comparatively unknown writer" whose work "had . . . been published in Paris to some high critical acclaim." It then argues there had been a second stage of development, bringing him from the status of a writer celebrated for "A successful London production . . . followed by a record run at the Pike Theater in Dublin" and "The Broadway *Godot,*" which "went far to establish Beckett in this country, as we know." Perhaps he had once been a "divine amateur," but now, as the fee-paying audience could attest, his work was a commercial venture. The contract for the "Evening with Beckett" gave Beckett a flat fee of fifty dollars; Rosset, Dekker, and Epstein received fifty dollars each plus "one-third of one-half of the income from single admissions above expenses" (as per the contract of July 16, 1956).

Between 1956 and the Nobel award in 1969 this process of commercial promotion was orchestrated in ways specifically designed to promote a particular Beckettian persona while selling books and adding to his international fame. Beckett would settle into a pattern of refusing honors and awards; but he would also participate (albeit behind the scenes) in a number of events specifically designed to glorify his reputation and add to his acclaim. And he *did* accept awards, retaining his reputation as a "reluctant prizeman" even as he became a doctor of letters at TCD and an honorary member of societies including the American Academy of Letters and the Modern Language Association. He gained the reputation of a reluctant prizeman, as a man who accepted honors and awards but who had no interest in the honors and awards he accepted, because his surrogates and sentinels repeated the claim whenever they had the microphone in their hand or the printing press at their disposal. One of his first refusals of an award was reported to Con Leventhal in a letter dated January 26, 1956, a few days after the Miami production of *Godot.* He turned down Seamus Sullivan's offer to nominate him as a member of the Irish Academy of Letters on the grounds that he was sickened by the thought of scholarly institutions, and that those situated in Ireland were especially anathema to him (HRHRC). But he was clearly interested in the award. The ambivalent refusal in this letter shifted when it was Leventhal who initiated the offer of an award from Trinity College in July 1959. Beckett attended the awards ceremony despite an ongoing disagreement concerning the performance of his plays in Ireland (in January 1958 *Act Without Words I and II* and a reading from *All That Fall* had been slated for a festival in Dublin, but Beckett withdrew them in protest when O'Casey and Joyce were cut from the program [February 20, 1958, SUL 20]).

However "reluctant" he might have been when he attended the TCD award ceremony, Beckett still posed for a photograph wearing his doctoral robes. Perhaps his lack of a hat is intended to communicate his disdain for the ceremony, but the photograph, taken by the *Irish Times,* became part of his press packet, turning any disdain he might have had into a selling point. The photograph featured in publicity for Alec Reid's seminar on Beckett at the Lantern Theatre in Dublin on July 26 and 27, 1971, advertising a lecture called "The Reluctant Prizeman: Something about Sam." The prize referred to in 1971 was, of course, the Nobel Prize for Literature. A revised version of the introductory essay in Grove Press's *All I Can Manage, More Than I Could,* this essay had its "germ" in a "conversation" with Beckett, underscoring how many received ideas about Beckett originated with Beckett himself (Reid 1971, 8). The photograph also appears on the academy-oriented cover of G. I. Papasakis's Greek edition of *Damned to Fame*. Again we see the pattern through which Beckett accepted an award but managed to give the impression he did so against his will, calling attention to his ostensible resistance to the game of fame even as he participated in this game.

We cannot properly conclude an analysis of the ways in which Beckett became an ostensibly reluctant but highly public presence in the literary marketplace without attending to a series of campaigns, activities, and events organized in his name during the decade or so preceding the Nobel award. Rosset's efforts to expand the audience for Beckett in the American marketplace continued apace, especially after he launched the *Evergreen Review* in 1957. Volume 1, number 1 of the review featured "Dante and the Lobster" and reprints of poems from *Echo's Bones,* and a cover photograph of a seductive adolescent girl reinforced Beckett's appeal to the "hippie" youth who had supported *Godot* during its New York run in 1956 (Rosset 1994, vii). While Rosset would work with Beckett to reprint previously published texts not readily available in the United States, including "The Expelled" (January–February 1962, no. 22) and "The Calmative" (June 1967, no. 47), he was obviously more interested in unpublished material he could associate with the "counterculture." Throughout, his main intention was to build a solid audience for his flagship author by associating him with the sexy icons of underground culture and the most cutting-edge politics of the day. For example, the third number in 1957 included the first accurate printing of "From an Abandoned Work" (it had been printed by *Trinity News* in June 1956, but the editors had been heavy-handed in "correcting" Beckett's text); this third volume again put Beckett in the same context as the nascent youth revolution, connecting him with the buzz over free speech and censorship generated by volume 1, number 2, with its focus on the "San Francisco Scene." Stories and poems by writers including Lawrence Ferlinghetti, Allen Ginsberg, Jack Kerouac, and Henry Miller had been challenged as "obscene" by customs officials, creating the sense that there was a literary movement with the *Evergreen Review* as its voice. As Ken Jordan put it in his August 1993 introduction to Rosset's *Evergreen Review Reader,* this second issue "brought the Beats and *Evergreen Review* to the forefront of the American stage" (Rosset 1994, i). Two issues after calling widespread attention to Beckett's prose in volume 3 of his review, Rosset scored another marketing coup: the summer 1958 (no. 5) issue featured a premiere publication of

Beckett's latest play, *Krapp's Last Tape.* Rosset took the opportunity to align Beckett with the most iconographic and rebellious figure in US culture in the 1950s, placing his name on the cover between James Dean and a naked mannequin (Rosset 1994, 48).

Beckett's deep respect for Rosset's contribution to the dissemination of his texts in the American literary marketplace is evident from his granting Rosset the right to publish "From an Unabandoned Work" in *Evergreen Review* (no. 14). A brief excerpt had appeared in *X: A London Magazine* in 1959 (no. 1), but the *Evergreen* printing was the first substantial piece of Beckett's first novel since he had finished *L'Innommable* in January 1950. The text represents an English-language draft of the opening ten pages of *Comment c'est/How It Is,* written before he decided to complete the novel in French. Published in fall 1960, this breakthrough text appeared with a cover calling attention to the contradiction between a postage stamp proclaiming "freedom of the press" and a post-office cancellation stamp encouraging customers to "report obscene mail to your postmaster" (Rosset 1994, 102). The implication is, of course, that Beckett had decided to "unabandon" his text in order to protest US obscenity laws. Again granted permission to release the premiere publication of a text in May-June 1963, the first English version of *Cascando,* Rosset put Beckett's work in a political context. This time he connected Beckett with the American movement for civil rights, printing a play in May beginning "in the month of May" (*GCE III,* 343). About "the reawakening" (348), *Cascando* appears in the context of a cover showing an activist holding a large sign with the word "NOW" (Rosset 1994, 218). Rosset's persistent effort to associate Beckett with the most current cultural and political issues is evident from an advertisement he crafted to publicize the February 1966 issue of *Evergreen Review* (vol. 10, no. 39). Barbarella, "the luscious heroine of the French comic strip for grown-ups . . . banned in her native land," is juxtaposed with a photograph of Beckett with the caption "Samuel Beckett is now appearing at your local newsstand" (see fig. 2). The issue contains the first American printing of "Imagination Dead Imagine" (first published in English in the *Sunday Times* on November 7, 1965) and uses a cover with a joke-cartoon of a ballerina who has discovered she is without underwear at the moment she performs a high kick in front of a packed house with a clear view up her skirt. This titillation is clearly designed to create a niche for Beckett made up of those who were not afraid of free expression, progressive politics, and open sexuality.

Rosset's aggressive marketing plan in the United States was complemented by Alan Schneider. Between 1956 and 1984 Schneider would help raise Beckett's profile through a steady stream of American productions, revivals, and tours. The American director began his career during World War II at Catholic University and made his name with production of plays by Eugene O'Neill, William Saroyan, Tennessee Williams, and Thornton Wilder on the Arena Stage in Washington DC in 1951–55. He established himself in New York with a blockbuster production of Wilder's *Skin of Our Teeth* at the American National Theater and Academy in August 1955. Schneider had seen *Godot* at the Théâtre Babylone in spring 1954 and immediately tried to contact Beckett to buy the American rights. Discovering the rights had already gone to Albery and Glenville and that "Mr Beckett seemed as far removed as Mr. Godot himself," he returned to New York with the plan to "forget all about *Warten Auf Godot*" (1987, 186). In fall 1954 Michael Myerberg invited him to direct the American premiere of *Godot* in Miami. As part of his preparation for the job, Schneider sailed to Europe in October 1955 to meet Beckett in Paris with a plan to travel to London to see the Albery/Glenville production. They met in the lobby of the Lancaster Hotel, a gaudy high-society establishment just off the Champs-Elysées. Schneider obviously knew Beckett's tastes because he presented him with a bottle of Lacrima Cristi, a sparkling wine from Naples; a scheduled thirty-minute meeting turned into three hours at Beckett's apartment followed by an all-night session at Fouquet's, an expensive restaurant Joyce frequented on the corner of the Champs-Elysées and Avenue George V. By the time they parted after another night together in Montparnasse, Schneider was hooked: "When I left him, I wanted nothing more than to please him. I came with respect and trepidation; I left with a greater measure of devotion than I have ever felt for a writer whose work I was translating for the stage" (225). The immediate bond between the two men is evident: within two days they met up again in London to see five performances of *Godot* at the Criterion Theatre.

Even though Schneider would be dropped by Myerberg after the Miami production of *Godot,* he became Beckett's preferred director, staging the US premieres of every subsequent play: as Schneider records in his memoirs, it was not long before "people were talking about 'the extraordinarily close collaboration' between Samuel Beckett [and] Alan Schneider" (1987, 277); edited by Maurice Harmon, *No Author Better Served: The Correspondence of Samuel Beckett and Alan Schneider* provides comprehensive proof of this intense collaboration, revealing Beckett's persistent behind-the-scenes, over-the-Atlantic grip on American productions of his plays over a thirty-year period. The key to the collaboration was Schneider's willingness to give the impression Beckett's plays were intended to be objets d'art rather than box-office hits: as we have seen from Shenker's "Moody Man of Letters" and the letters published in the *Village Voice* in 1958, Beckett was happy to reinforce this impression. This explains why histories of Beckett's career in the theater tend to emphasize the Schneider-directed "Miami fiasco" while downplaying Peter Hall's direction of the audience-pleasing production of *Godot* in London in 1955 and Herbert Berghoff's respectable run in New York in 1956. Together with the list of plays Schneider directed between 1956 and 1968, *No Author Better Served* illustrates Schneider's crucial role as Beckett's main point-person in the American theatrical marketplace in the period before he was awarded the Nobel Prize for Literature; after George Devine died in 1966 and up to his own death in 1984, Schneider was even more important, becoming Beckett's primary "go-to" English-language director. Although Beckett became increasingly active as a director of his own work after the 1961 production of *Happy Days* in London and, especially, after the 1964 production of *Play* in London, he mainly worked in Germany and France, taking full control of only three English language productions—*Footfalls* at the Royal Court in May 1976, *Happy Days* at the Royal Court in June 1979, and *Endgame* at Riverside Studios in May 1980. When Beckett was not directly involved as a co-director or director he used Schneider as his authorized directorial conduit. Schneider's reputation as "an off-Broadway director" did no harm at all to Beckett's self-fashioned image as an author who had no interest in being a celebrity (Schneider 1987, 278).

The list of Schneider's author-sanctioned productions is impressive. On January 28, 1958, he opened *Endgame* at the off-Broadway Cherry Lane Theatre on Commerce Street in Manhattan; on September 29, 1959, he produced a successful revival of *Godot* at the Alley Theatre in Houston; on January 14, 1960, he premiered *Krapp's Last Tape* at the Provincetown Playhouse in New York; on April 4, 1961, he did a revival of *Krapp* at the not-for-profit Arena Stage in Washington DC; on September 17, 1961, he directed the New York premiere of *Happy Days* at the Cherry Lane Theatre, taking the play to Princeton University's nonprofit McCarter Theatre on January 12, 1962; on February 11, 1962, he revived *Endgame* at the Cherry Lane; and on September 12, 1962, he paired a new production of *Krapp's Last Tape* with Edward Albee's *Zoo Story* at the East End Theatre in New York.

In the meantime, on July 10, 1962, he staged *Act Without Words II* at his alma mater, the University of Wisconsin. Eighteen months later, on January 4, 1964, he opened his production of *Play* at the Cherry Lane Theatre. He revived *Happy Days* at the Cherry Lane on September 28, 1965, and *Krapp's Last Tape* at the Billy Rose Theatre on October 1, 1968. Between 1968 and 1984 Schneider would direct fifteen different plays by Beckett with over thirty-five separate productions. The list includes the landmark production of *Not I* at Lincoln Center in New York on November 22, 1972; the premiere of *Rockaby* at the State University of New York in Buffalo on April 8, 1981; the English-language premiere of *Catastrophe* at the Harold Clurman Theatre in New York on June 11, 1983 (along with the English-language premiere of *What Where* and *Ohio Impromptu,* which he had premiered at Ohio State University on May 9, 1981); and a trilogy of plays for the inaugural performance at the Samuel Beckett Theatre in New York on February 16, 1984 (*Rockaby, Footfalls,* and *Enough,* all starring Billie Whitelaw). Schneider wrote to Beckett on March 2, 1984, to say "We are selling out the Samuel Beckett Theatre(!), turning away hundreds on weekends. We are the talk of the town" (Ackerley and Gontarski 2004, 179).

Long before the successful launch of the Samuel Beckett Theatre in New York, Beckett was well aware of Schneider's importance in boosting his status and turning him into a box-office phenomenon. In 1960 he had given him the right to film *Waiting for Godot* for PBS television, a right he had denied many others, including his close professional acquaintances at the BBC, and in 1964 he honored Schneider by traveling to New York to collaborate on location during the filming of *Film*. While in New York he paid homage to Schneider's Cherry Lane productions by making a pilgrimage to the theater. Schneider understood Beckett thoroughly enough to stay true to his vision of his work and to regret it when he erred from this vision, as he did when he slowed his production of *Play* in 1964 in response to demands by Edward Albee, Richard Barr, and Clinton Wilder. And he remained true to Beckett's image of himself when he described his attitude toward fame: "To this day he strongly dislikes interviews, cocktail parties, celebrity socializing, and all the other public concomitants of the literary life" (Schneider 1987, 225).

The situation on the stage in London was less driven by a single director and was, thus, less controlled by Beckett until he asserted himself by acting as a co-director and, eventually, as a director. Until he stepped up, there was much anxiety because the quality of productions was unpredictable. Peter Hall directed the English-language premiere of *Godot* in London from

August 3 to September 3, 1955, continuing at the Criterion from September 12, 1955 to March 24, 1956. This is the production Beckett saw with Schneider when he famously suggested it was off target, sitting in the audience making clear he thought it was "all wrong." Even though the production was crucial to Beckett's ongoing success in the marketplace, Hall's job as a Beckett director was finished. When the BBC's Third Programme produced *All That Fall* for broadcast on January 17, 1957, the director was Donald McWhinnie: Beckett seems to have been more comfortable with this choice because McWhinnie accepted Beckett as a genius and took his suggestions seriously, visiting him in Paris with Barbara Bray, chief script editor at the Third Programme, to make sure the production followed the author's wishes. Despite his complaints about the animal sounds in the BBC version of *All That Fall,* there is every indication Beckett thoroughly enjoyed listening to McWhinnie's production of his first radio play (Knowlson 1996, 389). The next Beckett production in London, *Endgame* at the Royal Court Theatre, opened on October 28, 1958. After months of negotiations with the Lord Chamberlain's office over the script, a license had been granted on August 6, 1958. This time George Devine directed, playing the role of Hamm alongside Jack MacGowran's Clov. It was not, for Beckett, a happy experience. He liked Devine and gave him lots of advice, attending the last few days of rehearsals when he was taking breaks from acting as an informal co-director on McWhinnie's production of *Krapp's Last Tape,* which was on the same bill. But the effect was awkward. Devine was caught between his own sense of the play and Beckett's overwhelming last-minute suggestions; MacGowran suffered from what Beckett saw as a lack of direction (Knowlson 1996, 410). Still, Beckett and Devine had established the basis of a long-term relationship marked by Devine's devotion to what he would, in a "last tribute," refer to as Beckett's "extraordinary mind and poetic vision" (Calder 1967, 99). McWhinnie's production of *Krapp* was more to Beckett's liking, mainly because he deferred to Beckett throughout. Subsequently the author agreed to let McWhinnie direct a television production of *Godot* for the BBC in 1961; however, the result was not, for Beckett, in keeping with the spirit of the play, which he thought ill-suited to television and described in disparaging terms (Knowlson 1996, 435). But his relationship with McWhinnie was cemented over whiskey and wine and the two would work together again fifteen years later on the BBC productions of *That Time* (1976) and *Ghost Trio* (1976).

In the meantime, Devine directed the London premiere of *Happy Days* at the Royal Court Theatre, opening on November 1, 1962, and the premiere of *Play* at the Old Vic, opening on April 7, 1964; in both cases, Beckett took a controlling role from the beginning, using his relationship with Devine to establish an enduring pattern of authorial control over British productions of his plays (the controversy over Fiona Shaw's 1994 production of *Rockaby* illustrates the ongoing effort by the Beckett estate to legislate Beckett's controlling influence after his death). As Cronin puts it, "Beckett was a perfectionist where productions of his work were concerned, a brooding presence in the stalls who distrusted actors and insisted on a meticulous obedience to his written stage directions" (1996, 529). Given the repeated claim about Beckett's lack of interest in the audience and his ostensible focus on producing an object, we could draw the conclusion Beckett was committed to "Art for Art's sake" (529). Beckett's obsession with the re-creation of his own vision for the plays was such that, in the case of *Happy Days,* he almost drove the actor playing Winnie, Brenda Bruce, to a nervous breakdown and had to back off until she recovered. With *Play* he was so "obtrusive" he ran headlong into arguments with the producer, Kenneth Tynan. But Devine took Beckett's side, arguing he would "perform the play as written," obeying the newly written injunction in the stage directions to use a "rapid tempo throughout," while Sir Laurence Olivier and Bamber Gascoigne defended Tynan, arguing that they were more interested in "producing the play not to satisfy Samuel Beckett but for an audience" (Ackerley and Gontarski 2004, 444). It would seem the author had no concern for the standard audience at the Old Vic. But he was more attuned to the theatrical marketplace than this apparent aestheticism suggests: he wanted a big audience and was happy for his plays to be performed on big stages, but his reputation as an avant-garde artiste led him to focus on those who rebelled against the strictures of the mainstream London stage. To do so he needed directors, like Schneider, who would serve him unequivocally: "The Letters about *Happy Days* . . . show how reliable Schneider was in getting as close as he could to Beckett's exact technical requirements as well as to the play's meanings" (Harmon 1998, x).

Devine was learning to serve in a similar capacity in England, but he suffered a severe heart attack and would pass away on January 20, 1966, shortly after providing John Calder with his "Last Tribute" to Beckett (Calder 1967, 99). At the time, Beckett had been ready to collaborate with Devine on the screenplay of *Eh Joe,* written in April 1965. With his most dependable English director no longer available, Beckett turned to Alan Gibson as his director for *Eh Joe*, recording the play with the BBC in January 1966, and screening it on BBC 2 on July 4, 1966, with MacGowran as

"Joe" and Sian Phillips as "Voice." On February 11, 1966, he told Schneider he was happy with the entire project (Harmon 1998, 198). Less than two years later, with Billie Whitelaw set to star in *Come and Go,* Beckett worked with William Gaskill for a performance at the Royal Festival Hall (December 9, 1968); a few months later he turned to yet another director, Deryk Mendel, a good friend who had directed a landmark production of *Play* in Ulm-Donau in June 1963, to reprise *Come and Go* at the Royal Festival Hall (March 23, 1969). Perhaps the best conclusion we can draw from the history of Beckett's pre-Nobel productions on the London stage is that the only consistency is to be found in his constant and increasing presence at these productions: in his correspondence Beckett repeatedly complained about his tiredness and expressed his ongoing disdain for the reception of his work, but he worked tirelessly to gain complete control over the staging of his plays. He knew his audience and he knew how to maintain his aestheticized reputation with this audience.

As we have seen, Rosset's success in cultivating an audience of young intellectuals for Beckett is evident from the *Evergreen Review* and his direct marketing campaign aimed at college professors and university bookstores (fig. 9). Harmon rightly suggests that Beckett had, by 1971, "become part of the university curriculum, his novels and plays studied in literature and drama courses, his work always in print" (1998, xi). Discomfort with academe was, of course, part of the image Beckett fashioned as he developed strategies to separate himself from Joyce: the process of intellectual decomposition narrated in *Molloy, Malone Dies,* and *The Unnamable* underscores this antiacademic persona and it was, of course, part of Rosset's campaign on Beckett's behalf (fig. 10). But Beckett, like Rosset, was conscious of the importance of sales on university campuses, and he was careful to develop close connections with scholars and selected academic institutions. This awareness explains why he accepted the honorary doctorate from Trinity College Dublin in 1959, why he collaborated with Francis Warner's project for a Samuel Beckett Theatre at Cambridge University, and why he was so generous in supporting the archive devoted to his work at Reading University. He further acknowledged the efficacy of this university-focused strategy in 1981, during celebrations of his seventy-fifth birthday: he supplied commissioned texts to the Center for Theatre Research in Buffalo, New York, and one of America's largest universities, Ohio State University in Columbus, Ohio. Both plays were directed by Schneider, with Billie Whitelaw performing in the Buffalo production of *Rockaby* on April 8,

1981, and with David Warrilow performing in *Ohio Impromptu* on May 9, 1981. Beckett's creative output faded in the 1980s, but he was determined to express his deepest gratitude to those who had turned him into a staple of the university curriculum.

A parallel campaign was waged in Britain by John Calder. His work in the UK market is evident in the Calder and Boyars collection at the Lilly Library in Bloomington, Indiana. Known as John Calder (Publishers) Ltd. between 1950 and 1964, changing its name to Calder and Boyars in 1964 and back to its original name in 1975 (when Calder and Marion Boyars were divorced), Calder's company made its name by publishing controversial books including Henry Miller's *Tropic of Cancer* (1963) and *Tropic of Capricorn* (1964), and Herbert Selby's *Last Exit to Brooklyn* (1966). As Calder writes in *In Defence of Literature,* "the latter was the subject of a much-publicized obscenity case at the Old Bailey. The company eventually won on appeal and reprinted twenty thousand copies of the book in response to widespread interest roused by the case" (Aster and Lane 1999, 37). In many ways, then, Calder built his company using strategies similar to Rosset's, tapping into the rapidly growing market for radical and morally questionable writing accompanying the youth revolution of the late 1950s and the 1960s. Along the way Calder founded "an anti-censorship society," the Defence of Literature and the Arts Society, and could legitimately claim "During the 60's I was perhaps the most fashionable publisher, one of the most talked about" (Aster and Lane 1999, 29). He is the publisher who introduced Beckett's nondramatic work to Britain and the Commonwealth. Like Rosset, he did so by appealing to young, antiestablishment intellectuals and by distributing his books through universities and offbeat bookshops.

By his own account, Calder wrote to Beckett during the first London run of *Godot* in 1955 but missed the opportunity to negotiate a contract to publish his plays when he sent the request to the wrong address. In the meantime Faber bought the rights to publish *Godot* and subsequent dramatic works (the one exception would be *Come and Go,* which Beckett specifically gave to Calder). When Faber decided the novels were too obscene, Calder stepped in, signing a contract for the rights to Beckett's prose and poetry in Britain and the commonwealth in 1956. He negotiated with Editions de Minuit to publish English translations of the French novels, publishing *Malone Dies* in 1958. Calder followed with the first collection of the postwar novels, *Three Novels* (1960), and the first collection of Beckett's poetry in English, *Poems in English* (1961). He also bought the rights for

Watt and *Murphy*, publishing both in 1963. He would then publish *How It Is* in 1964, *Proust* and "Three Dialogues with Georges Duthuit" in 1965, and *Molloy* and a reprint of *Three Novels* in 1966. In addition to the general publicity garnered by the more controversial texts, the publishing house also set out to promote Beckett as its flagship author. His strategy is clear from a note he included in *Waterstone's Guide to Books* (1990), defining his niche in "Creative literary publishing" in terms of "a missionary belief" designed to gain "the confidence and affection of his writers" so "he has a good chance of keeping his authors once they are established and profitable." He goes on to describe the crucial part of the plan: "to find at least one really unusual and important [author] whose name will become synonymous with the imprint" (Aster and Lane 1999, 37). In 1990 Calder identified Beckett as his "lucky genius, friend and guru" and, as we have seen, wrote an obituary lauding him as a "saint." But in 1960 he had been less willing to trust to luck and Beckett's spiritual potential; in 1960 he developed a marketing strategy designed to make Beckett's name synonymous with John Calder. Part of this plan is evident from a "Sketch of Plan for Beckett Symposium" he composed in the early days of his relationship with Beckett (it is dated 1960 by Breon Mitchell, director of special collections and curator of the Calder collection at the Lilly Library in Bloomington, Indiana). This document gives a sense of Calder's nascent campaign to boost sales of Beckett's work by recruiting academic and commercial advocates: he lists "possible contributors" who had already committed themselves to Beckett's cause and who might be enlisted as spokespeople: "Maurice Blanchot, Ruby Cohn, G. W. Stonier (?), Harold Hobson, Hugh Kenner, Austyn Wainhouse, and Patrick Bowles" (MS 2192, 1:42, Lilly).

As Beckett's sixtieth birthday approached, and with his list of Beckett publications now healthy enough to be displayed on publicity material, Calder put his plan into action. In March 1964 he orchestrated "An afternoon of readings and debate under the chairmanship of Martin Esslin," with readings by Jack MacGowran and Patrick Magee, at the Criterion Theatre, London. In 1965 he consulted with Beckett in the development of a revised program for performance at the Memorial Theatre in Stratford, the Traverse Theatre in Edinburgh, and the Arts Theatre in London in August through October 1965. This program became the basis of Calder's celebrations for Beckett's sixtieth birthday and eventually led to a new round of publications, including *Beckett at 60: A Festschrift*. It is clear Calder was determined to give Beckett a public profile worthy of a potential Nobel laureate. And

Beckett cooperated. Despite an ongoing medical problem, Beckett threw himself into his professional work with a vengeance in 1964 and 1965, jetting to Berlin, London, Paris, and New York to assist with productions of his plays, broadcasts of his nondramatic work, and the filming of *Film*. Together with the advertising by Rosset, the series of productions by Schneider, and the events organized by Calder, Beckett's efforts propelled him into a position of supreme celebrity (fig. 12).

A quick summary of Beckett's efforts in 1964 and 1965 suggests how his intense professional schedule supplemented the work of Rosset, Schneider, and Calder. In late 1963 he corresponded regularly with Alan Schneider during preparations for the New York production of *Play* (opened on January 4); he worked with MacGowran and Magee and a young director, Michael Blake, on a production of *Endgame* (rehearsed in London, the play was put on in Paris in February 1964); he consulted with Roger Blin before he took *Fin de partie* on a French tour that began in February 1964; he assisted Jean-Louis Barrault as he prepared a March 1964 Paris revival of *Fin de partie;* he went to London in March to work with George Devine on the Old Vic production of *Play* (opened on April 7, 1964, with Whitelaw as W2); he helped with the casting and rehearsals of Jean-Marie Serreau's Paris production of *Comedie* (opened on June 14, 1964); he spent time in London in late June and early July helping with the Royal Shakespeare Company's rehearsals of *Endgame* (directed by Donald McWhinnie, with MacGowran as Clov and Magee as Hamm); he flew to New York on July 10, 1964, to help with the making of *Film* (he flew back on August 6); he worked on the BBC production of *Cascando* (broadcast on October 6, 1964, with Devine directing and Magee as "Voice"); he went to London in December 1964 to help with the Royal Court revival of *Godot* (directed by Anthony Page, with Nicol Williamson as Vladimir); he went to Berlin in February 1965 to help Deryk Mendel overhaul an ailing version of *Warfen auf Godot,* took a quick break in London on February 18–21 to help MacGowran with his recording of "End of Day," and returned to Berlin to finish rehearsals at the Schiller-Theater for its February 25 opening. In the meantime, he found time to write *All Strange Away* in October 1964, *Imagine morte imaginez* in January 1965, and *Va–et-vient* and *Come and Go* (written simultaneously and finished on January 25, 1965). Exhausted with the theater after the Berlin production of *Godot,* he rested in anticipation of a second round of surgery on his jaw scheduled for July 19, 1965 (the first round, in November 1964, had left him with a hole in his palate; it would be August 1966 before the work of reconstruction and dentistry was complete). But Beckett's physical ailments only caused a temporary pause in his creative energies: he wrote *Eh Joe* in April 1965, finishing it on May 1 and translating it into French as *Dis Joe* in May; he translated *Words and Music* as *Paroles et musique* in July 1965; and he produced the first draft of *Le Dépeupleur* in November to December 1965.

Beckett's theater work certainly helped sales of Calder's publications by raising the author's public profile, but there was more to be done. Calder had already commissioned a book by Hugh Kenner designed as a reader's guide, *Samuel Beckett* (1968). And even though he would complain that "Books on Samuel Beckett's work are coming out like induced hailstorms to awaken the wasteland" and would suggest this was "caused by a fascination that Mr. Beckett would do much to be rid of" (Calder 1967, 1), in 1968 he released a revised edition of Kenner's book, again arranging United States distribution through the University of California. He would also contribute to the "hailstorm" by publishing *No's Knife* (Beckett 1967b), an anthology of easily digestible extracts from previously published texts. The effect was, of course, to make Beckett's prose more accessible, more marketable. Calder was clearly focused on the effort to promote broader interest in Beckett's prose by targeting theater-goers who identified with "a strange club" defined by "caustic humour or satisfying disgust" (Calder 1967, 3). The event at the Criterion in 1964 included extracts from the opening pages of *Watt* (MacGowran), an early section of *Molloy* (Magee) from "my mother never refused to see me" (page 17 in the Calder edition of *Three Novels*), a section from *Malone Dies* (MacGowran; starting on page 212), the full text of *From an Abandoned Work* (MacGowran), the final scene from *Endgame* (MacGowran and Magee), a selection of poems (MacGowran), an extract from the final pages of *The Unnamable* (Magee), and selections from the forthcoming novel *How It Is*. To ensure the attendees were aware of the next book to be issued by Calder and Boyars, the program repeatedly advertises *How It Is*, "to be published on April 30th." The program for the Criterion evening asserts once more that "he shuns every form of personal publicity" and goes on to promote Beckett as "the greatest master of the language since Joyce, and probably the greatest creative imagination writing today" (Lilly).

On June 25, 1965, Calder wrote asking Beckett's "approval" for a modification to the Criterion program, proposing to use *Krapp's Last Tape* and *Come and Go* before the interval, with readings from *Molloy*, "Three Dialogues," and a "repeat of *Come and Go* after the break," followed by a "discussion chaired by Martin Esslin." Calder's reasoning was that "this could be very successful and do a lot for book sales, etc." (Lilly). Beckett's reply on June 30 is effusive, explaining his deep gratitude for all the work Calder was doing on his behalf, giving the go-ahead for him to use whichever texts he chose, *except* "Three Dialogues" (Lilly). Subsequently, on July 29, 1965, Beckett advised Calder not to do *Come and Go* unless he was there to supervise (Lilly). Obedient to Beckett's instructions, Calder revised his plan, relying heavily on extracts from *Watt* and *Three Novels,* especially *Molloy,* replacing the plays with texts his company had published. Throughout, he corresponded with Beckett, reporting his intentions so that Beckett had time to exercise his power of veto. Again, Beckett played a crucial role in setting up the event; and again, he did so while remaining behind the scenes. Billed as "An Evening with Samuel Beckett" (though there was no chance at all that Beckett would actually appear) the revised program was performed at the Memorial Theatre, Stratford, on August 22, 1965. Introduced by Calder, it included two extracts from *Godot,* a few poems, the final scene from *Endgame,* and readings from *Molloy, Malone Dies, The Unnamable,* and *How It Is.* On September 3, 1965, Calder reported to Beckett: "the Stratford reading went extremely well" and "The Edinburgh readings are going extremely well to full houses and good reviews." His next step was to bring the program down to the Arts Theatre in London, where it played for "one week at 10:30 at night" (Lilly).

Calder's publicity campaign, specifically designed to win theater-goers over to Beckett's prose and, thus, to sell more books, continued with the November 7, 1965, publication of "Imagination Dead Imagine" in the *Sunday Times* (page 48). This exposed Beckett's most recent work to roughly five hundred thousand readers. Soon after this public relations coup, Calder began to develop a book designed as "a Birthday offering to Sam" (Leventhal to Calder, December 13, 1965, Lilly). Intended for publication in April 1966, but delayed until 1967, *Beckett at 60* (Calder 1967) is an homage by Beckett's professional acquaintances and collaborators including Arikha, Devine, Esslin, Hayden, Herbert, Leventhal, Lindon, MacGowran, Monteith, Pinter, Schneider, and Simpson. With so many personal notes, tributes, memoirs and reports, it functions as a formal celebration by a hard core of Beckett loyalists writing "more or less within the social framework demanded [of me] by the editor" (HRHRC).

Like the contributors to *Our Exagmination Round His Factification for Incamination of Work in Progress,* the celebration of Joyce's legacy published in 1929 by *his* publisher, Shakespeare and Company, the contributors to *Beckett at 60* were told what to write and were paid for their efforts. A few excerpts from almost fifty notes Calder wrote in December 1965 and January 1966 give us sufficient sense of his shaping influence on the "symposium of tributes" (as he called the collection in a January 4 letter to Nicol Williamson). In a brief letter to Jack MacGowran on December 2, 1965, he wrote, "I am putting together a birthday tribute for Sam's 60th birthday and I would like you to contribute an article of a maximum 1,500 words if you would like to on 'working with Beckett' from an actor's point of view. We can only pay a relatively modest fee of 8 guineas for a text of between 1,000 and 1,500 words." On the same day he wrote to Barbara Bray, "I am preparing a tribute for Samuel Beckett's 60th birthday next Spring. Would you be willing to write an article of about 1,500 words on his influence on younger writers in France for a fee of 12 guineas?" Again on the same day, he asked Lindon for an article "about how you first met Beckett, the excitement of discovering him and the first reception of the novels and of *Godot* in Paris" (curiously he omitted any mention of payment in his letter to Lindon). And, again on December 2, 1965, he asked Leventhal "if you would be willing to write an article of about 1,500 words or longer if you like on 'Beckett in the 30's', filling in some of the background of Beckett, Joyce, etc. A personal memoir is what I would really like here." His effort to produce a tapestry of intimate anecdotes is best exemplified by the relatively long note he wrote to Dumesnil on January 7, inviting her to write about "Sam before the war," about "Sam's wartime activities," or about "The period when you were going around publishers with his manuscripts" and giving her freedom "to write something quite different." Suzanne's refusal notwithstanding, Calder engineered a text giving "Beckett addicts" a fix of previously unreported biographical information about "Sam" at the same time that it functioned "as an introduction for new readers to one of the great seminal minds of our time" (all quotations in this paragraph are from the "Beckett at Sixty" file, 1965–67, Lilly).

In its published form the book is divided into three sections, "Reminiscences," "Critical Examinations," and "Tributes," and the introduction makes clear the book is designed as an homage to "the reluctant Beckett" (Calder 1967, 1). Calder confesses that the contributors "are all overawed . . . by the prophet from Dublin" (2) and goes on to say the book is being published not "for the benefit of its subject who will chuck it away in disgust" and "not for the benefit of the publisher," but "for the benefit of the contributors . . . who want to say basically that they love him, or admire him, or are grateful" (3).

There is no question *Beckett at 60* functioned as a marketing device in Britain: sales of what Calder called *The Trilogy* (1959) had already been sufficiently boosted by Calder's efforts in 1964 and 1965 to justify a reissue in 1966; after the festschrift, the same happened to Calder's editions of *Malone Dies* (1958) and *Poems in English* (1961), with new editions of both texts released in 1968. *Poems in English* also sold quickly, especially after the Nobel award, with a third printing appearing in 1971. Increased interest on college campuses created demand for a second edition of Kenner's *Samuel Beckett* with a revised introduction and afterword (1968). Sales of *Watt* and *Murphy* (1963), *How It Is* (1964), and *Molloy* (1966) also increased significantly as Calder's marketing efforts were complemented by the work he did "build[ing] up a little network of bookshops not just in Britain but in Australia, in New Zealand and European bookshops who sold English books" (Applefield 1999, 28). With a "network" of distributors ready to sell "the more intellectual authors" (1999, 28), Calder compiled *No's Knife: Collected Shorter Prose 1945–1966,* including "The Expelled," The Calmative," "The End," the complete series of "Texts for Nothing," "From an Abandoned Work," and three texts presented as "Residua": "Enough," "Imagination Dead Imagine," and "Ping." He released the collection in May 1967, shortly after organizing "An Evening of Music and Reading from the work of Samuel Beckett and Bertolt Brecht" at the Royal Court on April 30, 1967, as a "Gala Benefit in aid of the Free Art Legal Fund" (Aster and Lane 1999, 156). Calder was not as aggressive as Rosset, but he was persistent and took advantage of opportunities as they arose. Further, as the tributes of *In Defence of Literature* illustrate, Calder was a well-respected man, and he was prepared to use his reputation to associate Beckett's work with current political issues, broadening the market for his texts by positioning him as a leading light in the anticensorship movement. A good example of how Calder combined the marketing of Beckett with his political activism is evident from his use of *Come and Go,* which Beckett gave him in 1965. *Come and Go* gave Calder a showpiece for the winter season in 1968, elevating the status of his press and his political organization through a high-profile performance at the Royal Festival Hall on December 9, 1968. The performance was repeated at the same venue on March 23, 1969, as a fund-raising event for the Defence of Literature and the Arts Society. Both events gave him the opportunity to advertise the "special signed luxury editions on handmade paper" of *Poems in English, How It Is,* and *Imagination Dead Imagine* (March 2, 1967, to John Fletcher, Lilly). He also used the events to publicize the trade edition of *No's Knife,* which was supplemented with a special edition of two hundred, consisting of one hundred series A and one hundred series B, all signed by Beckett.

Before Calder's live performances, public interest in Beckett had been stimulated by BBC Radio productions of *Waiting for Godot* on April 27, 1960, and January 5, 1962, and *Endgame* on May 2, 1962. Again, Beckett benefited from the assistance of his professional friends and acquaintances. Collaborations with Barbara Bray, George Devine, John Fletcher, and Martin Esslin led to a series "of readings of non-dramatic texts by Beckett . . . throughout the sixties" (Esslin 1982, 139), reinforcing Calder's series of evenings "with Beckett." For example, MacGowran and Denys Hawthorne did radio broadcasts of Beckett's poems on March 9, 1966, and November 24, 1966, and, as already noted, MacGowran presented *Imagination Dead Imagine* on March 18, 1967. Sales of Beckett's nondramatic texts were bolstered again by the September 1967 issue of *A Samuel Beckett Reader* (published simultaneously by Calder in hardback and by the New English Library as a Signet paperback). As Calder put it in his preface to the chronological collection of extracts, the "reader" was specifically "designed to make the work of Samuel Beckett . . . more accessible to the average reader" (Beckett 1967a, 7). In other words, it was part of a strategy to expand the market for Beckett's work. As suggested above, *No's Knife* also attracted a broader audience for Beckett's prose, providing a sample of texts in a package structured like "End of Day" and "Beginning to End," taking the reader on a chronological journey through Beckett's career as a prose writer. Correspondence between Beckett and Calder proves Beckett's full collaboration in determining the contents, packaging, and title of a book composed of previously published material and designed to increase his accessibility and prominence in the marketplace: on December 7, 1966, he gave Calder the title for the book and explained how he wanted it to be structured, detailing a sequence based on four distinct phases of his postwar career (before writing *Godot;* after *L'Innommable;* after the success of *Godot;* after *How It Is*). Having outlined the exact order he wanted, he asked for the book to be presented with a minimalist framework, free of embellishments and with the least possible amount of contextualizing matter (Lilly, fig. 12).

By the time Francis Warner approached Beckett with his proposal for the Oxford Samuel Beckett Theatre, the author was, as they say, at the top of his game. He had a private secretary, trusted directors and publishers in France, Germany, and the United States; the power to co-direct his plays when he chose; a wife who was prepared to fly around Europe to check on productions of his plays; a custom-designed apartment in Paris; and a writer's retreat in Ussy. The spark of fame that came in 1953 with the Babylone *Godot* had been nurtured and fueled so that it was, by 1967, providing the energy for a network of devoted professionals who were promoting and glorifying his name across the globe. When Aidan Higgins described Beckett as "no smiling sixty-year-old public man" (March 30, 1966, Lilly), he simply reiterated the public image constructed by Beckett himself in 1937–50 and defended by his sentinels in the years of burgeoning fame. As we have seen, by 1967 Beckett's unsmiling face was iconographic, his public persona had become a matter of famous absence, and his professional friends and accomplices were prepared to celebrate his name in numerous venues with loving devotion. Calder was certainly extreme in calling Beckett "the prophet from Dublin" (1967, 2) but his tendency to place him on a pedestal is endemic. No matter how resistant the Beckett industry remains to the suggestion that their man "Sam" participated in the construction and dissemination of his public image, and no matter how often they repeat the mantra that he had no interest in money, publicity, or fame, facts should not be brushed under the carpet. It is time to put aesthetic and quasi-religious representations of Beckett's biography in the context of his life as a professional writer in the commercial marketplace.

Conclusion

> It is well known that Mr. Beckett cares little for the outward emblems of fame.
>
> —TCD Litt. D citation, 1959

> Beckett's purity as an artist was his trademark. With it went a rejection of worldly values, causing his wife to declare "Quelle catastrophe!" when he won the Nobel prize in 1969.
>
> —Shorter, *Unfathomable Truths*

Quelle Catastrophe?

Received understandings of the life of Samuel Beckett tell a dramatic tale about Dumesnil's response to Jérôme Lindon's telephone call on October 24, 1969, in which he informed her Beckett had won the Nobel Prize for Literature: her response has become central to Beckett mythology. "Quelle catastrophe," the phrase Dumesnil allegedly uttered, has taken on a life of its own, giving Bair a subtitle for a chapter about the period between 1966 and 1969 and Knowlson part of his title for a chapter called "Accident, Illness, and 'Catastrophe,' 1967–69." In many ways the response has become emblematic of Beckett's attitude toward fame, encapsulating his image as an amateur who preferred to tinker away without regard for public acclaim and with active fear his life would be ruined by the trappings of fame. In this view he was "appalled" by the Nobel award because "his long-term future" would be "disrupted by the celebrity" (Knowlson 1996, 505). We have seen how the success of *Godot* in 1953–56 made Beckett question his ability to write and have noted his repeated claims to debilitated exhaustion and a complete lack of professional acumen. We have also seen how his public image as "un célèbre inconnu" was framed in the mid-1950s using his own statements about his preference for failure and through the deployment of a growing network of professional colleagues who repeated talking points about his aversion to publicity, fame, money and the reception of his work (see fig. 5). We have noted substantial evidence of his participation in the construction of his authorial persona, both through his work with Samuel Johnson in 1937–40 and through the release of "Three Dialogues" in 1949, the Shenker interview in 1956, and the Schneider letters in 1958. Books and articles by professional acquaintances in academe and publishing, including Patrick Bowles, John Calder, Ruby Cohn, Martin Esslin, John Gruen, James Knowlson, Con Leventhal, and Richard Seaver, perpetuated this persona with frequent repetitions of bullet points about Beckett's aversion to celebrity. We have also witnessed his persistence in the face of the storm of professional commitments when he finally became successful. Once he had established a sustainable reputation, he accepted prizes and accolades, attending the award ceremony at Trinity College in July 1959, cooperating in the planning of the series of "Evenings" and "taster" texts designed to celebrate his work (fig. 12), actively participating in planning and fund-raising for the Samuel Beckett Theatre at Oxford (fig. 6), fully engaging in the complex negotiations involved in establishing the Samuel Beckett Library at Reading University. Clearly, his repeated claims to incompetence in his business affairs must be put in the context of his vigilant, detailed, untiring, and highly effective attention to these affairs.

Within days of the Nobel award, Beckett would be celebrated in the French press as "le grande anonyme" and as the master of "une grammaire neutre" (MS 3158, RUL). Again, he was represented as though he were a character in one of his own texts, passively resigned to a fate he could not avoid. As I have argued throughout, the evidence from his career is, however, to the contrary. Even though he often complained about being swamped with the petty details of his professional obligations (as he did, for example, in letters to Susan Manning on December 17, 1955, July 2, 1956, and October 30, 1957, HRHRC), he forged ahead with the determination of a man driven by a deeply ingrained work ethic. By 1959, when he accepted an honorary doctorate from TCD, he was "celebrated throughout the literary world as playwright, novelist, poet, satirist, critic, and translator" and had "established his right to be named among the outstanding men of letters educated in Trinity College—Congreve, Farquhar, Swift, Goldsmith, Wilde, and Synge." In a few years he had lifted his public profile from that of an Irish-associated Left Bank phenomenon to that of an international celebrity, but he had, at the same time, established a resilient reputation as a man averse to fame: "It is well known that Mr. Beckett cares little for the outward emblems of fame" (TCD Litt. D citation, HRHRC). As suggested above, this authorial persona was only possible with a careful strategy designed to manage relationships between his public and private lives, between the world of creativity and the world of business. Affluence combined with a supportive network of professionals gave him the freedom to fashion and disseminate a public image as a man of silence and solitude without sacrificing the benefits of solid contracts, a steady flow of royalties, deep engagement with the complicated processes of book and stage production, and an increasingly prominent public profile. The culmination of this carefully controlled fashioning and publicity is, of course, the authorized biography he initiated through his close friend and professional acquaintance James Knowlson: *Damned to Fame: The Life of Samuel Beckett* (1996).

After his custom-built cottage in Ussy was completed in 1953, he had a fail-safe retreat from unwanted stress, but "to keep in touch with the business side of his work" he had a telephone installed in 1954 (Knowlson 1996, 352). When he needed to get away from the interruptions and demands of city living, he took long vacations in Southern Europe and Northern Africa, often spending accumulated royalties in local currency, but he also took manuscripts with him and kept in constant contact with his professional affairs by sending frequent business-related telegrams and postcards to publishers and directors. As we have seen from his relationship with Brendan Behan, when he was in Paris and needed relief he retreated into the relative silence of his apartment, installing a telephone with an on/off switch so he could control the timing of incoming calls. But he also invited selected scholars, photographers, and other professional colleagues into his otherwise private spaces, allowing them to document where he worked, what his study looked like, how his bookshelves were stacked, what it was like to live as "Samuel Beckett."

His relationship with Lawrence E. Harvey during the 1960s, evidenced by Harvey's photographs of Beckett's cottage and study in Ussy sur Marne (Knowlson 1996; between pages 256 and 257) and by the "score of conversations in 1961–1962 and 1964–1965" that laid "the foundations of" *Samuel Beckett: Poet and Critic* (Harvey 1970), provides solid proof of Beckett's investment, before the Nobel award, in the effort to "throw light not only on his literary beginnings but also on the works of his artistic maturity" (Harvey 1970, xii). Although Harvey took copious notes (available at the Dartmouth College Library), no direct quotations from Beckett appeared in Harvey's book; again, the author shaped the reception of his poetry and criticism without seeming to do so. I have great respect for Harvey's groundbreaking work, but the "score of conversations" with Beckett are indistinguishable from Harvey's own interpretations, making it impossible to distinguish between Harvey's function as an academic and his function as a public mouthpiece for Beckett. Harvey's book gives us another clue to the success and longevity of Beckett's persona: the reason he continues to be regarded as "a reluctant biographical subject" (McDonald 2006, 6) who has, nonetheless, become "one of the world's most recognizable recluses" (2) is that he successfully created and managed a buffer zone between himself and the literary marketplace by enlisting people who would function as his loyal spokespersons. Hiding behind this trust-based buffer zone, he could function as though he were unknown, anonymous, letting Calder, Harvey, Knowlson, Lindon, Rosset, Schneider, and Whitelaw speak for him; but when he chose he could step into the limelight without compromising his reputation as someone who disliked publicity.

The success of Beckett's strategy and the resilience of his reputation is evident from McDonald's description of Beckett as a "reluctant biographical subject": any Beckett scholar writing after 1996 is fully aware of the comprehensive array of biographical accounts by numerous friends and acquaintances in Beckett's obituaries in 1989–90, the plethora of different photographs accompanying these obituaries, and Beckett's role in orchestrating the development of a major archive devoted to his life and work. Why would a "reluctant biographical subject" spend many hours during his final months on earth talking at length with a university professor he had designated as his "authorized biographer"? The only answer can be that he did so because he had great faith in academe and was perfectly willing to exert control over his biographical legacy by trusting this legacy to a professional academic.

Twenty years earlier, immediately after he was informed about the Nobel award in Nabeul, Tunisia, on October 23, 1969, Beckett called on his network of professional associates to protect him from public view, but he was already a celebrity and could not prevent the world's press from locating his secluded hotel within hours of the announcement. On October 25 Lindon rushed to his aid, speaking to the press in a crowded lobby on his behalf until, on October 26, Beckett decided to put an end to the media siege by showing his face. When he did so, he was dressed in a tailored jacket with a suave polo-neck sweater, smoking a four-inch cigar. He was tanned like a film star and was clearly in supreme control of his media representation (*Times* [London] 1969a). Flanked by his French publisher, he could remain silent while Lindon voiced a carefully calculated response to the award. The main talking point was Dumesnil's reaction; the statement was designed to create the public perception that the award was a disaster for Beckett. As we have already seen from its recurrence in the main biographies, the story would be repeated during the remainder of Beckett's life, influencing the overwhelming gamut of obituaries written on the occasion of Beckett's death and continuing to be a crucial part of Beckett mythology. The currency of the "quelle catastrophe" story is evident: Ackerley and Gontarski report it as an undisputed truth (2004, 407). McDonald cites the story on the first page of his introduction, treating it as a given (2006, 1), and sites across the Web continue to feature the story (see, for example, "Samuel-Beckett.com," plus pages devoted to Beckett on "themodernworld.com," "guardian.co.uk," "thisislondon.co.uk," and "time.com"; these more general sites demonstrate the ubiquity of the myth). The "quelle catastrophe" story has, without doubt, become intrinsic to the received biography: as Eric Shorter puts it, "Beckett's purity as an artist was his trademark. With it went a rejection of worldly values, causing his wife to declare 'Quelle catastrophe!' when he won the Nobel prize in 1969" (Shorter 1989).

Beckett's carefully calculated response to the Nobel award is emblematic of his response to fame. As this fame grew, he became very busy and was beset by a series of challenges, but he was rarely reduced to idleness. In fact, he took great care to avoid being overwhelmed by his professional obligations, successfully creating a highly controlled environment where he retained the ability to create, edit, and manage his work. Even when fame was relatively new, in 1953–58, Beckett was incredibly productive, working systematically to establish a post-*Godot* reputation on a level with the greatest Irish writers. In this very busy period he complained constantly about the stresses that came with success, but he managed to translate and publish *En attendant Godot, Molloy* (with Patrick Bowles), *Malone meurt,* and *L'Innommable.* He also wrote, translated, and published *Fin de partie;* completed two mimes in French, *Acte sans paroles I and II* (translating the first of these into English for publication with *Endgame* in 1958); and completed a stage play, two radio plays, and a new prose piece in English: *Krapp's Last Tape, All That Fall, Embers,* and *From an Abandoned Work.* During this period he also oversaw the publication of *Watt* (1953) and *Nouvelles et textes pour rien* (1955), co-translated *All That Fall* into French (with Robert Pinget), organized a collection of homages for Jack Yeats, and began the texts that became *Comment c'est/How It Is* and *Theatre I and II.* Furthermore, he began to work on German translations of *Fin de partie, Malone meurt,* and *Echo's Bones* and oversaw the Italian translations of *Godot* and *Molloy.* Again, this immense productivity was possible because he was incredibly focused on his career and took such great care in the management of his professional life. As we have seen, after 1958 his efforts continued unabated, and he had, by 1965, consolidated his status as "the greatest master of language since Joyce, and probably the greatest creative imagination writing today (Calder 1964). Even though he was a habitual moaner when it came to his business affairs, he managed these affairs very successfully without sacrificing control over his private life, his public image, and his posthumous legacy.

The "quelle catastrophe" story is so intrinsic to Beckett mythology it demands closer analysis. When the award was announced he was advised in a telegram from Lindon to go into hiding, "je vous conseille de vous cacher" (RUL). In response, Beckett started a rumor that he had moved hotels. But he arranged to have meals delivered discreetly and stayed in his room. Inevitably, the press corps tracked him down and besieged the lobby. In the meantime, his French publisher telephoned to say he was on his way to help sort things out (presumably this is the call when Suzanne said "quelle catastrophe"). Once he arrived, Lindon arranged a press conference to be conducted in the hotel lobby exactly as he and Beckett prescribed: photographs were allowed; Beckett would answer no questions and would leave when he chose. After avoiding the press for three days "he showed himself . . . and posed for photographs while refusing to comment on the award" (*Times* [London] 1969a): he thus provided the photo op and story required by the newspapers without giving up on the idea he was "publicity-shy" (Knowlson 1996, 506). True to the image he had helped create through the non-interview interview with Israel Shenker in 1956, he met reporters without compromising his reputation for silence. In other words, he and his publisher managed the Nobel Prize story with great care and deliberation, communicating the message that "Mr Beckett did not seek the prize or wish to be awarded it" while "he did not see any reason for rejecting it" (*Times* [London] 1969a). With the pithy story about Dumesnil's reaction plus this message about his reluctance noted, dispatched, and printed, the press corps departed. Beckett stayed in Nabeul until early December, then ambled his way back toward Paris through Portugal, arriving home in mid-January. During this three-month jaunt, his sentinels protected his private life and his public image: during this particular episode it was Calder, Dumesnil, Leventhal, Lindon, and Rosset who created the space to allow him to stay away from Paris, enabling him to avoid the media and the public except as he saw fit.

Reporting on the October 24, 1969, telephone call telling Beckett he had won the prize, Knowlson writes "Lindon telephoned the Nabeul hotel and spoke first to a distressed Suzanne, who genuinely regarded the award as a 'catastrophe'" (Knowlson 1996, 505). More dramatic than Knowlson, Bair reports, "She turned to face Beckett, a stricken look on her face and whispered 'Quelle catastrophe!'" (Bair 1990, 604). For his part, Cronin tells us, "On the 23rd October the telephone rang in their hotel room and Suzanne answered it. After listening for a few moments she turned to Beckett with a grave face and exclaimed, 'Quelle catastrophe!'" (Cronin 1996, 543). In *The Grove Companion to Samuel Beckett,* the story is used to corroborate the claim that the award was disastrous for Beckett because it was "the end of his anonymity": "Not wishing the attention, he saw it as a disaster; Suzanne's words after the call . . . were 'Quelle catastrophe'" (Ackerley and Gontarski 2004, 407). Given Beckett's reputation as an intensely private man, it is curious how this remarkably vivid scene became part of the public record. Apart from anything else, a telegram had been sent the previous day telling Beckett about the impending phone call. In this context, the reported reaction sounds overdramatic. Unless Beckett had kept news of the award to himself since he had received the telegram on October 23, it seems odd Suzanne should be "stricken" during a phone call on October 24.

In any case, as Knowlson puts it, "These appalled reactions . . . became public, with words like 'catastrophe' and 'distressed' finding their way into press reports" (Knowlson 1996, 505–6). Knowlson's use of passive voice is entirely in keeping with his author-approved thesis about Beckett being "damned to fame," but it is very clear from newspaper accounts that these words were deliberately planted in the media by Beckett's spokesman. The UPI report filed on October 24 (*Times* [London] 1969c) makes it clear that Lindon put the story in circulation, turning a private moment in a private space into a key part of Beckett's public mythology: "Mr. Jérôme Lindon, agent and long-time friend of the Irish playwright, said that Mr. Beckett and his wife were going 'into hiding' to avoid any publicity brought by the award" and "added 'Both of them were distressed by the announcement that Samuel had won the prize'" and "Mrs. Beckett had described it as a 'catastrophe.'" The story goes on to quote Lindon saying "Beckett has no interest in money and the prize itself means nothing to him," that he would not go to Stockholm because he would not want "the glare of publicity," and that "To refuse the prize would probably increase the publicity." It is, then, beyond doubt that the "appalled reactions with words like 'catastrophe' and 'distressed'" became public as a direct result of statements made by Beckett's French publisher. The man who had advertised *Molloy* in 1951 as evidence of "l'apparition d'un grand écrivain français" (the appearance of a great French writer) now sought to dampen any suspicion Beckett might be interested in the accolades and awards attendant on this greatness. Within days, however, Lindon arranged for "la publication exclusive d'un texte qui ne sera en librairie que le 15 Novembre" (the exclusive publication on November 15 of a text that has not appeared in bookstores). "Sans" appeared in *La Quinzaine littéraire* in its edition covering the period from November 1 to November 15, 1969. Lindon was obviously keen to perpetuate the established image of his "reluctant prizeman"; he was also keen to capitalize on his success.

In the context of Lindon's talk of Beckett's discomfort with "the glare of publicity," it is worth noting Lindon's exploitation of the Nobel award through the immediate publication of a previously unpublished text in a newsstand journal. In its first copy after the Nobel announcement, the entire front page of *La Quinzaine,* and thus every newsstand in Paris, was emblazoned with Beckett's face (a Guy Suignard shot from 1966) together with a banner-sized announcement of the award and a large-font announcement of the unprecedented publication. But this was simply a way to strike while the iron was hottest. Two weeks later he followed with the publication of *Sans* in a limited, numbered edition of 742 copies. Beckett's English publishers, Faber and Faber and Calder and Boyars, were equally bold in taking immediate advantage of the award in the literary marketplace: the first copy of the *Times Literary Supplement* following the announcement carried advertisements by both UK publishers, each with a photograph of Beckett (Faber used a Bauer shot from 1962; Calder used an Ozkok from 1961). Both advertisements listed the Beckett books they had published with prices and a banner statement about Beckett being "Winner of the Nobel Prize for Literature 1969" (October 30, 1969).

In February 1970 Calder negotiated a contract with Tom Parkinson of David Conyers Productions to produce MacGowran's *Beginning to End,* establishing Calder and Boyars as "head agents, allocating amounts pro rata to Faber and for the American production to Grove" (February 27, 1970, Lilly). Beckett agreed. By April 10, 1970, Calder was acting as head agent for the publicity campaign, finalizing contracts for a successful two-year tour of Europe, the UK, and the United States. Ever the opportunist, Calder also rushed to publish *Lessness*, a special "Signature" edition of Beckett's translation of *Sans*. The book appeared in June 1970, a few weeks after it had appeared in *New Statesman* (May 1, 1970); the edition took advantage of Beckett's refusal to do public book signings by putting an enlarged copy of his autograph on the front cover. Beckett wrote his name on a sheet in quick response to a request by Calder for "a bit of paper with your signature scrawled over it as large as possible for the cover" (May 12, 1970, Lilly). Author and publisher were fully aware of the enhanced value attached to Beckett's autograph by his decision to avoid public book signings; he compensated, and capitalized, by signing manuscripts for public consumption in the privacy of his study. For its part, Grove Press issued the first American edition of *Lessness* in *Evergreen Review*, volume 80, in July 1970. Grove Press had already been planning to publish the *Collected Works of Samuel Beckett* in January 1970, and it appeared on schedule: sales were surely not harmed by the Nobel award.

Far from being debilitated by the Nobel award, Beckett seems to have found a new lease on life. In addition to the quick release of *Sans* and *Lessness* within a few months of the award, Beckett completed negotiations for the publication of Grove editions of *More Pricks Than Kicks* and *Mercier and Camier*, a Minuit edition of *Mercier et Camier*, the performance of *Breath* in aid of the Samuel Beckett Theatre in Oxford, a revival of *La derniere bande* at the Theatre Recamier in Paris, and the publication of extracts from *Le Dépeupleur*. Needless to say, each publication and event was an occasion to profit from the Nobel award. Rather than being a catastrophic distraction, the Nobel sparked a flurry of activity by Beckett and his publishers, becoming a driving force for his creativity and a central part of the strategy to market his work. Beckett sustained his career, beginning to write *Pour finir encore* and maintaining control over his theater work by telling Lindon not to allow theater productions of *Dis Joe* or *Words and Music* (Pilling 2006, 182). At the same time, however, the "quelle catastrophe" story was used to reinforce his ostensible aversion to the publicity brought by the award, to the fame it underscored, and to the increased royalties it garnered.

Even though he had asked Lindon to communicate his lack of interest to the Nobel Foundation, he was loathe to put himself in the same scandalous position as Sartre, who had refused the Nobel in 1964, thus developing a reputation for ungraciousness. Beckett accepted, but he did so on his own terms, in a way designed to protect his reputation as an amateur writer with no interest in public recognition. From his correspondence it seems his immediate complaint was a niggling irritation at the interruption of a holiday he had taken after a grueling trip to Berlin (October 25, 1969, HRHRC). At this stage, the award was less a catastrophe than an inconvenience, an impediment to his ability to enjoy himself. A month later he was still in Nabeul and had returned to the remote control of his business affairs, using postcards, telegrams, and, presumably, the occasional telephone call to communicate his wishes. For example, on November 24 he asked Rosset to give Lawrence Harvey, an American academic, permission to quote from Grove publications, explaining he was actively working to survive his new circumstances (SUL). On the same day he received a note from Grove Press asking him to sign contracts for a production of *Breath* in London and a revival of *Godot* in New York (November 24, 1969, SUL). It was business as usual. Two days later, a letter to Con Leventhal gives a strong sense of his ironic, but ongoing, commitment to a career defined by his ostensible reluctance about professional correspondence and contracts. The letter describes his valiant effort to keep up with the avalanche of mail while also producing new work (November 26, 1969, HRHRC).

Let's recall that he was still in Tunisia ostensibly suffering from the catastrophe occasioned by the Nobel award. With this in mind, it is interesting to read his complaints about his London agents granting permission for a production at the Abbey Theatre. He laments his limited control, explaining he can only restrict the contract to a one-month run, protecting his rights when it came to television and preventing other commercial uses of the play. It is intriguing that, devastated as he was reported to be, he went on to express his misgivings about the prospect of a London production of *Godot* featuring the comedian Spike Milligan. He ended the detailed letter with a dig at Curtis Brown for taking his money to act as his agents while blithely proceeding to destroy his capital assets (November 26, 1969, HRHRC). The letter makes absolutely clear that Beckett's main priority was the protection of his property rights; rather than recoiling from the effects of the Nobel Prize, he asserted his right to profit from his art. Three days later he sent John Calder a note accepting the proposal for a German edition of *Proust* so long as it was published by Suhrkamp Verlag (November 29, 1969, SUL). Again, despite the supposed trauma of the Nobel award, Beckett continued to assert his proprietary rights in the literary marketplace. And he retained sufficient control over his private life to remain in Nabeul until December 13, 1969, six weeks after the world knew exactly where he was staying. He then headed for Portugal, taking the long way home. Writing to Leventhal from Cascais, Portugal on January 6, 1970, he revealed his ongoing command of his business affairs, showing his continued control over his agents and publishers as he moved homeward: he had just refused Peter O'Toole TV rights to *Godot* and was keenly aware of the deep crisis at Curtis Brown. He had had enough and was ready to go back to Paris to take an even firmer grip on his post-Nobel professional affairs. He needed medical attention, but that was not his only motivation for returning to his home base. His professional life had been supercharged by the Nobel award, and even though remote control worked for three months, by January 1970 it had become apparent he needed a more hands-on approach.

While Beckett was ambling his way back to Paris, Alec Reid and Barney Rosset had begun to organize "a composite exhibit . . . on the occasion of the 1969 Nobel prize for literature" (Grove advertising flyer, SUL), with Rosset agreeing "to make Beckett's *Film* available" for the July 1970 event. He also helped Reid "arrange a lecture engagement" during a visit to the States in March 1970 (January 26, 1970, SUL). As suggested above, by March 1970 Beckett had entered into correspondence with Calder and Boyars about MacGowran's one-man show, *Beginning to End,* and he was planning to work through the text with the actor, helping turn samples from a set of texts written for the page into a program of staged performances (March 26, 1970, SUL). Calder's February 27, 1970, letter explained Conyers's intentions:

> they want to do the show in Paris in May in English for a limited run, followed by two to three weeks in Stockholm, and are then going to America where they would like to open the show on Broadway in September. In January 1971 they will start a fifteen week tour of the College theatres. After that they want to bring the production to England, possibly a West End Theatre. (Lilly)

Clearly a show designed to exploit Beckett's new status, the production gave Beckett "7% of gross takings, rising to 10% after production costs have been recouped" (SUL). By April 1970, the basic contractual details had been hammered out with Beckett's approval. Calder and Boyars acted as Beckett's main agent, and David Conyers Productions organized the tour (there was a dispute between Calder and Conyers created by confusion over rights to dramatic as different from nondramatic texts, but Beckett initiated a solution, and the issue was resolved in Calder's favor on the eve of the first performance).

Beyond their collaboration on "the International Jack MacGowran Tour" (March 24, 1970, SUL), Calder and Rosset reacted to the award by increasing the print run of the forthcoming bilingual edition of Beckett's novels, expanding from six thousand to ten thousand copies. Correspondence between Dick Seaver in New York and John Calder in London shows how quickly they arrived at an agreement (the deal was worked out in a flurry of letters written between October 24 and November 18, 1969 [SUL]). Intent on exploiting the Nobel publicity, Grove also made immediate plans to publish an American edition of *Proust and Three Dialogues,* which had been published by Calder in 1967. Other publishing houses across Europe were quick to join the post-Nobel frenzy. Two examples from February 1970 give a sense of the effect of the prize on Beckett's marketability across Europe: the Hungarian publishers Europa Press approached John Calder for permission to publish "the plays of Samuel Beckett in Hungarian translation, in volume form," paying a royalty of 7 percent on a print-run of "about 6–8000 copies"; later in the month Beckett authorized a Spanish publication of *Proust* in exchange for an advance of $250 (February 14 and February 17, SUL). Rosset, who had fallen out with John Calder on numerous occasions because of disputes over distribution rights, continued to assert his economic interests in Beckett's increasingly marketable texts.

After years of bold expansion that made Grove worth seventeen million dollars on the stock exchange in 1969, Rosset had begun to see ominous signs: sales of *Evergreen Review* had stalled, and there was increased competition from Girodias's American Olympia Press and West Coast publishers such as Greenleaf Classics (Gontarski 2000, 14). As a consequence, Rosset was even more defensive than usual when approached by Karl Gierow, permanent secretary of the Swedish Academy, and Nils Ståhle, executive director of the Nobel Foundation, for approval to publish, in association with Helvetica Press, "a representative work" by Beckett in an English-language version of "an anthology titled *Les Prix de Littérature,* and followed by versions in Portuguese, Italian, and German" (February 16, 1970, SUL). Rosset turned them down on the argument Beckett was already widely available in America. He explained, "I am puzzled by your association with a profit making enterprise" (February 27, 1970, SUL). On being assured that "neither the Nobel Foundation nor the Swedish Academy has got any profit interest in the Nobel anthology series planned by Helvetica Press" and that their interest was "solely to assist in making justice to all Laureates and thereby—we believe—also best serving the reading public" (April 14, 1970, SUL), Rosset again replied in the negative, explaining, "we still do not understand why this commercial venture is being conducted under the name of the Nobel Foundation" (April 22, 1970, SUL). Finally, in response to a May 19, 1970, reminder by Alexis Gregory of Helvetica, Rosset expressed his final no: "I find it sad to see the prize commercialized and I will not join the effort" (May 21, 1970, SUL). For the record, the Helvetica Press edition came out with a list of the Nobel laureates in literature since 1901 and with contributions by Faulkner, O'Neill, and Steinbeck; rebuffed by Rosset, with his eye on profit margins and his refusal to aid a competitor, the Swedish Academy and Nobel Foundation came up with an alternative plan, going through Lindon to arrange the 1971 publication of a celebratory special issue of *Malone meurt* and *Oh les beaux jours* with illustrations by Avigdor Arikha, a portrait of Beckett by Michel Cauvet, and cover art by Picasso.

While Beckett did not participate in the literary marketplace in the ways that became standard after World War II, refusing invitations to do public readings, lectures, and book signings; complicating the genre of the author interview by preventing note taking and tape recording; and maintaining a strictly guarded (though strategically revealed) private life, we have seen that he *did* participate. He did so with the same level of care he brought to his published texts and staged productions. This carefully controlled participation in public relations is evident from a post-Nobel report called "In the Wilderness for 20 Years." While it begins with a familiar assertion, Beckett "has gone out of his way to avoid literary fame and the necessity to explain himself to importunate interviewers," the report goes on to give an intimate account of Beckett, "his life philosophy and his writings," quoting Beckett directly and describing his apartment in detail (Whitman 1969). John Banville's assertion that "He refused to take part in the cult of personality, maintaining an admirable reticence in the face of a gossip-obsessed world" (2006, 131) should, then, be tempered by noting how his presence in the popular press complemented and reinforced his personality as an artist who ostensibly transcended the world of gossip but who engaged with this world *on his own terms:* again, the "quelle catastrophe" story is a culmination and distillation of an approach to the literary marketplace that had been cultivated since the beginnings of Beckett's career.

By examining Beckett's social and educational upbringing, his early experience as a struggling writer, his deliberate construction of a post-Joycean authorial persona, his consolidation of his business affairs after 1950, his successful development of a post-*Godot* portfolio of publications, his ongoing engagement with contract negotiations and decisions about the nitty-gritty aspects of publishing, his willingness to collaborate in the development of public programs designed to celebrate and promote his work, his voluntary participation in countless photo shoots during play rehearsals and in his private rooms, and his enthusiasm for cheap paperback publications alongside limited editions and expensive livres d'artiste, we have developed a comprehensive understanding of the mentality Beckett brought to the business of writing. Beckett benefited from stylized representations by Europe's best photographers, but he also dismantled received ways of thinking about literary production and the isolated genius, puncturing the aesthetic balloon by posing on garbage (fig. 4), by sitting for a portrait as he engaged in a commercial enterprise (fig. 3), and by allowing his image to be used by Saatchi and Saatchi (fig. 1). Of course, he also punctured neo-Romantic principles in his work, from the beginning engaging with the laws of supply and demand (in "A Wet Night"), exchange and service (in *Watt*), writing for hire (in *Molloy*), public reception and interpretation (in *All That Fall* and *Happy Days*), the economy of desire (in *The Lost Ones*), and image construction and manipulation (in *Catastrophe*). The success of his professional achievement and his ability to achieve a much more stable and healthy life than Joyce, Behan, and other predecessors and peers derive from his ability to maintain an exquisite level of control over his private life, his personal relationships, and his professional collaborations. He achieved an effective balance of ambivalences, allowing him to sustain his professional career without compromising his status as an amateur, without becoming a purely cult figure, without being at the beck and call of his publishers and his public, and without becoming self-destructive. He achieved the image of perfect artistic detachment at the same time that he enjoyed and revealed the collaborative nature of the literary marketplace, making a healthy living for himself and others without any overt appearance of anything other than artistic effort. Beckett achieved a healthy lifestyle free of scandal and self-destructiveness, paparazzi, and unwanted seclusion.

We have seen how a range of Beckett's close acquaintances and associates did their utmost to promote his work. Some, including Patrick Bowles, Con Leventhal, and Richard Seaver did so while profiting directly from sales of Beckett's books: Bowles as co-translator of *Molloy,* Leventhal as his private secretary, Seaver as editor of *Watt* and the collection *I Can't Go On, I'll Go On.* We have also noted the long list of beneficiaries to Beckett's success, not just publishers but also artists, actors, directors, scholars, and a host of other professional workers. Beckett's coattails were long, and they continue to pull people along; he willingly encouraged and facilitated their use by trusted protectors of his legacy. As they rode in his wake, taking advantage of his currency in the literary marketplace as well as his ostensible avoidance of self-promotion (because the association with Beckett's "integrity" adds credibility to their work), many of these beneficiaries, including Walter Asmus, John Calder, Ruby Cohn, John Haynes, James Knowlson, John Pilling, and Billie Whitelaw continue to benefit from their privileged access to "Sam." They unanimously repeat the claim about his preference for anonymity and privacy; exactly because Beckett was so successful in creating the image of inaccessibility, those who gained access continue to underscore and protect the value of this access. Their careers have been significantly boosted by his explicit blessing, and it would hardly do for them to question the main selling propositions associated with his authorial persona.

The collections of photographs, prefaced with words to the effect that such collections are remarkable exactly because they give a treasured glimpse of a man who preferred not to be photographed, illustrate how a supposedly private characteristic functioned as an effective and durable marketing strategy. Just as Beckett's autograph carries more value because he was so careful about its use, so photographic portraits carry more value because he was so careful in regulating who was allowed into his presence with a camera. As I have already suggested, the claim he "loathed self-promotion in all its forms" wears a bit thin when so many people who worked so closely with "Sam" repeat the idea so often in such similar terms, using the idea to promote and protect his most distinctive and marketable characteristic. Similarly, the claim he did not like to be photographed wears a bit thin when we begin to gather the hundreds of posed and unposed shots of Beckett, noticing how many of them have been used to promote Beckett's life and work. An observation about his personality takes on the character of a coordinated campaign designed to consolidate a specific public image through the use of repeated talking points. The problem for me is that the mantralike repetition and the closely guarded investment in the idea that he loathed publicity effectively mystify Beckett's life and work, making it seem as though he were as absent from his professional career as "Godot" from his most famous play. "Godot Has Arrived" [*Times* (London) 1969b], is just one of many articles and books that frame understandings of Beckett's work in terms borrowed directly from Beckett's work (also see fig. 1).

Just as we cannot accept at face value that a man who worked ceaselessly to create a viable authorial voice was damned to fame, we cannot sit comfortably with the idea that a man photographed so often was troubled by the loss of "his anonymity." The Nobel award tested his public image, bringing publicity and money to an author who, ostensibly, preferred failure and poverty, but he had managed his affairs and his authorial image so carefully by 1969 that there was no real threat to his protected space or his public persona.

Again, whether or not he was "horrified" by news of the Nobel award (Knowlson 1996, 505), Beckett took it in his stride, maintaining control over his business affairs and public image even as he anticipated a derailing that never happened. Simply put, he was so well protected he could continue to be a productive professional writer in the months and years after the Nobel award, exploiting his new level of international prestige by sponsoring a series of even more expensive and ambitious artists' editions of his texts, establishing himself as the authoritative director of "definitive" versions of his plays (and authorizing a number of directors, actors, dramaturges, and scholars who would become spokespersons in his stead: the series of videotaped plays called *Beckett Directs Beckett* is misleading exactly because the author was not directly involved in the productions but *did* work with the directors on previous versions of the plays. As we have seen, Beckett also took effective control over his biographical legacy. Frankly, he managed his life so that he could enjoy his new-found status as a Nobel laureate, using the enhanced credibility associated with the award to elevate his work to unprecedented heights: he had already begun to control productions of his work before 1969, but now he could take command of a Beckett-devoted theater in Frankfurt and could assert absolute control over definitive productions of his plays in London and Paris. He enjoyed and exploited his new status. This enjoyment is evident from the UPI photograph published in the *Times* (London) on October 27, 1969. The photograph was taken during his brief audience with the press on October 26 (*Times* [London] 1969a, 4): he is tanned and relaxed, smoking a cigar, silently reveling in the attention and the honor. The glow lasted for a number of months. An anonymous photograph taken in Lancaster, England, in May 1970 shows him relaxed, smiling, even jaunty, his handmade suit and formal tie giving him the look of a suave professional who has reached the zenith of his career, the casual balance of his spectacles on his forehead giving him an aura of confidence and urbanity (see the cover of the Einaudi translation of *Damned to Fame;* also see Marie 1997, 51). We are left asking, "catastrophe, quelle catastrophe?"

Apart from the prestige it gave a man who had worked unceasingly since 1929 to make a living as a writer and who had built on his success with *En attendant Godot* by surrounding himself with an international network of professional collaborators, clearing a private domain that he could use to sustain his career, the Nobel award boosted sales, causing a significant increase in revenue from royalties. The publicity campaigns by Calder and Grove had already increased sales during the 1960s, and a new tag now appeared on every Beckett publication, "Winner of the Nobel Prize for Literature." We can follow the "damned to fame" logic of the Sam Club and say he allowed this marketing device to help his publishers, but we must surely acknowledge that what was good for Beckett's publishers was also good for Beckett and, eventually, for Beckett's highly profitable estate. The Grove reprint of the paperback version of the three-novel collection, *Molloy, Malone Dies,* and *The Unnamable* provides an excellent example of the steady increase in Beckett's marketability before October 1969 and the significant increase that followed. In 1965 the new printing sold 6,874 copies, giving Beckett a royalty payment of $99.25; in 1966 sales rose to 8,867, giving him $128.57; in 1967 sales again rose, reaching 10,709, pushing total sales to date to 26,450 and giving Beckett $217.85; in 1968 sales held steady, reaching 10,863, giving him $262.88; and in 1969, sales rose again, hitting 15,053, earning Beckett $364.28. Beckett's royalty statements show total sales of 52,366 copies by the end of December 1969.

This steady increase in sales during the 1960s together with a significant boost during the period of the Nobel award is matched by the American edition of *Godot.* Grove royalty statements show sales of 11,286 copies at $1.45 a copy in the first six months of 1963, giving Beckett a royalty payment of $1,527. At that stage the edition had sold 99,595 copies. By the final six months of 1966, the edition had sold 249,412 copies, now at $1.75, with 30,600 copies sold during the six-month period and with just over $5,000 going to Beckett. Sales held steady at 30,778 copies in the first six months of 1967, but then began to increase again, jumping to 48,417 copies in July–December 1967 and 49,162 in January–July 1968, before settling down to 44,527 copies in the final six months of 1968. Then, in the first six months of 1969 sales increased again, hitting a record of 52,692 copies for the period. From its publication in spring 1956 to June 30, 1969, the "one dollar *Godot*" had sold 474,988 copies. In the period that includes the Nobel announcement, sales jumped 20 percent, to 61,207 copies, with a threefold leap in foreign sales (from 3,082 in the first six months of 1969 to 9,311 in the final six months). In the first six months of 1970, sales held steady at 61,131 copies (5,769 foreign), so that the twelve-month period spanning the Nobel award produced sales of 122,338 copies, representing a 20 percent increase over the previous twelve months and adding more than 20 percent to the total sales of the book since 1956. If we add the amount Beckett earned from American sales of the paperback *Godot* in June 1969 to June 1970 to his earnings from American performance rights for the play during the same period (with no major professional performances in America), we can assess his one-year royalty income for these two items at roughly $10,000.

The other big money-spinner was *Endgame*. In the first six months of 1969 the Grove edition sold 8,629 copies, with sales of 107,604 from publication in 1958 to June 1969. In the final six months of 1969 sales leapt to 15,564; and in the first six months of 1970 the figure held steady at 15,193 copies, raising total sales of the Grove paperback edition to 138,361. American sales of the paperback edition of *Endgame* gave Beckett a royalty payment of more than $1,000 in June 1969 to June 1970.

Once we take into account royalty income from book sales and performances of his other plays and novels, including the amounts he earned from Samuel French, the Dramatist's Play Service, and the publishers of anthologies (such as Appleton-Century Crofts for its use of *All That Fall* in *Drama and Discussion*) and recordings (particularly the US branch of Claddagh Records), his annual income from American sources approaches $15,000 (the average annual income for an American worker in 1969 was approximately $8,500). Independently wealthy, with numerous sources of income and royalty checks flowing in from all corners of the world, Beckett was in a good position to give away the prize money of 375,000 Swedish kronor (30,000 pounds sterling; 45,000 US dollars). By doing so he could protect his image as a man with no interest in money without suffering any financial consequences. Simply put, he already had more money than he could spend and could afford to leave royalty money in the country where it was earned until he was ready to go and spend it. With nc plans to go to America after the 1964 trip, US royalties accumulated rapidly: on February 5, 1970, for example, Rosset wrote to inform him that "There is approximately $13,000 due to you for subsidiary income, and for royalties periods ending December 1968, June 1969, and December 1969." We should note that this does not include the check for $9,000 he received in Tunisia in October 1969 (acknowledged in a letter dated February 2, 1970, SUL), the $2,000 he received in Madeira in December 1968 (acknowledged in a letter dated December 5, 1968, SUL), and other amounts deducted from his tally such as the $1,000 he gave Judith Schmidt as a wedding gift in March 1970, the $500 he donated to the Horace Gregory award committee in June 1969, and sundry amounts including two donations of $50 to the Mexican journal, *El Corno Emplumado* in March and November 1968. Again, it is evident that long before the Nobel award Beckett was in a position to pay his own way in the currency of whichever country he visited; when he did not have local currency, he could rely on a transfer of any amount of dollars necessary to his needs.

Financial security aside, in the period after the Nobel award a much more important celebration and consolidation of Beckett's legacy developed. In 1970–71 Reading University organized an exhibition and began to build an archive. This eventually became the Beckett International Foundation, an author-supported professional organization dedicated to the preservation of Beckett's legacy. Organized by James Knowlson, James Edwards, and Carol Sanders, the exhibition laid the groundwork for Beckett's relationship with the man who would become his authorized biographer. The first contact came in a March 26, 1970, letter telling Beckett about the intended tribute: "As a small token of our admiration for your work, we are hoping to organize next February at the University of Reading an exhibition of your poetry, translations, novels and plays, together with photographs of productions, etc." Knowlson acknowledged up front his goal "to lay the foundation for a fairly substantial Samuel Beckett collection in the University Library, which can be added to later on." And while describing this as "a very modest undertaking compared with the vast project at St. Peter's College, Oxford" (a project to which Knowlson gives little regard in the biography he would write twenty years later), he announced an overall plan to "produce something of permanent, rather than merely temporary, interest" (MS 1227/1/2/1, RUL). The result was the magnificent collection at Reading University. An undated note from this period, signed by Beckett and generically addressed to whomever it might concern, provides sufficient evidence of Beckett's direct approval of the exhibition; it serves as a letter of introduction for Knowlson and Edwards as they gather materials, authorizing them to copy prepublication versions of his work in support of the exhibition at the University of Reading (MS 1574, RUL). By May 1970 Edwards and Knowlson were actively collecting materials and support, casting a wide net in order to "offer an exceptional opportunity to survey the whole range of Beckett's creative work up to the present" ("typescript of prospectus," MS 1227/8/2, RUL).

A May 1 letter from the organizers to the Society for Theatre Research in London requests "material from your own Theatrical Collection" and associates the event with "the appeal fund now being launched for a Beckett Theatre in Oxford." For his part, John Calder replied to a May 1 letter by promising "[w]e will certainly make everything in print available and we can probably supply on loan manuscripts, proofs and correspondence" (May 5, 1970, MS 1227/1/2/3, RUL). As Knowlson explained in a letter to Rosset dated July 9, 1970: "This exhibition will consist of printed books, manuscripts, photographs of his life and of first productions of his plays, playbills, programmes, etc. as well as critical studies of his novels, poems and plays, and unpublished recollections by Beckett actors and friends" (SUL). He goes on to explain, "we hope that the Beckett exhibition will reach an international public and receive international coverage," and he makes clear that the intention is to form "a special collection of Beckettiana . . . permanently available to scholars of Beckett's work" and that Beckett "is himself lending his advice and help in the preparation of the exhibition" (July 9, 1970, SUL 32). When Beckett was not available, Leventhal stepped up; on August 14, 1970, he wrote to Knowlson, "I hasten to assure you that I shall be glad to give you all the help I can to make your proposed exhibition a success" (RUL).

As previously noted, Leventhal had been Beckett's friend since the early 1930s and had functioned as his standby professional assistant since he resigned from TCD in 1963. He had become, by 1971, Beckett's closest personal representative, and it was entirely appropriate he should write the foreword for the exhibition catalog and give a keynote lecture on opening night in Reading. The catalog reinforces the authorial persona used to sell Beckett since the 1950s: Leventhal recites the idea Beckett "shuns publicity" and is "made of the stuff that will not compromise" (Knowlson 1971, 14). Defining Beckett in terms of "minority" appeal and as part of the "literary vanguard," Leventhal confirms his status as "a rare genius." With a neomodernist disdain for "the newspapers," which "find it easier to provide amusement by photographing the characters in the *Endgame* dustbins than to assess seriously the play's significance," he overlooks how newspapers and other organs of mass distribution, as well as high-profile limited editions and collectors' texts, had been used to ensure "Samuel Beckett has not had to wait as a long as Samuel Pepys for recognition" (13). Leventhal's investment in the idea that the Reading exhibition had taken a risk in supporting a controversial writer whose work is "only best for the few," leads him to turn a blind eye to the material surrounding him as he writes and speaks: the catalog is packed with evidence demonstrating the Beckett-approved promotional use of small magazines and newspapers, radio and television broadcasts, limited editions and staged readings.

In other words, the exhibition catalog underscores how Beckett achieved the celebrity status he ostensibly would have preferred to avoid, calling attention to the commercial media outlets he supposedly avoided. For example, the section on "Recent Prose Fiction" (111–15) lists the June 1956 *Trinity News* and 1957 *Evergreen Review* (vol. 1, no. 3) publications of "From an Abandoned Work" in addition to the December 1957 BBC reading of the text by Patrick Magee, the 1967 Les Editions de Minuit "limited edition of 222 copies" of *D'un ouvrage abandonné,* and the 1967 trade edition of *Têtes-mortes* (which included *D'un ouvrage abandonné*). Throughout, the list of exhibits illustrates the long-standing practice by Beckett and his publishers of publishing short extracts and limited editions in advance of the trade publication of any given novel. None of these promotional publications appeared without Beckett's prior knowledge and written approval.

As Beckett's fame was established, the two-pronged use of journal publications and limited editions had evolved into a sophisticated marketing strategy: the 1950s use of coterie journals such as *Transition* and *Evergreen Review* developed into the use of mass-market magazines and newspapers such as the *New York Times,* the *New Statesman,* the *Times of London,* and the *New Yorker;* the early use of special, signed hardback editions continued, but it was increasingly supplemented with expensive artists' editions (a good example being the November 1965 simultaneous publication of *Imagination Dead Imagine* in the *Sunday Times (London)* and in a hors commerce edition of 100 copies "on hand-made paper signed by the author" (Knowlson 1971, 113). As the catalog illustrates, this practice goes back to the October 1950 *Transition Fifty* publication of English translations of excerpts from *Molloy* and *Malone meurt* "a month before the appearance of the volume itself" (56) and the publication of "An extract entitled 'Mahood' . . . prior to the publication of the volume of *L'Innommable,*" in the *Nouvelle Revue Française* (57). With all three novels, the "taster" extracts anticipated editions of 3,000 copies together with some form of high-priced limited edition: there were 50 deluxe copies of each novel; in the case of *Molloy,* an additional 500 signed copies were distributed for "Les Amis des Éditions de Minuit" (Ackerley and Gontarski 2004, 376).

The practice of gaining advance publicity by publishing texts in trade magazines and newspapers continued with the publication of extracts from

Comment c'est in *X: A Quarterly Review* in November 1959 ("L'Image," one of these extracts, was included in the exhibition) and in *L/VII* in December 1959 (as "Découverture de Pim"), and the extract from *How It Is* published as "From an Unabandoned Work" in the September-October 1960 issue of *Evergreen Review* (page 112). Again, these texts anticipated the simultaneous publication of special editions and regular trade editions in hardback and paperback. In the case of *Comment c'est* (1961) Minuit released "100 signed copies on Alfa Mousse Navarre reserved for the 'Club de L'Edition Originale,'" and in the case of *How It Is* (1964) Calder released two series of "100 copies hors-commerce on hand-made paper," the first bound in vellum, the second bound in morocco (Knowlson 1971, 112). The exhibition also displayed some of the extracts published in advance of the 1970 trade issue of *Le Dépeupleur* by Les Editions de Minuit (10,000 copies, with 399 special numbered copies): "Dans le cylindre" from the January 1967 issue of *Livres de France; L'Issue* from the limited edition of 154 copies with illustrations by Arikha (Paris: Les Editions Georges Visat, 1968); and *Sejour* from the "limited edition of 175 copies" by Georges Richard (1970). As I have pointed out above, one of the more interesting examples is Beckett's translation of *Sans,* which first appeared (as noted above) in *Quinzaine litteraire* and then in an edition of 100 numbered copies hors commerce, plus an additional 642 copies also "printed on vélin cuve B.F.K Rives paper" (Knowlson 1971, 115); after first publication in *New Statesman* on May 1 1970 (635), the English translation appeared as *Lessness* with Beckett's signature "scrawled" across the front cover "as large as possible" (Calder to Beckett, May 12, 1970, Lilly). As further publicity, the text was broadcast on BBC Radio 3 on February 25, 1971, in a production directed by Beckett with Jack MacGowran as the voice.

Like Leventhal, Knowlson is invested in a neo-Romantic, "art-for-art's-sake" representation of Beckett's authorial persona. Explaining that "the whole notion of 'acceptance' . . . seems quite irrelevant to his activity as a writer," Knowlson quotes from Beckett's "Three Dialogues" to support his thesis: the author "has concentrated with great single-mindedness upon the exploration of what he once referred to as 'that whole zone of being that has always been set aside as something by definition incompatible with art'" (1971, 15). Knowlson's decision to represent Beckett's life and work in terms of "simplicity and starkness and by the use of numerous black and white photographs . . . to catch something of the dark, tragic-comic nature of his uncompromising vision" is part of a genuine effort to "record . . . forty years of dedicated creative activity" (15). But the design of the exhibition was clearly intended to communicate a particular understanding of Beckett's authorial persona and a particular interpretation of his work. His claim that "the exhibition requires no explanation" (15) is, of course, entirely consistent with Beckett's claim in the letters to Schneider published in the *Village Voice* as part of the publicity campaign for the New York premiere of *Endgame:* "My work is a matter of fundamental sounds . . . and I accept responsibility for nothing else" (Beckett 1984b, 109).

This purist representation is also at odds with the work of a writer whose entire canon challenges neat identifications and who fully understood the craftsmanship and significance of staging, design, and representation. Beckett may occasionally have argued the aesthetic line about literary genres being distinct, but his actual practice was to blur and merge genres, authorizing and orchestrating dramatic presentations of "prose" texts (as he did with *Lessness* in 1971), treating certain word clusters as prose in one context and poetry elsewhere (as he did when he wove the poem "Dieppe" into *Watt, GCE I,* 200), transforming stage plays into television plays (as he did with *Waiting for Godot, Not I, What Where,* and other plays), and going along with various adaptations of his work from one genre-specific venue to another (as he did when he worked with MacGowran to produce a stage show from various prose pieces). In November 1960 he actively supported Jay Ward Productions as they turned *Act Without Words* into a cartoon, and he profited from the conversion, receiving an advance of $250 against a royalty of 10 percent. To call Beckett "uncompromising" is to turn him into a much less interesting author than he actually was: as we will see later in this conclusion, *Catastrophe* illustrates that he had a much more complex understanding of the practicalities of the marketplace than a black-and-white aesthetic perspective allows.

Perhaps the best illustration of the tension between the public image Beckett propagated through his friends and his more complicated life as a professional writer is the framed photograph in the back office of the special collections room at Reading University Library. The photograph was taken by Guy Suignard during rehearsals for the February 1966 Theatre de France production of *Va et Vient,* directed by Beckett at L'Odeon. Reproduced in the Marval *Portraits* (Marie 1997, 41), it shows Beckett with head in hand, as though in despair. It seems to confirm his preference for failure. But the photograph is, in fact, direct evidence of Beckett's success; despite his pose of exasperation, the portrait demonstrates his voluntary participation in a high-profile production at one of the most prestigious and expensive venues in Paris. The production confirmed his status alongside Ionesco and anticipated his ascension to an even grander international status. The prominence of this photograph at the Reading archive is symptomatic of the received approach to Beckett's life and career: it isolates him, making him seem like "his 'people,' as they totter on the brink of silence and nothingness" (Knowlson 1971, 15). But it complicates this image by demonstrating his willingness to be represented as a philosopher-poet, a contemporary version of "the thinker," caught up in the solipsistic world of his private thoughts, craving isolation and peace. And it does so while showing him in the midst of the very success and fame he had worked so hard to achieve.

Like the photographs that show him signing limited edition texts and posing as "Beckett" on a pile of garbage in an alley, the Suignard image is, I would argue, a graphic illustration of Beckett's desire to expose the process of image construction. Again, like Joyce, who stood behind Beckett and the other writers as they advertised "Work in Progress" in *Our Exagmination,* and who then went one step beyond his "marshals" by parodying the process in the pages of his book ("Imagine the twelve deaferended dumbbawls of the whowl abovebeugled to be the contonuation through regeneration of the urutteration of the word in pregross" [Joyce 1939, 284]), Beckett used his professional acquaintances to establish ways of reading his life and work that he was careful to subvert and dismantle. He thus created an effective deconstructive analysis of the literary marketplace by playing both sides of the divide/interaction between art and commerce, privacy and publicity, insularity and fame.

The Distant Storm of Applause

Much remains to be done to develop a full understanding of Beckett's relationship with the literary marketplace: we might envision a series of projects looking at his career as a professional writer across Europe and beyond, with the situation in France, Germany, and Italy meriting comprehensive treatment. His work in the theater and with broadcast media, including arrangements with Claddagh Records; his relationship with the BBC, RTF, and German-based television companies; and his work on the radio deserve study because they promise to open new ways of thinking about his use of the mass media. His post-Nobel career demands much deeper analysis, and the period between his death in 1989 and the centenary celebrations in 2006 remains open to inquiry, as do the centenary celebrations and the regular festivals and conferences, galas and symposia devoted to his life and work. Much remains to be written about Beckett's public legacy, including the ways in which the Beckett estate and others continue to protect, and to profit from, this legacy. But to conclude this analysis, we will consider the immediate impact of the Nobel Prize in light of a late text that opens new ways of thinking about his status as a professional writer in the literary marketplace: *Catastrophe* (1982).

Written in early 1982 and first performed on July 21, 1982, at the Avignon Festival for "A Night for Vaclav Havel" organized by the International Association for the Defense of Artists (AIDA), the play was dedicated to Havel, the Czech writer who had been in prison since 1979 for violating Czechoslovakian censorship laws. It was first published in French in a limited edition of ninety-nine copies as *Solo suivi de Catastrophe* (1982) and then in *Catastrophe et autres dramaticules* (1982). English translations followed in the *New Yorker* in January 1983, in *Index on Censorship* in January 1984, in *Evergreen Review* in February 1984, and in *Three Plays* (1984). Specifically written as a political statement in support of a writer imprisoned for publicly violating the censorship rules governing the totalitarian regime in Soviet-controlled Czechoslovakia, *Catastrophe* explores the manipulation and response of a "protagonist" who has been put on a pedestal by a director who is driven by an uncompromising art-centered approach. In the play this approach is self-evidently totalitarian. "P" accepts his fate, as if passively, until the final moment, when he challenges the "Distant storm of applause" by raising his head. When he raises his head, he silences the taped audience with a face that directly recalls Beckett's face in the series of publicity photographs we have already examined.

Taking its title from the received story about how Suzanne Dumesnil responded to news of the Nobel award, using a "Protagonist" who suffers from Dupuytren's syndrome, an ailment Beckett endured; an "Assistant" who takes notes in a way that recalls Beckett's own "theatrical notebooks" (notebooks later marketed because they offer significant revisions of published texts); and a "Director" whose cigar connects him with the photograph of Beckett taken in the Nabeul hotel when he made his first public appearance after the Nobel award, the play explores the relationship between the creator and the created, emphasizing the importance of the mediating, script-altering "Assistant" and the "offstage" worker, "Luke, in charge of the lighting" (*GCE III*, 483–89). In other words, the play dramatizes the process of professional collaboration necessary to artistic expression by tapping into the historical moment, through a direct connection to Dumesnil's widely reported private reaction, when Beckett ascended to a new level of international fame: Beckett himself is invoked as a director-author, metonymically at least, through the Director's cigar. Beckett's demeanor as a director is also invoked through his resistance to "this craze for explicitation," his apparent indifference to the actor's suffering, his willingness to revise the script in rehearsal, and his concerted effort to create a definitive image. Beckett is also associated with the Protagonist, again metonymically, through the "Fibrous degeneration" of his hands and the isolation of his head (which recalls various head shots, especially the 1973 portrait by Haynes, fig. 8). The silent unliftability of his mouth seems to be a direct reference to Beckett's own description of his clenched jaws in a letter to Barney Rosset on August 12, 1957. In the context of the advertising poster designed by Saatchi and Saatchi in 1983 (fig. 1), the rejection of the Assistant's proposal to put a gag on the Protagonist seems to connect the play with yet another aspect of Beckett's life in the literary marketplace, his public image as an icon of stony silence, as the cigar-smoking man who refused to speak at the moment he publicly acknowledged his most prestigious award. Beckett was a highly complex man who was fully capable of representing different parts of himself in a play written when his creative flame was fading fast. Within a few years he would authorize a biography, but in the meantime, while he still had creative energy, he wrote a play that provides a vivid understanding of how he understood his life as a professional writer.

On the surface, *Catastrophe* is an allegorical representation of a silenced "protagonist" who is inextricably trapped in a neatly defined role scripted to create a "catastrophe," a dramatic denouement, out of the iconographic phenomenon of his isolated head. Manipulated throughout by the director and assistant as he stands on a pedestal, "P" seems to accept his lot as a paradoxical icon, as a figure celebrated for his acquiescence, as a "protagonist" with his head lowered in nonprotagonistic obeisance. He seems damned to his potential fame, passively accepting whatever audience reaction his appearance elicits. In this sense the character represents Beckett's oft-repeated indifference to audience response. At the same time, the "female assistant" seems to confirm a hierarchy of command from the Director to the Assistant to Luke, the lighting engineer, with the Protagonist at the mercy of all. Interestingly enough, in this descending hierarchy the audience, represented on a recording with applause that "falters" and "dies," is at the bottom of the pecking order. In this order of things, the Assistant does the Director's bidding while "P submits, inert." When, "[t]imidly," she asks, "What about a little . . . a little . . . gag?" the Director replies "For God's sake! This craze for explicitation! Every i dotted to death! Little gag! For God's sake!" She then asks "Sure he won't utter?" to which the Director replies "Not a squeak."

The Director seems to be in complete control of how the Protagonist is represented and, thus, of the carefully crafted image designed to form "our catastrophe." Accordingly, the Assistant seems entirely at the beck and call of the Director. But, even before the protagonist raises his head in defiance of the Director's orders, subverting the chain of command and releasing the actual, live audience into a surge of applause occasioned by its support of freedom of expression and its rejection of authoritarian manipulation (to recall the circumstances of the play's premiere in Avignon), the course of the play is marked by a series of moments indicating the chain of command is less rigid than it seems: the Assistant translates the Director's instructions into words her boss has not specifically used. In response to his question "Why hands in pockets?" she answers, "To have him all black"; he responds, "He mustn't," and she makes a note, "Hands exposed." The same pattern leads the Assistant to produce a series of imperative directions: "Hands limp," "Whiten cranium," "Whiten hands," "Raise pedestal," and "Whiten all flesh." She thus turns his negative comments into succinct stage directions. In other words, the projected final script, with instructions for staging written to be as imperative and unchangeable as Beckett's notoriously static stage directions, is a collaborative effort between the Assistant and the Director: he gives a general idea of what he wants to avoid; she creates specific directions, asserting a positive vision of the idealized image. The Assistant thus assumes an indispensable role as the mediator between director and audience. Even though the projected "catastrophe" is a "Terrific" finale designed to "have them on their feet," the actual play challenges the script, dismantling the isolation of the objet d'art: in sum, the play makes clear that its projected "catastrophe" depends on collaboration and communication between a network of professionals.

As such, the script seems to invite the kind of creative interpretation Vasek Simek developed in a March 1990 production at the John Houseman Studio Theater in New York. Simek supplemented the play's scripted conclusion with what he called "a few moments of my own and the actors' tribute to Vaclev Havel's fate, which I am convinced Beckett . . . would give a probable wink to" ("Director's Notes," MS 3730, RUL): in Simek's version, after the applause dies, the protagonist unfurls himself into a victory salute to the accompaniment of the National Anthem of Czechoslovakia (Program for "By and For Havel," MS 3720, RUL). Given the way the play (and Beckett's entire oeuvre) unsettles the relationship between the ongoing process and the final product, Rosset and Martin Garbus's argument in a March 23, 1990, letter to the *New York Times* that the "New Finale Would Appall Beckett" and that Simek's interpretation is "egregious" (A34) seems overly dramatic and unnecessarily rigid, representing only one side of Beckett's contribution to twentieth-century literature. As Gerard Raymond put it in a May 2–8, 1994, article responding to the Beckett estate's decision to challenge Deborah Warner's version of *Footfalls*, interpretations of Beckett's work are only offensive to "Beckett purists" who insist on "total fidelity to Beckett's precise stage directions." The danger with such purist approaches to Beckett's work is that they threaten to kill what they seem to defend; by rigidly applying black-and-white readings of Beckett's life and work, those who supposedly act in Beckett's interests reduce his representational possibilities, treating his life as a one-dimensional expression of artistic purity, reducing his plays to "museum pieces" (Raymond 1994).

As I have suggested throughout this book, purist understandings of the separation between art and commerce do a disservice to an author who shone a light on the process that constructs and exploits portraits of the famous in an age obsessed with celebrity. Such understandings also turn a blind eye to one of the more important aspects of his oeuvre—his Brechtian dismantling of neo-Romantic, art-for-art's-sake aestheticism and genius. By choosing to play with the relationship between rehearsal notes and a finished script, and by dramatizing a moment during which the actor-protagonist defies the actor-director, Beckett underscores his revision-based, intensely self-conscious and self-reflexive approach to literary expression. He thus underlines the fact that the theatrical apparatus involves more than the stage and the script, tying the fate of the artist to support networks that make art visible, public, marketable. In addition to baring the devices through the Pirandellian technique of presenting a play in rehearsal, *Catastrophe* incorporates an offstage lighting engineer, Luke; the Director is distracted from focusing on his job by his imminent "caucus"; and the canned applause calls attention to the artificiality, the "stagedness," of the play. Beckett thus puts the action on stage in the context of a work world involving committee meetings, administrative assistants, and mechanical aids and devices; the entire play is, in fact, self-consciously placed in the context of a dynamic exchange between different professionals.

Catastrophe illustrates how, just as Beckett exposed and dismantled the apparati of verbal and visual expression in his prose and drama, he deliberately revealed and complicated the business of authorial representation and exploitation, highlighting *and* subverting the great divide between art and commerce. Once more, we must recognize his deliberate effort to complicate the relationship between his private/personal and public/professional roles: he personally invited professional photographers into his private spaces to document the process through which his public image was created and disseminated. Numerous professional photographers including Jerry Bauer (1962), Henri Cartier-Bresson (1964), Gisèle Freund (1964), Lufti Ozkok (1963 and 1966), John Minihan (1980), Louis Monier (1985), Roger Pic (1977), and Marc Trivier (1983) were invited into his private space to take photographs: Cécile Marie's *Portraits d'auteurs: Samuel Beckett* (1997) provides an excellent sample of the images produced during these entirely voluntary sessions. Beckett's evident enthusiasm for private portraits contradicts the repeated claim that he loathed intrusions into his private life. And this enthusiasm is consistent with his explorations of the apparati of representation in *Catastrophe* and other texts. There is no better example of the coming together of the different ambivalences and tensions that comprise Beckett's legacy in the literary marketplace than the Saatchi and Saatchi poster (fig. 1), the T-shirt discussed in the introduction, and the play *Catastrophe.*

The public gagging of his famously silent mouth in an advertising image adds another turn to his self-conscious analysis of his public image. As noted in the introduction, the *Index on Censorship* advertising poster announced, "If Samuel Beckett had been born in Czechoslovakia, we'd still be waiting for Godot": in the advertisement, Godot, a silent figment representing whatever we are waiting for, becomes a symbol of free expression; as such, the image runs up against Beckett's notoriety as an uncompromising author who severely restricted directorial interpretations of his plays (except by himself and his authorized representatives such as Schneider and Asmus). The anti-censorship message was enabled because Beckett floated signifiers in ways anticipating and clarifying poststructuralist discourse (which is why Barthes, Derrida, Foucault, and Kristeva acknowledge their debt to Beckett), the word "Godot" referring not just to the inexistent, silent character but, at the same time, to the play that made Beckett famous by turning down-side-up the most basic assumptions of the theater. "Godot" also applies, of course, to Beckett himself, a figure notoriously absent and silent who was repeatedly merged with his fictional characters. Associated with the literature of silence and the postmodern turn long before Ihab Hassan's book on the subject, "the Godot man" becomes doubly mute. The Minihan photograph taken in the Hyde Park hotel in 1980 and modified by Saatchi and Saatchi in 1983 is, of course, part of the long tradition of photographs explored in our introduction. These publicity shots already represent Beckett as a silent figure; in the Saatchi modification his silence is, so to speak, silenced. Still, the ad works because this double muting is re-reversed by the pictorial eloquence of Beckett's physiognomy. The gagged icon of silence becomes a symbol of resistance to state censorship and a harbinger of political freedom, thus adding another interpretive turn to *Catastrophe*. But because the gagged mouth is Beckett's, the image represents the unstable function of the famous author in postmodern culture, silenced because his fame-bringing words issue from internal biochemistry; silenced because the meanings associated with the words he issues develop elsewhere, in realms of experience separate from his own; silenced because his life is not his own even when he is in a room of his own; silenced because, in the postmodern age of image manipulation and surveillance, the private is always public.

Works Cited

Index

Works Cited

Archival Sources

Calder and Boyars Archives. John Calder and the Lilly Library, Indiana University, Bloomington, Indiana.

Grove Press Records. Special Collections Research Center, Syracuse University Library, Syracuse, New York.

Samuel Beckett Archives at the Beckett International Foundation Library. Reading University, Reading, United Kingdom.

Samuel Beckett and Carlton Lake Archives. Harry Ransom Humanities Research Center, University of Texas, Austin, Texas.

Tom McGreevy correspondence. Special Collections, Trinity College, Dublin, Ireland.

Henry Wenning correspondence. Washington University Library, St. Louis, Missouri.

Published Sources

Abbott, H. Porter. 1996. *Beckett Writing Beckett: The Author in the Autograph.* Ithaca: Cornell Univ. Press.

Ackerley, C. J., and Stan Gontarski. 2004. *The Grove Companion to Samuel Beckett: A Reader's Guide to His Works, Life, and Thought.* New York: Grove.

"Advance-Guard Advance." 1953. *Newsweek.* March 30.

Albright, Daniel. 2003. *Beckett and Aesthetics.* Cambridge: Cambridge Univ. Press.

Arnold, Bruce. 2003. *The Spire and Other Essays in Modern Irish Culture.* Dublin: Liffey Press.

Aster, Howard, and Amy Lane, eds. 1999. *In Defense of Literature: For John Calder; Fifty Years of Publishing Literature, Politics, and the Arts.* London: Mosaic Press.

Aston, Frank. 1958. "One Report on 'Endgame.'" *New York World Telegram-Sun,* January 29.

Bair, Deirdre. 1990. *Samuel Beckett: A Biography.* New York: Simon and Schuster.

Banville, John. 2006. "Beckett's Last Words." In *Samuel Beckett: 100 Years; Centenary Essays.* Edited by Christopher Murray, 122–31. Dublin: New Island.

Beckett, Samuel. 1958. "Beckett's Letters on 'Endgame': Extracts from His Correspondence with Director, Alan Schneider." *Village Voice.* March 19, 8 and 15.

———. 1967a. *A Samuel Beckett Reader.* Edited by John Calder. London: Calder.

———. 1967b. *No's Knife: Collected Shorter Prose, 1945–1966.* London, Calder and Boyars.

———. 1976. *I Can't Go On, I'll Go On: A Selection from Samuel Beckett's Work.* Edited by Richard Seaver. New York: Grove. Re-issued in 1992 as *A Samuel Beckett Reader: I Can't Go On, I'll Go On.*

———. 1977a. *Collected Poems in English and French.* New York: Grove.

———. 1977b. *Collected Poems.* Edited by John Calder. London: John Calder.

———. 1979. *Imagination Dead Imagination.* London: John Calder (Copy 1 of 50 held by the Beckett International Foundation. RUL. Also published in the *Sunday Times* [London]. 1965. November 7).

———. 1984a. *The Collected Shorter Plays of Samuel Beckett.* New York: Grove.

———. 1984b. *Disjecta: Miscellaneous Writings and a Dramatic Fragment.* Edited by Ruby Cohn. New York: Grove.

———. 1988. *Beginning to End: A Selection of the Works of Samuel Beckett, Adapted by Samuel Beckett and Jack MacGowran.* With illustrations by Edward Gorey. New York: Gotham.

———. 1992. *Dream of Fair to Middling Women.* Edited by Eoin O'Brien and Edith Fournier. New York: Arcade Publishing.

———. 2006. *Samuel Beckett: The Grove Centenary Edition.* Volumes 1–4. Edited by Paul Auster. New York: Grove.

Begam, Richard. 1996. *Samuel Beckett and the End of Modernity.* Stanford: Stanford Univ. Press.

Benjamin, Walter. 1968. *Illuminations.* New York: Schocken Books.

Billington, Michael. 1989. "Master of the Game." *The Guardian,* December 27, 13.

Blake, Ian. 1968. "An Oxford Tribute to 'Our Greatest Living Writer': The Samuel Beckett Theatre." *Irish Times,* May 21.

Bowles, Patrick. 1958. "How Samuel Beckett Sees the Universe." *The Listener,* June 19, 1011–12.

Brater, Enoch, ed. 1986. *Beckett at 80/Beckett in Context.* Oxford: Oxford Univ. Press.

Braun, Stephen. 1989. "Samuel Beckett Dies at 83; 'Godot' Author, Nobelist." *Los Angeles Times,* December 27.

Bronowski, Joseph. 1931. *The European Caravan: An Anthology of the New Spirit in European Literature.* New York: Brewer, Warren and Putnam.

Brown, Stephen. 2006. "Fail Better! Samuel Beckett's Secrets of Business and Branding Success." *Business Horizons* 49, no. 2 (March-April): 161–69.

Bryden, Mary. 1992. "Figures of Golgotha: Beckett's Pinioned People." In *The Ideal Core of the Onion: Reading Beckett Archives,* edited by John Pilling and Mary Bryden, 45–62. Reading: Beckett International Foundation.

Butler, Lance St. John. 1984. *Samuel Beckett and the Meaning of Being: A Study in Ontological Parable.* New York: St. Martin's.

Calder, John. 1964. Program for "The Novels and Plays of Samuel Beckett: An Afternoon of Readings and Debate." Lilly.

———, ed. 1967. *Beckett at 60: A Festschrift.* London: Calder.

———. 1986. *As No Other Dare Fail: For Samuel Beckett on His 80th Birthday by His Friends and Admirers.* London: Calder.

———. 1990. "Samuel Beckett: A Saint Born on Good Friday." *Irish Times,* April 13, 7-8.

Chapsal, Madeleine. 1957. "Un Célèbre Inconnu: Samuel Beckett." *L'Express,* February 8, 26–27.

Clarksdale Press Register. 1955. "Grove Press Ranges Far and Wide, Forward and Backward in Book Quest." *Saturday Review,* February 19, 2.

Cohn, Ruby, ed. 1967. *A Casebook on Waiting for Godot.* New York: Grove.

———. 2001. *A Beckett Canon.* Ann Arbor: Univ. of Michigan Press.

Connor, Steven. 1988. *Samuel Beckett: Repetition, Theory, and Text.* New York: Blackwell.

———. 1989. *Postmodernist Culture: An Introduction to Theories of the Contemporary.* Cambridge: Blackwell.

Cronin, Anthony. 1996. *Samuel Beckett: The Last Modernist.* London: Harper Collins.

Daily Mail (London). 1958. "Beckett Comes Back to DEATH VALLEY." March 8.

———. 1968. "Generous Prince." May 29.

Dearlove, J. E. 1982. *Accommodating the Chaos: Samuel Beckett's Nonrelational Art.* Durham: Duke Univ. Press.

Derrida, Jacques, with Derek Attridge. 1992. *Acts of Literature.* New York: Routledge.

Dettmar, Kevin, and Steven Watt, eds. 1996. *Marketing Modernisms: Self-Promotion, Canonizations, Rereading.* Ann Arbor: Univ. of Michigan Press.

Dilks, Stephen. 1998. "Voices Out of the Air: Freedom, Death, and Constraint in *All That Fall.*" In *Samuel Beckett: A Casebook.* New York: Garland Press.

———. 2003. "Samuel Beckett's Samuel Johnson." *Modern Language Review* 98, no. 2 (April): 285–98.

———. 2004. "Selling Work in Progress." *James Joyce Quarterly* 41, no. 4 (Summer): 719–44.

Driver, Tom. 1961. "Beckett by the Madeleine." *Columbia University Forum* (Summer): 21–25.

Dukes, Gerry. 2002. *Samuel Beckett.* Overlook Illustrated Lives. Woodstock: Overlook.

Dumesnil, Suzanne. 1935. *Musique Jeux.* Paris: Henry Lemoine and Co.

Duthuit, Georges, ed. 1948. *Transition Forty-Eight.* Paris: Transition.

Ellmann, Richard. 1982. *James Joyce*. New York: Oxford Univ. Press.

Esslin, Martin. 1965. *Samuel Beckett: A Collection of Critical Essays*. Englewood Cliffs, N.J.: Prentice-Hall.

———. 1982. *Mediations: Essays on Brecht, Beckett, and the Media*. New York: Grove.

Ezard, John. 1970. "Experiments Under the Quad." *Daily Telegraph Supplement*, July 10, 7–10.

Fehsenfeld, Martha Dow, and Lois More Overbeck, eds. 2009. *The Letters of Samuel Beckett 1929–1940*. New York: Cambridge Univ. Press.

Foxrock Foundation. 1990. *Brochure, Deed of Covenant, and Banker's Order*. London: Foxrock Foundation.

Friedman, Melvin, ed. 1970. *Samuel Beckett Now: Critical Approaches to His Novels, Poetry, and Plays*. Chicago: Univ. of Chicago Press.

Gelb, Arthur. 1956. "Wanted: Intellects." *New York Times*, April 15, sec. 2.

Gierow, Karl Ragnar. 1969. "Presentation Speech: The Nobel Prize in Literature 1969." Translated from the Swedish. http://nobelprize.org/nobel_prizes/literature/laureates/1969/press.html.

Golden Theater. 1956. Advertisement for *Waiting for Godot*. *New York Times*, April 23, 23.

Gontarski, S. E. 2000. *Modernism, Censorship, and the Politics of Publishing: The Grove Press Legacy*. Chapel Hill: Univ. of North Carolina.

Gontarski, S. E., and Anthony Uhlmann, eds. 2006. *Beckett After Beckett*. Gainesville: Univ. Press of Florida.

Gordon, Lois. 1996. *The World of Samuel Beckett 1906–1946*. New Haven: Yale Univ. Press.

Gruen, John. 1969. "Samuel Beckett Talks about Beckett." *Vogue*, December, 210–11.

Gussow, Mel. 1996. *Conversations With and About Beckett*. New York: Grove.

Harmon, Maurice, ed. 1998. *No Author Better Served: The Correspondence of Samuel Beckett and Alan Schneider*. Cambridge, Mass.: Harvard Univ. Press.

Harrison, Kenneth. 1958. "Mr. Beckett Finds Himself." *Books and Bookmen*, April, 21.

Harvey, Lawrence. E. 1970. *Samuel Beckett: Poet and Critic*. Princeton: Princeton Univ. Press.

Hasan, Ihab. 1967. *The Literature of Silence*. New York: Knopf.

Hayman, Ronald. 1969. "The Most Courageous Writer Going." Beckett International Foundation, RUL.

Haynes, John, and James Knowlson. 2003. *Images of Beckett: Photographs by John Haynes, Text by James Knowlson*. Cambridge: Cambridge Univ. Press.

Hodgart, Matthew. 1967. "Saint Beckett." *New York Review of Books*, December 7, 2–4.

Hodson, Phillip. 1967. "Waiting for Productions." *The Isis*, November 1.

Holden, Anthony. 1970. "The Samuel Beckett Theatre." *Financial Times,* February 10.

Huyssen, Andreas. 1986. *After the Great Divide: Modernism, Mass Culture, Postmodernism.* Bloomington: Indiana Univ. Press.

Joyce, James. 1916. *A Portrait of the Artist as a Young Man.* New York: Viking.

———. 1934. *Ulysses.* New York: Modern Library.

———. 1939. *Finnegans Wake.* New York: Viking.

———. 1989. *Critical Writings.* Edited by Ellsworth Mason and Richard Ellmann. Ithaca: Cornell Univ. Press.

Keats, John. 2002. *Selected Letters of John Keats.* Edited by Grant Scott. Cambridge, Mass.: Harvard Univ. Press.

Kenner, Hugh. 1968. *Samuel Beckett: A Critical Study.* Berkley: Univ. of California Press.

———. 1989. "Samuel Beckett's Glimmers of Darkness: In Paris, Encounters with the Author." *Washington Post,* December 27, D1-2.

Knowlson, James. 1971. *Samuel Beckett: An Exhibition.* 1971. Exhibitions catalog. London: Turret Books.

———. 1989. "Gazette: Samuel Beckett." *The Independent,* December 27, 19.

———. 1996. *Damned to Fame: The Life of Samuel Beckett.* London: Bloomsbury.

Knowlson, James, and Elizabeth Knowlson, eds. 2006. *Beckett Remembering, Remembering Beckett: A Centenary Celebration.* New York: Arcade Publishing.

Kyncl, Karel. 1989. "Havel, Beckett: The Intolerable Shirt of Fame." *The Independent,* December 30, 39.

Lane, Richard, ed. 2002. *Beckett and Philosophy.* New York: Palgrave.

Lennon, Peter. 1990. "Evenings with Sam." *The Guardian,* January 25, 23.

Lovenheim, Barbara. 1990. "A Canvas Who Has Lost Her Paintbrush." *New York Times,* September 1.

MacRuairi, Tomas. 1989. "The Celebrity No One Knew." *Irish Press,* December. 25, 26, 27.

Marie, Cécile, ed. 1997. *Portraits d'auteurs: Samuel Beckett.* Paris: Marval.

McClain, John. 1958. "Beckett Fails in 'Endgame.'" *New York Journal,* January 30.

McDonald, Ronan. 2006. *The Cambridge Introduction to Samuel Beckett.* Cambridge: Cambridge Univ. Press.

McKenzie, D. F. 1999. *Bibliography and the Sociology of Texts.* Cambridge: Cambridge Univ. Press (Orig. pub. 1985).

Mercier, Vivian. 1977. *Beckett/Beckett.* New York: Oxford Univ. Press.

Minihan, John. 1996. *Samuel Beckett: Photographs by John Minihan* Introduction by Aidan Higgins. New York: George Braziller.

Mitchell, Breon, and Lois More Overbeck. 1999. *Word and Image: Samuel Beckett and the Visual Text.* Atlanta: Emory Univ.

"Molten Gloom." 1956. *Time,* October 15, 118.

Montague, John. 1989. "The Gloom and the Glory of Beckett." *The Guardian,* December 27, 13.

Murtagh, Tommy. 1989. "Memories of Samuel Beckett at the PLM St Jacques." *Irish Times,* December 30.

Nightingale, Benedict. 1989. "Bleak View of Human Suffering." *Times* (London), December 27.

O'Brien, Eoin. 1986. *The Beckett Country: Samuel Beckett's Ireland.* Dublin: Black Cat and Faber and Faber.

O'Donovan, Patrick. 1970. "Mr Fuller's Egg-Shaped Theatre." *The Observer,* February 22, 1970.

Pilling, John. 1990. "Beckett's Legacy to Reading." *Catalyst: Reading Magazine,* January 18–31.

———. 1997. *Beckett Before Godot.* London: Cambridge Univ. Press.

———. 2006. *A Samuel Beckett Chronology.* New York: Palgrave/Macmillan.

"Playwright Pictured." 1987. *Amateur Photographer,* December 12, 40.

Pope, Alexander. 1984. *The Poems of Alexander Pope.* Edited by John Butt. London: Methuen.

Prial, Frank. 2006. "At Beckett's Centenary, His American Discoverer Looks Back." *New York Times,* April 13, www.nytimes.com/2006/04/13/books/13ross.

Rainey, Lawrence. 1998. *Institutions of Modernism: Literary Elites and Public Culture.* New Haven: Yale Univ. Press.

Raymond, Gerard. 1994. "Censorship from the Grave: The Beckett Estate Kills a London Production of *Footfalls,* Starring Fiona Shaw." *Theater Week,* May 2–8.

Reid, Alec. 1971. *All I Can Manage, More Than I Could.* Rev. ed. 1968. New York: Grove.

Ricks, Christopher. 1993. *Beckett's Dying Words: The Clarendon Lectures, 1990.* New York: Oxford Univ. Press.

Robinson, Michael. 1969. *The Long Sonata of the Dead: A Study of Samuel Beckett.* New York: Grove.

Rosset, Barney, ed. 1994. *Evergreen Review Reader 1957–1966.* New York: Arcade.

Schneider, Alan. 1987. *Entrances: An American Director's Journey.* New York: Limelight.

Shenker, Israel. 1956. "Moody Man of Letters: A Portrait of Samuel Beckett, Author of the Puzzling 'Waiting for Godot.'" *New York Times,* May 6, sec. 10.

Shorter, Eric. 1989. "Beckett Takes with Him Unfathomable Truths of *Endgame* and *Godot.*" *Daily Telegraph,* December 27.

Smith, Sid. 1989. "Samuel Beckett Dies; Plays Inspired 'Theater of Absurd.'" *Chicago Tribune,* December 27.

Times (London). 1969a. "Beckett to Accept Prize." October 27, sec. 1.

———. 1969b. "Godot Has Arrived."October 24, sec. 1.

———. 1969c. "Samuel Beckett Goes into Hiding." October 25, sec. 1.

———. 1989. "Samuel Beckett: Unassuming Genius Who Probed the Quandary of Human Existence." December 27, 14.

Uhlmann, Anthony. 1999. *Beckett and Poststructuralism.* Cambridge: Cambridge Univ. Press.

U.S. News & World Report. 1990. "Merry Messenger of Doom." January 8, 18.

Variety. 1956. "B'way Up; 'Godot' $15,300." May 2, 71.

Wallach, Allan. 1989. "Samuel Beckett." *Newsday,* December 27, sec. 2.

Warner, Francis. 1970. Program for "A Beckett Evening: A Celebrity Gala in Aid of the Oxford Samuel Beckett Theatre Appeal." Published by The Oxford Playhouse, Oxford Univ., March 8, MS 1227/6/21, Lilly.

Whitelaw, Billie. 1995. *Billie Whitelaw: Who . . . He?* London: Hodder and Stoughton.

Whitman, Alden. 1969. "In the Wilderness for 20 Years." *New York Times,* October 24.

Williams, Raymond. 1996. *The Politics of Modernism: Against the New Conformists.* New York: Verso.

Willison, Ian, Warwick Gould, and Warren Cherniak, eds. 1996. *Modernist Writers and the Marketplace.* New York: St. Martin's.

Wynands, Sandra. 2007. *Iconic Spaces: The Dark Theology of Samuel Beckett's Drama.* Notre Dame: Univ. of Notre Dame Press.

Index

Page numbers in italics denote illustrations.